Credits

Author
Will Goldstone

Reviewers
Rune Skovbo Johansen
Mark Backler
David Fugère-Lamarre
Bastien Fontaine
Steffen Franz
Aaron Grove
Ben Lee

Acquisition Editor
Wilson D'souza

Development Editor
Maitreya Bhakal

Technical Editors
Aaron Rosario
Apoorva Bolar

Project Coordinator
Jovita Pinto

Proofreader
Aaron Nash

Indexer
Monica Ajmera Mehta

Production Coordinator
Melwyn D'sa

Cover Work
Melwyn D'sa

Foreword

When we began creating Unity, we were just three programmers working on a beautiful little game. There weren't any good game engines that one could license without putting down wads of cash, so we created our own. We eventually decided that we enjoyed the challenge of making great tools even more than making games, and after some soul searching we realized that the tools we had been creating—combined with a simple licensing structure and an open community—had the potential to change the way that developers create, distribute, and play games.

It wasn't always an easy road to where we are today. Ridiculously long days and late nights, gigs serving sandwiches and making websites for law firms, and general hardship. Once, we were told by a potential investor (he passed on the deal) that our dream of 'democratizing game development' had a 1 in 1000 chance of working out. We could think of nothing better to do than take on the odds!

Stuffing insanely complex technology into a polished package, and making it as simple as humanly possible was job one, and so we were thrilled to see the first book about our software, *Unity Game Development Essentials* released in 2009. The book helped many people get off the ground with Unity, and so when Will told me he was due to release an updated edition I was only too happy to be asked to write its foreword. A long standing member of the Unity community, we first met Will back in 2007 when he was teaching game development with Unity at UK based Bournemouth University. He went on to produce some of the first Unity video tutorials for his students and shared these on our forums, helping a generation of early adopters pick up Unity version 1.5 and upwards.

Now working with us at Unity Technologies, Will has retained much of his former career in teaching—helping us to grow adoption by new users through creating training materials, giving talks and keeping active in our community. The new *Unity 3.x Game Development Essentials* you hold in your hand (or read on your mobile or desktop!) is rewritten from the ground up—but holds on to everything that was so nice about the first edition: each part of the original has been expanded, improved or elaborated upon, and it also includes some of the many features we added to Unity since then. You will not only learn about new features however; Will thoroughly walks through the basics, through scripting, learning scripting, and even addresses that perpetual Unity conundrum: *Should I learn C# or Javascript?*—by covering both programming languages in parallel, his book lets you decide what makes the most sense for you.

Whether you are an artist, level designer, or simply a young person choosing game creation as a potential career, this book represents a fantastic start for learning Unity. Starting out by covering the essential elements of 3D, you'll learn everything from scratch—no prior knowledge is assumed, but the book moves at a pace that will keep you turning pages and writing code!

I'd like to personally welcome you to the Unity community, and hope you have as much fun reading this book as we do working on Unity.

David Helgason
CEO & Co-founder, Unity Technologies

About the Author

Will Goldstone is a longstanding member of the Unity community and works for Unity Technologies as a Technical Support Associate, handling educational content, marketing, community relations and developer support. With an MA in Creative Education, and many years experience as a lecturer in higher education, Will wrote the first ever Unity book, the original *Unity Game Development Essentials*, and also created the first ever external video tutorials for the package. Through his site `http://www.unity3dstudent.com`, Will helps to introduce new users to the growing community of developers discovering Unity everyday. He also blogs intermittently at `http://willgoldstone.com`.

I would like to thank the following parties for helping to produce this book, and being generally awesome—Teck Lee Tan (@LoTeKk) for creating the Art Assets in the book; all the Ninjas at Unity Technologies: Rune Skovbo Johansen, Nicholas Francis (@unitynich), David Helgason (@davidhelgason), Joachim Ante, Graham Dunnett, Andy Brammall (@andybrammall), Andy Stark, Charles Hinshaw, Roald Hoyer-Hansen (@brokenpoly), Carl Callewaert (@carlunity), Chris Pope (@CreativeChris1), Dave Shorter, Mark Harkness (@ IAmRoflHarris), Ricardo Arango, Rob Fairchild (@robfairchild), Olly Nicholson, Cathy Yates, Adam Buckner, Richard Sykes, Emil Johansen (@AngryAnt), Ethan Vosburgh, Joe Robins (@JoeRobins) ... and the many more awesome guys and girls I can't fit here!

Plus awesome Unity-powered friends Bob Berkebile (@ pixelplacement), Tom Jackson (@quickfingerz), Thomas Pasieka (@thomaspasieka), Cat Burton (@catburton), Mike Renwick (@ runonthespot), Mark Backler, Russ Morris (@therussmorris), Jasper Stocker (@jasperstocker), Paul Tondeur (@paultondeur), David Fugère-Lamarre, Benjamin Lee, Steffen Franz, Aaron Grove, Bastien Fontaine. And of course not forgetting Mum, Dad, Rach, Penny, and my awesome friends.

About the Reviewers

Rune Skovbo Johansen has been part of the development team at Unity Technologies since 2009, working on expanding the feature set of the editor and tightening the workflows and interface. He is based in Copenhagen, Denmark. Besides editor work he has developed procedural animation tools, written sections of the Unity documentation, and has been a programmer on several of the official Unity demos.

In general, Rune is passionate about creating solutions that make advanced and cool technology simple to use. He has a creative and cross-disciplinary approach to software development grounded in a Master's degree in Multimedia & Game Programming and an interest since childhood in graphics, animation, and coding.

Rune engages with the game development community online in various forums and blogs and offline through game jams and other events. He has been a speaker at the Game Developers Conference and Unity's own Unite Conference, and has helped organize the Nordic Game Jam.

In his spare time Rune enjoys the outdoor in parks and forests, daily biking, and reading. He also spends time working creatively with graphics and animation, and developing small games. He has a special interest in anything procedural and is persistently trying to find the best way to instruct his computer to generate giant sprawling worlds for him. He writes about his projects at `runevision.com`.

Mark Backler is a Game Designer who has been working in the games industry for over 5 years. He has worked at EA, Kuju and is currently at Lionhead Studios working on *Fable: The Journey*. He has worked on numerous games including *Harry Potter and the Order of the Phoenix*, *Milo and Kate* and the Bafta award winning *Fable* 2. He can be found on Twitter at @MarkBackler.

I would like to thank Will for writing this book, which has helped me get up to speed with Unity so quickly, Cat for putting us into contact in the first place, the talented and creative people at Lionhead from whom I'm still learning every day, and my friends, especially Anish, Tom and Chuck, and my family for being all round awesome.

David Fugère-Lamarre holds a Computer Engineering degree from the École Polytechnique de Montréal and a Master's degree in Engineering Management from the New Jersey Institute of Technology. His video game development experience started in 2004 when he worked for Behaviour Interactive (Artificial Mind & Movement) in Montreal, Canada as a game programmer on various console titles. In 2007 he worked for Phoenix Studio in Lyon, France again as a game programmer for a console title. In 2009 he co-founded Illogika Studios (`http://illogika.com/`), an independent game development company in Montreal specializing in Unity game development. He also teaches Unity pro training classes at the Centre Nad in Montreal and his involved with local colleges in creating game programming courses.

Bastien Fontaine is a 25 year old French game designer/scripter. He passed a two-year diploma from a university institute of computer science (C++, Java, PHP, SQL, and so on) at Nice, France, then a 3-year diploma on ARIES private school on Game Design/Video game jobs formation. He learned software such as Virtools, Maya, 3DS Max, Photoshop. He finished his studies with a 1-year diploma from "Université Lyon 2" (Gamagora)where he learned Level Design and tools such as Unreal Engine, Unity, Sketch Up, and improved his game design skills.

He worked with Unity at Creative Patterns (Strasbourg, France) to develop for iPhone and at *Illogika Studio* (Montreal, Canada) to develop for the iPhone too.

He also worked at *Illogika Studio* with David Fugère-Lamarre, another reviewer of this book.

Steffen Franz is currently the Technical Director at *HiveMedia* (`www.hivemedia.tv`) a branded social game company in the San Francisco Bay Area. He is also the Lead Engineer on *Deadliest Catch – The Social Game*, a Facebook game based on Discovery Channel's hit show. Since earning his B.S. in Visual and Game Programming at *The Art Institute of California*—San Francisco, Steffen has been developing on Unity for over three years, working on titles such as *Globworld*, a child friendly virtual world, Disney Online *TRON Legacy*, and *Cordy*, a 3D platformer for Google's Android mobile platform.

I would like to thank the author for this opportunity to share my knowledge and professional experience of the Unity engine. Most of all I would like to thank my family, especially our two year old toddler taking the occasional nap time, allowing me to review this book and hopefully give you more insight on how challenging, yet fun game development can be.

Aaron Grove is an award winning Visual Effects Supervisor with over 10 years experience, creating high-end visual effects for television commercials and music videos in Australia, United Kingdom and United States of America. Aaron's creativity and knowledge of 3D & visual effects (technical and artistic) combined with his passion for games gives him the drive to create and craft visually stunning games. In 2010, Aaron was the Visual Effects Supervisor on the award winning (2010 D&D Yellow Pencil Award) music video *Two Weeks* by *Grizzly Bear*. Currently Aaron is the creative director and co-founder of Blowfish Studios which is solely focused on Unity game development. More information can be found at `www.blowfishstudios.com`.

Ben Lee is a software engineer and has been working in the computer game industry for over 13 years on projects involving EA, Intel, nVidia and 3M. He has extensive experience with designing and programming computer game engines and all other aspects of game software development for a variety of hardware platforms. Most recently Ben co-founded Blowfish Studios(`www.blowfishstudios.com`) and has since been focused solely on Unity game development.

www.PacktPub.com

Support files, eBooks, discount offers and more

You might want to visit www.PacktPub.com for support files and downloads related to your book.

Did you know that Packt offers eBook versions of every book published, with PDF and ePub files available? You can upgrade to the eBook version at www.PacktPub.com and as a print book customer, you are entitled to a discount on the eBook copy. Get in touch with us at service@packtpub.com for more details.

At www.PacktPub.com, you can also read a collection of free technical articles, sign up for a range of free newsletters and receive exclusive discounts and offers on Packt books and eBooks.

http://PacktLib.PacktPub.com

Do you need instant solutions to your IT questions? PacktLib is Packt's online digital book library. Here, you can access, read and search across Packt's entire library of books.

Why Subscribe?

- Fully searchable across every book published by Packt
- Copy and paste, print and bookmark content
- On demand and accessible via web browser

Free Access for Packt account holders

If you have an account with Packt at www.PacktPub.com, you can use this to access PacktLib today and view nine entirely free books. Simply use your login credentials for immediate access.

Table of Contents

Preface

Game Engines such as Unity are the power-tools behind the games we know and love. Unity is one of the most widely-used and best loved packages for game development and is used by everyone from hobbyists to large studios to create games and interactive experiences for the web, desktops, mobiles, and consoles. With Unity's intuitive, easy to learn toolset and this book, it's never been easier to become a game developer.

Taking a practical approach, this book will introduce you to the concepts of developing 3D games, before getting to grips with development in Unity itself—prototyping a simple scenario, and then creating a larger game. From creating 3D worlds to scripting and creating game mechanics you will learn everything you'll need to get started with game development.

This book is designed to cover a set of easy-to-follow examples, which culminate in the production of a First Person 3D game, complete with an interactive island environment. All of the concepts taught in this book are applicable to other types of game, however, by introducing common concepts of game and 3D production, you'll explore Unity to make a character interact with the game world, and build problems for the player to solve, in order to complete the game. At the end of the book, you will have a fully working 3D game and all the skills required to extend the game further, giving your end-user - the player - the best experience possible. Soon you will be creating your own 3D games and interactive experiences with ease!

What this book covers

Chapter 1, Enter the Third Dimension: In this chapter, we will introduce you to the concepts of working in 3D and how game development works with Unity. Having covered how 3D development works, you will learn the core windows that make up the Unity Editor environment.

Chapter 2, Prototyping and Scripting Basics: In this chapter, we aim to get you started with a practical approach to learning Unity, by building a simple game mechanic prototype, and working with C# (pronounced C-Sharp) or Javascript scripting as you get to grips with your first Unity interaction.

Chapter 3, Creating the Environment: Now that you have a grasp on how to make use of Unity, and it's processes, in this chapter you will begin to design outdoor environments—using the Terrain toolset to create an island environment.

Chapter 4, Player Characters and Further Scripting: With our island environment completed, we will look at how Player Characters are constructed in Unity, looking at scripting for characters, and also learning further scripting concepts that will be essential as you continue to create further interactions in Unity.

Chapter 5, Interactions: This key chapter will teach you three of the most important processes in game design with Unity—interaction using Collisions, detection of objects using Ray casting, and collider intersect detection using Trigger areas.

Chapter 6, Collection, Inventory, and HUD: With a variety of interactions covered, we will put this knowledge into further practice as we learn how to make a simple inventory for the player, and an accompanying heads up display to record items collected.

Chapter 7, Instantiation and Rigidbodies: To put interaction into practice once more, we will make use of Unity's built-in physics engine, and learn how to combine this with animation to create a shooting mini-game.

Chapter 8, Particle Systems: Taking a break from scripting, we'll dive into some of Unity's visual effects to create a campfire using Particle systems-making systems for fire and smoke.

Chapter 9, Designing Menus: Every good game needs a user interface, and in this chapter we will take a look at two differing approaches to creating menus in Unity: with GUI Texture components and with the GUI scripting class.

Chapter 10, Animation Basics: To keep your Unity games looking dynamic, it's important to learn how to animate in Unity. In this chapter, we'll create a game ending sequence of titles and learn how to animate via scripting and also with Unity's Animation window.

Chapter 11, Performance Tweaks and Finishing Touches: Whilst it's important to get gameplay just right, it's also nice to make sure your game looks polished before it's ready to unleash on your audience. In this chapter, we'll look at further visual effects and optimization to make your game shine and perform well.

Chapter 12, Building and Sharing: In order to grow as a developer, it's really important to share your work with players, and get feedback. In this chapter, we'll learn how you can export your game as a standalone executable, and as a web player, so that you can do just that.

Chapter 13, Testing and Further Study: In this concluding chapter, we will look at ways of receiving feedback from your player, and give you some advice to stand you in good stead as you begin your career in development with Unity. This chapter also features some recommended further reading to cover as you progress from the confines of this book to becoming a fully-fledged game developer!

Glossary: The glossary contains descriptions of common terms that you might encounter and also serves as a handy reference.

The *Glossary* is not present in the book but is available as a free download from the following link:
`http://www.packtpub.com/sites/default/files/downloads/1444OT_Glossary_Final.pdf`

What you need for this book

For this book you will be required to download the free version of Unity, available at:

`http://www.unity3d.com/unity/download`

Your computer should also meet the following specifications, as stated on the Unity website:

- **Windows**: XP SP2 or later.
- **Mac OS X**: Intel CPU and "Leopard" 10.5 or later.
- Graphics card with 64 MB of VRAM and pixel shaders or 4 texture units. Any card made in this millennium should work.

For the latest requirements, see the Unity website:

`http://unity3d.com/unity/system-requirements.html`

Who this book is for

If you're a designer or animator who wishes to take their first steps into game development or prototyping, or if you've simply spent many hours sitting in front of video games with ideas bubbling away in the back of your mind, Unity and this book should be your starting point. No prior knowledge of game production is required, inviting you to simply bring with you a passion for making great games.

Getting help with the book and updates

This book is written with Unity version 3.4.2 in mind, and is tested for that version. However, in some rare cases, despite stringent checks of the text, book releases may feature errors that cause confusion to readers. Also, as Unity evolves and new versions of the software are released, parts of this book may need updating.

To keep you totally up to date, we're providing you with the following website in order to give you up to date changes to what is written in the book, and also any changes that are made to Unity itself - making sure that this book is always up to date with Unity's latest practices. So if you stumble upon a problem you think may have changed, or simply need help understanding the book, visit the following URL: `http://www.unitybook.net`

Conventions

In this book, you will find a number of styles of text that distinguish between different kinds of information. Here are some examples of these styles, and an explanation of their meaning.

Code words in text are shown as follows: "Set the `fps` variable to the Rounded value of frames."

A block of code is set as follows:

```
// Matches
private var haveMatches : boolean = false;
var matchGUIprefab : GUITexture;
```

Some code lines are long, and end up running onto new lines—make sure that you do not do this in your code. Remember that code lines are terminated by a semi-colon `;` so wherever possible, keep code on a single line. In the example below, space restraints forces this to be displayed on two lines but in your script editor, you should not place a new line to achieve this:

```
new Vector3(Mathf.Lerp(xStartPosition, xEndPosition, (Time.time-
startTime)*speed), transform.position.y,transform.position.z);
```

New terms and **important words** are shown in bold. Words that you see on the screen, in menus or dialog boxes for example, appear in the text like this: "Go to **File | Save** in the script editor, and switch back to Unity."

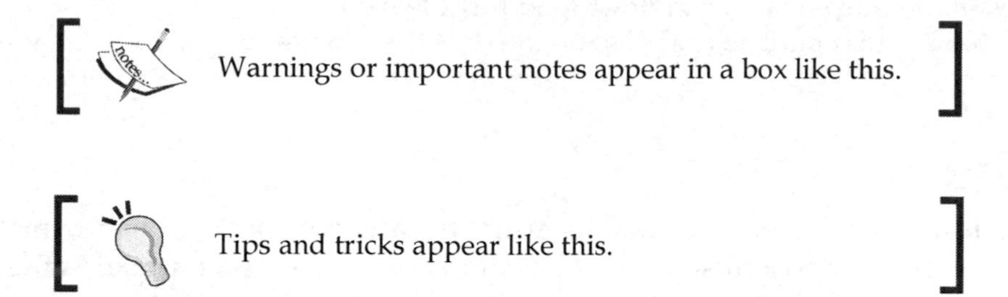

Reader feedback

Feedback from our readers is always welcome. Let us know what you think about this book—what you liked or may have disliked. Reader feedback is important for us to develop titles that you really get the most out of.

To send us general feedback, simply send an e-mail to `feedback@packtpub.com`, and mention the book title via the subject of your message.

If there is a book that you need and would like to see us publish, please send us a note in the **SUGGEST A TITLE** form on `www.packtpub.com` or e-mail `suggest@packtpub.com`.

If there is a topic that you have expertise in and you are interested in either writing or contributing to a book, see our author guide on `www.packtpub.com/authors`.

Customer support

Now that you are the proud owner of a Packt book, we have a number of things to help you to get the most from your purchase.

Downloading the book asset bundle

You can download the required files for all Packt books you have purchased from your account at `http://www.PacktPub.com`. If you purchased this book elsewhere, you can visit `http://www.PacktPub.com/support` and register to have the files e-mailed directly to you. An updated repository of the asset bundle for this book is also available at `http://unitybook.net/book_assets.unitypackage.zip`.

Downloading the color images of this book

We also provide you a PDF file that has color images of the screenshots used in this book. The color images will help you better understand the changes in the output. You can download this file from http://www.packtpub.com/sites/default/files/downloads/1444_Images.pdf

Errata

Although we have taken every care to ensure the accuracy of our content, mistakes do happen. If you find a mistake in one of our books—maybe a mistake in the text or the code—we would be grateful if you would report this to us. By doing so, you can save other readers from frustration and help us improve subsequent versions of this book. If you find any errata, please report them by visiting http://www.packtpub.com/support, selecting your book, clicking on the **errata submission form** link, and entering the details of your errata. Once your errata are verified, your submission will be accepted and the errata will be uploaded to our website, or added to any list of existing errata, under the Errata section of that title. Any existing errata can be viewed by selecting your title from http://www.packtpub.com/support and can also be viewed at http://unitybook.net/book-errata/.

Piracy

Piracy of copyright material on the Internet is an ongoing problem across all media. At Packt, we take the protection of our copyright and licenses very seriously. If you come across any illegal copies of our works, in any form, on the Internet, please provide us with the location address or website name immediately so that we can pursue a remedy.

Please contact us at copyright@packtpub.com with a link to the suspected pirated material.

We appreciate your help in protecting our authors, and our ability to bring you valuable content.

Questions

You can contact us at questions@packtpub.com if you are having a problem with any aspect of the book, and we will do our best to address it.

1
Enter the Third Dimension

Before getting started with any 3D package, it is crucial to understand the environment you'll be working in. As **Unity** is primarily a 3D-based development tool, many concepts throughout this book will assume a certain level of understanding of 3D development and game engines. It is crucial that you equip yourself with an understanding of these concepts before diving into the practical elements of the rest of this book. As such, in this chapter, we'll make sure you're prepared by looking at some important 3D concepts before moving on to discuss the concepts and interface of Unity itself. You will learn about:

- Coordinates and vectors
- 3D shapes
- Materials and textures
- Rigidbody dynamics
- Collision detection
- GameObjects and Components
- Assets and Scenes
- Prefabs
- Unity editor interface

Getting to grips with 3D

Let's take a look at the crucial elements of 3D worlds, and how Unity lets you develop games in three dimensions.

Coordinates

If you have worked with any 3D application before, you'll likely be familiar with the concept of the **Z-axis**. The Z-axis, in addition to the existing X for horizontal and Y for vertical, represents depth. In 3D applications, you'll see information on objects laid out in X, Y, Z format—this is known as the **Cartesian coordinate** method. Dimensions, rotational values, and positions in the 3D world can all be described in this way. In this book, as in other documentation of 3D, you'll see such information written with parenthesis, shown as follows:

(3, 5, 3)

This is mostly for neatness, and also due to the fact that in programming, these values must be written in this way. Regardless of their presentation, you can assume that any sets of three values separated by commas will be in X, Y, Z order.

In the following image, a cube is shown at location (3,5,3) in the 3D world, meaning it is 3 units from 0 in the X-axis, 5 up in the Y-axis, and 3 forward in the Z-axis:

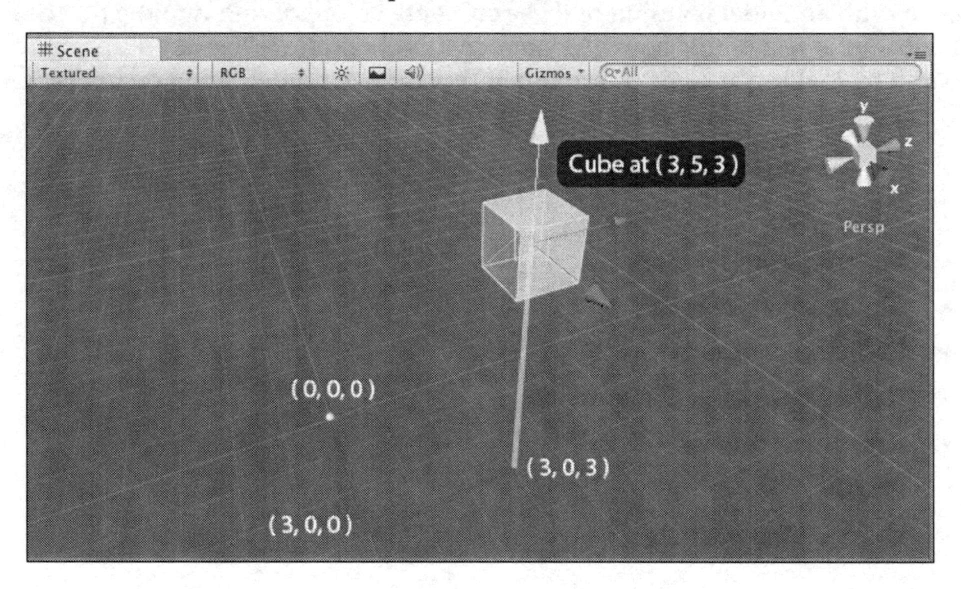

Local space versus world space

A crucial concept to begin looking at is the difference between local space and world space. In any 3D package, the world you will work in is technically infinite, and it can be difficult to keep track of the location of objects within it. In every 3D world, there is a point of origin, often referred to as the **'origin'** or **'world zero'**, as it is represented by the position (0,0,0).

All world positions of objects in 3D are relative to world zero. However, to make things simpler, we also use local space (also known as **object space)** to define object positions in relation to one another. These relationships are known as **parent-child relationships**. In Unity, parent-child relationships can be established easily by dragging one object onto another in the Hierarchy. This causes the dragged object to become a child, and its coordinates from then on are read in terms relative to the parent object. For example, if the child object is exactly at the same world position as the parent object, its position is said to be (0,0,0), even if the parent position is not at world zero.

Local space assumes that every object has its own zero point, which is the point from which its axes emerge. This is usually the center of the object, and by creating relationships between objects, we can compare their positions in relation to one another. Such relationships, known as parent-child relationships, mean that we can calculate distances from other objects using local space, with the parent object's position becoming the new zero point for any of its child objects.

This is especially important to bear in mind when working on art assets in 3D modelling tools, as you should always ensure that your models are created at 0,0,0 in the package that you are using. This is to ensure that when imported into Unity, their axes are read correctly.

We can illustrate this in 2D, as the same conventions will apply to 3D. In the following example:

- The first diagram (**i**) shows two objects in world space. A large cube exists at coordinates(**3,3**), and a smaller one at coordinates (**6,7**).
- In the second diagram (**ii**), the smaller cube has been made a child object of the larger cube. As such the smaller cube's coordinates are said to be (**3,4**), because its zero point is the world position of the parent.

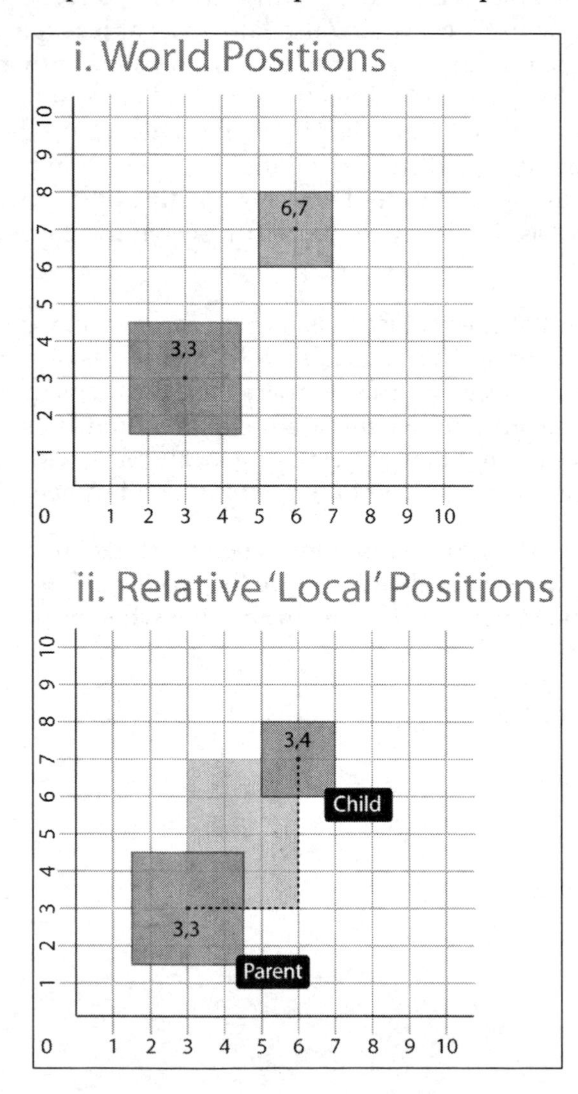

Vectors

You'll also see 3D vectors described in Cartesian coordinates. Like their 2D counterparts, 3D vectors are simply lines drawn in the 3D world that have a direction and a length. Vectors can be moved in world space, but remain unchanged themselves. Vectors are useful in a game engine context, as they allow us to calculate distances, relative angles between objects, and the direction of objects.

Cameras

Cameras are essential in the 3D world, as they act as the viewport for the screen.

Cameras can be placed at any point in the world, animated, or attached to characters or objects as part of a game scenario. Many cameras can exist in a particular scene, but it is assumed that a single main camera will always render what the player sees. This is why Unity gives you a Main Camera object whenever you create a new scene.

Projection mode—3D versus 2D

The Projection mode of a camera states whether it renders in 3D (Perspective) or 2D (Orthographic). Ordinarily, cameras are set to Perspective Projection mode, and as such have a pyramid shaped **Field of View (FOV)**. A Perspective mode camera renders in 3D and is the default Projection mode for a camera in Unity. Cameras can also be set to Orthographic Projection mode in order to render in 2D—these have a rectangular field of view. This can be used on a main camera to create complete 2D games or simply used as a secondary camera used to render **Heads Up Display (HUD)** elements such as a map or health bar.

In game engines, you'll notice that effects such as lighting, motion blurs, and other effects are applied to the camera to help with game simulation of a person's eye view of the world—you can even add a few cinematic effects that the human eye will never experience, such as lens flares when looking at the sun!

Most modern 3D games utilize multiple cameras to show parts of the game world that the character camera is not currently looking at—like a 'cutaway' in cinematic terms. Unity does this with ease by allowing many cameras in a single scene, which can be scripted to act as the main camera at any point during runtime. Multiple cameras can also be used in a game to control the rendering of particular 2D and 3D elements separately as part of the optimization process. For example, objects may be grouped in layers, and cameras may be assigned to render objects in particular layers. This gives us more control over individual renders of certain elements in the game.

Polygons, edges, vertices, and meshes

In constructing 3D shapes, all objects are ultimately made up of interconnected 2D shapes known as **polygons**. On importing models from a modeling application, Unity converts all polygons to polygon triangles. By combining many linked polygons, 3D modeling applications allow us to build complex shapes, known as meshes. Polygon triangles (also referred to as faces) are in turn made up of three connected **edges**. The locations at which these **edges** meet are known as points or **vertices**.

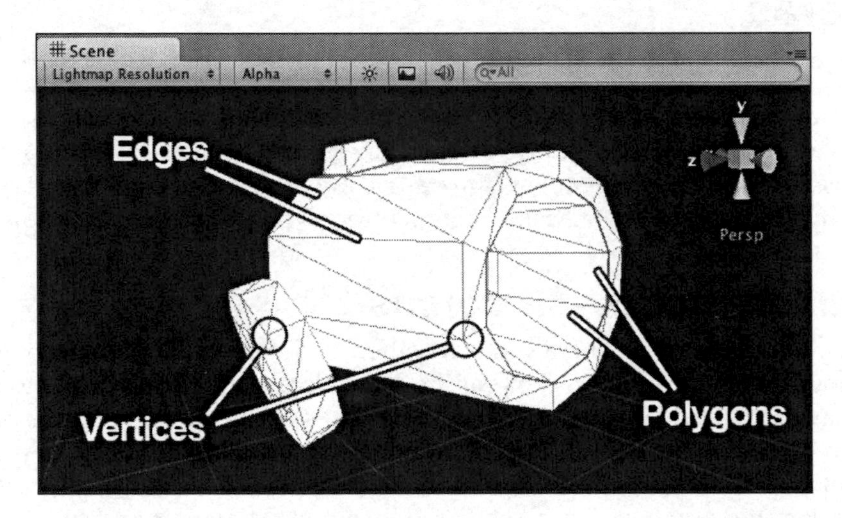

By knowing these locations, game engines are able to make calculations regarding the points of impact, known as **collisions**, when using complex collision detection with **Mesh Colliders**, such as in shooting games to detect the exact location at which a bullet has hit another object. In addition to building 3D shapes that are rendered visibly, **mesh** data can have many other uses. For example, it can be used to specify a shape for collision that is less detailed than a visible object, but roughly the same shape. This can help save performance as the physics engine needn't check a mesh in detail for collisions. This is seen in the following image from the Unity car tutorial, where the vehicle itself is more detailed than its collision mesh:

In the second image, you can see that the amount of detail in the **mesh** used for the collider is far less than the visible **mesh** itself:

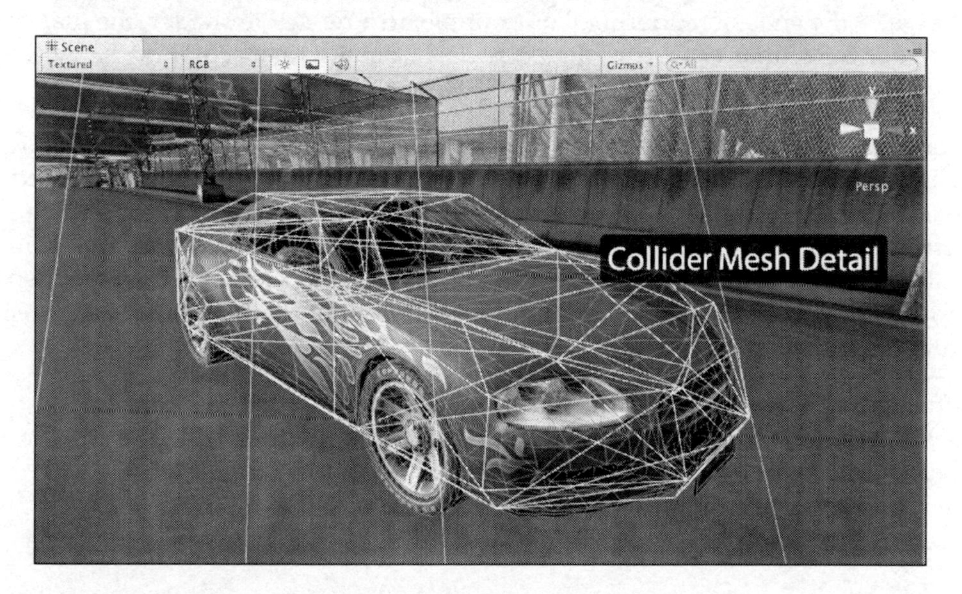

In game projects, it is crucial for the developer to understand the importance of the **polygon count**. The polygon count is the total number of polygons, often in reference to models, but also in reference to props, or an entire game level (or in Unity terms, 'Scene'). The higher the number of polygons, the more work your computer must do to render the objects onscreen. This is why we've seen an increase in the level of detail from early 3D games to those of today. Simply compare the visual detail in a game such as id's *Quake*(1996) with the details seen in Epic's *Gears Of War* (2006) in just a decade. As a result of faster technology, game developers are now able to model 3D characters and worlds, for games that contain a much higher polygon count and resultant level of realism, and this trend will inevitably continue in the years to come. This said, as more platforms emerge such as mobile and online, games previously seen on dedicated consoles can now be played in a web browser thanks to Unity. As such, the hardware constraints are as important now as ever, as lower powered devices such as mobile phones and tablets are able to run 3D games. For this reason, when modeling any object to add to your game, you should consider polygonal detail, and where it is most required.

Materials, textures, and shaders

Materials are a common concept to all 3D applications, as they provide the means to set the visual appearance of a 3D model. From basic colors to reflective image-based surfaces, materials handle everything.

Let's start with a simple color and the option of using one or more images—known as **textures**. In a single material, the material works with the **shader**, which is a script in charge of the style of rendering. For example, in a reflective shader, the material will render reflections of surrounding objects, but maintain its color or the look of the image applied as its texture.

In Unity, the use of materials is easy. Any materials created in your 3D modeling package will be imported and recreated automatically by the engine and created as assets that are reusable. You can also create your own materials from scratch, assigning images as textures and selecting a shader from a large library that comes built-in. You may also write your own shader scripts or copy-paste those written by fellow developers in the Unity community, giving you more freedom for expansion beyond the included set.

When creating textures for a game in a graphics package such as Photoshop or GIMP, you must be aware of the resolution. Larger textures will give you the chance to add more detail to your textured models, but be more intensive to render. Game textures imported into Unity will be scaled to a power of 2 resolution. For example:

- 64px x 64px
- 128px x 128px
- 256px x 256px
- 512px x 512px
- 1024px x 1024px

Creating textures of these sizes with content that matches at the edges will mean that they can be tiled successfully by Unity. You may also use textures scaled to values that are not powers of two, but mostly these are used for GUI elements as you will discover over the course of this book.

Rigidbody physics

For developers working with game engines, physics engines provide an accompanying way of simulating real-world responses for objects in games. In Unity, the game engine uses Nvidia's *PhysX* engine, a popular and highly accurate commercial physics engine.

In game engines, there is no assumption that an object should be affected by physics—firstly because it requires a lot of processing power, and secondly because there is simply no need to do so. For example, in a 3D driving game, it makes sense for the cars to be under the influence of the physics engine, but not the track or surrounding objects, such as trees, walls, and so on—they will remain static for the duration of the game. For this reason, when making games in Unity a Rigidbody physics component is given to any object that you wish to be under the control of the physics engine, and ideally any moving object, so that the physics engine is aware of the moving object, to save on performance.

Physics engines for games use the Rigidbody dynamics system of creating realistic motion. This simply means that instead of objects being static in the 3D world, they can have properties such as mass, gravity, velocity, and friction.

As the power of hardware and software increases, Rigidbody physics is becoming more widely applied in games, as it offers the potential for more varied and realistic simulation. We'll be utilizing rigid body dynamics as part of our prototype in this chapter and as part of the main game of the book in *Chapter 7, Instantiation and Rigid Bodies*.

Collision detection

More crucial in game engines than in 3D animation, collision detection is the way we analyze our 3D world for inter-object collisions. By giving an object a Collider component, we are effectively placing an invisible net around it. This net usually mimics its shape and is in charge of reporting any collisions with other colliders, making the game engine respond accordingly.

There are two main types of **Collider** in Unity—**Primitives** and **Meshes**. **Primitive shapes** in 3D terms are simple geometric objects such as **Boxes**, **Spheres**, and **Capsules**. Therefore, a primitive collider such as a **Box collider** in Unity has that shape, regardless of the visual shape of the 3D object it is applied to. Often, **Primitive colliders** are used because they are computationally cheaper or because there is no need for precision. A **Mesh collider** is more expensive as it can be based upon the shape of the 3D mesh it is applied to; therefore, the more complex the **mesh**, the more detailed and precise the collider will be, and more computationally expensive it will become. However, as shown in the Car tutorial example earlier, it is possible to assign a simpler mesh than that which is rendered, in order to create simpler and more efficient mesh colliders.

The following diagram illustrates the various types and subtypes of **collider**:

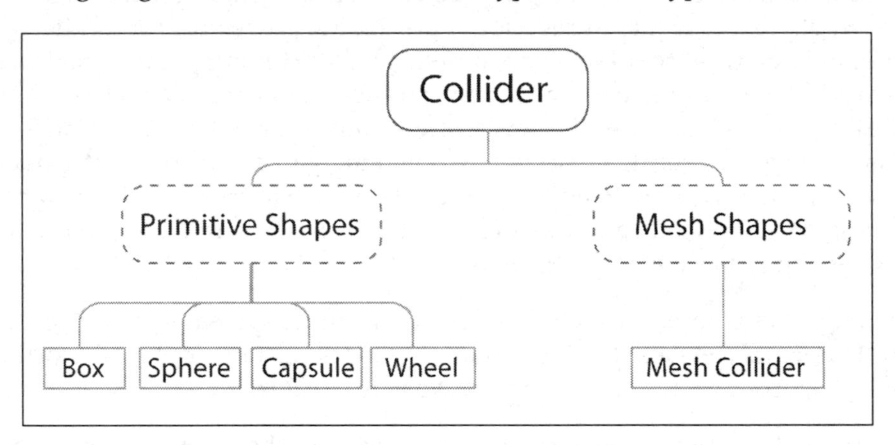

For example, in a ten-pin bowling game, a simple **Sphere collider** will surround the ball, while the pins themselves will have either a simple **Capsule collider**, or for a more realistic collision, employ a **Mesh collider**, as this will be shaped the same as the 3D mesh of the pin. On impact, the colliders of any affected objects will report to the physics engine, which will dictate their reaction, based on the direction of impact, speed, and other factors.

In this example, employing a **Mesh collider** to fit exactly to the shape of the pin model would be more accurate but is more expensive in processing terms. This simply means that it demands more processing power from the computer, the cost of which is reflected in slower performance, and hence the term expensive.

Essential Unity concepts

Unity makes the game production process simple by giving you a set of logical steps to build any conceivable game scenario. Renowned for being non-game-type specific, Unity offers you a blank canvas and a set of consistent procedures to let your imagination be the limit of your creativity. By establishing its use of the GameObject concept, you are able to break down parts of your game into easily manageable objects, which are made of many individual **Component** parts. By making individual objects within the game—introducing functionality to them with each component you add, you are able to infinitely expand your game in a logical progressive manner.

Component parts in turn have **Variables**—essentially properties of the component, or settings to control them with. By adjusting these **variables**, you'll have complete control over the effect that **Component** has on your object. The following diagram illustrates this:

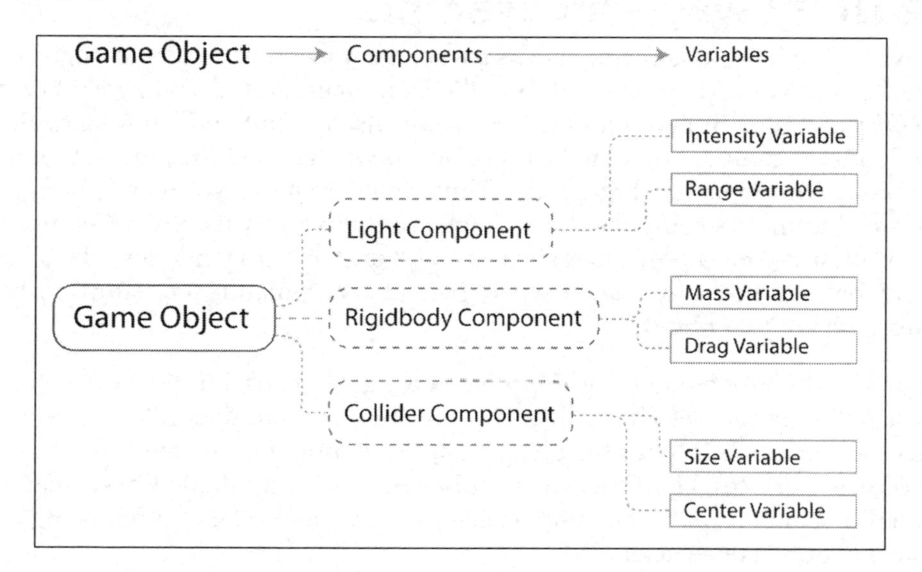

In the following image we can see a **Game Object** with a **Light Component**, as seen in the Unity interface:

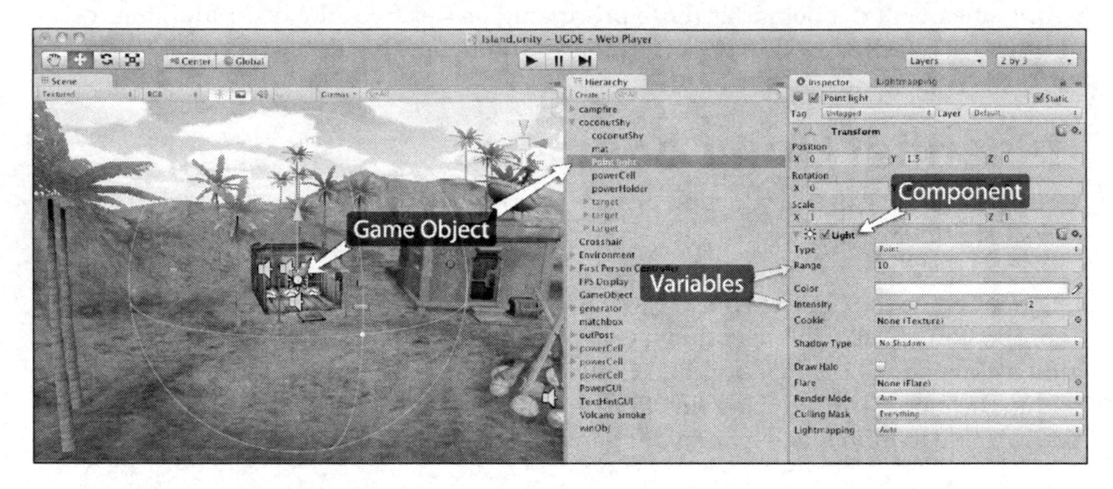

Now let's look at how this approach would be used in a simple gameplay context.

The Unity way—an example

If we wished to have a bouncing ball as part of a game, then we would begin with a sphere. This can quickly be created from the Unity menus, and will give you a new **GameObject** with a **Sphere mesh** (the 3D shape itself). Unity will automatically add a Renderer component to make it visible. Having created this, we can then add a Rigidbody component. A Rigidbody (Unity refers to most two-word phrases as a single word term) is a component which tells Unity to apply its physics engine to an object. With this comes properties such as mass, gravity, drag, and also the ability to apply forces to the object, either when the player commands it or simply when it collides with another object.

Our sphere will now fall to the ground when the game runs, but how do we make it bounce? This is simple! The collider component has a variable called **Physic Material**—this is a setting for the physics engine, defining how it will react to other objects' surfaces. Here we can select **Bouncy**—a ready-made Physic material provided by Unity as part of an importable package and voila! Our bouncing ball is complete in only a few clicks.

This streamlined approach for the most basic of tasks, such as the previous example, seems pedestrian at first. However, you'll soon find that by applying this approach to more complex tasks, they become very simple to achieve. Here is an overview of some further key Unity concepts you'll need to know as you get started.

Assets

These are the building blocks of all Unity projects. From textures in the form of image files, through 3D models for meshes, and sound files for effects, Unity refers to the files you'll use to create your game as assets. This is why in any Unity project folder all files used are stored in a child folder named `Assets`. This `Assets` folder is mirrored in the Project panel of the Unity interface; see *The interface* section in this chapter.

Scenes

In Unity, you should think of scenes as individual levels, or areas of game content—though some developers create entire games in a single scene, such as, puzzle games, by dynamically loading content through code. By constructing your game with many scenes, you'll be able to distribute loading times and test different parts of your game individually. New scenes are often used separately to a game scene you may be working on, in order to prototype or test a piece of potential gameplay.

Any currently open scene is what you are working on, as no two scenes can be worked on simultaneously. Scenes can be manipulated and constructed by using the Hierarchy and Scene views.

GameObjects

Any active object in the currently open scene is called a **GameObject**. Certain assets taken from the Project panel such as models and prefabs become game objects when placed (or 'instantiated') into the current scene. Other objects such as particle systems and primitives can be placed into the scene by using the **Create** button on the Hierarchy or by using the **GameObject** menu at the top of the interface. All **GameObjects** contain at least one component to begin with, that is, the **Transform** component. **Transform** simply tells the Unity engine the position, rotation, and scale of an object—all described in X, Y, Z coordinate (or in the case of scale, dimensional) order. In turn, the component can then be addressed in scripting in order to set an object's position, rotation, or scale. From this initial component, you will build upon GameObjects with further components, adding required functionality to build every part of any game scenario you can imagine.

In the following image, you can see the most basic form of a **Game Object**, as shown in the **Inspector** panel:

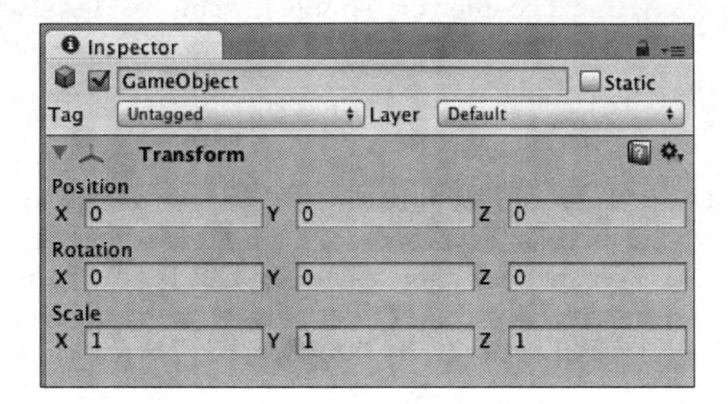

GameObjects can also be nested in the Hierarchy, in order to create the parent-child relationships mentioned previously.

Components

Components come in various forms. They can be for creating behavior, defining appearance, and influencing other aspects of an object's function in the game. By attaching components to an object, you can immediately apply new parts of the game engine to your object. Common components of game production come built-in with Unity, such as the Rigidbody component mentioned earlier, down to simpler elements such as lights, cameras, particle emitters, and more. To build further interactive elements of the game, you'll write scripts, which are also treated as components in Unity. Try to think of a script as something that extends or modifies the existing functionality available in Unity or creates behavior with the Unity scripting classes provided.

Scripts

While being considered by Unity to be components, scripts are an essential part of game production, and deserve a mention as a key concept. In this book, we will write our scripts in both C Sharp (More often written as 'C#') and Javascript. You should also be aware that Unity offers you the opportunity to write in Boo (a derivative of the Python language).We have chosen to primarily focus on C# and Javascript as these are the main two languages used by Unity developers, and Boo is not supported for scripting on mobile devices; for this reason it is not advised to begin learning Unity scripting with Boo.

Unity does not require you to learn how the coding of its own engine works or how to modify it, but you will be utilizing scripting in almost every game scenario you develop. The beauty of using Unity scripting is that any script you write for your game will be straightforward enough after a few examples, as Unity has its own built-in `Behavior` class called `Monobehaviour`—a set of scripting instructions for you to call upon. For many new developers, getting to grips with scripting can be a daunting prospect, and one that threatens to put off new Unity users who are more accustomed to design. If this is your first attempt at getting into game development, or you have no experience in writing code, do not worry. We will introduce scripting one step at a time, with a mind to showing you not only the importance, but also the power of effective scripting for your Unity games.

To write scripts, you'll use Unity's standalone script editor, Monodevelop. This separate application can be found in the Unity application folder on your PC or Mac and will be launched any time you edit a new script or an existing one. Amending and saving scripts in the script editor will immediately update the script in Unity as soon as you switch back to Unity. You may also designate your own script editor in the Unity preferences if you wish to, such as Visual Studio. Monodevelop is recommended however, as it offers auto-completion of code as you type and is natively developed and updated by Unity Technologies.

Prefabs

Unity's development approach hinges around the **GameObject** concept, but it also has a clever way to store objects as assets to be reused in different parts of your game, and then instantiated (also known as 'spawning' or 'cloning') at any time. By creating complex objects with various components and settings, you'll be effectively building a template for something you may want to spawn multiple instances of (hence 'instantiate'), with each instance then being individually modifiable.

Consider a crate as an example—you may have given the object in the game a mass, and written scripted behaviors for its destruction, and chances are you'll want to use this object more than once in a game, and perhaps even in games other than the one it was designed for.

Prefabs allow you to store the object, complete with components and current configuration. Comparable to the *MovieClip* concept in Adobe Flash, think of prefabs simply as empty containers that you can fill with objects to form a data template you'll likely recycle.

The interface

The Unity interface, like many other working environments, has a customizable layout. Consisting of several dockable spaces, you can pick which parts of the interface appear where. Let's take a look at a typical Unity layout:

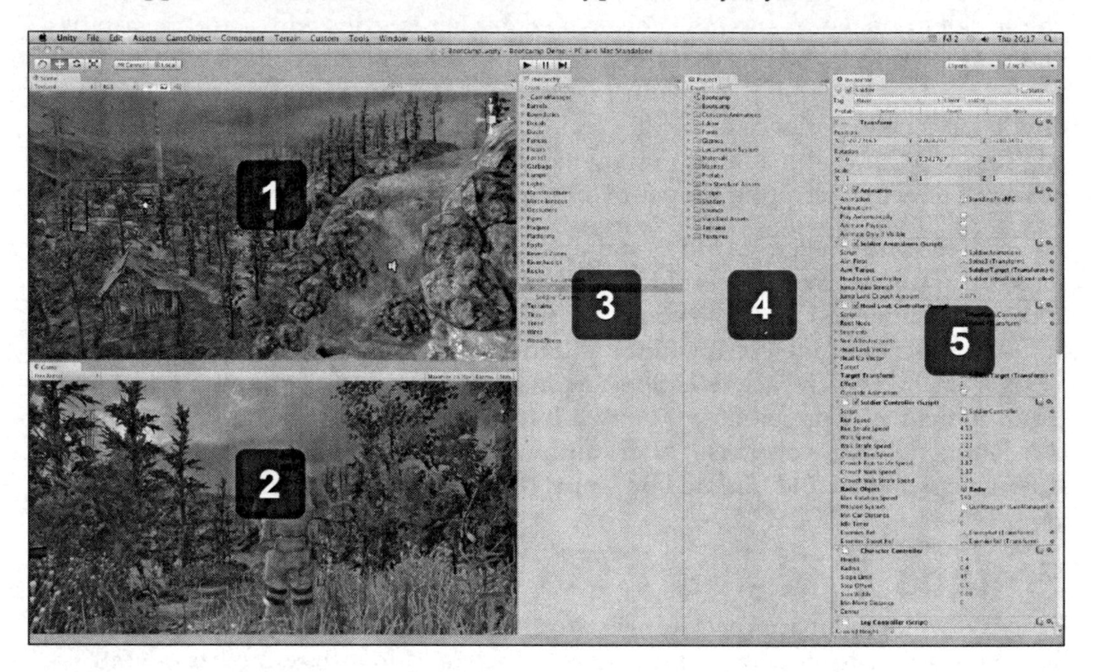

This layout can be achieved by going to **Window** | **Layouts** | **2 by 3 in Unity**.

As the previous image demonstrates (Mac version shown), there are five different panels or views you'll be dealing with, which are as follows:

Scene [1] – where the game is constructed.

Game [2] – the preview window, active only in play mode.

Hierarchy [3] – a list of GameObjects in the scene.

Project [4] – a list of your project's assets; acts as a library.

Inspector [5] – settings for currently selected asset/object/setting.

The Scene view and Hierarchy

The **Scene** view is where you will build the entirety of your game project in Unity. This window offers a perspective (full 3D) view, which is switchable to orthographic (top-down, side-on, and front-on) views. When working in one of the orthographic views, rotating the view will display the scene isometrically. The Scene view acts as a fully rendered 'Editor' view of the game world you build. Dragging an asset to this window (or the Hierarchy) will create an instance of it as a **GameObject** in the Scene.

The **Scene** view is tied to the **Hierarchy**, which lists all GameObjects in the currently open scene in ascending alphabetical order.

Control tools

The **Scene** window is also accompanied by four useful control tools, as shown in the following image:

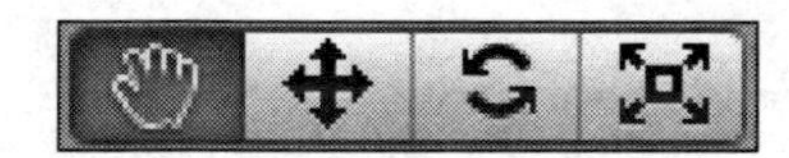

Accessible from the keyboard using keys *Q*, *W*, *E*, and *R*, these keys perform the following operations:

- **The Hand tool** [*Q*]: This tool allows navigation of the Scene window. By itself, it allows you to drag around in the Scene window with the left mouse button to pan your view. Holding down Alt with this tool selected will allow you left click to orbit your view around a central point you are looking at, and holding the Alt key with right click will allow you to zoom, as will scrolling the mouse wheel. Holding the Shift key down also will speed up both of these functions.
- **The Translate tool** [*W*]: This is your active selection tool. As you can completely interact with the **Scene** window, selecting objects either in the **Hierarchy** or **Scene** means you'll be able to drag the object's axis handle in order to reposition them.
- **The Rotate tool**[*E*]: This works in the same way as Translate, using visual 'handles' to allow you to rotate your object around each axis.
- **The Scale tool** [*R*]: Again, this tool works as the Translate and Rotate tools do. It adjusts the size or scale of an object using visual handles.

Having selected objects in either the **Scene** or **Hierarchy**, they immediately get selected in both. Selection of objects in this way will also show the properties of the object in the **Inspector**. Given that you may not be able to see an object you've selected in the **Hierarchy** in the **Scene** window, Unity also provides the use of the *F* key, to focus your **Scene** view on that object. Simply select an object from the **Hierarchy**, hover your mouse cursor over the **Scene** window, and press *F*. You can also achieve this by double-clicking the name of a game object in the Hierarchy.

Flythrough Scene navigation

To move around your Scene view using the mouse and keys you can use Flythrough mode. Simply hold down the right mouse button and drag to look around in first-person style, then use *W*, *A*, *S* and *D* to move and *Q* and *E* to descend and ascend (respectively).

Control bar

In addition to the control tools, there is also a bar of additional options to help you work with your Unity scenes, which is shown as follows:

Known as the Scene View Control Bar, this bar allows you to adjust (left to right):

- Draw mode (default is 'Textured')
- Render mode (default is 'RGB')
- Toggle scene lighting
- Toggle overlays—shows and hides GUI elements and Skyboxes and toggles the 3D grid
- Toggle audition mode—previews audio sources in the current scene
- Gizmos—use this pop-out menu to show or hide Gizmos, the 2D icons of cameras, lights, and other components shown in the scene.

Search box

While the **Scene** view is intrinsically linked with the Hierarchy, often you may need to locate an item or type of item in the **Scene** view itself by searching. Simply type the name or data type (in other words, an attached component) of an object into the search, and the **Scene** view will grey out other objects in order to highlight the item you have searched for. This becomes very useful when dealing with more complex scenes, and should be used in conjunction with *F* on the keyboard to focus on the highlighted object in the **Scene** window itself.

Create button

As many of the game assets you'll use in Unity will be created by the editor itself, the **Hierarchy** has a **Create** button that allows you to create objects that are also located within the top **GameObject** menu. Similar to the **Create** button on the Project panel, this drop-down menu creates items and immediately selects them so that you may rename or begin working with them in the **Scene** or **Inspector**.

The Inspector

Think of the **Inspector** as your personal toolkit to adjust every element of any GameObject or asset in your project. Much like the *Property Inspector* concept utilized by Adobe in Flash and Dreamweaver, this is a context-sensitive window. All this means is that whatever you select, the **Inspector** will change to show its relevant properties—it is sensitive to the context in which you are working.

The **Inspector** will show every component part of anything you select, and allow you to adjust the variables of these components, using simple form elements such as text input boxes, slider scales, buttons, and drop-down menus. Many of these variables are tied into Unity's drag-and-drop system, which means that rather than selecting from a drop-down menu, if it is more convenient, you can drag-and-drop to choose settings or assign properties.

This window is not only for inspecting objects. It will also change to show the various options for your project when choosing them from the **Edit** menu, as it acts as an ideal space to show you preferences—changing back to showing component properties as soon as you reselect an object or asset.

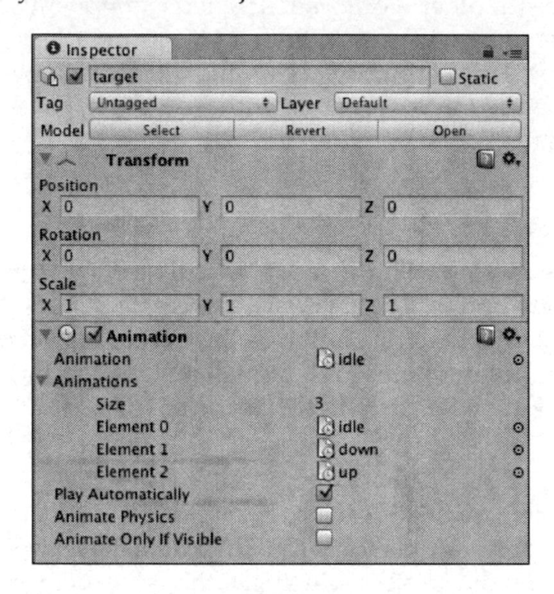

In this image, the **Inspector** is showing properties for a **target** object in the game. The object itself features two components—**Transform** and **Animation**. The **Inspector** will allow you to make changes to settings in either of them. Also note that in order to temporarily disable any component at any time, which will become very useful for testing and experimentation—you can simply deselect the checkbox to the left of the component's name. Likewise, if you wish to switch off an entire object at a time, then you may deselect the checkbox next to its name at the top of the **Inspector** window.

The Project window

The **Project** window is a direct view of the `Assets` folder of your project. Every Unity project is made up of a parent folder, containing three subfolders—`Assets`, `Library`, and while the Unity Editor is running, a `Temp` folder. Placing assets into the `Assets` folder means you'll immediately be able to see them in the **Project** window, and they'll also be automatically imported into your Unity project. Likewise, changing any asset located in the `Assets` folder, and resaving it from a third-party application, such as Photoshop, will cause Unity to reimport the asset, reflecting your changes immediately in your project and any active scenes that use that particular asset.

Asset management

It is important to remember that you should only alter asset locations and names using the **Project** window—using Finder (Mac) or Windows Explorer (PC) to do so may break connections in your Unity project. Therefore, to relocate or rename objects in your `Assets` folder, use Unity's **Project** window instead of your operating system.

The **Project** window, like the Hierarchy, is accompanied by a **Create** button. This allows the creation of any assets that can be made within Unity, for example, scripts, prefabs, and materials.

The Game view

The Game view is invoked by pressing the **Play** button and acts as a realistic test of your game. It also has settings for screen ratio, which will come in handy when testing how much of the player's view will be restricted in certain ratios, such as 4:3 (as opposed to wide) screen resolutions. Having pressed **Play**, it is crucial that you bear in mind the following advice:

Play mode—testing only!

In play mode, the adjustments you make to any parts of your game scene are merely temporary. It is meant as a testing mode only, and when you press **Play** again to stop the game, all changes made to active **GameObjects** during play mode will be undone. This can often trip up new users, so don't forget about it!

The Game view can also be set to **Maximize** when you invoke play mode, giving you a better view of the game at nearly fullscreen—the window expands to fill the interface. It is worth noting that you can expand any part of the interface in this way, simply by hovering over the part you wish to expand and pressing the *Space bar*.

In addition to using **Play** to preview your game, the live game mode can also be paused by pressing the *Pause* button at the top of the interface, and play can be advanced a frame at a time using the third button, **Advance Frame**, next to **Pause**. This is useful when Debugging—the process of finding and solving problems or 'bugs' with your game development.

Summary

Here we have looked at the key concepts you will need to understand and complete the exercises in this book. However, 3D is a detailed discipline that you will continue to learn not only with Unity, but in other areas also. With this in mind, you are recommended to continue to read more on the topics discussed in this chapter, in order to supplement your study of 3D development. Each individual piece of software you encounter will have its own dedicated tutorials and resources dedicated to learning it. If you wish to learn 3D artwork to complement your work in Unity, you are recommended to familiarize yourself with your chosen package, after researching the list of tools that work with the Unity pipeline and choosing which one suits you the best.

Now that we've taken a brief look at 3D concepts and the processes used by Unity to create games, we'll begin by completing a simple exercise before getting started on the larger game element of this book.

In the following chapter, we'll begin with a short exercise in which you will prototype a simple game mechanic using Primitive shapes generated by the engine itself, and some basic coding to get you started in C Sharp (C#)/ Javascript. It is important to kick-start your Unity learning with a simple example using primitives, as you will often find yourself prototyping game ideas in this manner once you feel more comfortable in using Unity.

After this, we'll move on to the larger exercise of the book, looking at game environments and getting to grips with the terrain editor. With a physical height painting approach, the terrain editor is an easy to use starting point for any game with an outdoor environment. We'll use this to build an island, and in the ensuing chapters we'll add features to the island to create a mini-game, in which the user must light a campfire by retrieving matches from a locked outpost. Let's get started!

2
Prototyping and Scripting Basics

When starting out in game development, one of the best ways to learn the various parts of the discipline is to prototype your idea. Unity excels in assisting you with this, with its visual scene editor and public member variables that form settings in the Inspector. To get to grips with working in the Unity editor, we'll begin by prototyping a simple game mechanic using primitive shapes and basic coding.

In this chapter, you will learn about:

- Creating a New Project in Unity
- Importing Asset packages
- Working with game objects in the **Scene** view and **Hierarchy**
- Adding materials
- Writing C Sharp (C#) and Javascript
- Variables, functions, and commands
- Using the `Translate()` command to move objects
- Using Prefabs to store objects
- Using the `Instantiate()` command to spawn objects

Your first Unity project

As Unity comes in two main forms—a standard, free download and a paid Pro developer license, we'll stick to using features that users of the standard free edition will have access to.

If you're launching Unity for the very first time, you'll be presented with a Unity demonstration project. While this is useful to look into best practices for the development of high-end projects, if you're starting out, looking over some of the assets and scripting may feel daunting, so we'll leave this behind and start from scratch!

In Unity go to **File | New Project** and you will be presented with the **Project Wizard** (Mac version shown); from here select the **Create New Project** tab.

Be aware that if at any time you wish to launch Unity and be taken directly to the **Project Wizard**, then simply launch the Unity Editor application and immediately hold the *Alt* key (Mac and PC). This can be set to the default behavior for launch in the Unity Preferences.

Click the **Set** button and choose where you would like to save your new Unity project folder on your hard drive. The new project has been named **UGDE** after this book, and I have chosen to store it on my desktop for easy access.

The **Project Wizard** also offers the ability to import many **Asset Packages** into your new project, which are provided free to use in your game development by Unity Technologies. Comprising scripts, ready-made objects, and other artwork, these packages are a useful way to get started in various types of new project. You can also import these packages at any time from the **Assets** menu within Unity, by selecting **Import Package**, and choosing from the list of available packages. You can also import a package from anywhere on your hard drive by choosing the **Custom Package** option here. This import method is also used to share assets with others, and when receiving assets you have downloaded through the **Asset Store**—see **Window | Asset Store** to view this part of Unity later.

From the list of packages to be imported, select the following (as shown in the previous image):

- **Character Controllers**
- **Skyboxes**
- **Terrain Assets**
- **Water (Basic)**

When you are happy with your selection, simply choose **Create Project** at the bottom of this dialog window. Unity will then create your new project and you will see progress bars representing the import of the four packages.

A basic prototyping environment

To create a simple environment, in which to prototype some game mechanics, we'll begin with a basic series of objects with which to introduce gameplay that allows the player to aim and shoot at a wall of primitive cubes.

When complete, your prototyping environment will feature a floor comprised of a cube primitive, a main camera through which to view the 3D world and a Point Light setup to highlight the area where our gameplay will be introduced. It will look something like this:

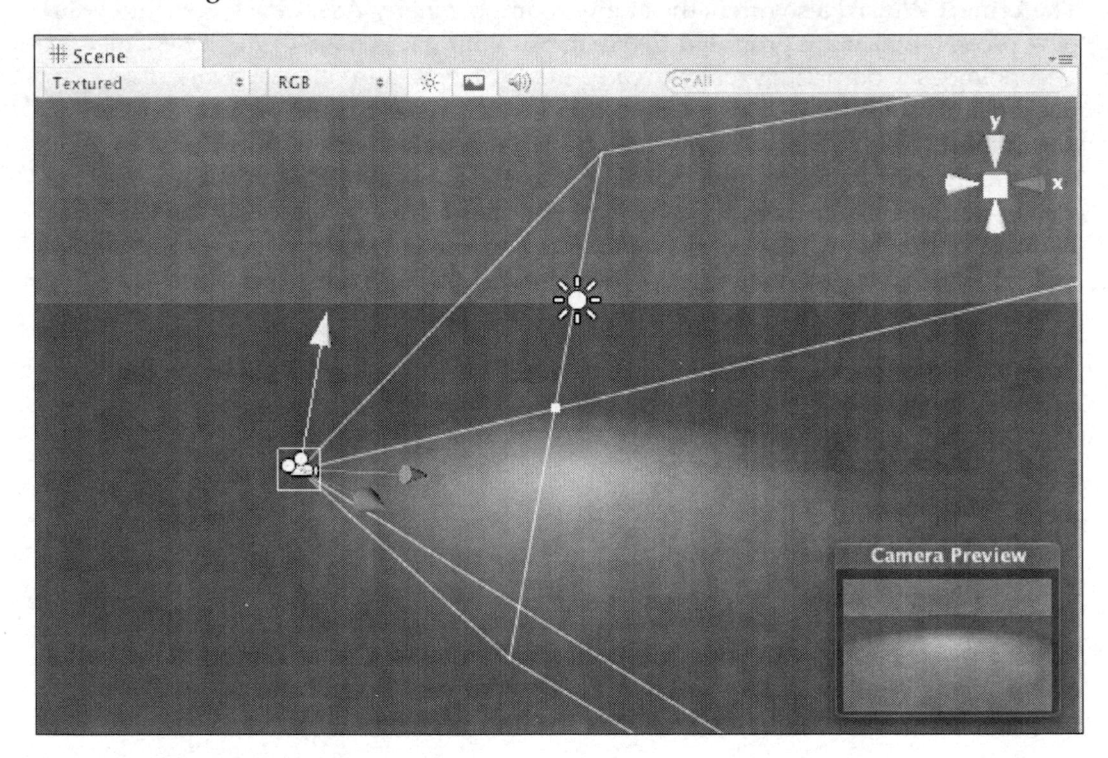

Setting the scene

As all new scenes come with a Main Camera object by default, we'll begin by adding a floor for our prototyping environment.

On the Hierarchy panel, click the **Create** button, and from the drop-down menu, choose **Cube**. The items listed in this drop-down menu can also be found in the **GameObject | Create Other** top menu. You will now see an object in the Hierarchy panel called a **Cube**. Select this and press *Return* (Mac) / *F2* (PC) or double-click the object name slowly (both platforms) to rename this object; type in **Floor** and press *Return* (both platforms) to confirm this change.

For consistency's sake, we will begin our creation at world zero—the center of the 3D environment we are working in. To ensure that the floor cube you just added is at this position, ensure it is still selected in the **Hierarchy** and then check the **Transform** component on the **Inspector** panel, ensuring that the position values for **X**, **Y**, and **Z** are all at 0; if not, change them all to zero, either by typing them in or by clicking the **Cog** icon to the right of the component, and selecting **Reset Position** from the pop-out menu.

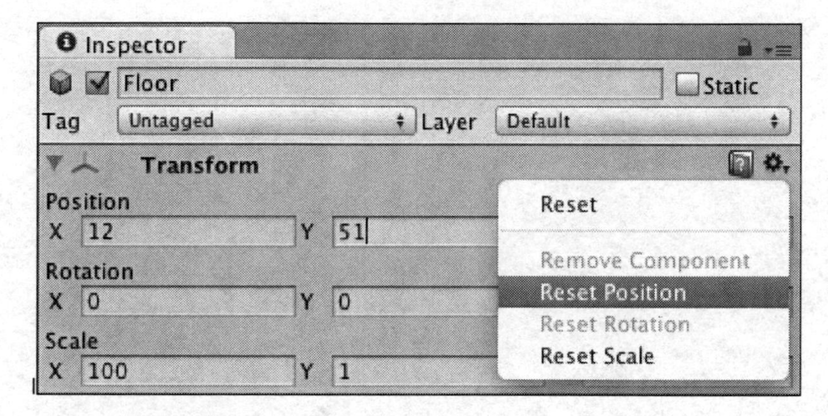

Next, we'll turn the cube into a floor, by stretching it out in the X and Z axes. Into the **X** and **Z** values under **Scale** in the **Transform** component, type a value of **100**, leaving **Y** at a value of **1**.

Adding simple lighting

Now we will highlight part of our prototyping floor by adding a Point Light. Select the **Create** button on the **Hierarchy** (or go to **Game Object | Create Other**) and choose **Point Light**. Position the new Point Light at (**0, 20, 0**) using the **Position** values in the **Transform** component, so that it is **20** units above the floor.

You will notice that this means that the floor is out of range of the light, so expand the **Range** by dragging on the yellow dot handles that intersect the outline of the Point Light in the **Scene** view, until the value for **Range** shown in the **Light** component in the **Inspector** reaches something around a value of **40**, and the light is creating a lit part of the floor object.

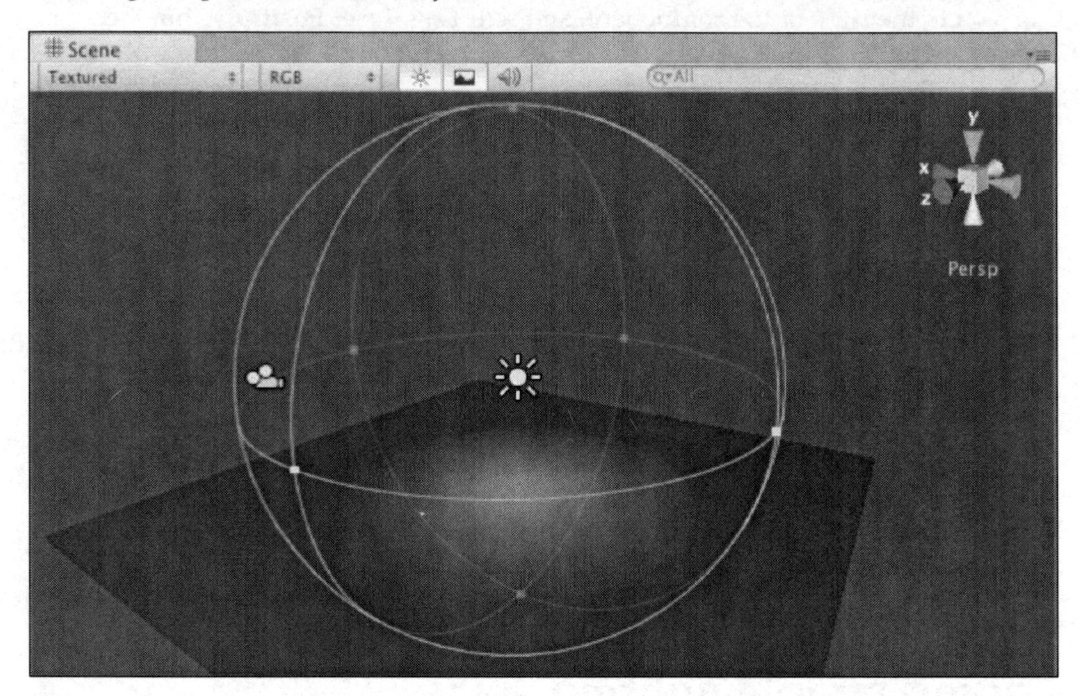

Bear in mind that most components and visual editing tools in the **Scene** view are inextricably linked, so altering values such as **Range** in the Inspector **Light** component will update the visual display in the **Scene** view as you type, and stay constant as soon as you press **Return** to confirm the values entered.

Another brick in the wall

Now let's make a wall of cubes that we can launch a projectile at. We'll do this by creating a single master brick, adding components as necessary, and then duplicating this until our wall is complete.

Building the master brick

In order to create a template for all of our bricks, we'll start by creating a master object, something to create clones of. This is done as follows:

1. Click the **Create** button at the top of the **Hierarchy**, and select **Cube**. Position this at **(0, 1, 0)** using the **Position** values in the **Transform** component on the **Inspector**. Then, focus your view on this object by ensuring it is still selected in the **Hierarchy**, hovering your cursor over the **Scene** view, and pressing *F*.
2. Add physics to your **Cube** object by choosing **Component | Physics | Rigidbody** from the top menu. This means that your object is now a Rigidbody—it has mass, gravity, and is affected by other objects using the physics engine for realistic reactions in the 3D world.
3. Finally, we'll color this object by creating a **Material**. Materials are a way of applying color and imagery to our 3D geometry. To make a new one, go to the **Create** button on the **Project** panel and choose **Material** from the drop-down menu. Press *Return* (Mac) or *F2* (PC) to rename this asset to **Red** instead of the default name **New Material**.
4. With this material selected, the **Inspector** shows its properties. Click on the color block to the right of **Main Color** [see image label 1] to open the **Color Picker** [see image label 2]; this will differ in appearance depending upon whether you are using Mac or PC. Simply choose a shade of red, and then close the window. The **Main Color** block should now have been updated.

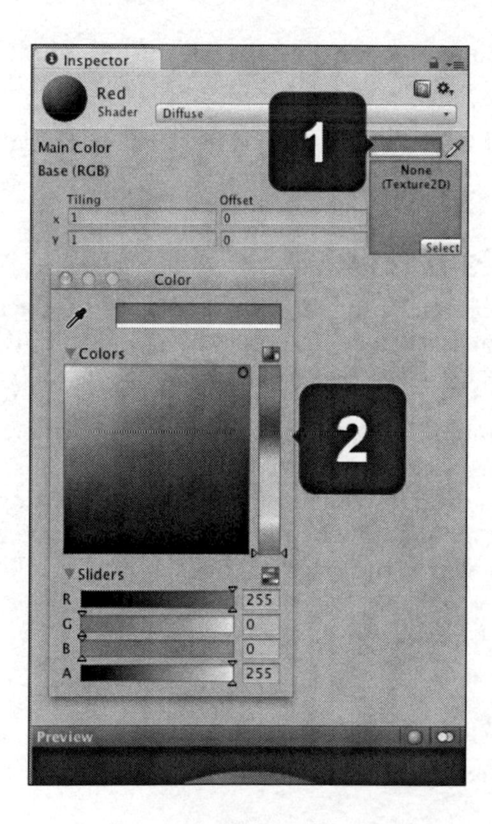

5. To apply this material, drag it from the **Project** panel and drop it onto either the cube as seen in the **Scene** view, or onto the name of the object in the Hierarchy. The material is then applied to the Mesh Renderer component of this object and immediately seen following the other components of the object in the **Inspector**. Most importantly, your cube should now be red! Adjusting settings using the **Preview** of this material on any object will edit the original asset, as this preview is simply a link to the asset itself, not a newly editable instance.
6. Now that our cube has a color and physics applied through the **Rigidbody** component, it is ready to be duplicated and act as one brick in a wall of many, before we do that however, lets have a quick look at the physics in action. With the cube still selected, set the **Y Position** value to **15** and the **X Rotation** value to **40** in the **Transform** component in the **Inspector**. Press **Play** (shortcut *Ctrl+P* [PC] *Command+P* [Mac]) at the top of the Unity interface and you should see the cube fall and then settle, having fallen at an angle.
7. Press **Play** again to stop testing. Do not press **Pause** as this will only temporarily halt the test, and changes made thereafter to the scene will not be saved.
8. Set the **Y Position** value for the cube back to **1**, and set the **X Rotation** back to **0**.

Now that we know our brick behaves correctly, let's start creating a row of bricks to form our wall.

And snap!—It's a row

To help you position objects, Unity allows you to snap to specific increments when dragging—these increments can be redefined by going to **Edit | Snap Settings**.

To use snapping, hold down *Command* (Mac) or *Control* (PC) when using the **Translate** tool (*W*) to move objects in the **Scene** view. So in order to start building the wall, duplicate the cube brick we already have using the shortcut *Command+D* (Mac) or *Control+D* (PC), then drag the red axis handle while holding the snapping key. This will snap by one unit at a time by default, so snap-move your cube one unit in the **X** axis to that it sits next to the original cube, shown as follows:

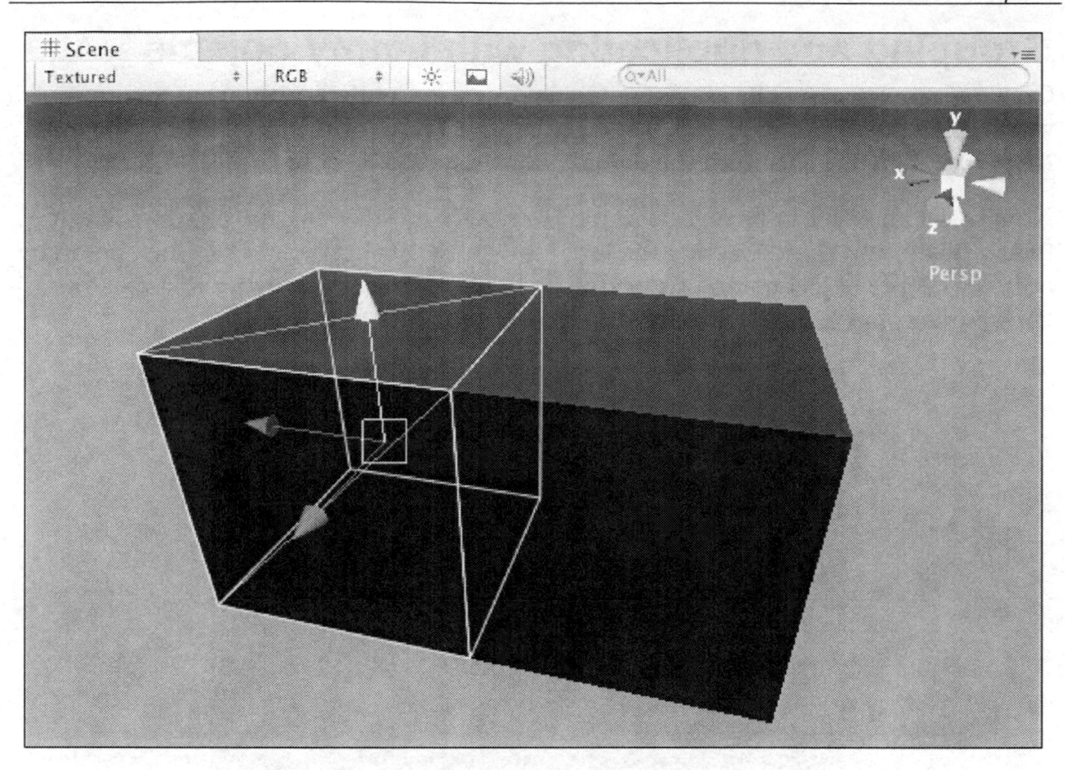

Repeat this procedure of duplication and snap-dragging until you have a row of 10 cubes in a line. This is the first row of bricks, and to simplify building the rest of the bricks we will now group this row under an empty object, and then duplicate the parent empty object.

Vertex snapping

The basic snapping technique used here works well as our cubes are a generic scale of 1, but when scaling more detailed shaped objects, you should use vertex snapping instead. To do this, ensure that the **Translate** tool is selected and hold down *V* on the keyboard; now hover your cursor over a vertex point on your selected object and drag to any other vertex of another object to snap to it.

Grouping and duplicating with empty objects

Create an empty object by choosing **GameObject** | **Create Empty** from the top menu, then position this at **(4.5, 0.5, -1)** using the **Transform** component in the **Inspector**. Rename this from the default name **GameObject** to **CubeHolder**.

Now select all of the cube objects in the **Hierarchy** by selecting the top one, holding the *Shift* key, and then selecting the last. Now drag this list of cubes in the Hierarchy onto the empty object named **CubeHolder** in the **Hierarchy** in order to make this their parent object; the **Hierarchy** should now look like this:

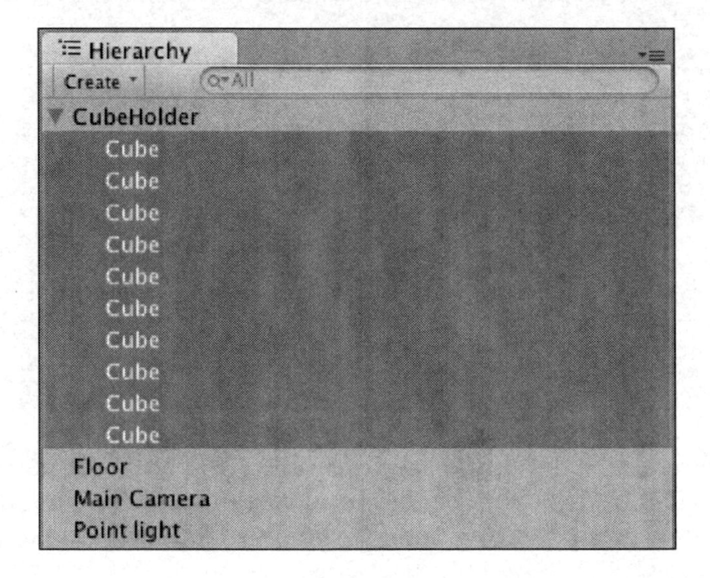

You'll notice that the parent empty object now has an arrow to the left of its object title, meaning you can expand and collapse it. To save space in the **Hierarchy**, click the arrow now to hide all of the child objects, and then re-select the **CubeHolder**.

Now that we have a complete row made and parented, we can simply duplicate the parent object, and use snap-dragging to lift a whole new row up in the Y axis. Use the duplicate shortcut (*Command/Control* + *D*) as before, then select the **Translate** tool (*W*) and use the snap-drag technique (hold *Command* on Mac, *Control* on PC) outlined earlier to lift by **1** unit in the **Y** axis by pulling the green axis handle.

Repeat this procedure to create eight rows of bricks in all, one on top of the other. It should look something like the following screenshot. Note that in the image all **CubeHolder** row objects are selected in the **Hierarchy**.

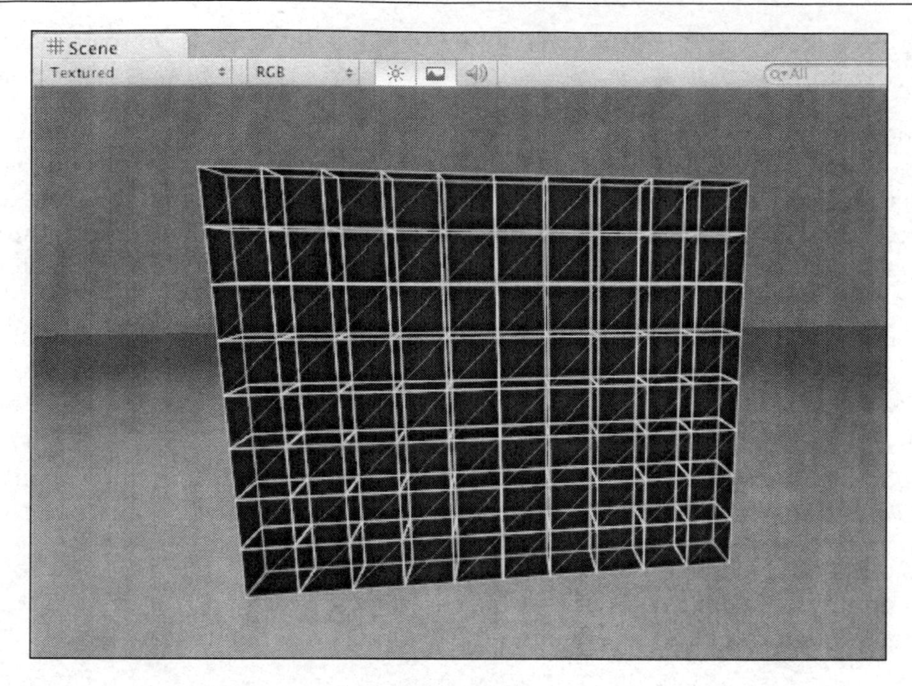

Build it up, knock it down!

Now that we have built a wall, let's make a simple game mechanic where the player can maneuver the camera and shoot projectiles at the wall to knock it down.

Setting the viewpoint

Set up the camera facing the wall by selecting the **Main Camera** object in the Hierarchy, and positioning it at **(4, 3, -15)** in the **Transform** component. Also ensure that it has no rotation values; they should all be set to **0**.

Introducing scripting

To take your first steps into programming, we will look at a simple example of the same functionality in both C Sharp(C#) and Javascript, the two main programming languages used by Unity developers. It is also possible to write Boo based scripts, but these are rarely used outside of those with existing experience in that language.

[To follow the next steps you may choose either Javascript or C#, then in the rest of this book continue with the chosen language your prefer.]

To begin, click the **Create** button on the Project panel, then choose either **Javascript** or **C# Script**.

Your new script will be placed into the Project panel named **NewBehaviourScript**, and show an icon of a page with either JS or C# written on it. When selecting your new script, Unity offers a preview of what is in the script already, in the view of the **Inspector**, and an accompanying **Edit** button that when clicked will launch the script into the default script editor—Monodevelop. You can also launch a script in your script editor at any time by double-clicking on its icon in the Project panel.

A new behaviour script or 'class'

Whether choosing C# or Javascript, it is recommended that you read through both parts of the ensuing section of the book as it contains overall information about scripting and may also help you decide as to which language you want to choose.

New scripts can be thought of as a new Class in Unity terms. If you are new to programming, think of a class as a set of actions, properties, and other stored information that can be accessed under the heading of its name.

For example, a class called `Dog` may contain properties such as '`color`', '`breed`', '`size`', or '`gender`' and have actions such as '`roll over`' or '`fetch stick`'. These properties can be described as **variables**, while the actions can be written in **functions**, also known as 'methods'.

In this example, to refer to the `breed` variable—a property of the `Dog` class, we might refer to the class it is in, `Dog`, and use a period (full stop) to refer to this variable in the following way:

```
Dog.breed;
```

If calling a function within the `Dog` class, we might say for example:

```
Dog.fetchStick();
```

We can also add arguments into functions—these aren't the everyday arguments we have with one another! Think of them as more like modifying the behavior of a function, for example,with our `fetchStick` function, we might build in an argument that defines how quickly our dog will fetch the stick. This might be called as follows:

```
Dog.fetchStick(25);
```

While these are abstract examples, often it can help to transpose coding into commonplace examples in order to make sense of them. As we continue in this book, think back to this example or come up with some examples of your own, to help train yourself to understand classes of information and their properties.

When you write a script in C# or Javascript, you are writing a new class or classes with their own properties (variables) and instructions (functions) that you can call into play at the desired moment in your games.

What's inside a new C# behaviour

When you begin with a new C# script, Unity gives you the following code to get started:

```
using UnityEngine;
using System.Collections;


public class NewBehaviourScript : MonoBehaviour {

  // Use this for initialization
  void Start () {

  }

  // Update is called once per frame
  void Update () {

  }
}
```

This begins with the necessary two calls to the Unity Engine itself:

```
using UnityEngine;

using System.Collections;
```

It goes on to establish the class named after the script. With C# you'll be required to name your scripts with matching names to the class declared inside of the script itself. This is why you will see:

`public class NewBehaviourScript : MonoBehaviour {` at the start of a new C# document, as `NewBehaviourScript` is the default name that Unity gives to newly generated scripts. If you rename your script in the Project panel when it is created, Unity will rewrite the class name in your C# script.

Code in classes

When writing code, most of your functions, variables, and other scripting elements will be placed within the class of a script in C#. *Within* – in this context – means that it must occur after the class declaration, and following the corresponding closing '}' of that, at the bottom of the script. So unless told otherwise, while following the instructions in this book, assume that your code should be placed within the class established in the script. In Javascript this is less relevant as the entire script is the class; it is not explicitly established. See the following section *What's inside a new Javascript behaviour?*

Basic functions

Unity as an engine has many of its own functions that can be used to call different features of the game engine, and it includes two important ones when you create a new script in C#.

Functions or methods as they are also known, most often start with the term `void` in C#. This is the function's return type – which is the kind of data a function may result in. As most functions are simply there to carry out instructions rather than return information, often you will see `void` at the beginning of their declaration, which simply means that a certain type of data will not be returned.

Some basic functions are explained as follows:

- `Start()`: This is called when the scene first launches, so is often used as it is suggested in the code, for initialization. For example, you may have a score variable that must be set to `0` when the game scene begins or perhaps a function that spawns your player character in the correct place at the start of a level.
- `Update()`: This is called in every frame that the game runs, and is crucial for checking the state of various parts of your game during this time, as many different conditions of game objects may change while the game is running.

Variables in C#

To store information in a variable in C#, you will use the following syntax:

```
typeOfData nameOfVariable = value;
```

For example:

```
int currentScore = 5;
```

Or:

```
float currentVelocity = 5.86f;
```

Note that the examples here show numerical data, with `int` meaning **integer**—a whole number, and `float` meaning **floating point**—a number with a decimal place, which in C# requires a letter f to be placed at the end of the value. This syntax is somewhat different from Javascript. See the following section, *Variables in Javascript*.

What's inside a new Javascript behaviour

While fulfilling the same functions as a C# file, a new empty Javascript file shows you less as the entire script itself is considered to be the class, and the empty space in the script is considered to be within the opening and closing of the class, as the class declaration itself is hidden.

You will also notice that the lines `using UnityEngine;` and `using System.Collections;` are also hidden in Javascript, so in a new Javascript you will simply be shown the `Update()` function:

```
function Update () {

}
```

You will notice that in Javascript, you declare functions differently, using the term `function` before the name. You will also need to write declaration of variables, and various other scripted elements with a slightly different syntax; we will look at examples of this as we progress.

Variables in Javascript

The syntax for variables in Javascript works as follows, and is always preceded by the prefix `var`:

```
var variableName : TypeOfData = value;
```

For example:

```
var currentScore : int = 0;
```

Or

```
var currentVelocity : float = 5.86;
```

As you will likely have noticed, the `float` value does not require a letter f following its value as it does in C#. You will notice as you see further scripts written in the two different languages that C# often has stricter rules about how scripts are written, especially regarding implicitly stating types of data that are being used.

Comments

In both C# and Javascript in Unity, you can write in comments using:

```
// two forward slashes symbols for a single line comment
```

Or:

```
/* forward-slash, star to open a multi line comments and at the end
of it,star, forward-slash to close */
```

You may wish to write comments in the code to help you remember what each part does as you progress through the book. Remember that because comments are not executed code, you can write whatever you like, including pieces of code; as long as they are contained within a comment they will never be treated as working code.

Wall attack

Now let's put some of your new scripting knowledge into action and turn our existing scene into an interactive gameplay prototype. In the **Project** panel in Unity, rename your newly created script **Shooter** by selecting it, pressing *Return* (Mac) or *F2* (PC), and typing in the new name.

If you are using C#, remember to ensure that your class declaration inside the script matches this name of the script:

```
public class Shooter : MonoBehaviour {
```

As mentioned previously, Javascript users will not need to do this. To kick-start your knowledge of using scripting in Unity, we will write a script to control the camera and allow shooting of a projectile at the wall that we have built.

To begin with, we will establish three variables:

- `bullet`: This is a variable of type Rigidbody, as it will hold a reference to a physics controlled object we will make
- `power`: This is a floating point variable number we will use to set the power of shooting
- `moveSpeed`: This is another floating point variable number we will use to define the speed of movement of the camera using the arrow keys

These variables must be **Public Member Variables**, in order for them to display as adjustable settings in the Inspector. You'll see this in action very shortly!

Declaring public variables

Public variables are important to understand as they allow you to create variables that will be accessible from other scripts—an important part of game development as it allows for simpler inter-object communication. Public variables are also really useful as they appear as settings you can adjust visually in the Inspector once your script is attached to an object. Private variables are the opposite—designed to be only accessible within the scope of the script, class, or function they are defined within, and do not appear as settings in the Inspector.

C#

Before we begin, as we will not be using it, remove the `Start()` function from this script by deleting `void Start(){}`. To establish the required variables, put the following code snippet into your script after the opening of the class, shown as follows:

```
using UnityEngine;
using System.Collections;
public class Shooter : MonoBehaviour {
  public Rigidbody bullet;
  public float power = 1500f;
  public float moveSpeed = 2f;

  void Update () {
  }
}
```

Note that in this example, the default explanatory comments have been removed in order to save space.

Javascript

In order to establish Public Member Variables in Javascript, you will need to simply ensure that your variables are declared outside of any existing function. This is usually done at the top of the script, so to declare the three variables we need, add the following to the top of your new **Shooter** script so that it looks like this:

```
var bullet : Rigidbody;
var power : float = 1500;
var moveSpeed : float = 5;

    function Update () {
    }
```

Assigning scripts to objects

In order for this script to be used within our game it must be attached as a component of one of the game objects within the existing scene.

Save your script by choosing **File** | **Save** from the top menu of your script editor and return to Unity. There are several ways to assign a script to an object in Unity:

1. Drag it from the **Project** panel and drop it onto the name of an object in the **Hierarchy** panel.
2. Drag it from the **Project** panel and drop it onto the visual representation of the object in the **Scene** panel.
3. Select the object you wish to apply the script to and then drag and drop the script to empty space at the bottom of the **Inspector** view for that object.
4. Select the object you wish to apply the script to and then choose **Component** | **Scripts** | and then the name of your script from the top menu.

The most common method is the first approach, and this would be most appropriate as trying to drag to the camera in the **Scene** view, for example, would be difficult, as the camera itself doesn't have a tangible surface to drag to.

For this reason, drag your new **Shooter** script from the **Project** panel and drop it onto the name of **Main Camera** in the **Hierarchy** to assign it, and you should see your script appear as a new component, following the existing Audio Listener component. You will also see its three Public Variables, **Bullet**, **Power**, and **Move Speed,** show in the **Inspector**, shown as follows:

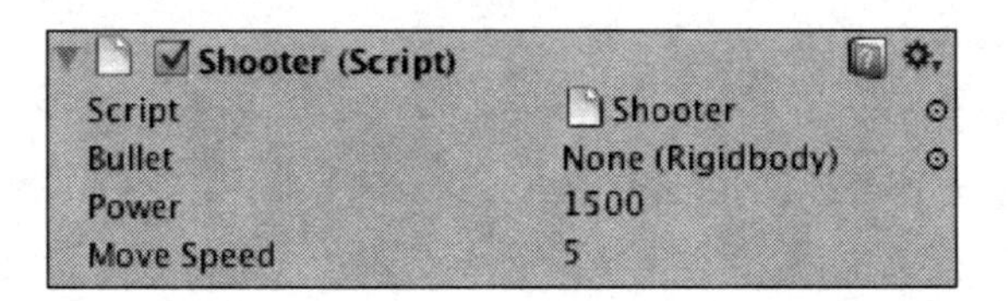

As you will see, Unity has taken the variable names and given them capital letters, and in the case of our `moveSpeed` variable, it takes a capital letter in the middle of the phrase to signify the start of a new word in the **Inspector**, placing a space between the two words when seen as a public variable.

You can also see here that the **Bullet** variable is not yet set, but it is expecting an object to be assigned to it that has a Rigidbody attached—this is often referred to as being a Rigidbody object. Despite the fact that in Unity all objects in the scene can be referred to as game objects, when describing an object as a `Rigidbody` object in scripting, we will only be able to refer to properties and functions of the `Rigidbody` class. This is not a problem however; it simply makes our script more efficient than referring to the entire `GameObject` class. For more on this, take a look at the script reference documentation for both the classes:

GameObject: `http://unity3d.com/support/documentation/ScriptReference/GameObject.html`

Rigidbody: `http://unity3d.com/support/documentation/ScriptReference/Rigidbody.html`

Be aware that when adjusting values of public variables in the **Inspector**, any values changed will simply override those written in the script, rather than replace them.

Let's continue working on our script and add some interactivity, so return to your script editor now.

Moving the camera

Next we will make use of the `moveSpeed` variable, combined with keyboard input in order to move the camera, and effectively create a primitive aiming of our shot, as we will use the camera as the point at which to shoot from.

As we want to use the arrow keys on the keyboard we need to be aware of how to address them in code first. Unity has many inputs that can be viewed and adjusted using the **Input Manager**—see **Edit** | **Project Settings** | **Input**.

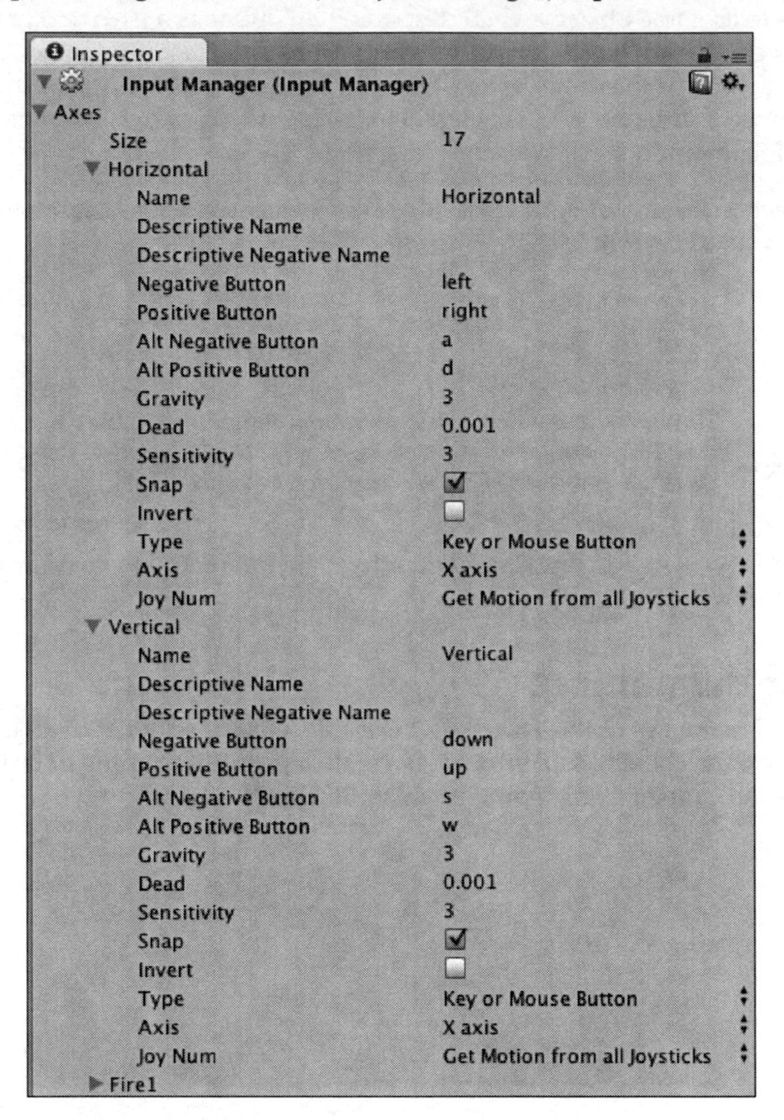

As seen in this screenshot, two of the default settings for **Input** are **Horizontal** and **Vertical**. These rely on an axis based input that when holding the **Positive Button** builds to a value of 1, and when holding the **Negative Button** builds to a value of -1. Releasing either button means that the **Input's** value springs back to 0, as it would if using a sprung analog joystick on a gamepad.

Because **Input** is also the name of a class, and all named elements in the **Input Manager** are axes or buttons, in scripting terms we can simply use:

```
Input.GetAxis("Horizontal");
```

This receives the current value of the horizontal keys—a value between -1 and 1 depending upon what the user is pressing. Let's put that into practice in our script now, using local variables to represent our axes.

By doing this we can modify the value of this variable later using multiplication, taking it from a maximum value of 1 to a higher number—allowing us to move the camera faster than 1 unit at a time.

This variable is not something we will ever need to set inside the **Inspector**, as Unity is assigning values based upon our key input. As such, these values can be established as **Local** variables.

Local, private, and public variables

Before we continue, let's take an overview of local, private, and public variables in order to cement your understanding:

- **Local variables**: These are variables established inside a function; they will not be shown in the **Inspector**, and are only accessible to the function they are within.
- **Private variables**: These are established outside of a function, and therefore, accessible to any function within your class - however they are also not visible in the **Inspector**.
- **Public variables**: These are established outside of a function, accessible to any function in their class, and also to other scripts as well as being visible for editing in the **Inspector**.

Local variables and receiving input

The local variables in C# and Javascript are shown as follows:

C#:

```
void Update () {
    float h = Input.GetAxis("Horizontal") * Time.deltaTime *
moveSpeed;
    float v = Input.GetAxis("Vertical") * Time.deltaTime * moveSpeed;
```

Javascript:

```
function Update () {
    var h : float = Input.GetAxis("Horizontal") * Time.deltaTime *
moveSpeed;
     var v : float = Input.GetAxis("Vertical") * Time.deltaTime *
    moveSpeed;
```

The variables declared here—`h` for `Horizontal` and `v` for `Vertical`, could be named anything we like; it is simply quicker to write single letters. Generally speaking, we would normally give these a name, because some letters cannot be used as variable names, for example, x, y, and z because they are used for coordinate values and therefore reserved for use as such.

As these axes' values can be anything from -1 to 1, they are likely to be a number with a decimal place, and as such we must declare them as floating point type variables. They are then multiplied using the `*` symbol by `Time.deltaTime`—this simply means that the value is divided by the number of frames per second (the `deltaTime` is the time it takes from one frame to the next or the time taken since the `Update()` function last ran), meaning that the value adds up to a consistent amount per second, regardless of the framerate.

The resultant value is then increased by multiplying it by the public variable we made earlier—`moveSpeed`. This means that although the values of `h` and `v` are local variables, we can still affect them by adjusting public `moveSpeed` in the **Inspector,** as it is part of the equation that those variables represent. This is common practice in scripting as it takes advantage of the use of publicly accessible settings combined with specific values generated by a function.

Understanding Translate

To actually use these variables to move an object, we will use the **Translate** command. When implementing any piece of scripting, you should make sure you know how to use it first.

Translate is a command which is part of the `Transform` class: `http://unity3d.com/`

`support/documentation/ScriptReference/Transform.html.`

This is a class of information that stores the position, rotation, and scale properties of an object, and also functions that can be used to move and rotate the object.

The expected usage of `Translate` is as follows:

```
Transform.Translate(Vector3);
```

The use of `Vector3` here means that `Translate` is expecting a piece of `Vector3` data as it's the main argument—`Vector3` data is simply information that contains a value for the X, Y, and Z coordinates; in this case coordinates to move the object by.

Implementing Translate

Now let's implement the `Translate` command by taking the `h` and `v` input values that we have established, placing them into Vector3 within the command.

C# and Javascript

Place the given line within the `Update()` function in your script; - meaning after the opening curly brace of `Update(){` and before the function closes with a right curly brace `}`. Note that this does not differ between languages:

```
transform.Translate(h, v, 0);
```

We can use just the word `transform` here because we know that any object we attach this script to will have a Transform component. Attached components of an object can be addressed using the lowercase version of their name, whereas accessing components on other objects requires use of the `GetComponent` command and their uppercase equivalent, for example:

```
GameObject.Find("OtherObjectName").GetComponent<Transform>.
Translate(h,v,0);
```

We do not need that in this instance. Accessing components on other objects is covered later in this book in *Chapter 4*, under *Inter-script communication and dot syntax*.

Here we are using the current value of `h` to affect the X axis, `v` to affect the Y axis, and simply passing a value of `0` to the Z axis, as we do not wish to move back and forth.

Save your script now by going to **File | Save** in your script editor and return to Unity. Save the scene we have worked on thus far also by going to **File | Save Scene As,** and name this scene **Prototype**.

Unity will prompt you to save into the `Assets` folder of your project by default and you should always ensure that you do not save outside of this folder as you will not be able to access the scene through the **Project** panel otherwise. You may also create a sub folder within `Assets` in which to keep your scenes if you wish to be extra tidy, this is not necessary but is generally considered to be good practice.

Testing the game so far

In Unity you can play test at any time, provided there are no errors in your scripts. If there are, Unity will ask you to fix all errors before allowing you to enter the Play Mode.

Once all errors are fixed—this will be signified by an empty or cleared **Console** bar at the bottom of the Unity interface. The **Console** bar represents the most recent entry into the Unity console. You can check this by choosing **Window | Console** (shortcut *Ctrl* + *Shift* + *C* [PC] *Command-Shift* + *C* [Mac]) from the top menu. All the errors will be listed in red, and double-clicking on the error will take you to the part of the script that will be causing the issue described. Most errors are often a forgotten character or simple misspelling, so always double check what you have written as you go.

If your game is free of errors, click the **Play** button at the top of the screen to enter the Play Mode. You will now be able to move the Main Camera object around by using the arrow keys—*Up*, *Down*, *Left*, and *Right* or their alternates *W*, *A*, *S*, and *D* as shown in the following image:

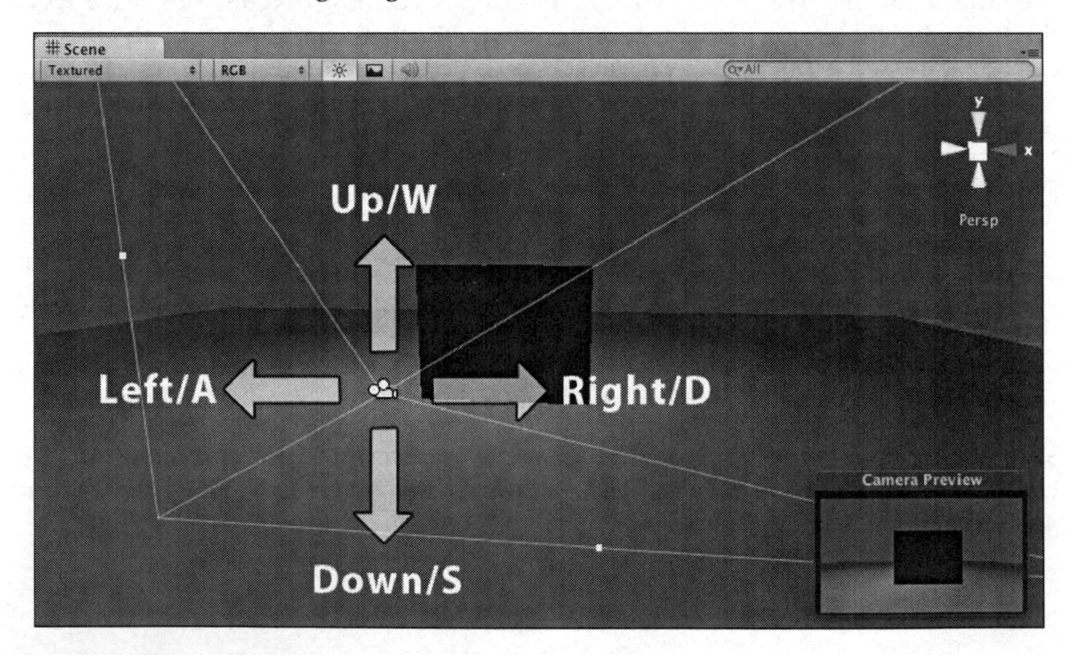

Once you have tested and confirmed that this works, press the **Play** button at the top of the interface again to switch off the Play Mode.

Switching off the Play Mode before continuing to work is important because settings of components and objects in the current scene that are adjusted during Play Mode will be discarded as soon as the Play Mode is switched off, so leaving Unity in Play Mode as you continue to work will mean you lose work.

Now let's finish our game mechanic prototype by adding the ability to shoot projectiles at the wall to knock it down.

Making a projectile

In order to shoot a projectile at the wall, we will need to first create it within the scene, and then store it as a **prefab**.

A prefab is a GameObject, stored as an asset in the project that can be instantiated—created during runtime and then manipulated, all through code.

Creating the projectile prefab

Begin by clicking the **Create** button at the top of the **Hierarchy**, and then select **Sphere** from the drop-down menu that appears. As mentioned previously, you can also access primitive creation from the **GameObject** | **Create Other** top menu.

Now ensure that the Sphere object is selected in the **Hierarchy** and hover your cursor over the **Scene** view and press *F* on the keyboard to focus your view on the Sphere.

If your Sphere has been created at the same position as one of your other objects, then simply change to the **Translate tool** (*W*) and drag the relevant axis handle until your Sphere is out of the way of the object blocking your view, then re-focus your view by pressing *F* again.

Taking a look at the **Inspector** panel, you will notice that when introducing new primitive objects to the scene, Unity automatically assigns them three new components in addition to the existing Transform component, which are as follows:

1. **Mesh Filter**: This is to handle the shape
2. **Renderer**: This is to handle the appearance
3. **Collider**: This is to manage interactions (known as collisions) with other objects

Creating and applying a material

We'll begin with the visual appearance of the projectile, and alter this by creating a material to apply to the renderer. Whenever you need to adjust the appearance of an object, you'll likely look to alter settings in some kind of Renderer component. For 3D objects it will be the Mesh Renderer, on Particle systems it will be a Particle Renderer, and so on.

To keep things neat, we'll make a new folder within our `Assets` folder to store all materials that we may create in this project. On the **Project** panel click the **Create** button and choose **Folder** from the drop-down menu. Rename this folder **Materials** by pressing *Return* (Mac) or *F2* (PC). Take the time now to place the Red brick material you made earlier inside this new folder.

To create any new asset inside of an existing folder in the **Project** panel, simply select the folder first and then create using the **Create** Button.

Now we will create the material we need and apply it to our object:

1. With the new `Materials` folder still selected click the **Create** button on the **Project** panel once again and this time choose **Material**. This creates a New Material asset that you should rename **bulletColor**—or something of your own choosing that reminds you that this asset is to be applied to the projectile.
2. With your new material still selected, click on this block to open the **Color Picker** window, select a shade of blue, and then close this window when you are happy with your selection.
3. Now that you have chosen your color for the material, drag and drop the **bulletColor** material from the **Project** panel and drop it onto the name of the Sphere object in the Hierarchy to assign it.

Note that, if you want to test how a material will look when applied to a 3D object in Unity, you can drag the material to the **Scene** view, hovering the cursor over meshes—Unity will show you a preview of what it will look like and you can then move the mouse away or press *Esc* if you wish to cancel, or release the mouse to apply.

Adding physics with a Rigidbody

Next we'll ensure that the physics engine has control of the projectile **Sphere** by adding a **Rigidbody** component. Select the **Sphere** in the Hierarchy panel and choose **Component** | **Physics** | **Rigidbody** from the top menu.

Your **Rigidbody** component is now added, with settings available to adjust in the **Inspector**. For the purpose of this prototype however, we needn't adjust any settings from the default.

Storing with prefabs

As we wish to fire this projectile when the player presses a key, we do not want the projectile to be in the scene by default, but instead want it to be stored and created when the key is pressed. For this reason we will store the object as a prefab, and use our script to instantiate (that is, create an instance of) it at the precise moment a key is pressed.

Prefabs are Unity's way of storing GameObjects that have been set up in a particular way; for example, you may have configured an enemy soldier with particular scripts and properties that behaves a certain way. You can store this object as a prefab and instantiate it when necessary. Similarly you might have a differing soldier that behaves differently, this might be a different prefab, or you might create an instance of the first, and adjust settings in the soldier's components, making him faster or slower upon instantiation for example; the Prefab system gives you a lot of flexibility in this regard.

Click the **Create** button at the top of the **Project** panel, and choose **Folder**, then rename this to **Prefabs**. Now drag the **Sphere** from the **Hierarchy** and drop it onto the **Prefabs** folder in the **Project** panel as show in the following screenshot. Dragging a GameObject such as this anywhere into the **Project** panel will save it as a prefab; we simply created this folder for neatness and good practice. Rename this new **Prefab** from **Sphere** to **Projectile**.

You can now delete the original Sphere object from the **Hierarchy** by selecting it, and pressing *Command+Backspace* (Mac) or *Delete* (PC); alternatively, you can right-click the object in the **Hierarchy** and choose **Delete** from the pop-out menu that appears.

Firing the projectile

Return to the **Shooter** script we have been working on so far by double-clicking its icon in the **Project** panel, or by selecting it in the **Project** panel and clicking the **Open** button at the top of the **Inspector**.

Now we will make use of the `bullet` variable we declared earlier, using it as a reference to the particular object we wish to instantiate. As soon as the object is created from our stored prefab, we will apply a force to it, in order to fire it at the wall in our scene.

After the line:

```
transform.Translate(h, v, 0);
```

Within the `Update()` function in your script, add the following code, regardless of whether you are using C# or Javascript:

```
if(Input.GetButtonUp("Fire1")){

}
```

This `IF` statement listens for the key applied to the `Input` button named **Fire1** to be released. By default, this is mapped to the *Left Ctrl* key or left mouse button, but you can change this to a different key by adjust settings in the **Input Manager (Edit | Project Settings | Input)**.

Using Instantiate() to spawn objects

Now within this `IF` statement—meaning after the opening { and before the closing `},` put the following line:

C#:

```
Rigidbody instance = Instantiate(bullet, transform.position,
transform.rotation) as Rigidbody;
```

Javascript:

```
var instance: Rigidbody = Instantiate(bullet, transform.position,
transform.rotation);
```

Here we are creating a new variable named `instance`. Into this variable we are storing a reference to the creation of a new object that is of type `Rigidbody`.

The Instantiate commands requires three pieces of information namely, `Instantiate(What to make, Where to make it, a rotation to give it);`

So in our example, we are telling our script to create an instance of whatever object or prefab is assigned to the `bullet` public member variable and that we would like it to be created using the values of position and rotation from the transform component of the object this script is attached to—the **Main Camera**. This is why you will often see `transform.position` written in scripts as it refers to the transform component's position settings of the object the script is attached to.

Note that in C# you must add as `Rigidbody` to specifically state the data type after the Instantiate command.

Adding a force to the Rigidbody

Having now created our object, we need it to be immediately fired forward using the `AddForce()` command. This commands works as follows:

```
Rigidbody.AddForce(Direction and amount of force expressed as a
Vector3);
```

So before we add the force, we will create a reference to the direction we wish to shoot in. The camera is facing the brick wall so it makes sense to shoot objects at the wall in the camera's forward direction. Following the instantiate line you just added, still within the `IF` statement, add the given code:

C#:

```
Vector3 fwd = transform.TransformDirection(Vector3.forward);
```

Javascript:

```
var fwd: Vector3 = transform.TransformDirection(Vector3.forward);
```

Here we have created a `Vector3` type variable called `fwd`, and told it to represent the forward direction of the current transform this script is attached to.

The `TransformDirection` command can be used to convert a local direction—that of the forward direction of the camera, to a world direction—as objects and the world each have their coordinate system, and the forward direction of an object may not necessarily match that of the world, so conversion is crucial. `Vector3.forward` in this context is simply a shortcut to writing `Vector3(0,0,1)`. It is one unit in length on the Z axis.

Finally, we will apply the force by first referring to our variable that represents the newly created object—`instance`, then using the `AddForce()` command to add a force in the direction of the `fwd` variable—multiplied by the public variable named `power` that we created earlier. Add the following line to your code beneath the last line you added:

C# and Javascript:

```
instance.AddForce(fwd * power);
```

Save your script and return to Unity.

Now before we can test play the finished game mechanic, we need to assign the **Projectile** prefab to the **Bullet** public variable. To do this, select the **Main Camera** in the **Hierarchy**, in order to see the **Shooter** script as a component in the **Inspector**.

Now drag the **Projectile** prefab from the **Project** panel, and drop it onto the **Bullet** variable in the **Inspector**, where it currently says **None (Rigidbody),** as shown in the following screenshot:

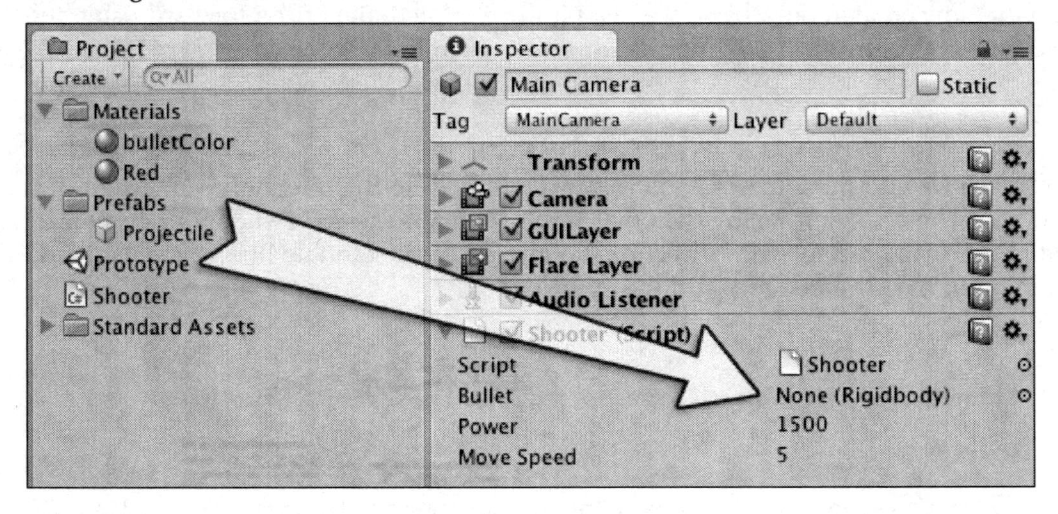

Once applied correctly, you will see the name of the projectile in this variable slot. Save the scene now (**File | Save Scene**) and test the game by pressing the **Play** button at the top of the interface.

You will now be able to move the camera around and fire the projectiles we created earlier using the *Left Ctrl* on the keyboard. If you wish to adjust how much power you give to the projectiles when they are fired, simply adjust the number in the **Power** public variable by selecting the **Main Camera**, and adjusting the value of **1500** currently assigned to it in the **Shooter (Script)** component, increasing or decreasing as you see fit. Remember to always press the **Play** button again to stop testing.

Summary

Congratulations! You have just created your first Unity prototype.

In this chapter, you should have become familiar with with the basics of using the Unity interface, working with Game Objects, components, and basic scripting. This will hopefully act as a solid foundation upon which to build further experience in Unity game development.

Now you might want to relax a little and take time to play your prototype or even create one of your own based on what you have learned. Or you may just be eager to learn more; if so, keep reading!

Let's move on to the main game of this book, now that you are a little more prepared on some of the basic operations of the Unity development.

In the next chapter, we will begin to create a game called *Survival Island*. In this, you will learn how to use the Terrain tools to create a tropical island, complete with its own volcano! Once you have created your island, you'll add a player character prefab and take a stroll around your newly created tropical paradise!

3

Creating the Environment

When building your 3D world, you'll be utilizing two different types of environment geometry—buildings, scenery, and props built in a third-party 3D modeling application, and terrains created using the Unity terrain editor.

In this chapter, we'll look at the use of the terrain editor, and how we can use its toolset to build the environment for our game—sculpting, geometry, and painting with textures to create an entire island terrain. We shall specifically be looking at:

- Working with the terrain tools to build an island
- Lighting scenes
- Using sound
- Importing packaged assets

Before we start making use of the terrain tools to build the island part of our environment, let's take an overview of what we are going to create in its entirety, in order to help you keep in mind the final goal as you work through this book.

Designing the game

In order to prepare you for the larger game you will make over the course of this book, let's first get a good idea of what you're going to make, so that you can better understand what we're doing and why at each step along the way.

The game we will design is called **Survival Island**—which you can of course rebrand and retitle if you wish! The basic concept is that your character has awoken on a desert island, with only an active volcano and a mysterious cabin for company. Your goal is to survive your night on the island by lighting a fire to signal for help and keep warm.

In order to light the fire you must acquire the matches that are locked away in the cabin. To unlock the cabin the player must pick up several power cells to fuel the generator that powers the door to the cabin. This would be simple except that the final power cell is locked into a minigame requiring the player to knock down timed targets at a coconut shy shooting gallery—knock them all down simultaneously, and you will win that all important final cell! The player will begin on a beach and seek out the buildings by following a path across the island.

Here is an overview of what the island will look like—naturally the buildings, campfire, and volcano aren't to scale!

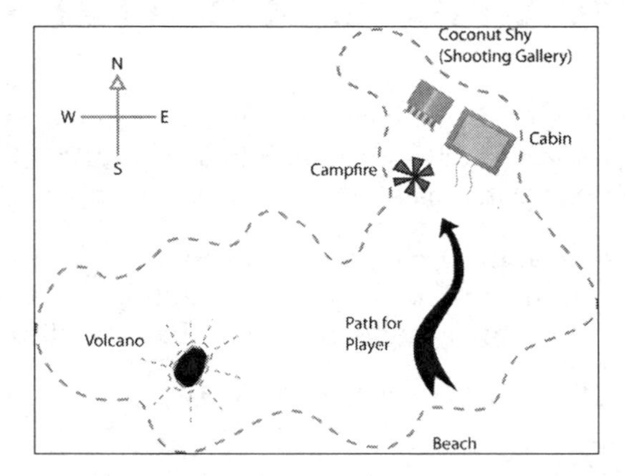

We will begin by using the Unity terrain tools to create and design the island:

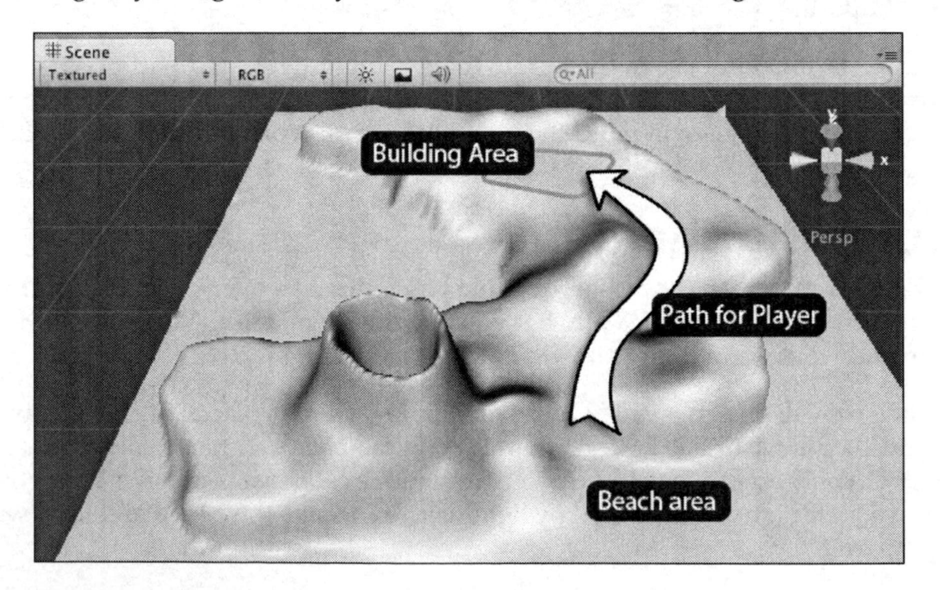

We will then import the rest of the elements of this game—the cabin, fuel cells, and other assets as an asset package specially created for this book. Towards the end of the book we will add further detail to the terrain; it will look something like the following image:

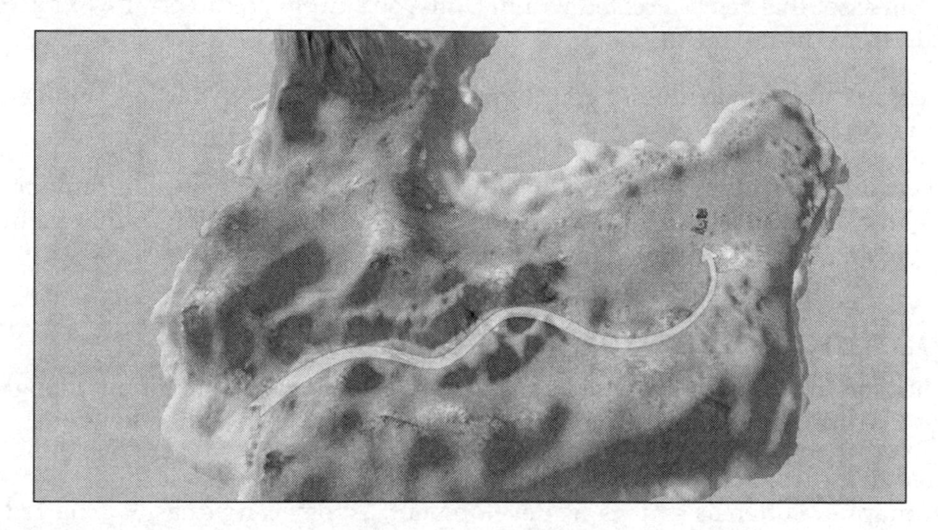

It may be useful to keep your prototype scene for reference so we will simply leave it within this project in a scene unrelated to our main game. Ensure that your prototype scene is saved and then go to **File** | **New Scene**. Now to go **File** | **Save Scene As** and save the scene into your `Assets` folder, naming it `Island`.

Naming conventions

Take note here that it is important to name elements in a case sensitive manner because, when writing code to address this scene for example, we will refer to the name 'Island' with a capital I.

Using the terrain editor

In building any game that involves an outdoor environment, a terrain editor is a must-have for any game developer. Unity has its own built-in terrain editor and this makes building complete environments quick and easy.

In Unity terms, think of a terrain as simply a game object that has a terrain toolkit component applied to it. Beginning as a plane—a flat, single-sided 3D shape—the terrain you'll create shortly can be transformed into a complete set of realistic geometry, with additional details such as trees, rocks, foliage, and even atmospheric effects such as wind.

Terrain menu features

In order to take a look at the features outlined in the following section, you will need to create a terrain. So let's begin by introducing a new terrain object to the game—this is an asset that can be created within Unity, so simply go to **Terrain** | **Create Terrain** from the top menu.

Before you can begin to modify your terrain, you should set up various settings for size and detail.

The **Terrain** menu at the top of Unity allows you to not only create a terrain for your game, but also allows you to perform the following operations (what follows is simply an overview; detailed instructions will follow.)

Importing and exporting heightmaps

Heightmaps are 2D graphics with light and dark areas to represent terrain topography and can be imported as an alternative to using Unity's height painting tools.

Created in an art package such as Photoshop and saved in a `.RAW` format, heightmaps are often used in game development, as they can be easily exported and transferred between art packages and development environments such as Unity.

As we will be using the Unity terrain tools to create our environment, we will not be utilizing externally created heightmaps as part of this book.

When using the Paint Height tools in Unity—you are creating a heightmap for your terrain behind the scenes. These tools make it easier than doing it in another tool. Readers from an art background may use this option to import or export existing maps they have made in other packages.

Setting the resolution

The following dialog window allows you to set a number of properties for any new terrain object you have created:

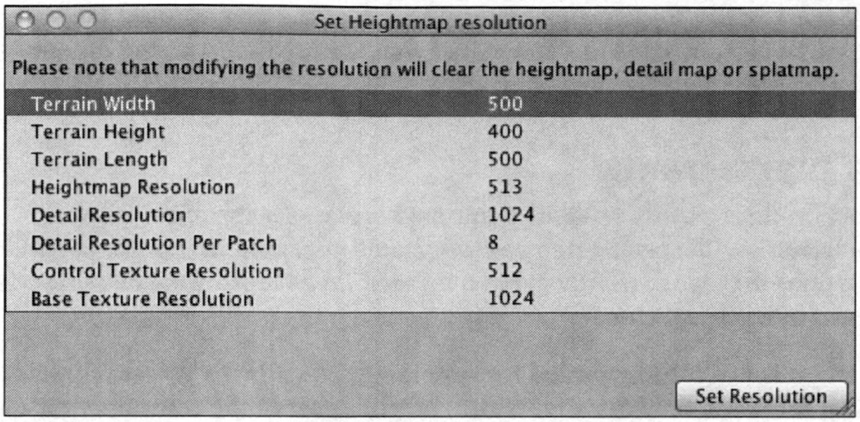

Set Heightmap resolution

Please note that modifying the resolution will clear the heightmap, detail map or splatmap.

Terrain Width	500
Terrain Height	400
Terrain Length	500
Heightmap Resolution	513
Detail Resolution	1024
Detail Resolution Per Patch	8
Control Texture Resolution	512
Base Texture Resolution	1024

Set Resolution

These settings should always be adjusted before the topography of the terrain is created, as adjusting them later can cause work on the terrain to be reset:

- **Terrain Width, Height,** and **Length**: Measured in meters. Note that, *Height* here sets the maximum height that the terrain's topography can feature.
- **Heightmap Resolution**: The resolution of the texture that Unity stores to represent the topography in pixels. Note that, although most terrain textures in Unity are created at a power of two dimension—128x128, 256x256, 512x512 and so on, heightmap resolutions always add an extra pixel because each pixel defines a vertex point; so in the example of a 4 x 4 terrain, four vertices would be present along each section of the grid, but the points at which they meet, including their endpoints would equal to five.
- **Detail Resolution**: The resolution of the graphic, known as a **Detail resolution map**, that Unity stores in your project metadata. This defines how precisely you can place details on the terrain. Details are additional terrain features such as plants, rocks, and bushes. The larger the value, the more precisely you can place details on the terrain in terms of positioning.
- **Detail Resolution Per Patch**: The resolution of each patch of the terrain, that is, painted on.
- **Control Texture Resolution**: The resolution of textures when painted onto the terrain. Known as **Splatmap** textures in Unity, the **Control Texture Resolution** value controls the detail of the gradients created between textures you paint on to the terrain. As with all texture resolutions, it is advisable to keep this figure lower to increase performance. With this in mind, it is a good practice to leave this value set to its default of **512**. The higher this value, the finer control you will get with edges between multiple textures in the same area.

- **Base Texture Resolution**: The resolution of the texture used by Unity to render terrain areas in the distance that are further from the in-game camera or on older performance hardware.

Mass place trees

This function does exactly what its name says—places a specified number of trees onto the terrain, with specific tree and associated parameters (width, height, density, and variation) that are currently set in the **Place Trees** area of the terrain script component in the **Inspector**.

This function is not recommended for general use, as it gives you no control over the position of the trees, only density, width, height as set in the component itself. It is recommended that you use the **Place Trees** part of the terrain tools instead, in order to manually paint a more realistic placement.

Flatten Heightmap

Flatten Heightmap is present to allow you to flatten the entire terrain at a certain height. By default, your terrain height begins at zero, so if you wish to make a terrain with a default height above this, such as we do for our island, then you can specify the height value here.

Refresh tree and detail prototypes

If you make changes to the assets that make up any trees and details that have already been painted onto the terrain, then you'll need to select **Refresh Tree and Detail Prototypes** to update them on the terrain.

The terrain toolset

Before we begin to use them to build our island, let's take a look at the terrain tools so that you can familiarize yourself with their functions.

As you have just created your **Terrain**, it should be selected in the **Hierarchy** window. If it is not selected, then select it now in order to show its properties in the **Inspector**.

Terrain Script

On the **Inspector**, the terrain toolset is referred to in component terms as the **Terrain (Script)**. The **Terrain (Script)** component gives you the ability to utilize the various tools and specify settings for the terrain in addition to the functions available in the terrain menu outlined earlier.

The **Terrain (Script)** component has seven sections to it, which are easily accessible from the icon buttons at the top of the component. Before we begin, here is a quick overview of their purpose in building terrains.

Raise height

This tool allows you to raise areas by painting with the **Transform** tool (Shortcut—*W* key):

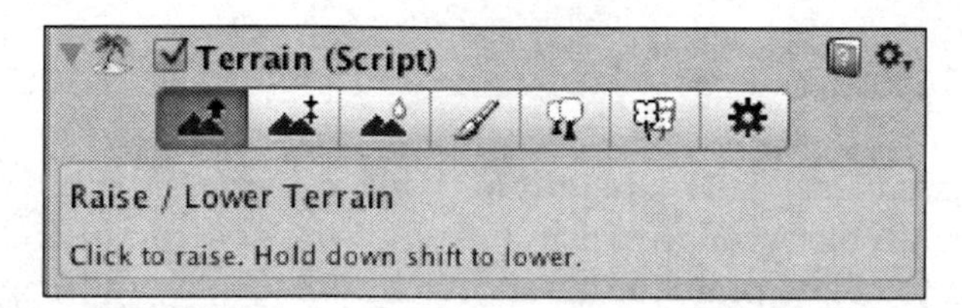

You also have the ability to specify **Brush** styles, **Size,** and **Opacity** (effectiveness) for the deformation you make. Holding the *Shift* key while using this tool causes the opposite effect—lowering height—as shown in the following image:

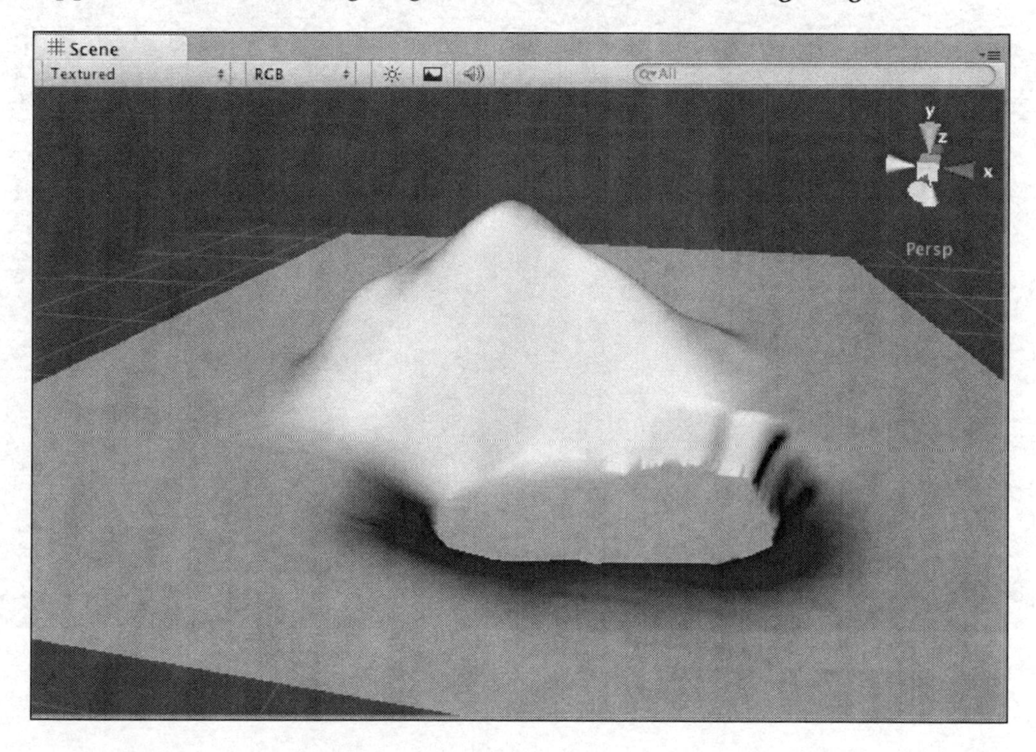

Paint height

This tool works similarly to the **Raise Height** tool, but gives you an additional setting—height:

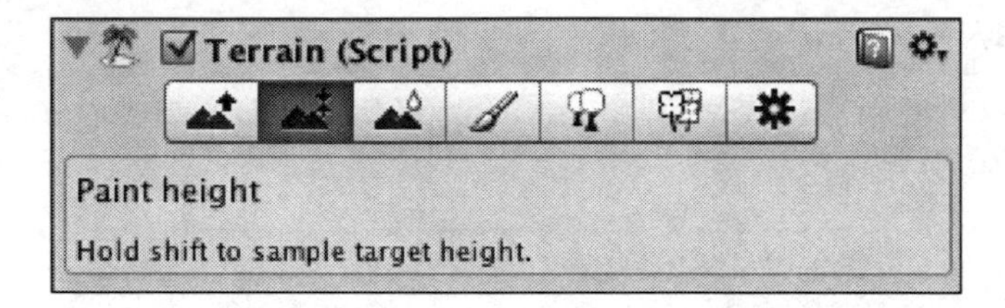

This means that you can specify a height to paint towards, which means that when the area of the terrain that you are raising reaches the specified height, it will flatten out, allowing you to create plateaus, as shown in the following image:

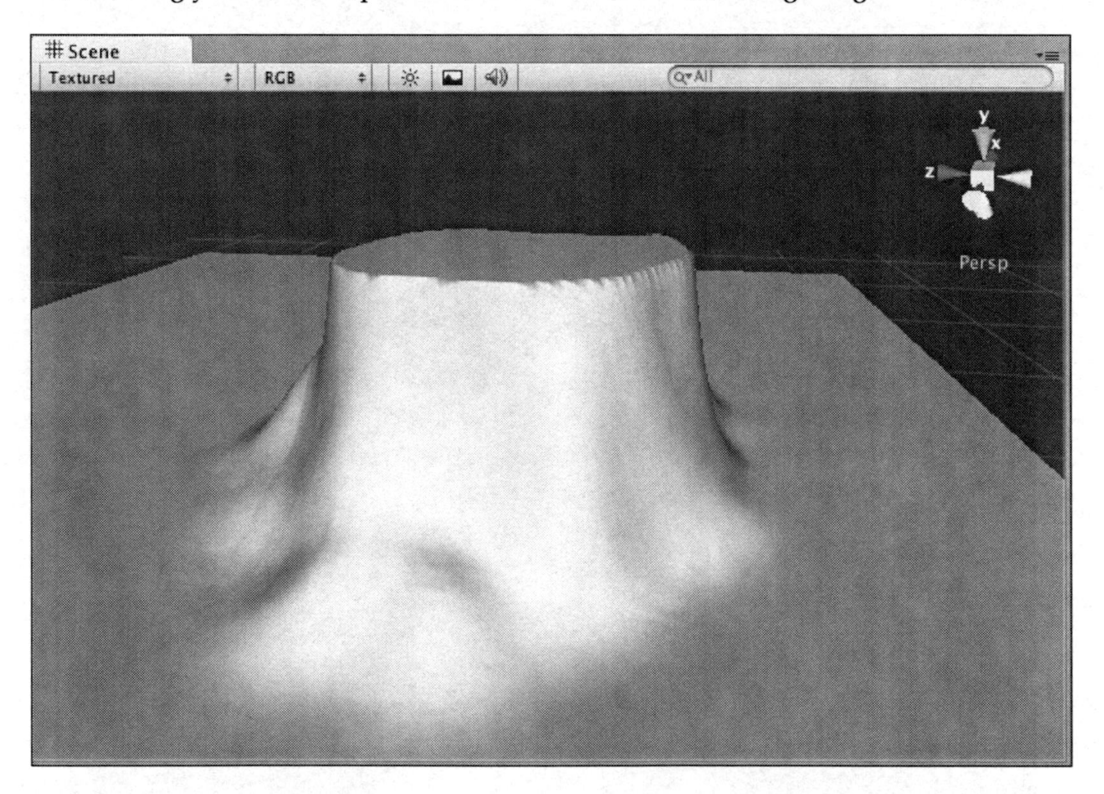

Smooth Height

This tool is used mostly to complement other tools such as Paint height in order to soften steep areas of topography.

For example, in the previous plateau, the land goes straight up, and should I wish to soften the edges of the raised area, I would use this tool to round off the harsh edges, creating the result shown in the following image:

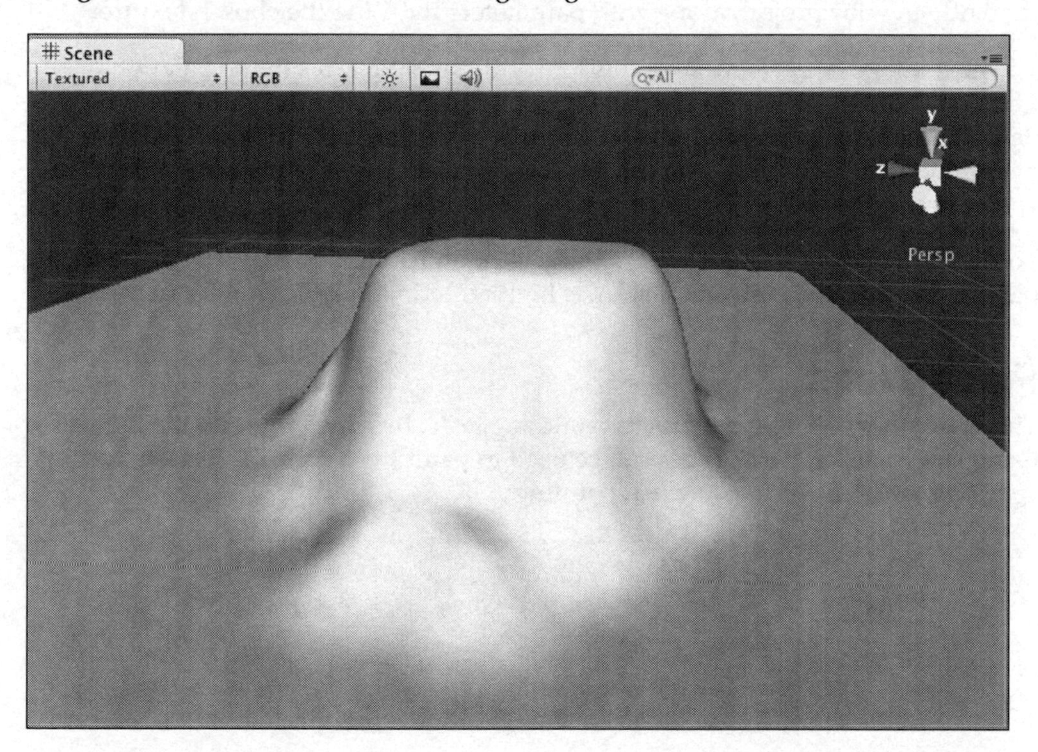

Paint Texture

Paint Texture is the tool used to brush textures—referred to as *Splats* in Unity terrain terms—onto the surface of the terrain:

In order to paint with textures, the textures must first be added to the palette in the **Textures** area of this tool. Textures can be added by clicking on the **Edit Textures** button and selecting **Add Texture**, which will allow you to choose any texture file currently in your project, along with parameters for tiling the chosen texture.

The next image is an example of this tool with three textures in the palette. The first texture you add to the palette will be painted over the entire terrain by default. Then, by combining several textures at varying opacities and painting manually onto the terrain, you can get some realistic areas of the kind of surface you're hoping to get.

To choose a texture to paint with, simply click on its thumbnail in the **Textures** palette. The currently chosen texture is highlighted with a blue underline.

Place Trees

This is another tool that does as its name suggests. By brushing with the mouse, or using single clicks, **Place Trees** can be used to paint trees onto the terrain, having specified which asset to use when painting.

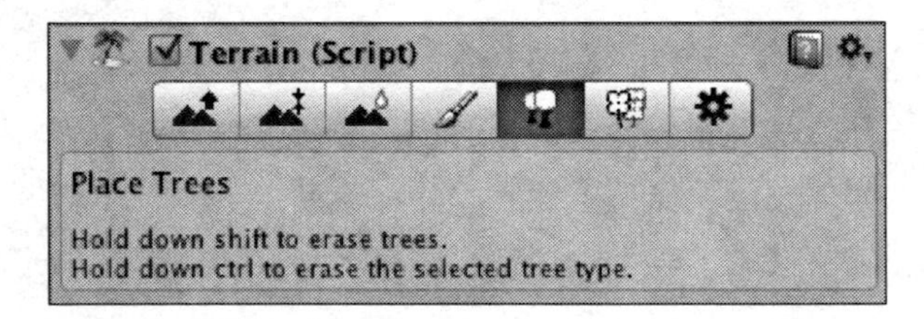

In the same way as specifying textures for the **Paint Texture** tool, this tool gives you an **Edit Trees** button to add, edit, and remove assets from the palette. These assets will be prefab tree game objects. In this book you will use the palm tree prefab game object that was imported with the terrain assets when you created the new project at the start of the book.

In its **Settings**, you can specify:

- **Brush Size**: The amount of trees to paint per click
- **Tree Density**: The proximity of trees placed when painting
- **Color Variation**: Applies random color variation to trees when painting several at once
- **Tree Width/Height**: Sizes the tree asset you are painting with
- **Tree Width/ Height Variation**: Gives you random variation in sizing to create more realistically forested areas

This tool also utilizes the *Shift* key to reverse its effects. In this instance, using *Shift* erases painted trees and can be used in conjunction with the *Ctrl* key to only erase trees of the type selected in the palette.

Paint Details

This tool works in a similar manner to the **Place Trees** tool but is designed to work with detail objects such as flowers, plants, rocks, and other foliage:

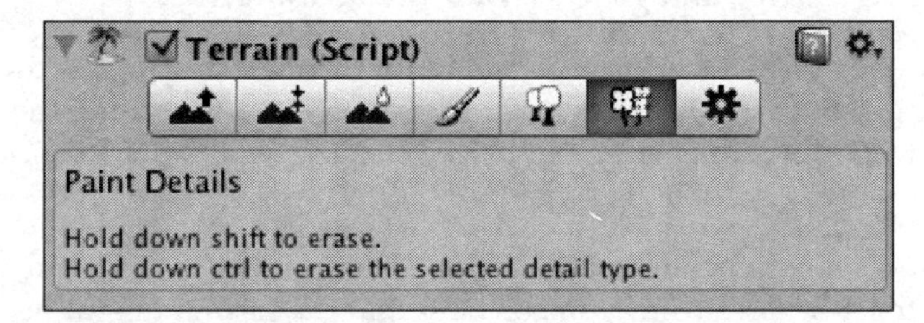

Terrain Settings

The **Terrain Settings** area of the **Terrain (Script)** contains various settings for the drawing of the terrain by the computer's **GPU** (**graphical processing unit**):

Here you can specify various settings that affect the **Level of Detail** (**LOD**).

Level of Detail in game development defines the amount of detail specified within a certain range of a player. In this example—a terrain—we need to be able to adjust settings such as **Draw Distance**, which is a common 3D game concept that renders less detail after a certain distance from the player in order to improve performance.

In **Terrain Settings**, for example, you can adjust **Base Map Distance** in order to specify how far away until the terrain replaces high resolution graphics with lower resolution ones, making objects in the distance less expensive to render.

We'll look at the terrain settings further as we begin to build our terrain.

Creating the island—sun, sea, and sand

Now let's dive into the toolset, and create our island!

Step 1—Setting up the terrain

Now that we have looked at the tools available to create our terrain, let's get started by setting up our terrain using the **Terrain** top menu. Ensure that your terrain is still selected in the **Hierarchy**, and go to **Terrain | Set Resolution**.

As we don't want to make too large an island for our first project, set the terrain **width** and **length** both to **500**. Remember to press *Enter* after typing these values, so that you've effectively confirmed them before clicking on the **Set Resolution** button to complete.

Next, our island's height needs to begin at its ground level, rather than at zero, which is the default for new terrains. If you consider that the terrain height of zero should be the sea bed, then we can say that our ground level should be raised to be the surface height of the island. Go to **Terrain | Flatten Heightmap**.

Click inside the **Height** box, and place in a value of **30** meters, and then press *Enter* to confirm. Click on **Flatten** to finish.

This change is a blink-and-you'll-miss-it difference in the **Scene** view, as all we've done is shift the terrain upward slightly. However, the reason we've done this is that it is a great time saver—as we can now flatten around the edges of the terrain using inverse **Raise Height** to leave a raised island in the centre of the terrain. This is a more time-efficient method than beginning with a flat zero-height terrain and raising the height in the centre.

Step 2—Creating the Island outline

On the **Inspector** for the terrain object's **Terrain (Script)** component, choose the **Raise Height** tool—the first of the seven buttons.

Select the first brush in the palette, and set its **Brush Size** to **100**. Set **Opacity** for the brush to **75**.

Change your view in the **Scene** panel to a top-down view by clicking on the **Y-axis** (green spoke) of the view gizmo in the top-right.

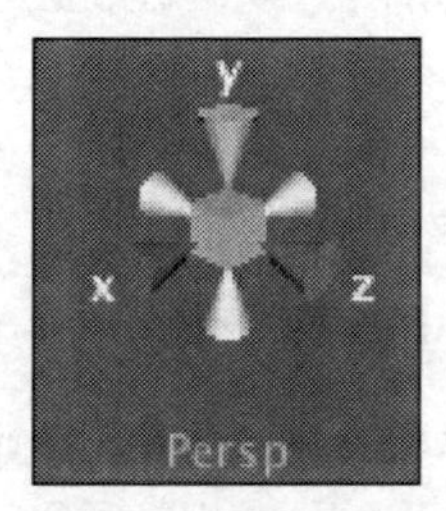

Using the *Shift* key to **lower height**, paint around the outline of the terrain, creating a coastline that descends to zero height—you will know it has reached zero as the terrain will flatten out at this minimum height.

While there is no need to exactly match the outline of the island suggested at the start of this chapter, try not to make a wildly different shape either, as you will need a flat expanse of land later for buildings. If you need a guide for the shape, either look at the following diagram or the map diagram shown earlier in the chapter. Once you have painted around the entire outline, it should look something like the following image:

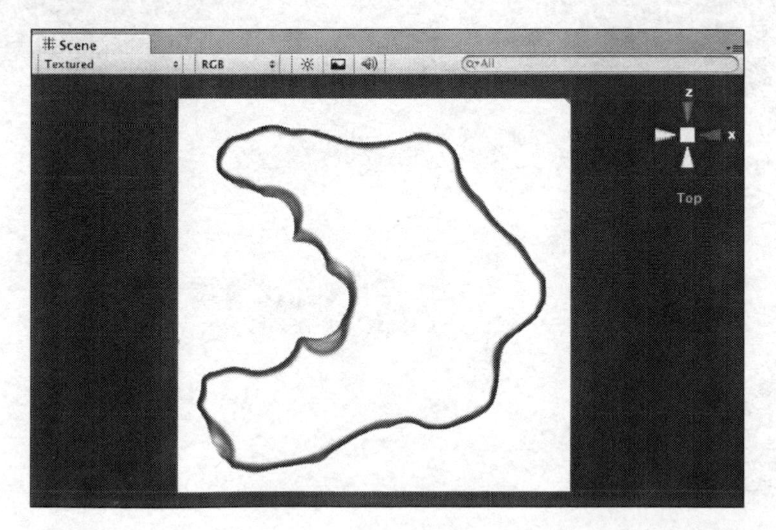

Now switch back to a **Perspective** (3D) view of your **Scene** by clicking on the center cube of the view gizmo in the top-right of the **Scene** window and admire your handiwork.

Now spend some time going over the island, using the **Raise Height** tool to create some further topographical detail, and perhaps using lower height (with the *Shift* key) to add a lake. Then make use of the **Smooth Height** tool to go around the edge of the terrain and soften some of those steep cliff edges. Leave a flat area in the south-west of your terrain (lower-left in the earlier image) and one free corner of your map in which we are going to add our volcano!

Step 3—Volcano!

Now to create our volcano! For this we will combine the use of the **Paint Height**, **Raise Height**, and **Smooth Height** tools. First, select the **Paint Height** tool.

Choose the first brush in the palette, and set the **Brush Size** to **75**, **Opacity** to **50,** and **Height** to **100**. Select the **Top** view again using the **view gizmo**, and paint on a plateau in the south-west that you left free on your terrain. Remember that this tool will stop affecting the terrain once it reaches the specified height of **100**.

Your island should now look like the following image in the **Perspective** view:

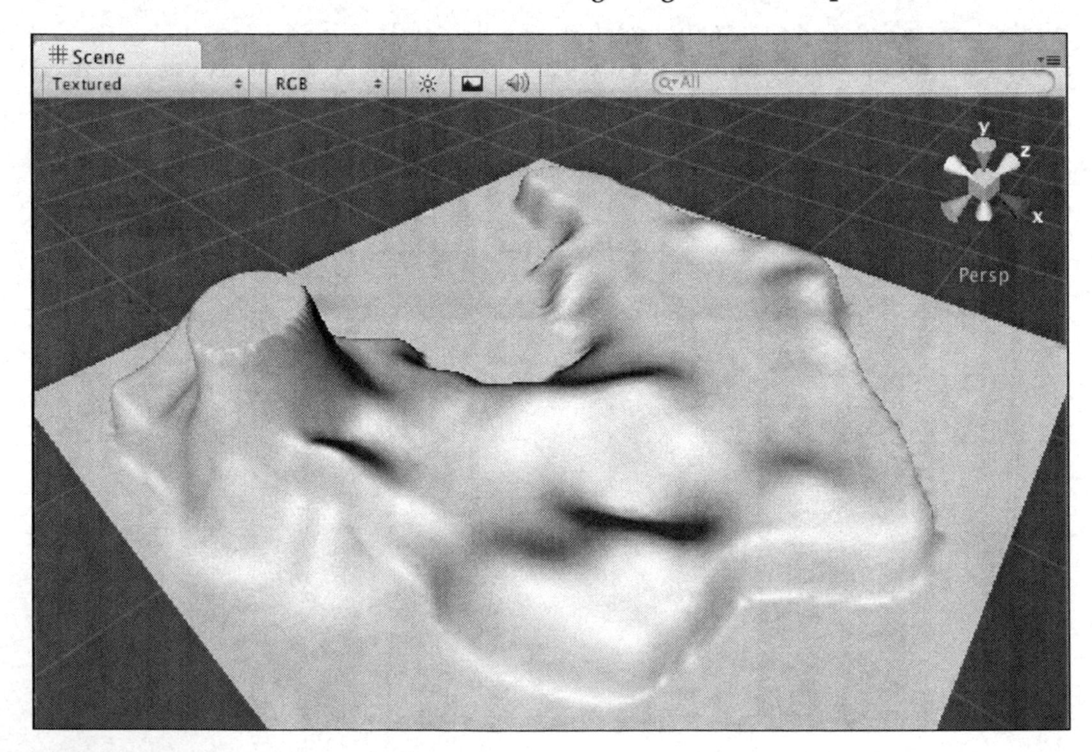

Now this plateau may look crude—we'll rectify this with smoothing shortly, but first we need to create the volcano mouth. So now with the **Paint Height** tool still selected, change the **Height** setting to **20** and the **Brush Size** to **30**. The next step will also be easier to accomplish using a top-down view, so click the Y-axis spoke of the **view Gizmo** to change the **Scene** view.

Now hold down the mouse and start painting from the center of the volcano plateau outwards towards its edge in every direction, until you have effectively hollowed out the plateau, leaving a narrow ridge around its circumference, as shown in the following image:

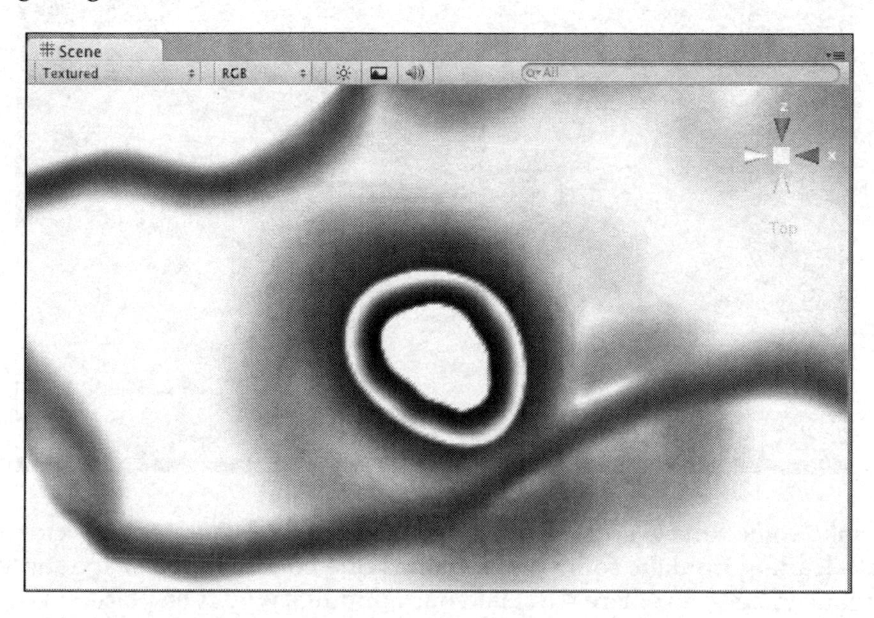

We still have a fairly solid edge to this ridge, and when switching to the **Perspective** view, you'll see that it still doesn't look quite right. This is where the **Smooth Height** tool comes in. Select the **Smooth Height** tool and set the **Brush Size** to **30** and **Opacity** to **100**. Using this tool, paint around the edge of the ridge with your mouse, softening its height until you have created a rounded soft ridge, as shown in the following image:

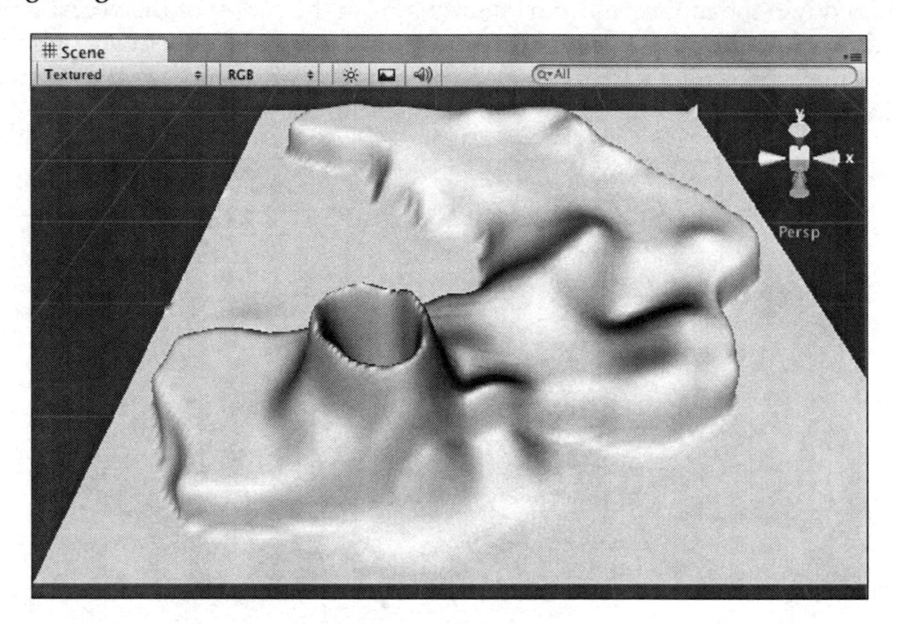

Finally, take some time to create a few ridges around the island terrain, leaving space for a path leading from the south of the island—the bottom of the shape shown in the previous image—to where we stated our buildings would be placed in the map illustration earlier in this chapter.

Now that our volcano has started to take shape, we can begin to texture the island to add realism to our terrain.

Step 4—Adding textures

When texturing your terrain, it is crucial to remember that the first texture you add will cover the terrain entirely. With this in mind, you should ensure that the first texture you add to your texture palette is the texture that represents the majority of your terrain.

In the **Terrain Assets** Package we included when we started the project, we are given various assets with which to customize terrains. As such, you'll find a folder called **Standard Assets** in your **Project** panel that contains the folder **Terrain Assets**. Expand this down by clicking on the gray arrow to the left of it, and then expand the subfolder called **Terrain Textures** - in here you'll find four texture files.

These are the four textures we'll use to paint our island terrain, so we'll begin by adding them to our palette. Ensure that the **Terrain** game object is still selected in the **Hierarchy**, and then select the **Paint Texture** tool from the **Terrain (Script)** component in the **Inspector**.

Painting procedure

To introduce the four textures for our terrain, begin by clicking on the **Edit Textures** button, and select **Add Textures** from the menu that pops out. This will launch the **Add Textures** dialog window in which you can select any texture currently in your project. Click on the circle selection button to the far right of the **Splat** setting (see following image) to open an **Asset Selection** window showing you a list of all available textures, and select the texture called **Grass (Hill)**. This **Select** dialog is searchable, so if you like, start typing the word **Grass** in order to narrow down the textures you are shown:

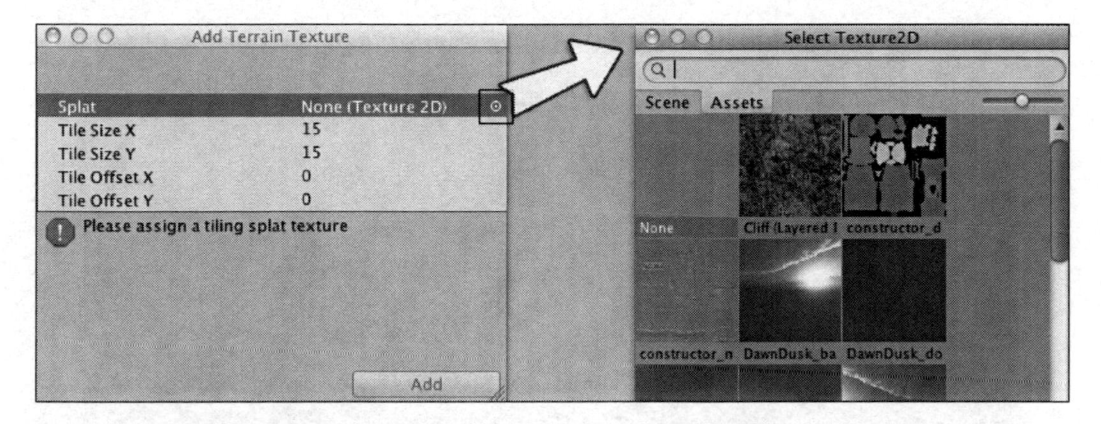

Leave the **Tile Size X** and **Y** values on **15** here, as this texture will cover the entire map, and this small value will give us a more detailed-looking grass. The **Tile Offset** values can be left on 0 as this texture is designed to tile as standard, so does not need offsetting.

Click on **Add** to finish. This will cover your terrain with the grass texture, as it is the first one we have added. Any future textures added to the palette will need to be painted on manually.

Repeat the previous step to add three further textures to the palette, choosing the textures named **Grass&Rock**, **GoodDirt**, and **Cliff (Layered Rock)**—while leaving the **Tile Size** settings unchanged for all except the **Cliff (Layered Rock)** texture, which should have an **X** and **Y Tile Size** of **70**, as it will be applied to a stretched area of the map and will look distorted unless tiled at a larger scale.

Sandy areas

You should now have all four textures available in your palette. Matching the above settings, choose the texture called **GoodDirt**—and it should become highlighted by a blue underline as shown in the preceding image. Set the **Brush Size** to **60**, **Opacity** to **50**, and **Target Strength** to **1**. You can now paint around the coast of the island using either the **Top** or **Perspective** view.

If you are using the **Perspective** view to paint textures, it will help to remember that you can use the *Alt* key while dragging the mouse, with either the **Hand** (Shortcut – *Q*) or **Transform** (Shortcut – *W*) tools selected, in order to rotate your view. You can also maximize any of the panels in the interface by hovering and pressing the *Spacebar* to toggle maximization.

When finished, you should have something like the following image:

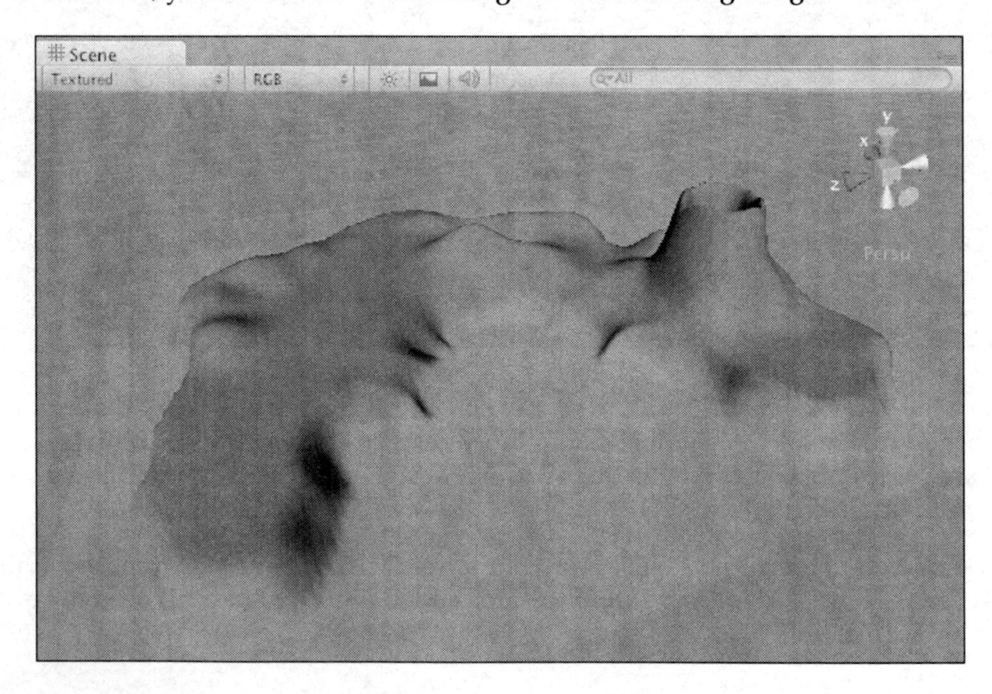

If you make a mistake while painting, you can either use **Edit** | **Undo** to step back one brush stroke, that is, a single-held mouse movement, or select the texture from the palette that you wanted and re-paint over your mistake with that.

Grass & Rock

Next select the **Grass & Rock** texture by clicking on the second thumbnail in the palette. Set the **Brush Size** to **25**, **Opacity** to **30**, and **Target Strength** to **0.5**. Now brush over any hilly areas on your terrain and around the top half of the volcano.

Volcanoes rock!

Now we need to make our volcano look more realistic by adding the **Cliff (Layered Rock)** texture to it. Select the cliff texture from the palette, and set the **Brush Size** to **20**, **Opacity** to **100**, and **Target Strength** to **1**.

Paint over the top outer half and the entire inner with these settings and then slowly decrease the **Opacity** and **Brush Size** values as you work your way down the outside of the volcano so that this texture is applied more subtly towards the ground. With a lower opacity, you may also want to paint over the tops of some of your taller hilled areas on the terrain.

While this will take some experimentation, when finished, your volcano should look something like the following image:

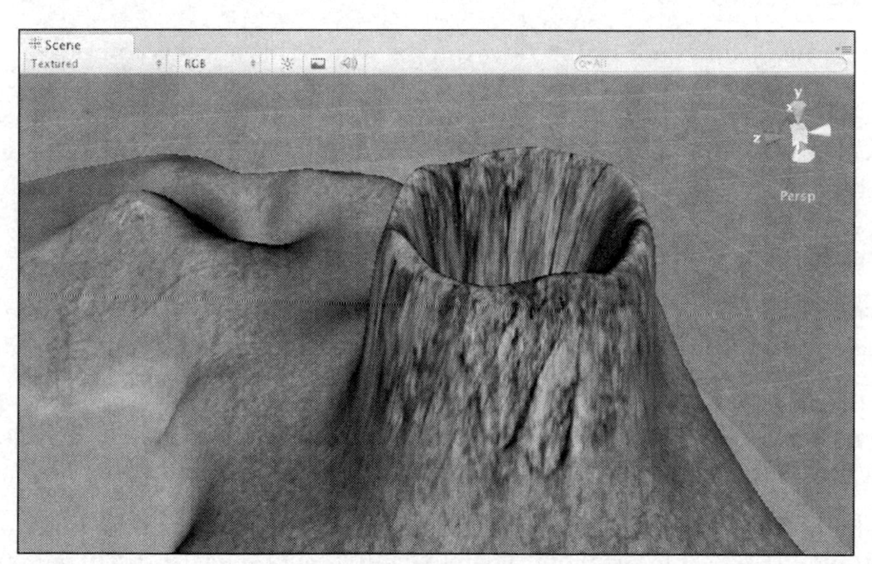

Step 5—Tree time

Now that we have a fully textured island, we need to spruce up the place a little with some trees. In our `Terrain Assets` package, there is a tree provided to get us started with the terrain editor, and thankfully for us, it is a palm tree asset. There is a Tree creator available in Unity, which you should try after this book, once you have more experience in Unity. For more information on this, visit: `http://unity3d.com/support/documentation/Components/class-Tree.html`

For now we will make use of the palm tree we have already created. Select the **Place Trees** tool of the **Terrain (Script)** component, and click on the **Edit Trees** button. From the drop-down menu that appears, choose **Add Tree**.

The **Add Tree** dialog window appears. As with some of the other terrain tools, this *Add* dialog allows us to select from any object of an appropriate type from our `Assets` folder.

This is not restricted to trees provided in **Terrain Assets**, which means that you can model your own trees by saving them into the `Assets` folder of your project in order to use them with this tool (see the documentation on Trees for further details). However, we are going to use the Palm tree provided by the terrain assets. Click on the circle selection button to the far right of the **Tree** setting—as with the texture painting earlier, this will open an **asset selection** window from which you can choose the **Palm** tree.

Bend factor here allows our trees to sway in the wind. This effect is computationally expensive, and any value will likely incur a performance reduction when play-testing your game. If you experience poor performance, return to this setting and replace it with a value of 0. For now we'll simply use a low number for a small amount of tree sway—type in a value of 2 and press *Enter* to confirm. If you find that this is causing low performance later in development, then you can always return to this setting and set it back to 0. Click on the **Add** button to finish.

With your palm tree in the palette, you should see a small preview of the tree with a blue background to show that it is selected as the tree to place.

Set the **Brush Size** to **15** (painting 15 trees at a time) and the **Tree Density** to **40** (giving us a wide spread of trees). Set **Color Variation** to **0.4** to give us a varied set of trees and **Tree Height / Width** to **50** with their **Variation** settings at **30**.

Using single-clicks, place trees around the coast of the island, near the sandy areas that you would expect to see them. Then to complement the island's terrain, place a few more palm trees at random locations inland.

Remember that if you paint trees incorrectly at any time, you can hold the *Shift* key and click, or paint (drag) with the mouse to erase trees from the terrain.

Step 6—The grass is always greener

Now that we have some trees on our island, we'll add a small amount of grass to complement the grass textures we covered the terrain with.

Select the **Paint Details** section of the **Terrain (Script)** component and click on the **Edit Details** button. Select **Add Grass Texture** from the pop-out menu.

The `Terrain Assets` package provides us with a grass texture to use, so click the circle selection button to the right of the **Detail Texture** setting, then in the asset selection window that appears, select the texture simply called **Grass**.

Having chosen the **Grass** texture, leave the **Width** and **Height** values at their default and ensure that **Billboard** is selected at the bottom of this dialog. As our grass detail textures are 2D, we can employ **billboarding**, a technique in game development that rotates the grass texture to face the camera during game play in order to make the grass seem less two-dimensional.

Using the color-picker boxes, ensure that the **Healthy** and **Dry** colors are of a similar shade of green to the textures we have painted onto the terrain, because leaving them on the default bright green will look out of place:

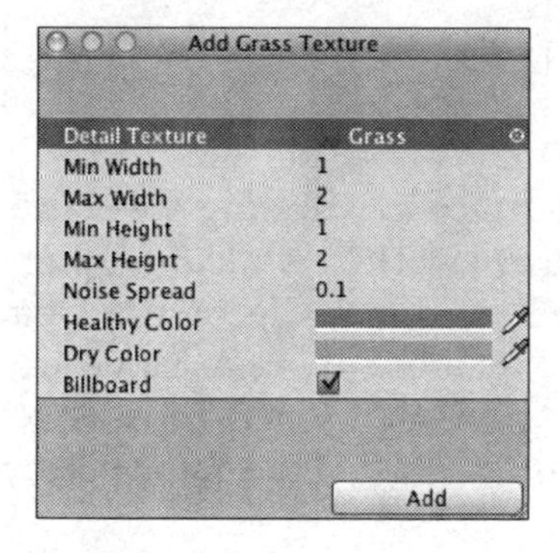

Click on the **Add** button at the bottom of the dialog window to confirm adding this texture to your palette.

To paint grass onto our map, we can yet again use mouse-based brushing in a similar way to the other terrain tools. Firstly, we'll need to choose a brush and settings in order to ensure a wide and disparate painting of grass detail onto our map. Given that rendering grass is another expensive feature for the computer to render, we'll keep the grass to a minimum by setting the **Brush Size** to **100**, but **Opacity** to **0.1**, and **Target Strength** to **0.3**. This will give a wide spread with very little grass, and by choosing a stipple brush (see the next image) we can paint on patchy areas of grass:

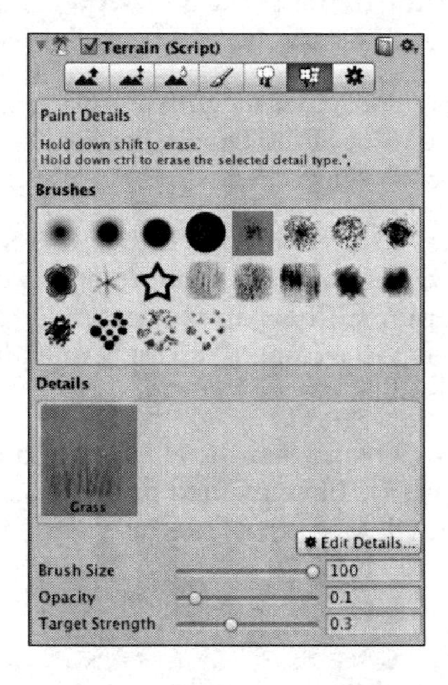

Now zoom into the terrain surface by selecting the **Hand** tool, and holding the *Command* key (Mac) or the *Ctrl* key (PC) while dragging the mouse to the right. Once at a close level of zoom, you'll need to reselect **Paint Details** on the Terrain tools and then click the mouse to paint on areas of grass. Move around the island painting on a few grassy areas—do this sparingly for performance reasons—and later you can always come back and add more grass if the game performs well.

It is crucial to zoom in on your terrain while painting details as the Unity Editor's **Scene** view does not render them visibly when zoomed out in order to save memory—so often it'll seem that when you have zoomed out, your grass and other details will disappear—do not worry, they are still there!

Step 7—Let there be lights!

Now that our island terrain is ready to explore, we'll need to add lighting to our scene. When first approaching lighting in Unity, it's best to be aware of what the three different light types are used for:

1. **Directional light**: Used as the main source of light, often as sunlight, a directional light does not emanate from a single point, but instead simply travels in a single direction.
2. **Point light**: These lights emanate from a single point in the 3D world and are used for any other source of light, such as indoor lighting, fires, glowing objects, and so on.
3. **Spot light**: Exactly what it sounds like, this light emanates from a single point, but has a radius value that can be set, much like focusing a flashlight.

Creating sunlight

To introduce our main source of light, we'll add a directional light. Click the **Create** button on the **Hierarchy** (or to **GameObject** | **Create Other** from the top menu) and choose **Directional Light**. This adds the light as an object in our scene, and you will see that it is now listed in the **Hierarchy**.

As the directional light does not emanate from a point, its position is ordinarily irrelevant as it cannot be seen by the player—only the light it casts is seen. However, in this tutorial, we're going to use the directional light to represent the sun, by applying a light flare to the light.

In order to represent the sun, we'll position the light high above the island, and to ensure that it is consistent with the direction of the light it casts, we'll position the light away from the island in the Z-axis.

Position the light at **(0, 250, -200)** by typing the position values into the **Inspector Transform** component. Set the **X rotation** to **15** in order to tilt the light downward in the X-axis, and this will cast more light onto our terrain.

Next, we'll need to make the light visible. To do this, we'll make use of some light flares. Unity provides these as a standard package we can import, to practice importing a new `Asset` package; I did not ask you to include these when we began our new project!

Let's introduce that package now by choosing **Assets** | **Import Package** | **Light Flares** from the top menu.

An **Importing Package** dialog window appears and you can simply click the **Import** button to confirm the addition of this package; it's that simple!

Now you can click the circle selector button to the far right of the **Flare** setting in the **Light** component—this will open an asset selection window, from which you can choose from the various light flares we just imported—choose the one titled **Sun** and close the asset selection window.

In *Chapter 10*, we will make use of the Lightmapping tool, which will take the lighting we have added here and in other parts of the book, and 'bake' it onto the environment, giving great quality shadows and great performance for your game.

Step 8—What's that sound?

An oft-overlooked area of game development is sound. For a truly immersive experience, your player needs to not only see the environment you've made, but hear it too.

Sound in Unity is handled through two components—the **audio source**, and the **audio listener**. Think of the source as a speaker in your game world, and the listener as a microphone or the player's ear. By default, camera game objects in Unity have an **audio listener** component. So given that you always have a camera in your game, chances are you'll only ever have to set up sound sources. It is also worth noting that the **audio listener** component has no properties to adjust—it just works. Unity will inform you with an error if you accidentally remove the only listener in any scene, or have more than one active listener at any time.

Sounds—2D versus 3D

Unity assumes by default that your sound files should be treated as 3D sounds—sounds that play realistically within the 3D space—becoming quieter as you move away from them and panning as you move to either side of them.

This means that Unity will automatically fade sounds as you move further from them, which in the case of ambient sound is something you may not want, and in the case of the hillside audio we are working on, is definitely something we need to change to 2D sound as this will give us a consistent audio volume, regardless of where the audio listener, that is, the player's ears—happen to be.

For example, for the following purposes:

- **In game music**: 2D sound would be best, as it would remain constant, no matter where the player's listener goes in the game.

- **Sound effect of a jukebox inside a building**: 3D sound would be best. Although you may be playing music as your sound effect, using 3D audio will make the sound play spatially, allowing the sound source to become louder the the player gets closer to it and pan as they move the audio listener to either side of it, for a more immersive experience.

Audio file formats

Unity will accept the most common audio formats—WAV, MP3, AIFF, and OGG. Upon encountering a compressed format such as MP3, Unity converts your audio file to the OggVorbis file format, while leaving uncompressed sounds such as WAVs unconverted. Remember that all compression settings can be changed in the **Inspector**, when selecting an asset in the project panel.

As with other assets you import, audio files simply get converted as soon as you switch between another program and Unity, as Unity scans the contents of the `Assets` folder each time you switch to it to look for new files. The option to compress to another format however, is not available to already compressed files such as MP3s that you may add to your project.

The hills are alive!

To make our island feel more realistic, we'll add a sound source playing constant outdoor ambience using a 2D sound.

Begin by selecting the terrain object in the **Hierarchy**. Go to **Component | Audio | Audio Source** from the top menu. This adds an **Audio Source** component to the **terrain** object. As the volume remains constant when using 2D sounds, and position is irrelevant, we could place the ambience sound source on any object—it simply makes logical sense that ambient sound of the terrain should be attached to that game object.

In the **Inspector** of the terrain, you will now see the **Audio Source** component with which you may either choose a file to play, or leave blank if you are planning to play sounds through scripting. Before you assign a sound, we'll need to get the relevant clip, and the other assets for this book.

Importing the book's asset package

For this step, you'll need to download the custom-made asset package for this book from the book page at `http://www.packtpub.com/support`. Visit this page and select this book from the list of titles on the menu. You will then be able to enter your e-mail address and you will be e-mailed a direct link to the asset package download. Once you receive this e-mail and download the compressed file, unzip the package and you will be left with a file with the extension `.unitypackage`. Now return to Unity and go to **Assets | Import Package | Custom Package**.

You will be presented with a file selection **Import Package** dialog window, from which you should navigate to the location on your hard drive that you saved the downloaded `.unitypackage` file. Select it, and then click on **Open** to choose it.

Click on **Import** to confirm adding these files to your project and after a short conversion progress bar, you should see them in your Project panel—contained within a parent folder named **Book Assets**. Within this, you'll need to open the `Sounds` folder you've added by clicking on the gray arrow to the left of it in order to see the `hillside` sound file; select it here in order to see the **Import settings** for this asset in the **Inspector**.

In the **Import Settings** for the **hillside** sound file, uncheck the box for **3D Sound** to switch this file back to 2D, and click the **Apply** button at the bottom of the **Import** settings to confirm this change. You will see a progress bar as Unity re-imports the sound file with this new setting.

The **hillside** file is now ready to be applied to the **Audio Source** component of the terrain.

Click on the circle selection button to the far right of the **Audio Clip** setting in the **Audio Source** component of the **terrain** object. This will present you with an asset selection window, showing a list of all available audio files in your project. Select the **hillside** audio file and then close the asset selection window.

Further audio settings

The **Audio Source** component has various settings to control how the audio clip sounds, as well as how it plays back. For our ambient hillside sound, simply ensure that the checkboxes for **Play On Awake** and **Loop** are selected.

This will play the ambience sound clip when the player enters the scene (or level) and continually loop the clip until the scene is exited.

Your **Audio Source** component should look like this:

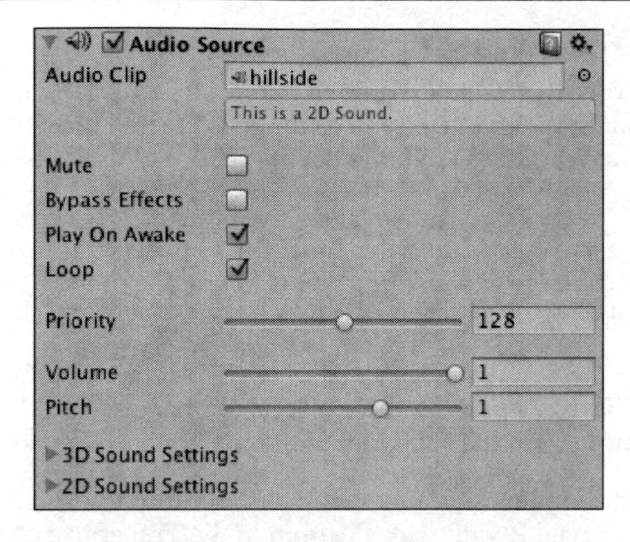

Step 9—Look, there! Up in the skybox!

In creating 3D environments, the horizon or distance is represented by the addition of a **skybox**. A skybox is a **cubemap**—a series of six textures placed inside a cube and rendered seamlessly to appear as a surrounding sky and horizon. This cubemap sits around the 3D world at all times, and much like the actual horizon, it is not an object the player can ever get to.

To apply a skybox to your scene, go to **Edit | Render Settings**. The Inspector area of the interface will now change to show the preferences for the rendering of this scene. To the right of the **Skybox Material** setting, click the circle selection button to open an asset selection window titled **Choose Material**. This is because technically a cubemap is a type of material—a way to apply textures to meshes in the game. From this selection window, choose **Sunny 2 Skybox**. This will apply the skybox, but it is crucial to understand that any skybox you add will only be shown in the **Game View** panel by default, unless you click the **Game Overlay** button at the top of the **Scene** view.

This is the second of the three buttons as shown in the following image:

Step 10—Open water

As we have constructed an island terrain, it follows that our land mass should be surrounded by water. Water in Unity free edition is created using an animated material applied to a surface—Pro users get the chance to use a more realistic `Pro Water` package.

While it is possible to create further dynamic water effects by utilizing particles, the best way to add a large expanse of water is to use one of the water materials provided by Unity.

The `Water (basic) assets` package gives us two readymade surfaces with the water material applied. Saved as prefabs, these objects can be introduced easily from the **Project** panel. Simply open the subfolder of **Standard Assets** called **Water Basic**.

Drag the **Daylight Simple Water** prefab into the scene and position it at (**250**, **4**, **250**) by filling in the X, Y, and Z values for **Position** in the **Transform** component in the **Inspector**. In order to expand the scale of the water prefab to form a sea around the island, simply increase both the **X** and **Z** values under **Scale** to **1600**.

This places the water in the center of the map and four meters above the sea-bed. This will cover up the corners of your island, and mask the terrain's true square-based nature. It should look like the following image:

Step 11—Going walkabout

In the **Project** panel, expand the `Standard Assets` folder,and then expand the subfolder called **Character Controllers**. In here you will find a two prefabs—a readymade **First Person Controller** and a **3rd Person Controller** object. We'll be making a First Person viewed game, so select the **First Person Controller**.

In the **Scene** view, zoom in to a part of the island you wish to drop your First Person Controller player object onto. Your view should look something like the following image:

Drag this prefab from the **Project** panel onto the **Scene** view and you should note that Unity tries to position your object on top of any collider it encounters—in this instance, the inbuilt Terrain Collider. When you release the mouse however, focus your view on the newly placed **First Person Controller** by hovering over the **Scene** view and pressing *F*.

You may notice that the object is dug in half way into the ground. This is simply because Unity places the center of the object (or from where it's axes emerge) onto the surface of the collider you drop onto. This is shown in the following image:

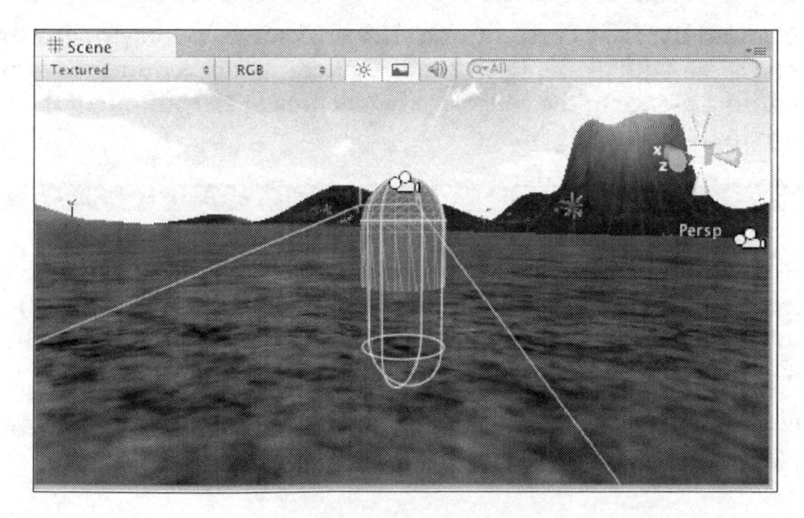

This is a problem because the game scene should always start without any colliders intersecting, as Unity must decide what to do in order to resolve the intersection, and the collider on the **First Person Controller** may be inactive until it is in a valid position. Because this object has its own script applied gravity, the object may be forced downward and fall through the map.

To avoid this issue, simply select the **Translate** tool (*W*) and then drag the green Y-axis handle up to ensure that the green capsule outline of the collider is above the ground.

Now that your **First Person Controller** object is an active game object, you can see it listed in the **Hierarchy** and its component parts listed in the **Inspector**.

Now press the **Play** button to test the game, and you should be able to walk around on your island terrain!

The default controls for the character are as follows:

- *Up arrow/W*: Walk forward
- *Down arrow/S*: Walk backward
- *Left arrow/A*: Sidestep left (also known as *Strafing*)
- *Right arrow/D:* Sidestep right
- Mouse: Look around/turn the player while walking

Once you've had a good stroll around the island, stop testing the game by pressing the **Play** button again.

Step 12—Final tweaks

As we have added the **First Person Controller** object, we no longer need the object that our scene came with by default—**Main Camera**. Unity reminds us of this by showing an info message in the console preview area at the bottom of the screen. This is shown in the following image:

There are 2 audio listeners in the scene (Main Camera). Please ensure there is always one audio listener in the scene.

To rectify this, simply remove the Main Camera object, as we no longer need it. To do this, select it in the Hierarchy, and press Command + Backspace (Mac) or Delete (PC), or - on either platform - right-click this object's name in the Hierarchy and choose Delete from the pop-out menu that appears.

Now that this object is gone, your island terrain is complete. Save your scene so that you do not lose any work—go to **File** | **Save Scene.**

Congratulations, your island terrain is ready for exploration, so hit the **Play** button again and go exploring! Just remember to press **Play** again to stop when you are finished.

Summary

In this chapter, we've explored the basics of developing your first environment. Beginning with nothing but a flat plane, you have now created a completely explorative island terrain in a short space of time. We've also looked at lighting and sound, two core principles that you'll apply in every kind of game project you encounter.

Remember, you can always return to the terrain tools covered in this chapter at any time in order to add more detail to your terrain - we will do this in chapter 10 - Performance tweaks, optimisation and final touches. Once you feel more confident with sound, we will also return to adding further audio sources to the island later in the book.

As you continue to work through this book, you'll discover all types of additional nuances that you can bring to environments in order to further suspend disbelief in the player.

We'll be looking at adding a dynamic feel to our island when we look at the use of particles, adding campfires, and even a plume of smoke and ash from our volcano!

In the next chapter, we'll place an outpost building into our scene, and look at how we can trigger its animation of a door opening when the player approaches it. To do this, we'll expand upon your new knowledge of scripting for Unity, and take our first leap into developing real game interactions.

4
Player Characters and Further Scripting

In this chapter, we'll expand the island scenario that we created in the previous chapter by taking a look at the construction of the player character that you have already added to the island. This object is an example of a first-person perspective player character. But how does its combination of objects and components achieve this effect?

We will take a look under the hood of this prefab while looking at how each of the components work together to create our player character.

As we have already added our prefab to the game scene, it would be all too easy to continue with the development and accept that this object just works. Whenever you are implementing any externally created assets, you should make sure that you always try to understand how they work—even if you cannot recreate them yourself just yet. Otherwise, if anything needs adjusting or goes wrong, you'll be in the dark, which can be detrimental when asking others for help.

With this in mind, we'll take a look at the following topics in order to help you understand how combining just a few objects and components can create a fully-fledged character:

- Working with the **Inspector**
- Anatomy of a character—an overview
- Parent-child relationships in objects
- The **Character Controller** component
- Public member variable adjustment in the **Inspector**
- Using cameras to create the viewpoint
- Further scripting
- Scripting for player movement

Working with the Inspector

As we are dissecting an object's details in the **Inspector**, let's begin by looking at the features of the **Inspector** that are common to game objects in the active scene and prefabs in the project.

At the top of the **Inspector**, you will see the name of the object that you have currently selected, along with a game object or prefab icon (red, green, and blue-sided cube or light blue cube respectively) and a checkbox to allow you to temporarily deactivate the object.

For example, when newly creating a game object (not from an existing prefab) with our **Directional light**, the top of the **Inspector** appears as follows:

Here, you can see the red, green, and blue icon, which represents a standard game object. It is also worth noting that the name box of this part of the **Inspector** can be used to rename an object simply by clicking and typing, as an alternative to renaming in the **Hierarchy** panel as we have done so far.

To the right of the name field is the **Static** checkbox. Checking this box tells Unity that a particular object in your scene will not be moving during the game, and as such can be lightmapped. We will make use of the **Lightmapping** tool later in the book to improve the aesthetics of our scene. This tool allows us to **Bake**—semi-permanently render the lighting of a scene into its textures to add depth and realism.

Check the box for **Static** on the **Directional light** now as we will include this light in our **lightmapping** later.

Following the icon, the active checkbox, and the name, you will see the **Tag** and **Layer** settings.

Tags

Tags are simply keywords that can be assigned to a game object. By assigning a tag, you can use the chosen word or phrase to address the game object (or objects) to which it is assigned within your game scripting (one tag can be used many times). If you have worked with Adobe Flash before, then you might liken tags to the *instance name* concept in Flash—in that they are keywords used to represent objects in a scene.

Adding a tag to a game object is a two-step procedure—firstly your tag must be added to a list within the **Tag Manager**, and then applied to your chosen object.

To help you get used to using tags, let's make and apply our first tag to the **Directional light** object. With this object selected in the **Hierarchy** panel, click on the **Tag** drop-down menu where it currently says **Untagged**.

You will now see a list of existing tags. You can either choose one of these or make a new one. Select **Add Tag** at the bottom in order to add a tag to the list in the **Tag Manager**:

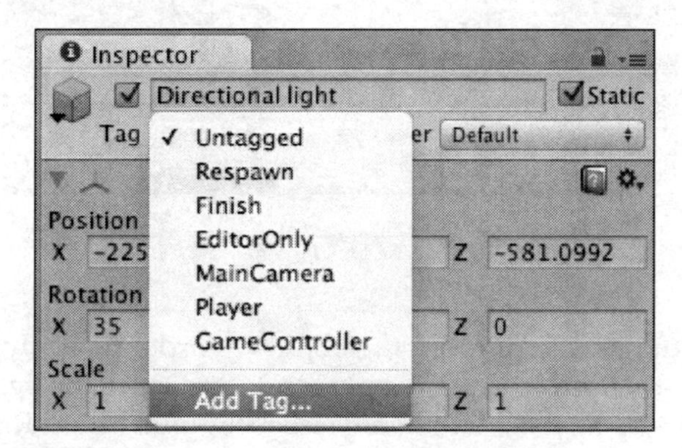

The **Inspector** panel will now switch to displaying the **Tag Manager**, rather than the components of the object that you previously had selected.

The **Tag Manager** shows both **Tags** and **Layers**. To add a new tag, you'll need to click on the gray arrow to the left of **Tags** in order to see the **Size** and **Element** fields. Once you have done this, you will be able to type in the space to the right of **Element 0**.

Type in the name **Sunlight** (tags may be named whatever you please), and press *Enter/Return* to confirm. Note that, as soon as you press *Enter/Return*, the **Size** value increments to the next number, and adds a new **Element** field—you need not fill this in, as it's simply available for the next tag you wish to add.

The **Size** parameter here is simply the amount of tags currently set up. Unity uses the **Size** and **Element** system for many different menus, and you'll encounter it as we continue to work with the **Inspector**.

You have added a tag to the list. However, it has not yet been assigned to the **Directional light** object. Therefore, reselect this object in the **Hierarchy** panel, and then click again on **Untagged** next to **Tag** at the top of the **Inspector**. You will now see your newly created tag called **Sunlight** at the bottom of your tag list. To apply it, simply select it from the drop-down menu, as shown in the following image:

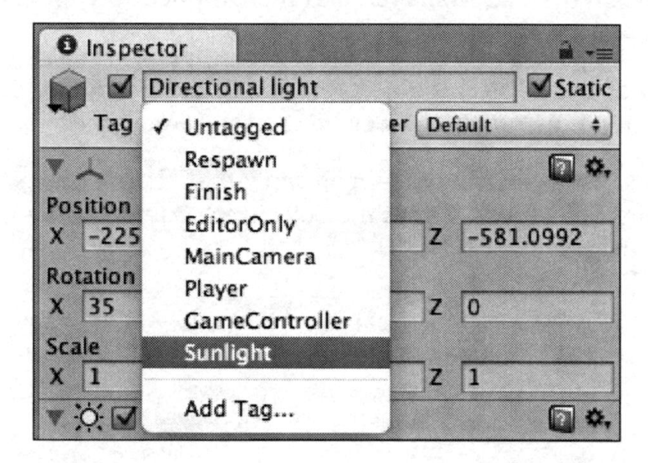

Layers

Layers are an additional way of grouping objects in order to apply specific rules to them. They are mostly used to group-apply rendering rules for lighting and cameras. However, they can also be used with a physics technique called **Raycasting** in order to selectively ignore certain objects. We will look at using Raycasting in the next chapter on *Interactions*. Another common usage of layers for physics is to place objects on the same layer that should interact with one another—effectively creating collision layers with objects that should collide on the same layer.

By placing objects on a layer, for example, they can be deselected from a light's **Culling Mask** parameter, which would exclude them from being affected by the light. Layers are created in the same manner as tags, and are accessible from the **Tag Manager**, seen listed in the following list of **Tags**.

Prefabs and the Inspector

If the active game object you select from the **Hierarchy** panel originates from a prefab, then you will be shown some additional settings, as shown in the following image:

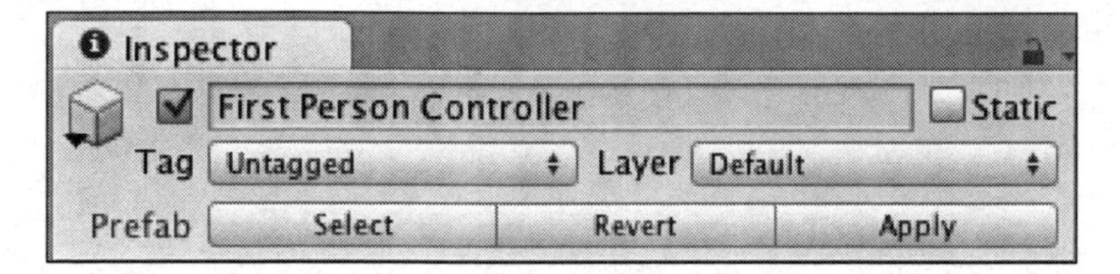

Beneath the **Tag** and **Layer** fields, you can see three additional buttons for interacting with the object's originating **prefab**:

1. **Select**: This simply locates and highlights the prefab the object belongs to in the Project panel.
2. **Revert**: This reverts any settings for components in the active object back to the settings used in the prefab in the **Project** panel.
3. **Apply**: Changes the settings of the prefab to those used in the currently selected instance of that prefab. This will update any other instances or 'Clones' of this prefab wherever they exist, in either the active or other scenes.

Now that you are aware of the additional settings available on the **Inspector**, let's start using it to inspect our player character.

Anatomy of a character

To get an overview of the characters available in the `Character Controllers` package we have imported into our project, let's take a look at how the First and Third Person prefabs work in Unity terms.

The following diagram shows the core components that make up these characters:

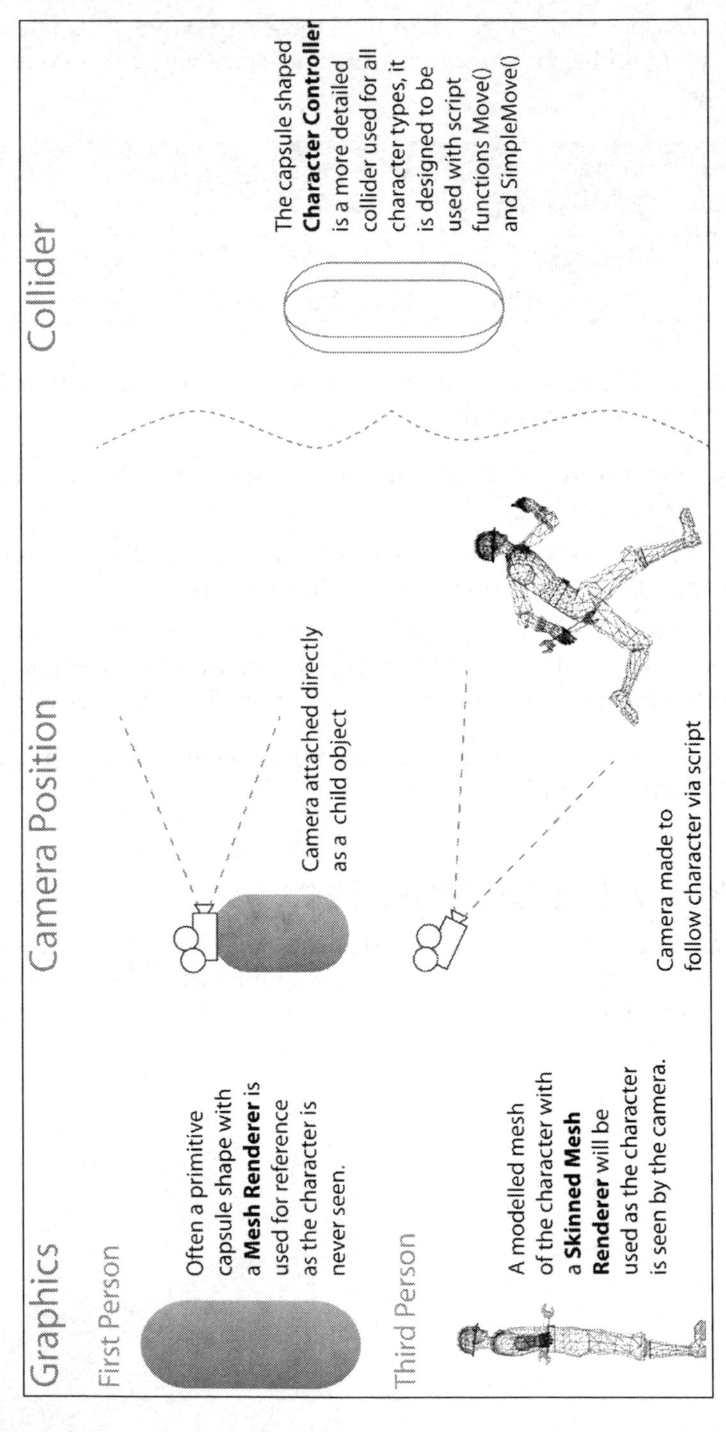

Deconstructing the First Person Controller object

Let's begin by looking at the objects that make up our **First Person Controller** (**FPC**) before we look into the components that make it work.

Click on the gray arrow to the left of **First Person Controller** in the **Hierarchy** in order to reveal the objects nested underneath. When objects are nested in this way, we say that there is a **parent-child relationship**. In this example, **First Person Controller** is the parent, while **Graphics** and **Main Camera** are its child objects. In the **Hierarchy**, child objects are indented to show their parenting, as shown in the following image:

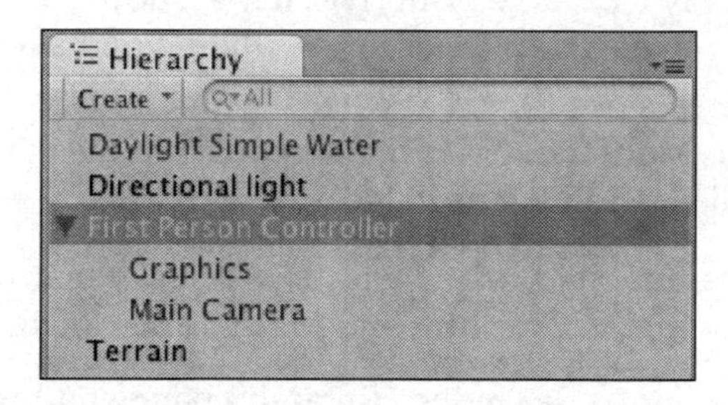

Parent-child issues

When considering nested or child objects, you should note that there are some key rules to remember. As discussed in the first chapter, parent-child relationships are important in complex objects that contain a hierarchy. In the case of the FPC they are particularly pertinent as wherever the parent object moves and rotates, the child objects—most importantly the Main Camera-moves with it. Refer to *Chapter 1, Enter the Third Dimension* for more information on this.

A child object's position and rotation values are relative to their parent. This is referred to as **local position** and **local rotation**. For example, you may consider your parent object to exist at (500, 35, 500) in world coordinates, but when selecting a child, you'll notice that while its position may be a lot closer to the value (0,0,0), it still appears to be in the same position as the parent. This is what we mean by relative to. By placing a child object at (0,0,0), we are telling it to be at the origin of its parent, or relative to the parent's position.

In the **Hierarchy** panel, click on **Graphics** beneath the FPC parent object, and you'll see this in action—the FPC is in a random world position on the island, yet our **Graphics** object has **Transform Position** values of (0,0,0).

As a result of this relativity, you should also be aware that whenever the parent object is moved, its children will follow, while maintaining their local positions and rotations according to the parent's position and rotation in the game world.

First Person Controller object

The three parts of this object are as follows:

1. **First Person Controller**: The FPC object, or parent of the group, which has the main scripting and Character Controller collider applied to it and is in control of how it behaves. This object has scripts applied for movement using the keyboard and rotation when moving the mouse left and right.
2. **Graphics**: Simply a capsule primitive shape (shown in the following image), which allows you as a developer to see where you have placed the FPC.
3. **Main Camera**: It is positioned at where you would expect the player's eye level to be. The Main Camera is there to provide the viewpoint, and has scripting applied, allowing us to look up and down.

Bearing in mind the parent-child relationship, we can say that wherever the FPC object moves or rotates to, the **Graphics** and **Main Camera** will follow.

Select the **First Person Controller** in the **Hierarchy** panel, and with your mouse cursor over the **Scene** window, press the *F* key to focus the view on that object. You should now see the FPC, a white capsule with green collider outline.

Now press the **Play** button, click anywhere on the **Game** window, and start to move the character while watching it in the **Scene** window. You should notice that as you move the character with the keys and rotate it with your mouse, the child objects also move. If your Unity layout is not set up to show both the **Game** and **Scene** views simultaneously, try the **2 by 3** layout by choosing **Window | Layouts | 2 by 3** from the top menu.

Object 1: First Person Controller (parent)

With the **First Person Controller** still selected in the **Hierarchy** window, take a look at the components attached to it in the **Inspector**.

You will see that there are five components making up the FPC parent object—**Transform, CharacterController, Mouse Look (Script), Character Motor (Script),** and **FPSInput Controller(Script)**.

Transform

As with all active game objects, the FPC has a **Transform** component, which shows, and allows adjustment of, its position, rotation, and scale parameters.

Character Controller

This acts as a collider (a component giving our object a physical presence that can interact with other objects) and is specifically designed for character movement and control within the world. It features the following parameters:

- **Height**: The height of the character, which defines how tall the capsule-shaped character collider will be.
- **Radius**: How wide the capsule-shaped collider will be—this has a default radius that matches the radius of the **Graphics** child object. However, if you wish to make your character wider, either to restrict movement or in order to detect collisions with a larger space, then you could increase the value of this parameter.
- **Slope Limit**: Taking into account uphill movement, this parameter allows you to specify how steep an incline can be before the character can no longer walk up to it. By including this parameter, the **Character Controller** stops the player from simply walking up vertical walls or steep areas of land, which would of course seem unrealistic.
- **Step offset**: As your game world may well feature stairs, this parameter allows you to specify how far from the ground the character can step up—the higher the value, the larger the distance they can step up.
- **Skin Width**: As the character will collide with other game objects in the scene, often at speed, this parameter is provided to let you specify how deeply other colliders may intersect with the character's collider without reacting. This is designed to help reduce conflicts with objects, the result of which can be a jittering (a slight but constant character shake) or the character getting stuck in walls. This occurs when two colliders suddenly intersect, without allowing the game engine time to react accordingly—rather than crashing, the engine will switch off colliders to halt control or force the colliders apart unpredictably. Unity Technologies recommends that you set skin width to 10 percent of your character's radius parameter.
- **Min Move Distance**: This is the lowest amount by which your character can be moved. Usually set to zero, setting this value to a larger number means that your character cannot move unless they will be moved beyond that value. This is generally only used to reduce jittering, but in most situations it is set to **0**.

- **Center**: Set as a `Vector3` (x,y,z values). It allows you to position the character collider away from its local central point. Usually at zero, this is more often used for third-person characters, which will have a more complex look than a simple capsule. By allowing you to move the Y-coordinate, for example, it enables you to account for where the character's feet hit the floor—as it is the Character Controller collider that defines where the player object rests on the ground, and not the visual mesh of the character's feet.

The Character Controller collider is represented in the **Scene** view by a green capsule-shaped outline, in the same way as other colliders in Unity.

Mouse Look (Script)

Written in C#, this script is in charge of turning our character as we move the mouse, leaving the horizontal move keys to handle side-stepping or strafing as it is also known. This script has a number of public member variables exposed for adjustment:

- **Axes**: Set to **MouseX** in this instance. This variable allows you to choose **MouseX**, **MouseY**, or **MouseXAndY**. In our FPC, we need this instance of the **MouseLook** script (the other instance being a component of the **Main Camera** child object) to be set to the X-axis only, as this will allow mouse movement in the left and right direction in order to rotate the entire character—the **MainCamera** child object included.

  You may be wondering why we do not simply have **MouseXAndY** axes chosen on the **MouseLook** component for the **MainCamera** object. The problem with this approach would be that while it would allow the camera to tilt and pan in both the axes, it would not keep the character facing where we are looking—it would simply rotate the camera locally. As a result, we could look around, but when we move the character with the keys, we would run off in the forward direction, rather than what we assume is forward, based on where the camera is facing. By having this instance of the **MouseLook** script on the parent object (**First Person Controller**), we are allowing it to rotate the character, which in turn pans the camera because it is a child and will match its parent's rotation.

- **SensitivityX/SensitivityY**: As we are only using the X-axis of this script, this variable will only control how much the left/right movement of the mouse affects the rotation of the object. If the **Axes** variable was set to include the Y-axis, then this would control how sensitive the up or down movement of the mouse was at affecting the camera tilt. You will notice that **SensitivityY** has been set to **0**, as we are not using it, while **SensitivityX** is set to **15**—the higher the value here, the faster the rotation.

- **MinimumX/MaximumX**: This allows you to restrict the amount you can pan around, as this script is in charge of turning the character. These amounts are set to **-360** and **360** respectively, allowing you to turn the player completely around on the spot.
- **MinimumY/MaximumY**: Again, we are not using the Y-axis, so this variable is set to **0** here, but ordinarily it would restrict the player when looking up and down, as it does in the instance of this script, which is applied to the **Main Camera** child object.

Character Motor (Script)

This script, written in Javascript, provides a basis for various different types of character control in Unity. Provided by Unity Technologies as part of the `Character Controllers asset` package that we imported earlier, this script is the motor that drives both the First and Third Person character prefabs.

This script is highly complex but has comments written in the code by developers at Unity, so it is recommended that after completing this book you return to this script and read through it as an exercise in further reading. You'll be surprised how much you begin to understand!

The core exposed public variables allow the following adjustments in the **Inspector** or through scripting:

- **Can Control**: This is a simple boolean (true or false) variable to allow control input to be enabled or disabled. This could be used for example when switching on a pause menu to allow the player to utilize the control keys for other means such as navigating a menu, or simply to avoid moving the player around accidentally.
- **Use Fixed Update**: `FixedUpdate()` is a similar function to `Update()` that we used earlier, but instead of every frame, Fixed Update updates with every **Physics step**—meaning that it is tied directly to the physics engine. As such anything that uses Rigidbodies or realistic movement should use Fixed Update; this is why this checkbox is set to true by default.
- **Movement**: This is an instance of the `CharacterMotorMovement` class in the script, which contains variables for moving, falling, and halting inertia both in the air and on the ground.
- **Jumping**: An instance of the `CharacterMotorJumping` class in the script, this class contains variables for differentiating how the character behaves during jumps, and also provides a boolean toggle to disable jumping entirely.

- **Moving Platform**: As the Character Controller is not a Rigidbody object, it's common practice to simply script for gravity, as it occurs in the **Character Motor script**. It requires additional coding in order to make it respond to other objects such as moving platforms. If you need your character to land on and move with platforms or be transported in lifts for example, then these settings enable the part of the script that allows moving objects to affect the character, transferring motion from objects the Character Controller is in contact with.
- **Sliding**: As the character controller is already capsule shaped, and designed to deal with steps and slopes, it is expected that moving down a curved hill may take the form of a slide. This set of features simply enhances this behavior, ensuring a smooth gliding motion; you may wish to turn this off for simpler platform games where ledges and precise jumping are important. Note also, that sliding comes into effect when the character is on a surface that is steeper than the Slope Limit set on the **Character Controller** component, and it prevents the character from climbing steep surfaces by jumping repeatedly.

FPSInput Controller (Script)

This script, written in Javascript, allows the character to move backward and forward using the vertical axis keys (Up arrow/Down arrow or W/S), to move side-to side (or strafe) with the horizontal axis keys (Left arrow/Right arrow or A/D), and to jump using the Jump input key, which by default is the Space bar. This script works in conjunction with the **Character Motor script**, and simply provides Input information for that script.

This is why you will find variables in the script that make use of the `Input` class we used in our prototype exercise in *Chapter 2, Prototyping and Scripting Basics*. For example, in the script you'll see the following:

```
var directionVector = new Vector3(Input.GetAxis("Horizontal"), 0,
Input.GetAxis("Vertical"));
```

This takes the `Horizontal` axis for the X-coordinate of a new direction Vector `Vector3` variable and `Vertical` axis for the Z value. This is what allows us to use the *Up* and *Down* (or *W* and *S*) keys to move the character back and forth and *Left* and *Right* (or *A* and *D*) to sidestep. Remember here that the mouse is in charge of which direction we are facing and thus turning is done by a separate script—the **MouseLook (Script)** component.

This script is also commented in full by the developers, so you can read through it to find out how it works. Again, to avoid being overwhelmed it is recommend that you wait until you have worked through this book before attempting this, unless you have prior scripting experience.

Object 2: Graphics (child)

Because of the first person nature of this character object, the player will never see their own body, as represented by the capsule. It is merely included in this prefab to help you, the developer, to easily spot the object in the **Scene** window when developing and testing the game. Often, developers will switch off the rendering of the capsule mesh by disabling the **MeshRenderer** component in the **Inspector**. This is to ensure that the capsule stays hidden, especially in games where the player's character is viewed from another angle during cut scenes.

Select the **Graphics** child object in the **Hierarchy** panel, and take a look at the **Inspector** to view its components.

We'll take it as read that this object has a **Transform** component and that its position is (0,0,0), as it sits centrally with the parent object, **First Person Controller.** As this object's only purpose is to represent our player visually, it simply has the two key components that make it visible, a **Mesh Filter** and a **Mesh Renderer**. But what do these two components do?

Mesh filter

A **MeshFilter** is simply a component containing the mesh—the 3D shape itself. It then works with the renderer to draw a surface based on the mesh. It is named **polySurface2** in this instance. The name of the **MeshFilter** component in any 3D mesh is usually the name of the mesh asset that it represents. Therefore, when you are introducing externally created models, you will notice that each **Mesh Filter** component is named after each part of the model.

Mesh Renderer

A **Mesh Renderer** must be present in order to draw surfaces onto the mesh of a 3D object. It is also in charge of the following:

- How the mesh responds to lighting
- Materials used on the surface to show color or textures

Mesh renderers have the following parameters:

- **Cast Shadows**: Whether light cast onto this object will cause a shadow to be cast on the other surfaces (only available in Unity Pro version).
- **Recieve Shadows**: Whether shadows cast by other objects are drawn onto this object (only available in Unity Pro version).

  In this example of the **Graphics** capsule, neither box is checked. Firstly, this is because we will never see the capsule, so we need not receive shadows.

Secondly, the player does not think that their character has a body shaped like a capsule, so seeing a capsule-shaped shadow following them around would look rather odd.

- **Materials**: This area uses the **Size/Element** system seen in the **TagManager** earlier in this chapter. It allows you to specify one or more materials and adjust settings for them directly without having to find out the material in use, and then adjust it separately in the **Project** panel.

As our **Graphics** object requires features and not color or texture, there is no material to preview, so you are shown a **Default Diffuse** look—a simple basic material preset for new primitive objects.

Object 3: Main Camera (child)

The **MainCamera** acts as your viewport. In the **First Person Controller** prefab, the **Main Camera** is positioned at the eye level (at the top of the **Graphics** capsule) and is controlled by scripts, allowing the player to move the entire parent object and the camera independently. This allows the player to look and also walk around at the same time.

Ordinarily, camera game objects are made up of three key components—**Camera**, **GUILayer**, and **FlareLayer**, in addition to the usual **Transform** component. Cameras also come with an **Audio Listener** for receiving sound, but this is usually removed from anything other than the main camera, as Unity requires that you only have one listener per scene.

Our camera has its own instance of the **MouseLook(Script)** we looked at earlier, which handles up/down tilt rotation for the camera, based on the input from the mouse. To understand camera views better, let's take a look at how the core components work.

Camera

While ordinarily accompanied by the **GUILayer** and **FlareLayer** components, the **Camera** component is the main component in charge of establishing the viewpoint. In order to understand how the **Camera** component forms our viewpoint, we will examine its parameters, which are shown in the following image:

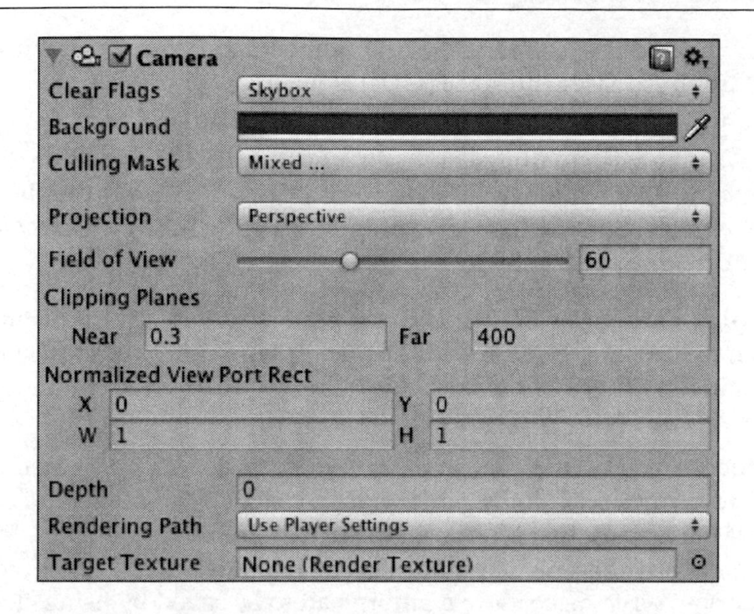

- **Clear Flags**: Ordinarily this will be set to its default, **Skybox**, to allow the camera to render the skybox material currently applied to the scene. But in order to allow you, the developer, to manage the use of multiple cameras to draw the game world, the **Clear Flags** parameter exists to allow you to set specific cameras, as well as to render specific parts of the game world. However, it is unlikely that you will begin utilizing techniques such as this until you have gotten to grips with more of the basics of Unity.
- **Background**: The background color is the color rendered behind all game objects if there is no skybox material applied to the scene. Clicking on the color block will allow you to change this color using the color picker as we did with the color for our material in the prototype exercise, or you may use the ink dropper icon to the right of the color block in order to sample color from somewhere onscreen.
- **Normalized View Port Rect**: This parameter allows you to specifically state dimensions of and position for the camera view. Ordinarily, this is set to fit the entire screen, and this is also true in the example of the **Main Camera** attached to our player.The **X** and **Y** coordinates being set to **0** means that our camera view begins in the bottom-left of the screen. Given that the **Width** and **Height** values are set to **1**, our view from this camera will fill the screen, because these values are in Unity's screen coordinates system, which ranges from 0 to 1.

You will see this system in other 2D elements that you work with in Unity, like **Graphical User Interface** (**GUI**) elements.

The advantage of being able to set the size and position of our viewport is that we may wish to utilize more than one camera in our game. For example, in a racing game you may wish to have a camera viewport in the top corner of the screen showing the view behind the car, to allow the player to spot other drivers approaching.

- **Clipping Planes (Near/Far)**: The **clip planes** are effectively distances in which to draw the game world. The near plane being the closest distance to begin drawing, and the far plane being the furthest, or rather where drawing ends.

  In order to save on memory in the graphical buffer (a part of memory used to store information on the game world's visuals), clip planes are often used to cut off the scenery that is far from the player. In older 3D games, this technique was more obvious, as computers back then had less RAM and graphics memory to write to, so more memory had to be saved by using closer far clip planes in order to make the game run smoothly. In general, it is recommended to only extend the far clip plane as far as it's visually necessary.

- **Field of view**: This parameter sets the width of the camera's viewport in degrees. This angle is set to **60** in our main camera object, as this is a sensible value in order to give the effect of a human eye view.
- **Orthographic** and **Orthographic size**: Toggling this setting would switch your camera to an orthographic view, as opposed to the standard 3D view, referred to as **Perspective** view. Orthographic cameras are most often used in games, such as isometric real-time strategy games, or true 2D platform games.
- **Depth**: The **Depth** parameter can be utilized when using multiple cameras. This allows you to specify a priority order for, or 'layer', camera views; that is, a camera with a higher depth value will render in front of a camera with a lower depth value. **Depth** can also work in conjunction with the **Normalized View Port Rect** setting in order to allow you to place smaller camera views over the main view of the game world. In the example of the rear-view mirror of a racing game, the rear-view camera would need to have a higher depth value than the main camera in order to be rendered in front of the main forward view of the game world.
- **Culling Mask**: This parameter works with Unity's layers, as discussed previously, in order to allow you to render selectively. By placing certain elements of your game on a particular layer, you can deselect the layer that they are on from the **Culling Mask** drop-down menu in order to exclude them from being rendered by the camera. Currently our **Main Camera** is set to render everything, as it is the only camera in the game.

GUILayer and Flare Layer

These two components have no parameters, but simply allow rendering of additional visual elements. The **GUILayer** allows the rendering of 2D elements such as GUI Text and GUI Texture objects. The **Flare Layer** allows the camera to render lighting flares such as the one we added to our **Directional light** in *Chapter 3, Environments*.

Mouse Look (Script)

This is the second instance of the **MouseLook(Script)** component that we have seen so far—the other being on the parent **First Person Controller**. However, this time its **Axes** parameter is set to **MouseY**, and as a result, it is simply in charge of looking up and down by rotating the main camera object around its X-axis. This, combined with the other instance of the **MouseLook** script, which rotates the parent object, gives us the effect of a totally free look using the mouse, because by rotating the parent object our main camera is rotated left and right also.

Audio listener

The audio listener acts as our ears and allows us to hear any audio sources placed in the game. By having the audio listener on the main camera in a first-person view game, 3D sounds that occur to the left of the player will be heard in the left ear, allowing you to create an environment with real-world immersion.

Now that we have explored the component parts of the **First Person Controller**, let's take a more in-depth look at scripting, before we move on to its use in the next chapter, *Interactions*. This section of the book is designed to expand and reinforce what you have already learnt in the prototyping exercise we completed earlier.

Further scripting

Scripting is one of the most crucial elements in becoming a game developer. While Unity is fantastic at allowing you to create games with minimal knowledge of game engine source code, you will still need to understand how to write code that commands the Unity engine. Code written for use with Unity draws upon a series of ready built classes, which you should think of as libraries of instructions or behaviors. By writing scripts, you will create your own classes by drawing upon commands in the existing Unity engine.

In this book, you will be introduced to the basics of scripting in both C# (pronounced *C-Sharp*) and Javascript, and it is highly recommended that you read the Unity *Scripting Reference* in parallel to it. This is available as part of your Unity installation in a `documentation` subfolder, and also online at:

`http://unity3d.com/support/documentation/ScriptReference/`

Problems encountered while scripting can often be solved with reference to this, and if that doesn't work, then you can search for your query on Unity answers:

`http://answers.unity3d.com`

Or you can ask for help on the Unity forums:

`http://forum.unity3d.com`

Or in the **Internet Relay Chat** (**IRC**) channel for the software. For more information, visit:

`http://unity3d.com/support/community`

When writing a new script or using an existing one, the script will become active only when attached to a game object in the current scene—though scripts attached to objects can call **static** (global) functions in scripts not attached to objects. By attaching a script to a game object, it becomes a component of that object, and the behavior written in the script can apply to that object. However, scripts are not restricted to calling (the scripting term for *activating* or *running*) behavior on the game object they belong to, as other objects can be referenced by a name or a tag and can also be given instructions.

In order to get a better understanding of the scripts we are about to examine, let's take a look at some core scripting principles.

Commands

Commands are instructions written in a script. Although commands may be loose inside a script, you should try and ensure that they are contained within a function to give you more control over when they are called. All commands in both languages must be terminated (stated as finished) with a semicolon as follows:

```
speed = 5;
```

This tells the script to expect another command or part of the next script.

Variables

Variables are simply containers for information. Variables may be named anything you like, provided that:

- The name does not conflict with an existing word in the Unity engine code.
- It contains only alphanumeric characters and underscores and does not begin with a number. For example, the word *transform* already exists to represent the **Transform** component of a game object, so naming a variable or function with that word would cause a conflict.

Variables may contain text, numbers, and references to objects, assets, or components. Here is an example of a variable declaration:

C#:

```
float speed = 9.0f;
```

Javascript:

```
var speed = 9.0;
```

Our variable's name—`speed`, is then set (given a value) using a single equals symbol and is terminated like any other command with a semicolon.

Variable data types

When declaring variables in Javascript, you should also state what kind of information they will store by defining a data type. Using our previous example, here is the same variable declaration including its data type:

```
var speed : float = 9.0;
```

Before the variable is set, we use a colon to specify the data type. In this example, the value that the variable is being set to is a number with a decimal place, and we state that it should have the data type `float` (short for 'floating point'—meaning a number with a decimal place).

You should note that in C#, the data type—in this case the word `float`, prefixes the variable instead of the word `var` and therefore explicitly applies a data type to the new variable.

By specifying the data type for any variable we declare, we are able to make our scripting more efficient, as the game engine does not need to decide upon an appropriate type for the variable it is reading. Here are a few common data types you will encounter when starting scripting with Unity (case sensitive differences in language are noted):

- **String (js) / string (c#)**: A combination of text and numbers stored in quotation marks "like this"
- **int**: Short for integer, meaning a whole number with no decimal place
- **float**: A floating point or a decimal placed numeric value
- **boolean (js) / bool (c#)**: A true or false value commonly used as a switch
- **Vector3**: A set of XYZ values—a three dimensional vector—technically this vector is made up of 3 float values—data types are often made up of other data types in this way

Using variables

After declaring variables, the information they contain may then be retrieved or set, simply by using the variable name. For example, if we were trying to set the `speed` variable, then we would simply say:

```
speed = 20;
```

We can also query or use the value of a variable in parts of our script. For example, if we wished to store a value that was half of the current speed variable, then we could establish a new variable, as shown in the following example (C# shown):

```
float speed = 9.0f;
float halfSpeed;
halfSpeed = speed/2.0f;
```

Also, notice that where the `halfSpeed` variable is declared, it is not set to a value. This is because a value is given to it in the command following it by dividing the existing speed variable's value by two. Note here, that we could have set the value for the variable when establishing it for efficiency, in which case it would have looked like the following code snippet:

```
float speed = 9.0f;
float halfSpeed = speed/2.0f;
```

Public versus private variables

Variables can be public or private members of a script, but only public variables will automatically show up as parameters of the script when it is viewed as a component in the **Inspector**. Typically these variables should only be used if adjustment through the **Inspector** is necessary, because otherwise the values of variables will be locked to what is written in the **Inspector**—not what is written in the script. Because of this you may find when starting out that you are adjusting values in a script after having applied it to an object, and they are not changing behavior. Therefore, if a variable's value is only going to be assigned by the script, then ideally it should be private.

Public variable conflicts

It is worth noting that if you establish a variable as public, then its value is controlled by the value written into the **Inspector**. If you rewrite your script later, changing its declared value within the script itself—then you should ensure that the value seen in the **Inspector** is not overriding your new value. You may wish to reconsider keeping this value public, or simply update the **Inspector** declared value to avoid this conflict.

If you wish to have a public variable in order to let other scripts read / assign its value, you can hide it from appearing in the **Inspector** by not serializing it. This means placing the following line before it when establishing it:

- **C#**:

  ```
  [System.NonSerialized]
  public float runSpeed = 8.0f;
  ```

- **Javascript**:

  ```
  @System.NonSerialized
  var runSpeed : float = 8.0;
  ```

Declaring public and private variables

The following section shows how you can declare public and private variables in C# and Javascript:

C#: Whether within or outside of a function, a variable in C# is private. It must have a `public` prefix to make it visible / adjustable in the **Inspector**.

```
public float gravity = 20.5f; // this is public
private float gravity = 20.5f; // this is private
float gravity = 20.5f; // this is also private in C#
```

Javascript: Javascript works somewhat differently. When a variable is declared within a function it is private and only accessible within that function, but when declared outside of a function, it is inherently public and requires a `private` prefix to hide it in the Inspector.

```
public var gravity : float = 20.0; // this is public
var gravity : float =20.0; // this is also public in Javascript
private var gravity : float = 20.0; //this is private
```

Full example

In the following image, we see a C# script applied to an object. Within the **Rocket** class, a public variable **moveSpeed** and a private variable **blastSpeed** are declared. The private variable is not given a value when declared but is assigned one in the **Update()** function, where it is given the value of the public variable **moveSpeed**, multiplied by 2. The value of this private variable is then used in a new **Vector3** variable as the Z-coordinate, which in turn is used to set the velocity value of a Rigidbody object:

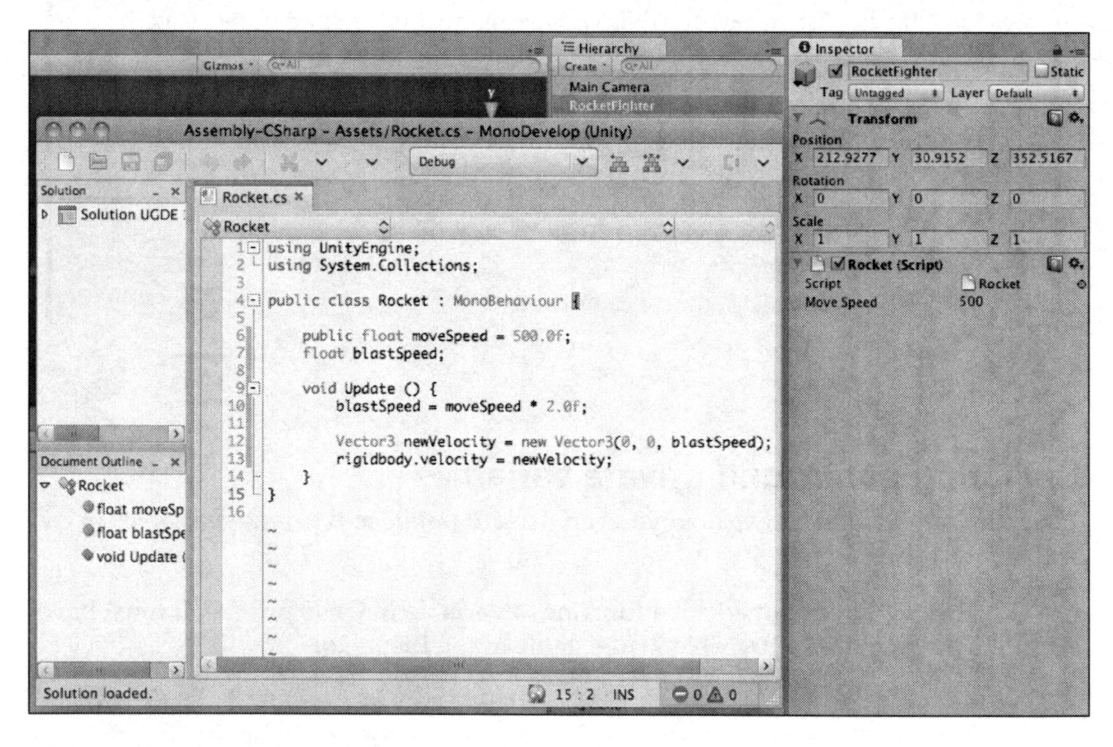

Be aware that any value adjusted in the **Inspector** will override the original value given to a variable within the script. It will not rewrite the value stated in the script, but simply replaces it when the game runs. You can also revert to the values declared in the script by clicking on the Cog icon to the right of the component and choosing **Reset** from the drop-down menu that appears.

Functions

Functions, or methods as they are also known, may be described as sets of instructions that can be called at a specific point in the game's runtime. A script may contain many functions and each one may call any function within the same script or other external scripts. In Unity scripting, there are many built-in functions ready made to carry out your commands at predefined points in time or as a result of user input. You may also write your own functions and call them when you need to carry out specific sets of instructions.

All functions are declared by the prefix `function` in Javascript, and typically by the prefix `void` in C#. This is followed by the function name and a set of brackets into which the developer may pass additional arguments if necessary. A function's span then ranges from the opening { curly brace and the closing } brace.

Let's look at some examples of the existing functions that you may use.

Update()

A new C# or Javascript file created in Unity begins with the `Update()` function, as we saw in our earlier exercise:

C#:

```
void Update(){
}
```

Javascript:

```
function Update(){
}
```

Games run at a certain number of **Frames Per Second** (**FPS**), and the `Update()` function is called when each frame of the game is rendered. As a result, it is mostly used for any commands that must be carried out constantly or for detecting changes in the game world that occur in real time, such as input commands—key presses or mouse clicks. As emphasized by the **CharacterMotor** script, when dealing with physics-related commands, the alternative function `FixedUpdate()` should be used instead, as it is a function which keeps in sync with the physics engine, whereas `Update()` itself can be variable depending on the frame rate.

OnMouseDown()

As an example of a function that is called at a specific time, **OnMouseDown()** is only called when the player's mouse clicks on a game object's collider or on a GUI element in the game.

This is most often used for mouse controlled games or detecting clicks in menus. Here is an example of a basic `OnMouseDown()` function (Javascript shown), which when attached to a game object, will quit the game when the object is clicked on:

```
function OnMouseDown(){
  Application.Quit();
}
```

There are also a variety of similar mouse functions such as `OnMouseUp()`, `OnMouseEnter()`, and more—search for *Mouse* in the script reference to see what you can do.

Writing custom functions

In creating your own functions, you will be able to specify a set of instructions that can be called from anywhere within the scripts you are writing. If we were setting up some instructions to move an object to a specified position in the game world, then we may write a custom function to carry out the necessary instructions so that we may call this function from other functions within a script.

Return type

Functions that you create to perform a specific task may not simply carry out instructions, but instead return information. For example, if we needed to create a function that carried out arithmetic and returned it, we could write something like the following code snippet:

C#:

```
float currentAmount;

float DoSums(){
  float amount = 5.0f + 55.8f;
  return amount;
}
void Update () {
  if(Input.GetButtonUp("Jump")){
    currentAmount = DoSums();
  }
}
```

Javascript:

```
private var currentAmount : float;

function DoSums() : float{
  var amount : float = 5.0 + 55.8;
  return amount;
}
```

Here we have a custom function called `DoSums()` which we have given a `return` type—like a data type in variable declaration, which means it will return data of type `float`. In order to get this function to return a value, we have given it this type and also used the `return` command, which means that when this function is used in another part of the script, its resultant value is returned, much like using a variable, but with more power, as its value may change depending upon what occurs within the function.

In the example given, a sum is calculated and assigned to the `currentAmount` variable when the player releases the *space bar* (the default for Input `"Jump"`). So in this simple example, `currentAmount` will be set to `60.8`, as this is the returned value of this function.

It is worth noting that to declare a custom function in C#, you simply begin with the return data type instead of `void`, and in Javascript, the data type is declared after the name of the function, in the same way as variable declaration.

Arguments

Arguments are variables within a function that allow you to send differing information to the function in order to alter what it does—this means you needn't repeat the same function with differing commands.

For example, on falling into a trap, a player character may need to be moved if they have died and are returning to the start of a level. Rather than writing the player relocation instructions onto every part of the game that causes the player to die, the necessary instructions can be contained within a single function that is called many times. The advantage here is that we can modify the behavior of this function simply by providing part of its command as an argument.

Typically, arguments are declared in the function in the following manner:

C#:

```
void FunctionName(DataType argument1, DataType argument2){
  //commands here that may use the value of arguments
}
```

Javascript:

```
function FunctionName(argument1 : DataType, argument2 :DataType){
  //commands here that may use the value of arguments
}
```

Within the parentheses you simply declare each new argument, separating them with commas, in a similar style to declaring variables, with the name of the variable and the datatype.

Declaring a custom function

To illustrate this further, you could be creating a function called `SpawnEnemy()`, which might look like the following code snippet:

C#:

```
void SpawnEnemy(GameObject enemy, Transform spawnTrans, string
enemyName){
  GameObject newEnemy = Instantiate(enemy, spawnTrans.position,
  spawnTrans.rotation) as GameObject;
  newEnemy.name = enemyName;
}
```

Javascript:

```
function SpawnEnemy(enemy : GameObject, spawnTrans : Transform,
enemyName : String){
    var newEnemy : GameObject = Instantiate(enemy,
  spawnTrans.position, spawnTrans.rotation);
    newEnemy.name = enemyName;
}
```

Calling a custom function

In this example, in order to call the function we would need to write the name of the function and then within its parentheses, three pieces of data that correspond to the arguments in the declaration of the function shown earlier, for example:

C#:

```
public GameObject enemyPrefab1;
public Transform spawn1;
public Transform spawn2;
int enemyCount = 0;
  void Update(){
    if(enemyCount < 1){
      SpawnEnemy(enemyPrefab1, spawn1, "Ogre");
      enemyCount++;
    }
  }
```

Javascript:

```
var enemyPrefab1 : GameObject;
var spawn1 : Transform;
var spawn2 : Transform;
var enemyCount : int = 0;

function Update(){
  if(enemyCount < 1){
    SpawnEnemy(enemyPrefab1, spawn1, "Ogre");
    enemyCount++;
  }
}
```

In this example, the `SpawnEnemy()` function is called and its arguments are given the following values:

- `enemy`: This argument is of type `GameObject`, and we are feeding it whatever game object is assigned to a public variable called `enemyPrefab`. It is likely that we would assign this in the **Inspector**; because it is public we can simply drag-and-drop a prefab onto it.
- `spawnTrans`: This argument has `Transform` as its data type, and it uses this information to declare position and rotation for the instantiate command (see the declaration in the earlier section). We feed it the value of `spawn1`, a public variable that we'll also likely drag-and-drop the transform of an empty game object, in order to mark a spawn position.

- `enemyName`: We simply give this argument the value `Ogre`, as it is a `string` data type.

These function arguments rely on being written in the correct order. For example, if we got them in the wrong order when calling the function like the following code snippet:

```
SpawnEnemy("Ogre", enemyPrefab1, spawn1);
```

We would get an error in our script telling us that this line of code has some invalid arguments. This simply means that we have offered data to the function that does not match what it expects, as in the declaration it is expecting (pseudo code).

```
SpawnEnemy(enemy - a game object,  spawnTrans - a transform, enemyName
- a "string" of information);
```

But by getting the order wrong, the script compilation will halt at the first problem, that we would be feeding a `string` where a `GameObject` is expected.

Here is the script in full in both the languages, as a recap:

C#:

```
using UnityEngine;
using System.Collections;

public class test : MonoBehaviour {

  public GameObject enemyPrefab1;
  public Transform spawn1;
  public Transform spawn2;
  int enemyCount = 0;

  void Update(){
    if(enemyCount < 1){
      SpawnEnemy(enemyPrefab1, spawn1, "Ogre");
      enemyCount++;
    }
  }

  void SpawnEnemy(GameObject enemy, Transform spawnTrans, string
enemyName){
    GameObject newEnemy = Instantiate(enemy, spawnTrans.position,
spawnTrans.rotation) as GameObject;
    newEnemy.name = enemyName;
  }
}
```

Javascript:

```
var enemyPrefab1 : GameObject;
var spawn1 : Transform;
var spawn2 : Transform;
private var enemyCount : int = 0;

function Update(){
  if(enemyCount < 1){
    SpawnEnemy(enemyPrefab1, spawn1, "Ogre");
    enemyCount++;
  }
}

function SpawnEnemy(enemy : GameObject, spawnTrans : Transform,
enemyName : String){
  var newEnemy : GameObject = Instantiate(enemy, spawnTrans.position,
spawnTrans.rotation);
  newEnemy.name = enemyName;
}
```

Apart from aforementioned differences between the languages—a new one appears here in the form of the data type `String`—in Javascript this is declared starting with a capital `S`, and in C# a lowercase `s` must be used.

If else statements

An **if statement** is used in scripting to check for conditions. If its conditions are met, then the `if` statement will carry out a set of nested instructions. If they are not, then it can default to a set of instructions called `else`. In the following examples, the `if` statement is checking whether the `boolean` variable `grounded` is set to `true`:

C#:

```
bool grounded = false;
float speed;

  void Update(){
    if(grounded==true){
          speed = 5.0f;
    }
  }
```

Javascript:

```
var grounded : boolean = false;
var speed : float;
function Update(){
  if(grounded==true){
    speed = 5.0;
  }
}
```

If the condition in the `if` statement's brackets is met, that is, if the `grounded` variable becomes `true`—as a result of this being assigned in this script by another function for example, then the `speed` variable will be set to `5`. Otherwise it will not be given a value.

As we are checking if a `boolean` variable is true here, we could simply write the following code:

```
if(grounded){}
```

This means exactly the same as writing `if(grounded == true)`. To check if this was false we could write the following code:

```
if(!grounded){}
```

Because the use of an exclamation mark simply serves to say not, so we would be saying if grounded is not true.

Note that when setting a variable, a single equals symbol '=' is used, but when checking the status of a variable, we use two '= ='. This is known as a comparative equals—we are comparing the information on either side of the equals symbols.

If you wish to say NOT equal to, you may replace the first equals symbol with an exclamation mark, like the following:

```
if(grounded != true){}
```

If we wanted to set up a fallback condition, then we could add an `else` statement after the `if`, which is our way of saying that if these conditions are not met, then do something else:

C# and Javascript:

```
if(grounded==true){
    speed = 5.0f;
}else{
    speed = 0.0f;
}
```

So unless `grounded` is `true`, `speed` will equal `0`.

To build additional potential outcomes for checking conditions, we can use an `else if` before the fallback `else`. If we are checking values, then we could write the following code snippet:

```
if(speed >= 6){
  //do something
}
else if(speed >= 3){
    //do something different
}
else{
    //if neither of the above are true, do this
}
```

Be sure to remember that wherever you see two forward slashes `//`, this simply denotes code that is not called, this is known as creating a comment (non-executed code).

Multiple conditions

We can also check for more than a single condition in one `if` statement by using two ampersand symbols—**&&**.

For example, we may want to check on the condition of two variables at once and only carry out our instructions if the variables values are as specified. We would write the following code snippet:

```
if(speed >= 3 && grounded == true){
  //do something
}
```

If we wished to check for one condition or another being true, then we can use two vertical lined characters '||' in order to mean **OR**. We would write this as follows:

```
if(speed >= 3 || grounded == true){
  //do something
}
```

This means that the commands within the `if` statement will run if at least one of the conditions is met.

For loops

Often in scripting you will need to carry out sets of instructions repetitively, until certain conditions are met. For these situations, it is often best to make use of `for` loops.

A `for` loop has three parameters within its parentheses which are as follows:

```
for(declaration of integer variable; condition to continue;
instruction to carry out at the end of each loop);
```

Unlike arguments in a function declaration, these are separated by a semi-colon instead of a comma. For example, a simple for loop that adds to a counter would look like the following:

C#:

```
public int counter = 0;
void Start() {
  for(int i=0; i<=10; i++){
    counter++;
    Debug.Log(counter);
  }
}
```

Javascript:

```
var enemyCount : int = 0;

function Start() {
  for(i=0; i<=10; i++){
    enemyCount++;
    Debug.Log(enemyCount);
  }
}
```

The `for` loop itself begins with an integer variable simply titled `i`, which is set to `0`; the loop then continues so long as the value of `i` is less than or equal to `10`, and with each loop we increment `i` by `1`—this is done using `++`, which is the same as writing `+=1`.

As the loop's variable `i` has a starting value of `0` and a continue value that is less than or equal to `10`, the loop will run 11 times, and therefore, any commands in the loop will be carried out this many times.

In this example, we are creating a public variable called `enemyCount` that is incremented with each loop. We then use `Debug.Log()` to print the value of this variable in the **Console**. This command is useful, as it will allow you to check on the value of variables as the scripts run. The console in Unity shows its latest value in the bar at the bottom of the interface where errors and warning in scripts, editor warnings, and `Debug.Log` information are shown. The console window itself can be accessed from the top menu **Window | Console**.

`For` loops like this are useful for various purposes such as dynamically creating prefabs at the start of a game—for example, by instantiating and altering a position variable with each loop, a row or grid of objects could be instantiated.

Inter-script communication and Dot Syntax

In order to create games effectively, you'll often need to communicate between scripts in order to pass data around, adjust variables, and call functions in external scripts—by external here we can mean either a separate script or one attached to a different object than the given script.

Accessing other objects

Often you may be in a situation where your script is located on one object, and you wish to communicate with a script on another object—for example, your player character may shoot an enemy and this results in the need for their health to decrease, but each enemy has an independent script storing its own health, so a script on the player or bullet must address the script on the enemy that its health is stored within.

To do this, prior to accessing the script, you'll need to refer to the object, which can be done in various ways including using the `Find()` and `FindWithTag()` commands or in the case of a collision, by referring to the collided with object, or in a basic sense by using public variables to establish references to an object.

Find() and FindWithTag()

A computationally more expensive way to refer to an object is to use the find commands, not something which should be done often; so avoid using these within `Update()` or other functions that run each frame where possible. Often this is best used to set a particular variable to an object using a `Start()` or `Awake()` function.

For example, we may set up a non-serialized or private variable (so that it is not altered by the **Inspector**) within our script to represent a particular game object, then set it when the game begins.

The `Find()` command itself expects to be given the name of a game object within its parentheses—using its hierarchical name as a string, while the `FindWithTag()` command is looking for the tag applied to an object, also written in a string which is shown as follows:

```
GameObject.FindWithTag("tagName");
```

Here is a quick example using `Find()` to address an object in the hierarchy called **ship_object**:

C#:

```
GameObject enemyShip;
void Start(){
  enemyShip = GameObject.Find("ship_model");
}
```

Javascript:

```
private var enemyShip : GameObject;
function Start(){
  enemyShip = GameObject.Find("ship_model");
}
```

Here the variable `enemyShip` is assigned the `ship_object` game object thanks to the use of `Find()`, by addressing its hierarchical name.

We now have a reference to our `ship_model` object in the current scene, and can refer to it using the `enemyShip` variable. Now we can use this to access scripts on that object.

SendMessage

A basic way of calling instructions on another object is to simply write a custom function in a script, and then use the `SendMessage()` command to call the instructions on that object.

For example, in our previous section on *Writing Custom Functions*, we created a function called `SpawnEnemy`, which had three arguments. For the purposes of simplifying this example, lets look at a function with just one argument:

C#:

```
void Renamer(string newName){
  gameObject.name = newName;
}
```

Javascript:

```
function Renamer(newName : String){
  gameObject.name = newName;
}
```

The single argument `newName` here can of course be set when calling the function. If we were calling this from the same script we could simply write the following:

```
Renamer("Steve");
```

However, if this function occurred in a script external to a script we were working in then we could use `SendMessage()` to call it. For this we would refer to an object and then `SendMessage()`, which is shown as follows:

C# and Javascript:

```
GameObject.Find("target").SendMessage("Renamer", "target_down");
```

Note here that we have not needed to name the script at all, as Unity simply looks at the object specified. In this case an item in the current scene called `target`, and it seeks a function in any of that object's attached scripts called `Renamer`. When it finds it, it executes it, sending the value `"target_down"` to the `newName` argument of the function.

GetComponent

`GetComponent()` works slightly differently but is more flexible as it is used to address all manner of components. We'll demonstrate here how to use it to perform the same function as we just saw with `SendMessage()`.

Firstly let's imagine that our `Renamer()` function is inside a script called `Setter`. This is attached to an object called `target` in the current scene, and we need to address the object, then use `GetComponent()` to refer to that particular script, and finally call the function itself.

C#:

```
GameObject.Find("target").GetComponent<Setter>().Renamer("target_
down");
```

Javascript:

```
GameObject.Find("target").GetComponent(Setter).Renamer("target_down");
```

Note here that regardless of language, we're using a dot to separate each action of the command, in this style:

```
FindTheObject.GetTheComponent.PerformAnAction;
```

This approach of drilling down to the specific part using dots to separate between classes and variables is an example of using what is called **Dot Syntax**.

Programming for Mobile

It is also worth noting that when coding in this style for mobile, it is important to break down an operation such as this into two steps, for example:

C#:

```
GameObject theTarget = GameObject.Find("target");
theTarget.GetComponent<Setter>().Renamer("target_down");
```

Javascript:

```
var theTarget : GameObject = GameObject.Find("target");
theTarget.GetComponent(Setter).Renamer("target_down");
```

Dot Syntax

In the previous example, we have used a script technique called Dot Syntax. This is a term that may sound more complex than it actually is, as it simply means using a dot (or full stop / period) to separate elements you are addressing in a hierarchical order.

Starting with the most general element or reference, you can use the Dot Syntax to narrow down to the specific parameter you wish to set.

For example, to set the vertical position of the game object, we would need to alter its Y coordinate. Therefore, we would be looking to address the position parameters of an object's **Transform** component. If adjusting the **Transform** component's `Position` property of an object on which a script is attached—we would write the following:

C#:

```
transform.position= new Vector3(0f, 5.5f, 4f);
```

Javascript:

```
transform.position = Vector3(0, 5.5, 4);
```

If addressing this component on another object however, we would need a reference to it first, either through the creation of a public variable which has a game object assigned to it through drag-and-drop, or through use of a function such as `Find()`. For example if using a public variable, we could write the following:

C#:

```
public GameObject theTarget;
theTarget.transform.position = new Vector3(0f, 5.5f, 4f);
```

Javascript:

```
var theTarget : GameObject;
theTarget.transform.position = Vector3(0, 5.5, 4);
```

We would then simply assign the object to this public variable in the **Inspector**, making the variable `theTarget` valid for use in the script.

This could be made even more efficient if we were only using this variable to set parameters of the **Transform** component itself, or carry out functions of the `Transform` class, by making a variable of type `Transform`; we can then skip the reference to that component.

C#:

```
public Transform theTarget;
theTarget.position = new Vector3(0f, 5.5f, 4f);
```

Javascript:

```
var theTarget : Transform;
theTarget.position = Vector3(0, 5.5, 4);
```

This would also mean that the script itself would be more efficient programmatically as it would not need to store as much data as a reference to the entire `GameObject` class.

This means that any parameter can be referenced by simply finding the component it belongs to by using the dot syntax. To further illustrate this, if we wished to adjust the intensity value of a light, we could write the following parameter:

```
light.intensity = 8;
```

As illustrated earlier, if we wished to adjust a light on an external object, we would simply use dot syntax to address that object first, and then use the same approach as shown earlier:

```
GameObject.Find("streetlight").light.intensity = 8;
```

Null reference exceptions

If a variable is left unassigned at any time in scripting, it is considered null—meaning 'not set'. You may encounter this when forgetting to assign objects or prefabs in Unity. The editor will give an error stating **Null Reference Exception**. This may seem confusing at first glance but makes sense when you understand that null means not set, reference refers to a variable or parameter, and exception simply means a problem causing a part of the script to be invalid.

You will also be told which part of a particular script is causing this, and you can even safeguard against it occurring or halting a script by first checking if a reference is not null (that is set) first, for example:

C#:

```
public Transform theTarget;
  if(theTarget){
    theTarget.position = new Vector3(0f, 5.5f, 4f);
  }
```

Javascript:

```
var theTarget : Transform;
  if(theTarget){
    theTarget.position = Vector3(0, 5.5, 4);
  }
```

Here we are using `theTarget` within an `if` statement—we're querying it in a similar way to if we were checking a Boolean variable, but here we are simply checking that it is not null.

Comments

In many prewritten scripts, you will notice that there are some lines written with two forward slashes prefixing them. These are simply comments written by the author of the script. It is generally a good idea, especially when starting out with scripting, to write your own comments in order to remind yourself how a script works. There are two ways to comment, single line and multi line:

```
// This is a single line comment
/* This is a multiline comment and will continue to be a comment until
it is closed by a star and another forward-slash, in other words, the
reverse of how it began */
```

Further reading

As you continue to work with Unity, it is crucial that you get used to referring to the *Scripting Reference* documentation, which is installed with your copy of Unity and also available on the Unity website at the following address:

`http://unity3d.com/support/documentation/ScriptReference/`

You can use the scripting reference to search for the correct use of any class, function, or command in the Unity engine.

Now that you have got familiar with the basics of scripting, let's take a look at another example script for character movement. This script is a simpler version of the CharacterMotor that you have imported with the `Character Controllers` asset package. Called **FPSWalker**, this script is a Javascript example, but the principles can be easily translated to C#.

Scripting for character movement

This script is an example of a character control script that uses the `Input` class and `CharacterController` class' `Move` command to create character movement by manipulating a `Vector3` variable.

Deconstructing the script

To test how much you have learned so far, take a look at the script in its entirety first, to see how much you can understand, then read on to see each part deconstructed.

Full script (Javascript)

The full deconstruction of the script is as follows:

```
var speed : float = 6.0;
var jumpSpeed : float = 8.0;
var gravity : float = 20.0;
private var moveDirection : Vector3 = Vector3.zero;
private var grounded : boolean = false;
function FixedUpdate() {
  if (grounded) {
```

```
    moveDirection = Vector3(Input.GetAxis("Horizontal"), 0,
  Input.GetAxis("Vertical"));
    moveDirection = transform.TransformDirection(moveDirection);
    moveDirection *= speed;

    if (Input.GetButton ("Jump")) {
      moveDirection.y = jumpSpeed;
    }
  }
  moveDirection.y -= gravity * Time.deltaTime;

  var controller : CharacterController
  GetComponent(CharacterController);
  var flags = controller.Move(moveDirection * Time.deltaTime);
  grounded = (flags & CollisionFlags.CollidedBelow) != 0;
}
@script RequireComponent(CharacterController)
```

Variable declaration

As with most scripts, `FPSWalker` begins with a set of variable declarations from lines 1 to 6, as shown in the following code snippet:

```
var speed : float = 6.0;
var jumpSpeed : float = 8.0;
var gravity : float = 20.0;
private var moveDirection : Vector3 = Vector3.zero;
private var grounded : boolean = false;
```

Lines 1 to 3 are public member variables used later in the script as values to multiply by. They have decimal places in their numbers, so they ideally would feature data types set to float. Lines 5 and 6 are private variables, as they will only be used within the script.

The private variable `moveDirection` is in charge of storing the player's current forward direction as a `Vector3` (set of X,Y,Z coordinates). On declaration, this variable is set to (0,0,0)—using the shorthand `Vector3.zero` in order to stop the player from facing an arbitrary direction when the game begins.

The private variable `grounded` is data typed to a `boolean` (`true` or `false`) data type. It is used later in the script to keep track of whether the player is resting on the ground, in order to allow movement and jumping, which would not be allowed if they were not on the ground (that is, if they are currently jumping).

Storing movement information

The script continues on line 8 with the opening of a `FixedUpdate()` function. Similar to the `Update()` function discussed earlier, a fixed update is called every fixed framerate frame. This means that it is more appropriate for dealing with physics-related scripting, such as Rigidbody usage and gravity effects, as standard `Update()` will vary with game frame rate dependent upon hardware.

The `FixedUpdate()` function runs from lines 8 to 26, so we can assume that as all of the commands and `if` statements are within it, they will be checked after each frame.

In the book, you may occasionally come across a single line of code appearing on two different lines. Please note that this has been done only for the purpose of indentation and due to space constraints. When using such code make sure it's on one line in your script file.

The first `if` statement in the function runs from lines 9 to 17:

```
if (grounded) {

  moveDirection = new Vector3(Input.GetAxis("Horizontal"), 0,
Input.GetAxis("Vertical"));
  moveDirection = transform.TransformDirection(moveDirection);
  moveDirection *= speed;

  if (Input.GetButton ("Jump")) {
    moveDirection.y = jumpSpeed;
  }
}
```

By stating that its commands and nested `if` statement (line 14) will only run `if(grounded)`, this is shorthand for writing:

```
If(grounded == true){
```

When `grounded` becomes `true`, this `if` statement does three things with the variable `moveDirection`.

Firstly, it assigns it a new `Vector3` value, and places the current value of `Input.GetAxis("Horizontal")` to the X coordinate and `Input.GetAxis("Vertical")` to the Z coordinate, leaving Y set to `0`:

```
moveDirection = new Vector3(Input.GetAxis("Horizontal"), 0,   Input.
GetAxis("Vertical"));
```

As we saw in the *Chapter 2*, earlier in this book, the `Input.GetAxis` commands here are simply representing values between `-1` and `1` according to horizontal and vertical input keys, which by default are:

- *A/D* or Left arrow/Right arrow—horizontal axis
- *W/S* or Up arrow/Down arrow—vertical axis

When no keys are pressed, these values will be `0`, as they are axis-based inputs to which Unity automatically gives an 'idle' state. Therefore, when holding the Left arrow key, for example, the value of `Input.GetAxis("Horizontal")` would be equal to -1, when holding the Right arrow, it would be equal to 1, and when releasing either key, the value will count back towards 0.

In short, the following line gives the variable `moveDirection` a `Vector3` value with the X and Z values based upon key presses, while leaving the Y value set to `0`:

```
moveDirection = new Vector3(Input.GetAxis("Horizontal"), 0,   Input.
GetAxis("Vertical"));
```

Next, our `moveDirection` variable is modified again on line 11:

```
moveDirection = transform.TransformDirection(moveDirection);
```

Here, we set `moveDirection` to a value based upon the **Transform** component's `TransformDirection`. The `TransformDirection` command converts local XYZ values to world values. So in this line, we are taking the previously set XYZ coordinates of `moveDirection` and converting them to a set of world coordinates. This is why we see `moveDirection` in the brackets after `TransformDirection` because it is using the value set on the previous line and effectively just changing its format.

Finally, `moveDirection` is multiplied by the `speed` variable on line 12:

```
moveDirection *= speed;
```

Because `speed` is a public variable, multiplying the XYZ values of `moveDirection` by it will mean that when we increase the value of `speed` in the **Inspector**, we can increase our character's movement speed without editing the script. This is because it is the resultant value of `moveDirection` that is used later in the script to move the character.

Before our `if(grounded)` statement terminates, there is another nested `if` statement from lines 14 to 16 which is shown as follows:

```
if (Input.GetButton ("Jump")) {
  moveDirection.y = jumpSpeed;
}
```

This `if` statement is triggered by a key press with the name `Jump`. By default, the jump button is assigned to the *Space bar*. As soon as this key is pressed, the Y-axis value of the `moveDirection` variable is set to the value of variable `jumpSpeed`. Therefore, unless `jumpSpeed` has been modified in the **Inspector**, `moveDirection.y` will be set to a value of `8.0`.

This sudden addition from `0` to `8.0` in the Y-axis would give the effect of jumping. But how does the character return to the ground? Character controller objects do not use **Rigidbody** components, so are not controlled by gravity in the physics engine.

This is why we need line 19, on which we subtract from the value `moveDirection.y`:

```
moveDirection.y -= gravity * Time.deltaTime;
```

You'll notice that we are not simply subtracting the value of gravity here, as the result of doing that would not give the effect of a jump, but instead take us straight up and down again between two frames. We are subtracting the sum of the `gravity` variable multiplied by a command called `Time.deltaTime`.

By multiplying any value within an `Update()` function by `Time.deltaTime`, you are overriding the frame-based nature of the function and converting the effect of your command into seconds. So by writing the following we are actually subtracting the value of gravity every second, rather than every frame, meaning that actions will not be frame-rate-specific:

```
moveDirection.y -= gravity * Time.deltaTime;
```

Moving the character

Lines 21 to 23 are in charge of the character's movement.

Firstly, on line 21, a new variable named `controller` is established and given the data type `CharacterController`. It is then set to represent the `Character Controller` component, by using the `GetComponent()` command we looked at earlier:

```
var controller : CharacterController =   GetComponent
(CharacterController);
```

So now, whenever we use the variable reference `controller`, we can access any of the parameters of that component and use the `Move` function in order to move the object.

On line 25, this is exactly what we do. As we do so, we place this movement into a variable called `flags`, shown as follows:

```
var flags = controller.Move(moveDirection * Time.deltaTime);
```

The `CharacterController.Move` function expects to be passed a `Vector3` value—in order to move a character controller in directions X, Y, and Z—so we utilize the data that we stored earlier in our `moveDirection` variable and multiply by `Time.deltaTime` so that we move in meters per second, rather than meters per frame.

Checking grounded

Our `moveDirection` variable is only given a value if the Boolean variable `grounded` is set to `true`. So how do we decide if we are grounded or not?

Character Controller colliders, like any other colliders, can detect collisions with other objects. However, unlike the standard colliders, the character controller collider has four specific collision shortcuts set up in a set of responders called `CollisionFlags`. These are as follows:

- None
- Sides
- Above
- Below

They are in charge of checking for collisions, with the specific part of the collider they describe—with the exception of None, which simply means no collision is occurring.

These flags are used to set our `grounded` variable on line 23:

```
grounded = (flags & CollisionFlags.CollidedBelow) != 0;
```

This may look complex due to the multiple equals symbols, but is simply a shorthand method of checking a condition and setting a value in a single line.

Firstly, the `grounded` variable is addressed, and then set using an equals symbol. Then, in the first set of brackets, we use a **bit mask** technique to determine whether collisions in the variable `flags` (our controller's movement) match the internally defined `CollidedBelow` value:

```
(flags & CollisionFlags.CollidedBelow)
```

The use of a single ampersand symbol here specifies a comparison between two values in binary form, something that you need not understand at this stage because Unity's class system offers shorthand for most calculations of this type.

If our controller is indeed colliding below, and therefore, must be on the ground, then this comparison will be equal to 1.

This comparison is followed by `!=0`. An exclamation mark before an equals symbol means "does not equal". Therefore, this comparison evaluates to true if the values are different and false if they are the same, so if `(flags & CollisionFlags.CollidedBelow)` is not the same as 0 then it will evaluate to true, and true is thus assigned to the grounded variable.

@Script commands

The `FixedUpdate()` function terminates on line 24, leaving only a single command in the rest of the script, that is, an `@script` command shown as follows:

```
@script RequireComponent(CharacterController)
```

`@script` commands are used to perform actions that you would ordinarily need to perform manually in the Unity Editor.

In this example, a `RequireComponent()` function is executed, which forces Unity to add the component specified in brackets, should the object the script is being added to not currently have one.

Because this script uses the **CharacterController** component to drive our character, it makes sense to use an `@script` command to ensure that the component is present and, therefore, can be addressed. It is also worth noting that `@script` commands are an example of a command that need not be terminated with a semicolon.

Summary

In this chapter, we've taken a look at the first interactive element in our game so far—the **First Person Controller**. We have also taken a broad look at scripting for Unity games, an important first step that we will be building on throughout this book.

In the next chapter, you will have more hands-on time with your own scripts and look further into interactions in Unity, learning about collision detection, triggers, and ray casting.

To do this, we'll be introducing our first model to the island game, an outpost that the player can interact with using a combination of animation and scripting.

5
Interactions

In this chapter, we'll be looking at further interactions and dive into three of the most crucial elements of game development, namely:

- **Collision Detection**—detecting interactions between objects by detecting when their colliders collide with one another
- **Trigger Collision Detection**—detecting when colliders set to trigger mode have other colliders within their boundary
- **Ray Casting**—drawing a line (or vector) in the 3D world from one point to another, in order to detect potential collisions without two colliders colliding or intersecting

In order to learn about these three topics, we will introduce an outpost model to our island, and learn how to write code for interactions by making the outpost's door open when the player character walks towards it. We will look at how to achieve this with each of the listed techniques, before choosing the most appropriate one for use in our game. First let's look at the relevant import settings for our outpost, and then add the outpost to the island terrain that we have created.

External modeling applications

Given that 3D design is an intensive discipline in itself, it is recommended that you invest in a similar tutorial guide for your application of choice. If you're new to 3D modeling, then here is a list of 3D modeling packages currently supported by Unity:

1. Maya
2. 3D Studio Max
3. Cheetah 3D
4. Cinema 4D
5. Blender

6. Carrara
7. Lightwave
8. XSI
9. Modo

These are the nine most suited modeling applications as recommended by Unity Technologies. The main reason for this is that they export models in a format that can be automatically read and imported by Unity, once saved into your project's `Assets` folder. These application formats will carry their meshes, textures, animations, and character rigging across to Unity, whereas some smaller packages may not support export of character rigs upon import to Unity.

For a full view of the latest compatibility chart, visit: `http://unity3d.com/unity/features/asset-importing`.

Common settings for models

In the Project panel, expand the **Book Assets** folder to show the **Models** folder inside it. Inside you should find a model called **outPost**. Select this model to see its Import settings in the Inspector.

Before you introduce any model to the active scene, you should always ensure that its settings are as you require them to be in the Inspector. When Unity imports new models to your project, it is interpreting them with its **FBXImporter** component.

By using the **FBXImporter** component in the **Inspector**, you can select your model file in the **Project** window and adjust settings for its **Meshes**, **Materials**, and **Animations** before your model becomes part of your game, and even reinterpret the model once it is added to the scene.

Meshes

In the **Meshes** section of the **FBXImporter**, you can specify:

- **Scale Factor**: Depending on the scale of models exported by your chosen modeling application, this may need to be set to a value of 1, 0.1, 0.01, or something similar—the simplest way to approach this is to export a cube primitive. To ensure that your model matches the size of the cube primitive you can create in Unity itself. This will allow you to setup your modeling application with an appropriate scale. If you wish your models to be scaled differently, then you can adjust them here before you add the model to the scene. However, you can always scale objects once they are in your scene using the **Transform** component's **Scale** settings.

- **Mesh Compression**: This drop-down menu allows you to specify settings to compress the complexity of your mesh as it is interpreted by Unity. This is useful for optimizing your game and generally should be set to the highest setting possible without the models' appearance being affected too drastically.
- **Generate Colliders**: This checkbox will find every individual mesh of the model and assign a **Mesh Collider** to it. A mesh collider is a complex collider that can fit to complex geometric shapes and, as a result, is the usual type of collider you would expect to want to apply to all parts of a map or 3D model of a building. However, mesh colliders are also the most computationally expensive way of adding colliders to a model, and as such should not be used when primitive shaped colliders will suffice.
- **Swap UVs**: Sometimes when importing 3D models that will be lightmapped, the wrong channel is picked up by Unity, resulting in a failure to map correctly, this checkbox switches to the correct channel to correct this problem.
- **Generate Lightmap UVs**: This checkbox means that Unity will plot coordinates from the mesh to allow the Lightmapping tool to successfully bake a texture based upon the shape of an object. If you are an artist and wish to see more information on the advanced settings here, it is recommend that you read the Lightmapping UVs section of the Unity manual, located here:

  `http://unity3d.com/support/documentation/Manual/LightmappingUV.html`

Normals and Tangents

- **Normals and Tangents:** These settings define how the normals and tangents of a model are interpreted, giving you the opportunity to optimize your game by disabling, calculating, or importing these aspects of 3D models.
- **Split Tangents**: This setting allows corrections by the engine for models imported with incorrect Bump Mapped lighting. Bump Mapping is a system utilizing two textures, one a graphic to represent a model's appearance and the other a height map. By combining these two textures, the bump map method allows the rendering engine to display flat surfaces of polygons as if they have 3D deformations. When creating such effects in third-party applications and transferring to Unity, sometimes lighting can appear incorrectly, and this checkbox is designed to fix that by interpreting their materials differently.

Materials

The **Materials** section allows you to choose how to interpret the materials created in your third-party 3D modeling application. The user can choose either **Per Texture** (creates a Unity material for each texture image file found) or **Per Material** (creates Materials only for existing materials in the original file) from the **Generation** drop-down menu.

Animations

The **Animations** section of the Importer allows you to interpret the animations created in your modeling application in a number of ways. From the **Generation** drop-down menu, you can choose the following methods:

- **Don't Import**: Set the model to feature no animation
- **Store in Original Roots**: Set the model to feature animations on individual parent objects, as the parent or root objects may import differently in Unity
- **Store in Nodes**: Set the model to feature animations on individual child objects throughout the model, allowing more script control of the animation of each part
- **Store in Root**: Set the model to only feature animation on the parent object of the entire group

The **Animation Wrap Mode** drop-down menu allows you to choose several different settings for how animations will play back (once, in a loop, and so on)—these can be set individually on the animations themselves, so if you do not wish to adjust a setting for all, then this can be left on Default.

Checking **Split Animations** will mean that when creating models to be used with Unity, animators create timeline-based animation, and by noting their frame ranges, they can add each area of animation in their timeline by specifying a name and the frames in which each animation takes place. The specified animation name can then be used to call individual animations when scripting.

Animation Compression

The **Animation Compression** section handles compression and correction of errors that may occur on import from a 3D modeling app.

The **Animation Compression** drop-down menu has three settings—**Off**, **Keyframe Reduction**, and **Keyframe Reduction and Compression**.

It is not recommended that you set this to **Off** unless you need total precision in your animations, as by default Unity would reduce keyframes to save memory using **Keyframe Reduction**. By using compression also, Unity will also attempt to save on file size, and as this may result in errors, with this selected you can then use the three 'Error' values to set the precision you'd like, with smaller numerical values giving tighter, more precise animation.

Now that we've given an overview, let's get started with our first externally created model asset, the outpost.

Setting up the outpost model

In the **Project** panel, open the **Book Assets** folder and within the **Models** folder, select **outPost**. We'll use the **FBXImporter component** in the **Inspector** to adjust settings for the outpost. Aside from the defaults, ensure that:

- Under **Meshes—Scale Factor** is set to **1.5**, and **Generate Colliders** and **Generate Lightmap UVs** are selected
- Under **Materials—Generation** is set to **Per Texture**
- Under **Animations—Split Animations** is selected

Now using the table based area at the bottom of the Animations section, add three animation clips by clicking on the **+** (Plus symbol) button to the right:

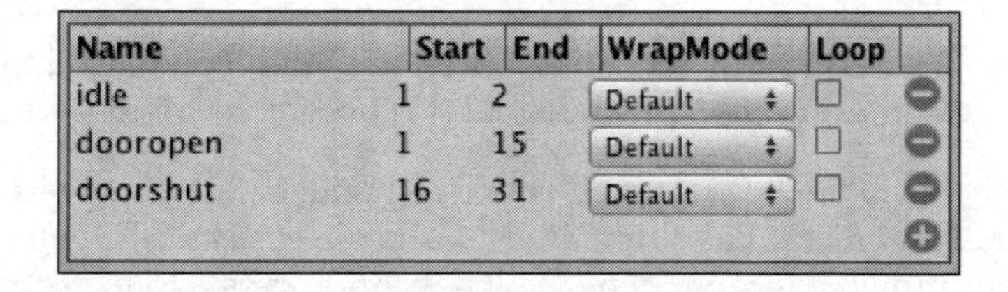

The first animation is automatically named **idle**, which is fine, but you'll need to specify the frame range. Therefore, under **Start**, place a value of **1** to tell Unity to start on frame **1**, and under **End**, specify a value of **2**.

Repeat this step to add two further animations:

- **dooropen**—from frames 1 to 15
- **doorshut**—from frames 16 to 31

Bear in mind that these animation names are case sensitive when it comes to calling them with scripting, so ensure that you write yours literally as shown throughout this book.

The **Loop** field of the Animations table can be misleading for new users. It is not designed to loop the particular animation you are setting up—this is handled by the particular animation's **Wrap Mode** setting on the Animation component of an object. Instead, this feature adds a single additional frame to animations that should loop, but the start and end frames of which do not match up in Unity after importing them from modeling applications.

Provided that your outpost model is set up as described above, click on the **Apply** button to confirm these import settings, and you're all done—the model should be ready to be placed into the scene and used in our game.

Adding the outpost

Before we begin to use both collision detection and ray casting to open the door of our outpost, we'll need to introduce it to the scene.

To begin, drag the **outPost** model from the **Project** panel to the **Scene** view and drop it onto an empty area of land. You'll notice that when dragging 3D objects to the Scene view, Unity positions them by dropping them onto any collider that it finds beneath your dragged cursor.

In this instance, it's the in-built Terrain Collider, but often you'll need to do your own tweaking of position using the **Translate** tool (*W*) once your objects are in the scene.

Once the outpost is in the **Scene**, you'll notice its name has also appeared in the **Hierarchy** panel and that it has automatically become selected. To get a better look at it, hover your mouse over the Scene view now and press *F* to focus the view on this object.

Positioning

As your terrain design may be somewhat different to the one shown in the images in this book, select the **Transform** tool and position your **outPost** in a free, flat area of land by dragging the axis handles in the scene. If you do not have a flat area, go back to the Terrain tools by selecting the **Terrain** object in the Hierarchy and use the tools we looked at in *Chapter 3* to flatten a particular area by using the **Paint Height** tool to paint to the ground height level of **30** meters.

In the above image, the outPost game object is at position of (213, 30, 380)—see the Transform component—but you may need to reposition your object manually. Remember that once you have positioned using the axis handles in the **Scene** window, you can enter specific values in the **Position** values of the **Transform** component in the **Inspector**.

Rotation

Whilst not essential in a functional sense, for aesthetic purposes we will make sure that the front of the building is facing the sunlight from our Directional Light. To do this, simply rotate the object by **180** degrees in the Y-axis using the **Transform** component in the Inspector.

Adding colliders

In order to open the door, we need to identify it as an individual object when it is collided with by the player—this can be done because the object has a collider component and through this we can check the object for its name or a specific tag. Expand the **outPost** parent object by clicking on the dark gray arrow to the left of its name in the **Hierarchy** panel.

You should now see the list of all child objects beneath it. Select the object named **door** and then with your mouse cursor over the **Scene** window, press *F* on the keyboard to focus your view on it. If you are not shown the door face-on, simply hold the *Alt* key and drag to rotate your view around until you can see what you want.

You should now see the door in the **Scene** window, and as a result of selecting the object, you should also see its components listed in the **Inspector** panel. You should notice that one of the components is a **Mesh Collider**. This is a detailed collider assigned to all meshes found on the various children of a model when you select **Generate Colliders**, as we did for the **outPost** asset earlier.

The mesh collider is assigned to each child element, as Unity does not know how much detail will be present in any given model you could choose to import. As a result, it defaults to assigning mesh colliders for each part, as they will naturally fit to the shape of the mesh they encounter. Because our door is simply a cube shape, we should replace this mesh collider with a simpler and more efficient box collider. This is a very important step when importing even simple meshes, as you will often see better performance with primitive colliders rather than mesh colliders.

From the top menu, go to **Component | Physics | Box Collider**.

You will then receive two prompts. Firstly, you will be told that adding a new component will cause this object to lose its connection with the parent asset in the **Project** panel. This dialog window, titled **Losing Prefab**, simply means that your copy in the **Scene** will no longer match the original asset, and as a result, any changes made—with the exception of Scale—to the asset in the **Project** panel in Unity will not be reflected in the copy in the **Scene**. Simply click on the **Add** button to confirm that this is what you want to do.

This will happen whenever you begin to customize your imported models in Unity, and it is nothing to worry about. This is because, generally, you will need to add components to a model, which is why Unity gives you the opportunity to create prefabs—more on these later.

Secondly, as the object already has a collider assigned to it, you will be prompted, asking you whether you wish to **Add**, **Replace**, or **Cancel** the application of this collider to your object. Generally, you'll use a single collider per object, as this works better for the physics engine in Unity. This is why Unity asks if you'd like to **Add** or **Replace** rather than assuming the addition of colliders.

As we have no further need for the mesh collider, choose **Replace**.

You will now see a green outline around the door representing the **Box Collider** component that you have added:

A **Box Collider** is an example of a **Primitive Collider**, so called as it is one of several scalable primitive shape colliders in Unity—including Box, Sphere, Capsule, and Wheel—that have predetermined collider shapes, and in Unity, all primitive colliders are shown with this green outline. You may have noticed this when viewing the character controller collider, which is technically a capsule collider shape and as such also displays in green.

Finally, we need to tag the door object, as we will need to address this object in our scripting later. With the door child object still selected, click on the Tag drop-down at the top of the **Inspector** panel, and choose **Add Tag**. In the **Tag Manager** that replaces your current **Inspector** view, add the tag **playerDoor**, as shown in the following image:

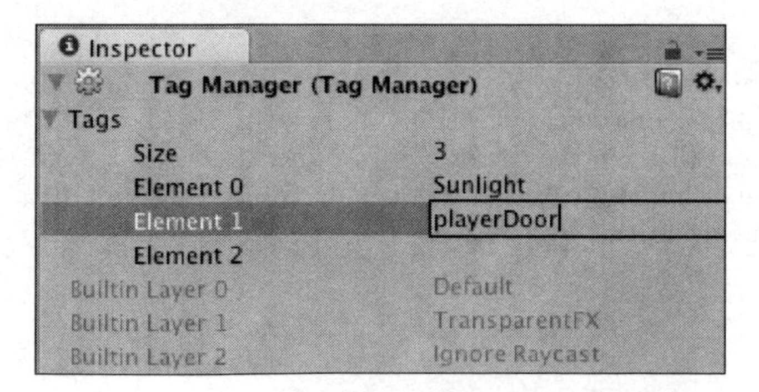

Because adding tags is a two step process, you will need to reselect the **door** child object in the **Hierarchy** panel, and choose your newly added **playerDoor** tag from the **Tag** drop-down menu to finish adding the tag:

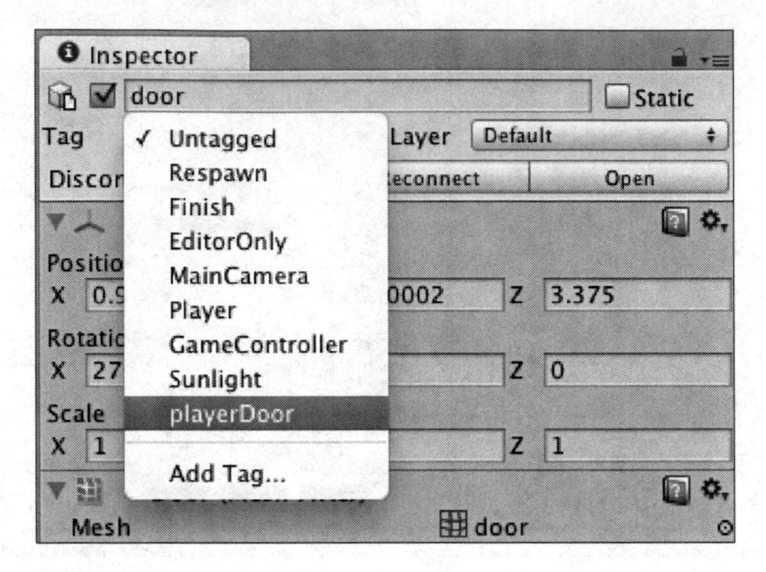

Adding the Rigidbody

Now that we have a more efficient collider on the object, we should also add a Rigidbody component to our door. Although we are not using physics to animate our door, the physics engine should still be aware of the movement of this object as it has a collider attached—otherwise performance will suffer as the physics engine must recalculate *non-moving* object's positions—which it considers to be any object without a Rigidbody.

With the **door** child object still selected, go to **Component | Physics | Rigidbody**. To ensure that the physics engine does not attempt to control the motion of the door itself, uncheck **Use Gravity**, and check **Is Kinematic**.

Adding audio

As the door will be automatically opening and closing, we'll need to add an audio source component to allow the door to emit sound effects as its being opened and closed. With the **door** child object still selected, choose **Component | Audio | Audio Source** from the top menu.

Disabling automatic animation

By default, Unity assumes that all animated objects introduced to the scene will need to be played automatically. Although this is why we create an idle animation—in which our asset is doing nothing, allowing Unity to play automatically will sometimes cause animated objects to appear a frame into one of their intended animations. To correct this issue, we can simply deselect the **Play Automatically** checkbox in the **Inspector** for the parent object of our model. Ordinarily, we would not need to do this if our asset was simply a looped animation constantly playing in the game world, a billowing flag or rotating lighthouse lamp for example. But we do not need our door to animate until the player reaches it, so we should avoid automatically playing any animation.

To do this, reselect the parent object called **outPost** in the **Hierarchy** panel, and in the **Animation** component in the **Inspector** panel, uncheck the **Play Automatically** checkbox.

The **Inspector** panel view of the **outPost** object should now appear similar to this image:

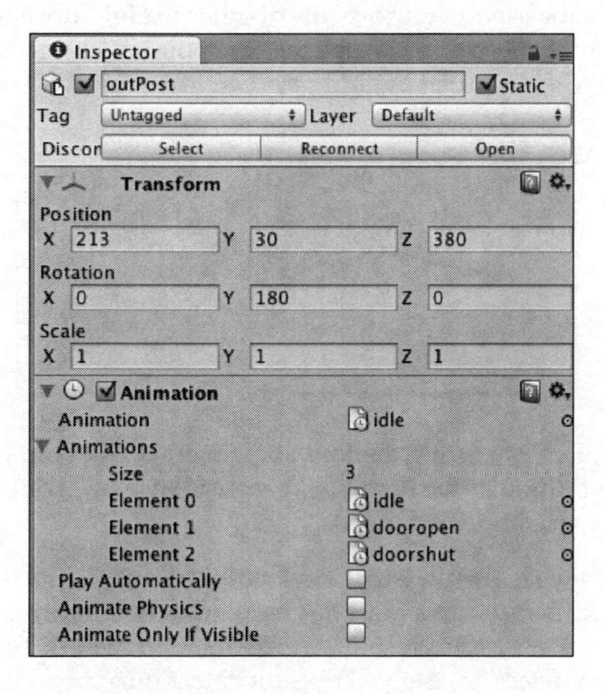

Note that in this image, the **Animations** parameter is expanded in the **Animation** component to show the animation states currently applied to this object.

The outpost object is now ready to be interacted with by our player character, so we will need to begin scripting for collision detection.

Collisions and triggers

To detect physical interactions between game objects, the most common method is to use a collider component—an invisible net that surrounds an object's shape and is in charge of detecting collisions with other objects. The act of detecting and retrieving information from these collisions is known as collision detection.

Not only can we detect when two colliders interact (collision detection), but we can also detect when particular colliders are intersecting (trigger-mode collision detection) and even pre-empt a collision and perform many other useful tasks by utilizing a technique called **Ray Casting**. Ray casting, in contrast to detecting intersecting 3D shaped colliders, draws a Ray—put simply, an invisible (non-rendered) vector line between two points in 3D space—which can also be used to detect an intersection with a game object's collider.

Ray casting can also be used to retrieve lots of other useful information such as the length of the ray (therefore, distance), and the point of impact of the end of the line—for example where a bullet might impact another object in a game scenario.

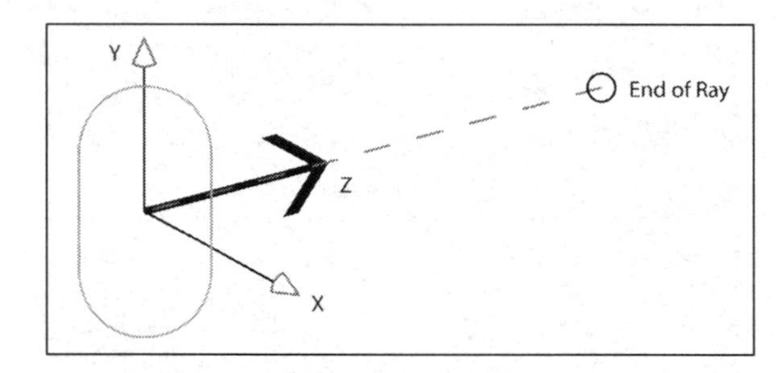

In the given example, a ray facing the forward direction from our character is demonstrated. In addition to the direction, a ray can also be given a specific length, or allowed to cast until it finds an object.

Over the course of the chapter, we will work with the outpost model that we have added to the terrain. Because this asset has been animated for us, the animation of the outpost's door opening and closing is ready to be triggered. This can be done either with collision detection, trigger collision detection, or ray casting, and we will explore what you will need to do in order to implement each approach.

Let's begin by looking at collision and trigger detection; when it may be appropriate to use a trigger-mode collider, or ray casting instead of, or in complement to standard collision detection. In the early part of this chapter we will look at these three approaches in the context of opening the **outPost** door, before going on to implement each approach.

When objects collide in the game engine, information about the **collision event** becomes available. By recording a variety of information upon the moment of impact, the engine can respond in a realistic manner. For example, in a game involving physics, if an object falls to the ground from a height, then the engine needs to know which part of the object hit the ground first. With that information, it can correctly and realistically control the object's reaction to the impact.

Of course, Unity handles these kinds of collisions and stores the information on your behalf, and you only have to retrieve it in order to do something with it.

In the example of opening a door, we would need to detect collisions between the player character's collider and a collider on or near to the door. It would make little sense to detect collisions elsewhere, as we would likely need to call the animation of the door when the player is near enough to walk through it, or to expect it to open for them.

As a result, we would check for collisions between the player character's collider and the door's collider. However, we would need to extend the depth of the door's collider so that the player character's collider did not need to be pressed up against the door in order to trigger a collision, as shown in the following illustration. However, the problem with extending the depth of the collider is that the game interaction with it becomes unrealistic.

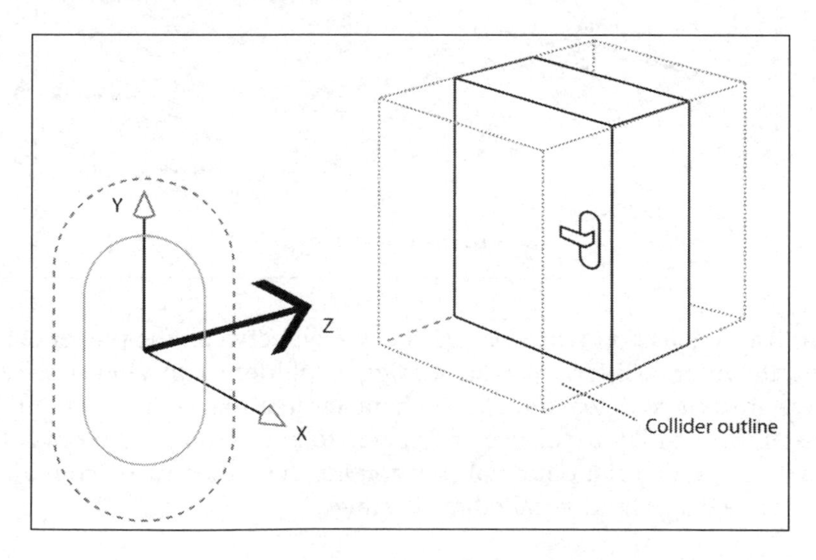

In the example of our door, the extended collider protruding from the visual surface of the door would mean that we would bump into an invisible surface, which would cause our character to stop in their tracks; and although we would use this collision to call the opening of the door through animation, the initial bump into the extended collider would seem unnatural to the player and thus detract from their immersion in the game.

In order to avoid this, colliders can be set to **Trigger** mode, a mode where colliders intersecting the trigger collider can be detected, but will not be repelled as if they were a physical object—these are often used to detect when a player character is in a particular area. With this approach two colliders may be used—one collider placed on the door that fits its exact shape and size, whilst another larger collider is placed around this object and set as a trigger (see the next diagram).

In this approach, we would use the trigger collider to detect the presence of the player, and therefore call actions on the door, such as the animation when it opens. Meanwhile, the standard collider on the door itself will react to objects hitting the door directly, perhaps if the player character runs into the door before the animation finishes or if an object is thrown at the door and must bounce off.

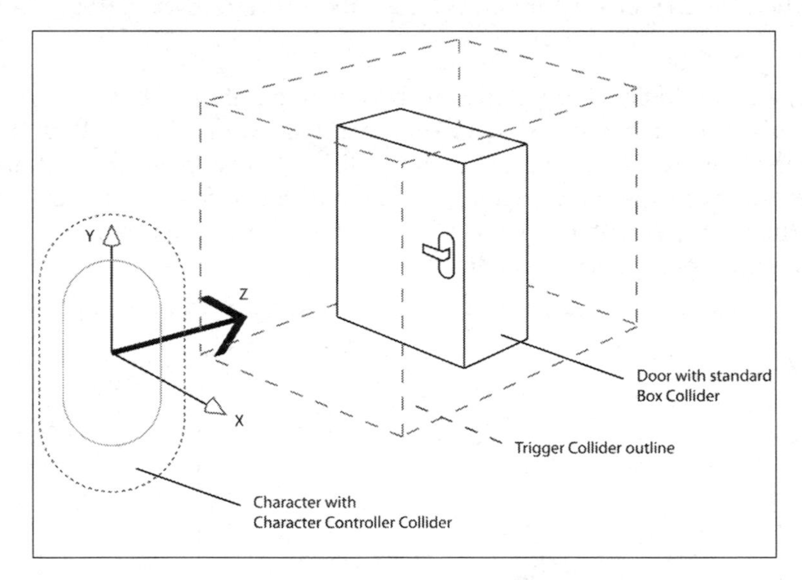

So while collision detection will work perfectly well between the player character collider and the door collider, by using a Trigger collider occupying space around the door, we are able to detect the player character in advance of them bumping into the door itself. In addition to the use of Triggers to detect intersection of colliders, sometimes we must detect a potential collision much further away from an object, for this we can use a technique called ray casting.

Ray casting

Whilst we can detect collisions between the player character's collider and a collider that fits the door object, or a trigger collider near to the door—we can also check whether the player is about to intersect a collider by casting a ray forward from where the player is facing. This means that when approaching the door, the player need not walk right up to it—or walk into an extended trigger collider—in order for it to be detected.

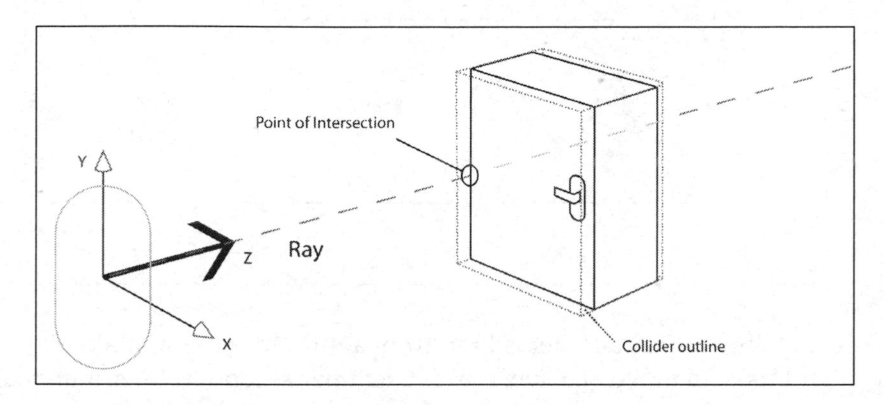

However, the drawback of this approach is that it means the player must be facing the door's collider in order for the ray to intersect it (given that the ray is cast in the forward direction of the player), which as you'll likely know is not how an automatic door works—it simply detects motion near to it.

Despite the drawbacks of this and the collision detection approach, as you will discover in your time learning game development in Unity, it is often good to try a number of approaches to a problem in order to decide which is the most efficient. For this reason we will learn collision detection and ray casting to open the door alongside the more appropriate trigger collision detection.

It is also important to learn ray casting as it is often used in other parts of game development to solve specific problems, such as pre-empting a potential collision where two colliders intersecting may not be appropriate. Let's look at a practical example of this problem.

The frame miss

In the example of a gun in a 3D shooter game, ray casting is used to predict the impact of a gunshot when a gun is fired. Because of the speed of an actual bullet, simulating the flight path of a bullet heading toward a target is very difficult to visually represent in a way that would satisfy and make sense to the player. This is down to the frame-based nature of the way in which games are rendered.

If you consider that when a real gun is fired, it takes a tiny amount of time to reach its target—and as far as an observer is concerned it could be said to happen instantaneously—we can assume that even when rendering over 25 frames of our game per second, the bullet would need to have reached its target within only a few frames.

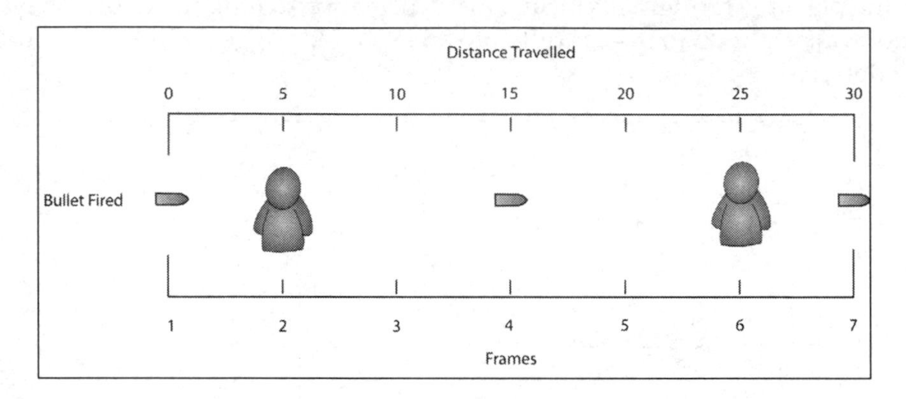

In the previous illustration, a bullet is fired from a gun. In order to make the bullet realistic, it will have to move at a speed of 500 feet per second. If the frame rate is 25 frames per second for example, the bullet will move at 20 feet per frame. The problem with this is that a person is about two feet in diameter, which means that the bullet will very likely miss the enemies shown at 5 and 25 feet away that the player would expect to hit. This is where prediction comes into play.

Predictive collision detection

Instead of checking for a collision with an actual bullet object, we find out whether a fired bullet will hit its target. By casting a ray forward from the gun object (thus using its forward direction and therefore the bullet's trajectory) on the same frame that the player presses the fire button, we can immediately check which objects intersect the ray.

We can do this because rays are drawn immediately. Think of them like a laser pointer—when you switch on the laser, we do not see the light moving forward because it travels at the speed of light—to us it simply appears.

Rays work in the same way, so that whenever the player in a ray-based shooting game presses fire, they draw a ray in the direction that they are aiming. With this ray, they can retrieve information on the collider that is hit. Moreover, by identifying the collider, the game object itself can be addressed and scripted to behave accordingly. Even detailed information, such as the point of impact, can be returned and used to affect the resultant reaction, for example, causing the enemy to recoil in a particular direction.

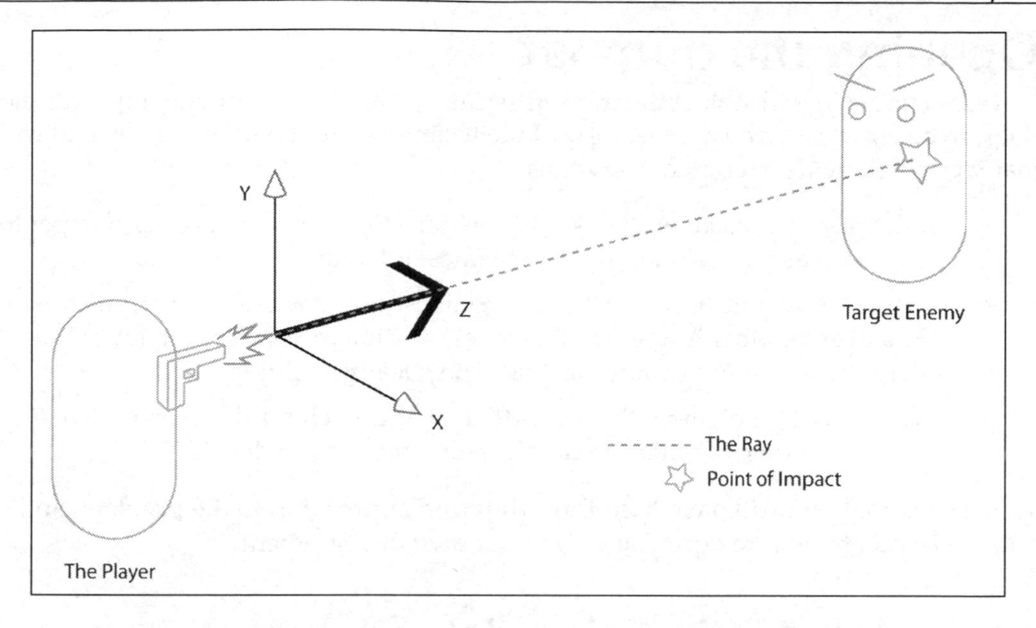

In our shooting game example, we would likely invoke scripting to kill or physically repel the enemy whose collider the ray hits, and as a result of the immediacy of rays, we can do this on the frame after the ray collides with, or *intersects* the enemy collider. This gives the effect of a real gunshot because the reaction is registered immediately.

> **Continuous collision detection**
>
> If you are working with projectiles that are fast moving, but not at the speed of a bullet, the frame miss problem may still occur. This can be corrected by setting the **Collision detection** type of your Rigidbody component to **Continuous** or **Continuous Dynamic,** depending on what other objects your Rigidbody interacts with.

Now let's return to focusing on our door example and make use of the approaches we just outlined in order to make the door of the **outPost** game object interactive.

Opening the outpost

In this section, we will look at the three differing approaches for interacting with the door, in order to give you an overview of the techniques that will become useful in many other game development situations:

- In the first approach, we'll use collision detection—a crucial concept to get to grips with as you begin to work on games in Unity.
- In the second approach, we'll implement a simple ray cast forward from the player, another important skill to learn—that means we can detect interactions without colliders actually physically colliding.
- Finally, we'll implement the most efficient approach for this scenario—using a separate Trigger collider to call the animation on the door.

This means that you will have tried three differing approaches to the problem, and will have code to refer to once you begin your own development.

Approach 1—Collision detection

To begin writing the script that will play the door-opening animation and thereby grant access to the outpost, we need to consider which object to write a script for.

In game development, you should see your player character as a unique entity that all other objects are awaiting interaction with. Rather than establishing a master script for the player that will account for all eventualities, we can write smaller scripts that simply know what to do when they encounter the player.

However, when detecting standard (non-trigger) collisions involving the **Character Controller** collider, you must make use of the function `OnControllerColliderHit()`. This function specifically detects collisions between the character controller and other objects, and therefore must be placed in a script that is attached to an object with a character controller component. This, although incongruous with the logic for script attachment outlined earlier, serves as an exercise to learn this function before we move on to using other more efficient approaches that will not involve scripting directly onto the player's character.

Creating new assets

Before we introduce any new kind of asset into our project, it is good practice to create a folder in which we will keep assets of that type. In the **Project** panel, click on the **Create** button, and choose **Folder** from the drop-down menu that appears.

Rename this folder **Scripts** by selecting it and pressing *Return* (Mac) or by pressing *F2* (PC). Move your **Shooter** script file into this folder by dragging and dropping now, to keep things neat.

Next, create a new C# or Javascript file within this folder simply by leaving the **Scripts** folder selected and clicking on the **Project** panel's **Create** button again, this time choosing the relevant language.

> By selecting the folder that you want a newly created asset to be in before you create them, you will not have to create and then relocate your asset, as the new asset will be made within the selected folder.

Rename the newly created script from the default—`NewBehaviourScript`—to `PlayerCollisions`. Script files have the file extensions such as `.cs` for C# or `.js` for Javascript but the Unity **Project** panel hides file extensions, so there is no need to attempt to add it when renaming your assets.

> You can also spot the file type of a script by looking at its icon in the **Project** panel. Javascript files have a 'JS' written on them, C# files simply have 'C#' and Boo files have an image of a Pacman ghost, a nice little informative pun from the folks at Unity Technologies!

Scripting for character collision detection

To start editing the script, double-click on its icon in the **Project** panel to launch it in the default script editor—MonoDevelop.

Working with OnControllerColliderHit

By default, all new scripts include the `Update()` function (C# users will also see the `Start()` function), and this is why you'll find it present when you open the script for the first time. However, we are about to take a look at another Unity function called `OnControllerColliderHit`, a collision detection function specific to character controllers, such as the one that drives our player character.

> C# users—always remember to ensure that the class name of the script matches the file name before you continue working—it should have been automatically changed from **NewBehaviorScript** to **PlayerCollisions**.

Let's kick off by declaring variables that we can utilize throughout the script.

Our script begins with the definition of two private variables and three public variables. Their purposes are as follows:

- `doorIsOpen`—a private `true/false` (Boolean) type variable acting as a switch for the script to check if the door is currently open.
- `doorTimer`—a private floating-point (decimal-placed) number variable, which is used as a timer so that once our door is open, the script can count a defined amount of time before self-closing the door.
- `doorOpenTime`—a public floating-point (potentially decimal) numeric public member variable, which will be used in order to allow us to set the amount of time that we wish the door to stay open in the **Inspector.**
- `doorOpenSound/doorShutSound`—two public member variables of data type `AudioClip`, for allowing sound clip drag-and-drop assignment in the **Inspector** panel.

Define these variables by writing the following at the top of the **PlayerCollisions** class; remember that in Javascript this simply means at the top of the script because Javascript hides the class declaration, and in C# this means after the opening `public class PlayerCollisions : MonoBehaviour {` line:

C#:

```
bool doorIsOpen = false;
float doorTimer = 0.0f;
public float doorOpenTime  = 3.0f;
public AudioClip doorOpenSound;
public AudioClip doorShutSound;
```

Javascript:

```
private var doorIsOpen : boolean = false;
private var doorTimer : float = 0.0;
private var currentDoor : GameObject;

var doorOpenTime : float = 3.0;
var doorOpenSound : AudioClip;
var doorShutSound : AudioClip;
```

Next, we'll leave the `Update()` function briefly while we establish the collision detection function itself. Move down two lines from:

C#:

```
void Update () {
}
```

Javascript:

```
function Update(){
}
```

And write in the following function:

C#:

```
void OnControllerColliderHit(ControllerColliderHit hit){

}
```

Javascript:

```
function OnControllerColliderHit(hit : ControllerColliderHit){


}
```

This establishes a new function called `OnControllerColliderHit`. This collision detection function is specifically for use with player characters such as ours, which use the **CharacterController** component. Its only argument—`hit`—is a variable of type `ControllerColliderHit`, which is a class that stores information on any collision that occurs. By addressing the `hit` variable, we can query information on the collision, including—for starters—the specific game object our player has collided with.

We will do this by adding an `if` statement to our function. So within the function's curly braces—that is, between { and }, add the following `if` statement:

C# and Javascript:

```
if(hit.gameObject.tag == "playerDoor" && doorIsOpen == false){

}
```

In this `if` statement, we are checking two conditions, firstly that the object we hit is tagged with the tag `playerDoor` and secondly that the variable `doorOpen` is currently set to `false`. Remember here that two equals symbols (`==`) are used as a comparative, and the two ampersand symbols (`&&`) simply say 'and also'.

The end result means that if we hit the door's collider that we have tagged and if we have not already opened the door, this `if` statement may carry out a set of instructions.

We have utilized the dot syntax to address the object that we are checking for collisions with by narrowing down from `hit` (our variable storing information on collisions) to `gameObject` (the object hit) to the `tag` on that object.

If this `if` statement's conditions are met, then we need to carry out a set of instructions to open the door. This will involve playing a sound, playing one of the animation clips on the model, and setting our Boolean variable `doorOpen` to `true`.
As we are going to call multiple instructions—and may need to call these instructions as a result of a different conditions later when we implement the ray casting approach—we will place them into our own custom function called `OpenDoor`.

We will write this function shortly, but first, we'll call the function in the `if` statement we have, by adding:

```
OpenDoor();
```

So your full collision function should now look like this:

C#:

```
void OnControllerColliderHit(ControllerColliderHit hit){
  if(hit.gameObject.tag == "playerDoor" && doorIsOpen == false){
    OpenDoor(hit.gameObject);
  }
}
```

Javascript:

```
function OnControllerColliderHit(hit: ControllerColliderHit){
  if(hit.gameObject.tag == "playerDoor" && doorIsOpen == false){
    OpenDoor(hit.gameObject);
  }
}
```

OpenDoor() custom function

Storing sets of instructions you may wish to call at any time should be done by writing your own functions. Instead of having to write out a set of instructions or "commands" many times within a script, writing your own functions containing the instructions means that you can simply call that function at any time to run that set of instructions again. This also makes tracking mistakes in code—known as **Debugging**—a lot simpler, as there are fewer places to check for errors.

In our collision detection function, we have written a call to a function named `OpenDoor`. The brackets after `OpenDoor` are used to store parameters we may wish to send to the function—using a function's brackets, you may set additional behavior to pass to the instructions inside the function. We looked at an example of this earlier in the book; to remind yourself, see *Writing custom functions* in *Chapter 4*.

We'll take a look at this in more detail later in this chapter. The brackets of `OpenDoor()` contain a single argument—a `GameObject` type reference which is sending the currently collided with object by using `hit.gameObject` as a reference.

Declaring the function

To write the function that we need to call, below the closing } curly brace of the `OnControllerColliderHit` function, begin by writing the following:

C#:

```
void OpenDoor(GameObject door){

   }
```

Javascript:

```
function OpenDoor(door : GameObject){


}
```

Here, the function has the corresponding argument named door, which is awaiting a reference of type GameObject— which we already know is being sent to it by the collision detection we just wrote.

Much in the same way as the instructions of an `if` statement, we place any instructions to be carried out when this function is called within its curly braces.

Checking door status

One condition of the `if` statement within our collision detection function was that our Boolean variable `doorIsOpen` must be `false`. In order to stop this function from recurring—the first command inside our `OpenDoor()` function is to set this variable to `true`.

This is because the player character may collide with the door several times when bumping into it, and without this Boolean, they could potentially trigger the `OpenDoor()` function many times, causing sound and animation to recur and restart with each collision.

By adding in a variable that when `false` allows the `OpenDoor()` function to run and then disallows it by setting the `doorIsOpen` variable to `true` immediately, any further collisions will not re-trigger the `OpenDoor()` function.

Add the following line to your `OpenDoor()` function now by placing it between the curly braces:

C# and Javascript:

```
doorIsOpen = true;
```

Playing audio

Our next instruction is to play the audio clip assigned to the variable called `doorOpenSound`. To do this, add the following line to your function by placing it within the curly braces:

C# and Javascript:

```
door.audio.PlayOneShot(doorOpenSound);
```

Here we are addressing the **Audio Source** component attached to the game object currently contained in the `door` argument—which you'll remember is the `playerDoor` tagged object that is hit in the collision detection.

Addressing the audio source using the term `audio` gives us access to four functions, `Play()`, `Stop()`, `Pause()`, and `PlayOneShot()`. We are using `PlayOneShot` because it is the best way to play a single instance of a sound, as opposed to playing a sound and then switching clips, which would be more appropriate for continuous music than sound effects. In the brackets of the `PlayOneShot` command, we pass the variable `doorOpenSound`, which will play whatever sound file is assigned to that variable in the **Inspector**.

Testing the script

Before we continue to write the script, assuming that it works thus far—let's save it and test it out. So far all that our script should do is detect a collision between the Player object—**First Person Controller**, and the door child object of the **outPost**. When this occurs, it is set to play a sound that we must assign to our **doorOpenSound** public variable.

Go to **File | Save** in MonoDevelop and switch back to Unity. We must assign this script to our **First Person Controller**, but first, ensure that it is free of errors. Check the bar at the bottom of the Unity interface, as this is where any errors made in the script will be shown. The bottom bar of the interface shows the latest line output by the Console panel in Unity (**Window | Console**). If there are any errors, then double-click on the error and ensure that your script matches the previous snippets.

As you continue to work with scripting in Unity, you'll get used to using error reporting to help you correct any mistakes that you may make.

> The best place to begin double-checking that you have not made any mistakes in your code is to ensure that you have an even number of opening and closing curly braces—this means that all functions and statements are correctly closed.

If you have no errors, then simply select the object you wish to apply the script to in the **Hierarchy**—the **First Person Controller** object.

Apply the script to this object using one of the various methods we looked at in the previous chapter on prototyping—the simplest method is just to drag the script's icon and drop it onto the name of the object that you wish to apply it to—the **First Person Controller**.

Unity will now prompt you with a **Losing prefab** dialog window—this simply asks whether you wish to make the object in your scene different to the original asset in the Project. This is standard practice, so just click on **Continue** here.

Now select the **First Person Controller** in the Hierarchy and you should then see the script appearing as a component of that object in the **Inspector** panel.

Now expand the **Book Assets | Sounds** folder in the Project panel and you will see audio clips named **door_open** and **door_shut**. Keep the **First Person Controller** object selected so that you can see the **Door Open Sound** and **Door Shut Sound** public variables on the **Player Collisions (Script)** component, and drag-and-drop these audio clips from the Project panel to the relevant public variables in the Inspector. Once assigned they should look like this:

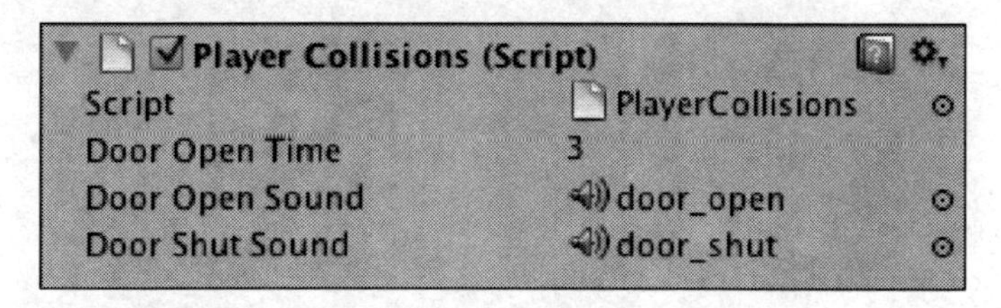

Now we're ready for some action! Go to **File | Save Scene** in Unity to update our scene, and then test the game by pressing the **Play** button at the top of the interface.

If we had not assigned a clip to the **Door Open Sound** public variable, when the collision occurred in the script, it would attempt to play an audio clip but find that none was assigned—this would result in a **Null Reference Exception** error—literally speaking a reference, that is null—meaning not set. This can often occur if you set a variable to public and forget to assign it, or if you have set up a reference in a script but it is not assigned.

Walk the **First Person Controller** over to the **outPost** and try and interact with the door. You'll notice you cannot interact with the door collider until the **First Person Controller** is pressed up against it. Once the colliders touch you should hear the audio clip for the door opening—no animation just yet however, as we have not called it in our script. Remember that if you want to check on what is occurring in the game, you should watch the Scene view as you test your game with the Game view.

Extending colliders

We can make this interaction occur sooner by extending the collider—let's try this out now. Press the **Play** button at the top of the interface again to stop testing.

Select the **door** child object of the **outPost**, and focus your view on it by hovering over the Scene view and pressing *F*. Switch to Top view by clicking the **Y** (green) handle of the View Gizmo in the top right of the Scene view.

Now, hold the *Shift* key, and drag the green collider boundary dots on the front and back of the door in order to extend the collider as shown:

Now that our collider is extended, we will collide with it as we approach the steps. Play test once more and confirm that this works as expected, remembering to press the Play button again to stop testing before you continue working. Now let's get that door open; it's animation time!

Playing animation

One of the tasks we performed in the import process at the beginning of this chapter was setting up animation clips using the **Inspector**. By selecting the asset in the **Project** panel, we specified in the **Inspector** that it would feature three clips:

- `idle` (a 'do nothing' state)
- `dooropen`
- `doorshut`

In our `OpenDoor()` function, we'll call upon a named clip using a **String** of text to refer to it. However, first we'll need to state which object in our scene contains the animation we wish to play. Because the script we are writing is attached to the player, we must refer to another object before referring to the animation component. We can do this yet again by referring to the object hit by our player character. In our `OpenDoor()` function we have an argument that receives the door object from the `OnControllerColliderHit()` function—we just used this to play a sound file on the door by saying `door.audio.PlayOneShot("doorOpenSound");` but unfortunately our animation component is not attached to the door itself, but instead to the parent object, the outPost object.

To address the parent of an object, we can simply use the shortcut `transform.parent` when referring to the door. Inside the `OpenDoor()` function, beneath the last command you added—`door.audio.PlayOneShot(doorOpenSound);`—add the following line:

C# and Javascript:

```
door.transform.parent.animation.Play("dooropen");
```

This line simply says "find the door's parent object, address the animation component on this object, and play the animation clip named dooropen". So let's try this out—Go to **File | Save** in MonoDevelop and switch back to Unity.

Press Play at the top of the interface, and play test your game. Walking up to the collider on the door should cause the sound and animation of the door to now play. As always, stop play testing before you continue your development.

Reversing the procedure

Now that we have created a set of instructions that will open the door, how will we close it once it is open? To aid playability, we will not force the player to actively close the door themselves but instead establish some code that will cause it to shut after a defined time period.

This is where our `doorTimer` variable comes into play. We will begin counting as soon as the door becomes open by adding a value of time to this variable, and then check when this variable has reached a particular value by using an `if` statement.

Because we will be dealing with time, we need to utilize a function that will constantly update, such as the `Update()` function we had awaiting us when we created the script earlier.

Create some empty lines inside the `Update()` function by moving its closing curly brace } a few lines down.

Firstly, we should check if the door has been opened, as there is no point in incrementing our timer variable if the door is not currently open. Write in the following `if` statement to increment the timer variable with time if the `doorIsOpen` variable is set to `true`:

C# and Javascript:

```
if(doorIsOpen){
        doorTimer += Time.deltaTime;
}
```

Here we check if the door is open (if the `doorIsOpen` variable has been set to true)—this is a variable that by default is set to `false`, and will only become `true` as a result of a collision between the player object and the door. If the `doorIsOpen` variable is `true`, then we add the value of `Time.deltaTime` to the `doorTimer` variable. Bear in mind that simply writing the variable name as we have done in our `if` statement's condition is the same as writing `if(doorIsOpen == true)`.

`Time.deltaTime` is a property that will count independent of the game's frame rate. This is important because your game may be run on varying hardware when deployed, and it would be odd if time slowed down on slower devices and was faster when better hardware ran it. As a result, when adding time, we can use `Time.deltaTime` to calculate the time taken to complete the last frame and with this information, we can automatically correct real-time counting.

Next, we need to check whether our timer variable, `doorTimer`, has reached a certain value, which means that a certain amount of time has passed. We will do this by nesting an `if` statement inside the one we just added—this will mean that the `if` statement we are about to add will only be checked if the `doorIsOpen` `if` condition is valid.

Add the following code below the time incrementing line inside the existing `if` statement:v

C# and Javascript:

```
if(doorTimer > doorOpenTime){
    ShutDoor();
    doorTimer = 0.0f;
}
```

This addition to our code will be constantly checked as soon as the `doorIsOpen` variable becomes `true` and waits until the value of `doorTimer` exceeds the value of the `doorOpenTime` variable, which, because we are using `Time.deltaTime` as an incremental value, will mean three real-time seconds have passed. This is of course unless you change the value of this variable from its default of `3` in the **Inspector**.

Once the `doorTimer` has exceeded a value of `3`, a function called `ShutDoor()` is called, and the `doorTimer` variable is reset to zero so that it can be used again the next time the door is triggered. If this is not included, then the `doorTimer` will get stuck above a value of `3`, and as soon as the door is opened it would close as a result.

Now, you should notice that the `ShutDoor()` function has no argument—this is because we need to establish a variable in which to store a reference to the current door we are interacting with. We did not need to do this earlier, because the call to the `OpenDoor()` function was within the collision detection function—in which we had a reference to the door in the form of variable `hit.gameObject`.

However, as we are writing code to call a `ShutDoor()` function within `Update()`, the variable `hit` does not exist there, so we should establish a private variable at the top of the script that any function can access, and that is set by our collision detection. Beneath the other variables at the top of your script, add the following variable:

C#:

```
GameObject currentDoor;
```

Javascript:

```
private var currentDoor : GameObject;
```

Now, within your collision detection function, add in a line that assigns this variable a value, and then amend the call to `OpenDoor()` as follows:

C#:

```
void OnControllerColliderHit(ControllerColliderHit hit){
    if(hit.gameObject.tag == "playerDoor" && doorIsOpen == false){
      currentDoor = hit.gameObject;
      OpenDoor(currentDoor);
    }
}
```

Javascript:

```
function OnControllerColliderHit(hit: ControllerColliderHit){
  if(hit.gameObject.tag == "playerDoor" && doorIsOpen == false){
    currentDoor = hit.gameObject;
    OpenDoor(currentDoor);
  }
}
```

Now we have this established variable, place `currentDoor` in as the argument of your call to `ShutDoor()` in the `Update()` function:

C# and Javascript:

```
ShutDoor(currentDoor);
```

Your completed `Update()` function should now look like this:

C#:

```
void Update () {
  if(doorIsOpen){
    doorTimer += Time.deltaTime;

    if(doorTimer > doorOpenTime){
      ShutDoor(currentDoor);
      doorTimer = 0.0f;
    }
  }
}
```

Javascript:

```
function Update(){
   if(doorIsOpen){
      doorTimer += Time.deltaTime;
```

```
            if(doorTimer > doorOpenTime){
                ShutDoor(currentDoor);
                doorTimer = 0.0f;
            }
        }
    }
```

Now, add the `ShutDoor()` function itself below the existing `OpenDoor()` function—place your cursor at its ending } and move down to the next line. Because it largely performs the same function as `OpenDoor()`, we will not discuss it in depth. Simply observe that a different animation is called on the outpost and that our `doorIsOpen` variable gets reset to `false` so that the entire procedure may start over:

C#:

```
    void ShutDoor(GameObject door){
      doorIsOpen = false;
      door.audio.PlayOneShot(doorShutSound);
      door.transform.parent.animation.Play("doorshut");
    }
```

Javascript:

```
    function shutDoor(door : GameObject){
      doorIsOpen = false;
      door.audio.PlayOneShot(doorShutSound);
      door.transform.parent.animation.Play("doorshut");
    }
```

It's testing time again! Go to **File | Save** in MonoDevelop and return to Unity and test your game as before. Now that the timer is established, once your player character has collided with the door, three seconds should pass before it is automatically closed again.

Code maintainability

Now that we have a script in charge of opening and closing our door, let's look at how we can expand our knowledge of custom functions to make our scripting more maintainable.

Currently we have two functions we refer to as custom or bespoke—`OpenDoor()` and `ShutDoor()`. These functions perform the same three tasks—they play a sound, set a Boolean variable, and play an animation. So why not create a single function and add arguments to allow it to play differing sounds and have it choose either `true` or `false` for the Boolean and play differing animations? Making these three tasks into arguments of the function will allow us to do just that.

After the closing curly brace of `ShutDoor()` in your script, add the following function:

C#:

```
void Door(AudioClip aClip, bool openCheck, string animName,
  GameObject thisDoor){
    thisDoor.audio.PlayOneShot(aClip);
    doorIsOpen = openCheck;
    thisDoor.transform.parent.animation.Play(animName);
}
```

Javascript:

```
function Door(aClip : AudioClip, openCheck : boolean,
  animName : String, thisDoor : GameObject){
    thisDoor.audio.PlayOneShot(aClip);
    doorIsOpen = openCheck;
    thisDoor.transform.parent.animation.Play(animName);
}
```

You'll notice that this function looks similar to our existing `OpenDoor` and `ShutDoor` functions, but has four arguments in its declaration—`aClip`, `openCheck`, `animName`, and `thisDoor`. These are effectively variables that get assigned when the function is called, and the values assigned to them are used inside the function. For example, when we wish to pass values for opening the door to this function, we would call the function and set each parameter by writing the following:

```
Door(doorOpenSound, true, "dooropen", currentDoor);
```

This feeds the variable `doorOpenSound` to the `aClip` argument, a value of `true` to the `openCheck` argument, string of text `"dooropen"` to the `animName` argument, and sends the Game Object assigned to variable `currentDoor` to the `thisDoor` argument.

Now we can replace the call to the `OpenDoor()` function inside the collision detection function. First, remove the following line that calls the `OpenDoor()` function inside the `OnControllerColliderHit()` function:

```
OpenDoor(currentDoor);
```

Replace it with the following line:

C# and Javascript:

```
Door(doorOpenSound, true, "dooropen", currentDoor);
```

Now we have a single function that is called with its four arguments being sent –

- `doorOpenSound`—as the sound to play
- `true`—as the value to give `doorIsOpen`
- `dooropen`—as the animation to play
- `currentDoor`—as the object we're currently interacting with

Finally, because we are using this new method of opening and closing the doors, we'll need to amend the door closing code within the `Update()` function. Within the `if` statement that checks for the `doorTimer` variable exceeding the value of the `doorOpenTime` variable, replace the call to the `ShutDoor(currentDoor)` function with this line:

C# and Javascript:

```
Door(doorShutSound, false, "doorshut", currentDoor);
```

You may now delete the original two functions—`OpenDoor()` and `ShutDoor()`, as our customizable `Door()` function now supersedes both of them. By creating functions in this way, we are not repeating ourselves in scripting, and this makes our script shorter, simpler to read and therefore to debug, and saves time writing two functions.

If you would like to keep these functions to remind you of what you have done, you may comment them out. When turned into comments, they are no longer executable parts of the script—so simply place `/*` before the opening of your `OpenDoor()` function and `*/` after the closing curly brace of the `ShutDoor()` function. In your script editor, the code will change color to show that it has been made into a multi-line comment. Be sure to save your script in MonoDevelop now.

Switch back to Unity now and press Play to test your game; you should now see that your door opens and closes, but we still have the issue of bumping into our extended collider.

Drawbacks of collision detection

Our first implementation of the door opening is complete. Making use of `OnControllerColliderHit()` works perfectly but is still not the most efficient method of creating this door opening mechanic.

The main drawbacks here are:

- Code is stored on the player object, and means that as we create further interaction code, this script becomes long and difficult to maintain

- The Collider extension means that the player bumps into an invisible surface that will open the door but cause the player to stop in their tracks, which interrupts gameplay

We will now move on to try our second of the three approaches, using ray casting.

Approach 2—Ray casting

In this section, we will implement our second approach to opening the door. Although character controller collision detection may be a valid approach, by introducing the concept of ray casting, we can try an approach where our player only opens the door of the outpost when they are facing it, because the ray will always face the direction that the First Person Controller is facing, and as such not intersect the door if, for example, the player backs up to it.

Disabling collision detection with comments

To avoid the need to write an additional script, we will simply comment out—that is, temporarily deactivate part of the code that contains our collision detection function. To do this, we will add characters to turn our working collision code into a comment.

Ensure that you still have the **PlayerCollisions** script open in the script editor and then before the following line:

C#:

```
void OnControllerColliderHit(ControllerColliderHit hit){
```

Javascript:

```
function OnControllerColliderHit(hit: ControllerColliderHit){
```

Place the following characters:

```
/*
```

Remember that putting a forward slash and asterisk into your script begins a multi line comment (as opposed to two forward slashes that simply comment out a single line). After the collision detection function's closing right curly-brace }, place the reverse of this, that is, an asterisk followed by a forward slash—`*/`. Your entire function should have changed the syntax color in the script editor to show that it has been **commented out**.

Migrating code—writing a DoorManager script

Now that we are about to use a ray to open the door, we should reconsider where the code for opening the door is placed. Our current door opening code is located on the player, and as the player may encounter many objects within our game, we should consider that the logic for the door opening and closing would be better stored on the door itself, meaning that the door need only be aware of its own functions, and the requirement to open for the player. We can then make use of the raycast in this approach, and the trigger in our third approach to call upon the opening code on the door object.

In Unity, click the **Create** button on the Project panel, and choose the relevant language you are working with. Name your new script **DoorManager**, and then launch it in MonoDevelop.

Here we are going to migrate the majority of our door logic from the **PlayerCollisions** script. Because you have already covered what this code does, simply place all of the code below into your new **DoorManager** script, and we will then discuss any differences and also what has changed in **PlayerCollisions** itself.

C#:

```
using UnityEngine;
using System.Collections;

public class DoorManager : MonoBehaviour {

  bool doorIsOpen = false;
  float doorTimer = 0.0f;
  public float doorOpenTime  = 3.0f;
  public AudioClip doorOpenSound;
  public AudioClip doorShutSound;

  void Start(){
    doorTimer = 0.0f;
  }

  void Update(){
   if(doorIsOpen){
     doorTimer += Time.deltaTime;
     if(doorTimer > doorOpenTime){
       Door(doorShutSound, false, "doorshut");
       doorTimer = 0.0f;
   }
 }
```

```
    }

    void DoorCheck(){
      if(!doorIsOpen){
        Door(doorOpenSound, true, "dooropen");
      }
    }

    void Door(AudioClip aClip, bool openCheck, string animName){
      audio.PlayOneShot(aClip);
      doorIsOpen = openCheck;
      transform.parent.gameObject.animation.Play(animName);
    }
  }
```

Javascript:

```
private var doorIsOpen : boolean = false;
private var doorTimer : float = 0.0f;
var doorOpenTime : float = 3.0f;
var doorOpenSound : AudioClip;
var doorShutSound : AudioClip;

function Start(){
  doorTimer = 0.0f;
}

function Update(){
  if(doorIsOpen){
    doorTimer += Time.deltaTime;

    if(doorTimer > doorOpenTime){
      Door(doorShutSound, false, "doorshut");
      doorTimer = 0.0f;
    }
  }
}

function DoorCheck(){
  if(!doorIsOpen){
    Door(doorOpenSound, true, "dooropen");
  }
}
```

```
function Door(aClip : AudioClip, openCheck : boolean, animName :
String){
  audio.PlayOneShot(aClip);
  doorIsOpen = openCheck;
  transform.parent.gameObject.animation.Play(animName);
}
```

The key change from the code in **PlayerCollisions** is the addition of the `DoorCheck()` function. By adding this we now have a function that can be called easily, without need for additional arguments that check if the door is not currently open:

```
  if(!doorIsOpen){
    Door(doorOpenSound, true, "dooropen");
  }
```

It then goes on to call the `Door()` function with its opening arguments. This switches on the `Update()` function's timer, which will reset the door as before. Now we can remove the duplicate code from **PlayerCollisions**, and implement our raycast.

Tidying PlayerCollisions

Now that we have our **DoorManager** script handling the door's state, we can cut the **PlayerCollisions** script code down to very simple elements. Given that you are learning Unity, as stated before, you may wish to comment out code done previously instead of deleting it, but in the following example, only the remaining code is shown - instead of showing you what should be commented also, so it is your choice whether to delete code or comment it.

Regardless, you should remove (delete or comment-out) code from **PlayerCollisions** so that you are only left with the following:

C#:

```
using UnityEngine;
using System.Collections;

public class PlayerCollisions : MonoBehaviour {

  GameObject currentDoor;

  void Update () {

  }
}
```

Javascript:

```
private var currentDoor : GameObject;

function Update(){

}
```

Now we have only the `Update()` function—this is where we will cast our ray—and a private variable to hold a reference to the door that we're currently interacting with.

Let's add the ray cast to call upon the `DoorCheck()` function in our **DoorManager**.

Casting the ray

Still in the **PlayerCollisions** script, move your cursor a couple of lines down from the opening of the `Update()` function. We place ray casts in the `Update()` function, as we need to technically cast our ray forward every frame, because at any time the player's direction may change. Add in the following code:

C#:

```
RaycastHit hit;

if(Physics.Raycast (transform.position, transform.forward,
  out hit, 3)) {
    if(hit.collider.gameObject.tag=="playerDoor"){
      currentDoor = hit.collider.gameObject;
      currentDoor.SendMessage("DoorCheck");
    }
}
```

Javascript:

```
var hit : RaycastHit;

if(Physics.Raycast (transform.position, transform.forward,
  hit, 3)) {
    if(hit.collider.gameObject.tag=="playerDoor"){
      currentDoor = hit.collider.gameObject;
      currentDoor.SendMessage("DoorCheck");
    }
}
```

At the outset, a ray is created by establishing a local variable called `hit`, which is of type `RaycastHit`. Note that it does not need to be made private in order to not be seen in the Inspector—it is not seen because it is a local variable (declared inside a function). This will be used to store information on the ray when it intersects colliders. Whenever we refer to the ray, we use this variable.

Then we use two `if` statements. The parent `if` is in charge of casting the ray and uses the variable we created. Because we place the casting of the ray (the `Physics.Raycast()` function) into an `if` statement, we are able to only call the nested `if` statement if the ray hits an object, making the script more efficient.

Our first `if` contains `Physics.Raycast()`, the actual function that casts the ray. This function has four arguments within its own brackets:

- The position from which to create the ray (`transform.position`—the position of the object that this script applies to—the **First Person Controller**)
- The direction of the ray (`transform.forward`—the forward direction of the object that this script applies to)
- The `RaycastHit` data structure we set up called `hit`—the ray stored as a variable
- The length of the ray (`3`—a distance in the game units, meters)

Note that in C# we must use a precursor `out` parameter before the variable `hit` in order to get the function to assign data to it, this is done implicitly in Javascript by simply naming the variable to use.

Then we have a nested `if` statement that first checks the `hit` variable for collision with colliders in the game world, specifically whether we have hit a collider belonging to a game object tagged `playerDoor`, so:

```
hit.collider.gameObject.tag == "PlayerDoor"
```

Once both `if` statements' conditions are met, we simply set the `currentDoor` variable to the object stored in `hit` and then call the `DoorCheck()` function by making use of Unity's **SendMessage()** function.

By using SendMessage we can call a function on an object, without a reference to the particular script, simply by naming the function:

```
currentDoor.SendMessage("DoorCheck");
```

`SendMessage()` here simply checks any scripts attached to the object assigned to the `currentDoor` variable, finds the `DoorCheck()` function and calls it.

For more information on `SendMessage()`, see the Unity script reference at: `http://unity3d.com/support/documentation/ScriptReference/GameObject.SendMessage.html`

Save your script and return to Unity now. All that is left now is to apply our **DoorManager** to the door. Ensure that the **outPost** parent object is expanded in the Hierarchy so that you can see the **door** child object, then drag-and-drop your **DoorManager** script from the Project panel onto the **door** child object in the Hierarchy.

Assign the **door_open** and **door_shut** audio clips to the public variables on the script component in the Inspector as you did previously when they were members of **PlayerCollisions**.

Resetting the collider

Now that we are using raycasting to look ahead of the player—we no longer need our expanded collider on the door—it can be reset to its default dimensions—those of the mesh that it is applied to. To do this, simply select the **door** child object in the Hierarchy and then in the **Box Collider** component, click the Cog icon to the right-hand side, and choose **Reset** from the pop-out menu that appears.

Now let's see it in action! Play test by pressing the **Play** button at the top of the Unity interface and you will notice that when approaching the door, it not only opens before you bump into it, but also only opens when you are facing it, because the ray that detects the door is cast in the same direction that the player character faces.

Ray casting can be used in this way to detect colliders near to other objects, or in their line of sight in many other game mechanics. It is recommended that when you finish this book, you should try prototyping some ideas that make use of techniques such as this because of how valuable they are in practical usage.

However, as stated previously, this is not the expected behavior for a door, as we expect it to simply detect a person within its vicinity—consider the behavior of a security light motion detector or a burglar alarm sensor as an ideal example. For this reason, let's move on to approach number 3—the most efficient approach to opening our door—using a Trigger collider.

Approach 3—Trigger collision detection

Because our first two approaches had drawbacks—bumping into a collider with standard `OnControllerColliderHit()` and only opening the door when facing it with our Ray cast —using a Trigger collider should be considered the best approach to creating a door opening mechanic, because there is no physical collider to bump into, and it will be triggered regardless of the direction the player is facing.

As previously stated, we will leave our existing Box Collider on the door so that it has a physical presence that objects can collide with if necessary. This means that we should place a Box Collider set to trigger mode on a separate object—this is also important because our door is animated to move, and we do not want our trigger area to move when the door is opened. For this reason, we can attach our Box Collider to the parent object—**outPost**, and then simply position this collider as a large trigger area around the door, as shown in the illustrations at the beginning of this chapter.

Once this is positioned, we can apply a new short script that uses the `OnTriggerEnter()` function—simply a function that detects other colliders entering a trigger mode collider. We will use this function to call upon the same `DoorCheck()` function as the ray in our second approach.

This will make our **PlayerCollisions** script obsolete for now, meaning that the logic for our door is entirely self-contained—this is considered good practice in development.

Creating and scaling the trigger zone

Select the parent object named **outPost** in the Hierarchy, and choose **Component | Physics | Box Collider** from the top menu.

Your **Box Collider** will be created at the standard (1,1,1) Cube primitive scale, but we can use the *Shift-Drag* method in the Scene view in order to resize and reposition it. You will also notice that it has been created at the center of the **outPost** model at its base—this is simply where the axes of this model were in the package it was created in:

Ensure that you have the Hand Tool (*Q*) selected—as this hides the Axis handles for the object—making it easier to adjust the collider boundaries. Hold the *Shift* key and drag the boundary dots on the sides of the Box Collider in the Scene view until you have something that looks like the next image. It will help to use the Orthographic (top, side) views to achieve this:

Side View

Perspective View

Now we will ensure that this is no ordinary collider! In the Inspector view for this object, check the **Is Trigger** checkbox on the **Box Collider** component.

Scripting for trigger collisions

Now that we have a trigger collider in place, we simply need to detect our player entering the trigger area (also sometimes referred to as a trigger *zone*). In the Project panel, click on the **Create** button, and create a new script in your chosen language of **C#** or **Javascript**.

Rename your new script **TriggerZone** and launch it in MonoDevelop. Our Trigger code will be applied to the parent **outPost** object, and is very simple, as all we need to do is:

- Detect the player
- Find the child object of the **outPost** named **door**
- Send a message to the door to call the `DoorCheck()` function

Let's begin by establishing an `OnTriggerEnter()` function in our script:

C#:

```
void OnTriggerEnter(Collider col){

}
```

Javascript:

```
function OnTriggerEnter(col : Collider){

}
```

This will look familiar as it works in a similar way to the `OnControllerColliderHit()` function we wrote earlier, but the information stored by the collision event is the particular `Collider` that the trigger collider has collided with or *intersected*. This is stored in a variable we have called `col` for simplicity.

From this we can check the object as before by using an `if` statement. Simply add the following to your `OnTriggerEnter()` function now:

C# and Javascript:

```
if(col.gameObject.tag == "Player"){
  transform.FindChild("door").SendMessage("DoorCheck");
}
```

Here we check the argument `col` as to whether the collider belongs to a game object with a tag `Player`. This tag was already present on the **First Person Controller** when we imported it as a prefab when we began working. Equally we could also use the Hierarchical name:

```
if(col.gameObject.name == "First Person Controller"){
```

But making use of the tag is quicker and will remain consistent should we rename our First Person Controller at any point.

When the `if` condition is met, we locate the `door` child object using the `transform.FindChild()` command—more efficient than `gameObject.Find()` as it only searches children of the object this script is attached to, where `gameObject.Find()` searches the entire Hierarchy. This is also useful as there may be other buildings in our scene with a door and we want to ensure that we are only sending the message to the door on the building whose trigger the player is currently stood within. Finally, `SendMessage()` is used as before to call the `DoorCheck()` function in the `DoorManager` script attached to the door.

Save your script in MonoDevelop and switch back to Unity now.

In Unity, attach your new **TriggerZone** script to the **outPost** object by dragging it from the Project panel and dropping it onto **outPost** in the Hierarchy.

Removing PlayerCollisions

Your new trigger is ready to use, but we should remove our previous approach in the **PlayerCollisions** script. You may keep the current state of **PlayerCollisions** in your Project for future reference, but currently, we no longer need it applied to the player. Select the **First Person Controller** in the Hierarchy and locate the **PlayerCollisions (script)** component. To remove the component, click the **Cog** icon to the right-hand side of the component and choose **Remove** from the pop-out menu that appears.

Okay, let's play! Choose **File | Save Scene** from the top menu and then click on the **Play** button and test your new trigger zone. Now the outPost door will open whenever the player enters the trigger zone, regardless of the direction they are facing—the ideal way to have the door open in our game. In development terms, we would call this an ideal approach because it does not rely on the player checking for an object it is interacting with; the outPost simply knows that if the player approaches then it must open its door.

Summary

In this chapter, we have explored three key methods for detecting interactions between objects in 3D games:

- Collision detection
- Ray casting
- Trigger collision detection

These three techniques have many individual uses, and they are key skills that you should expect to reuse in your future use of Unity.

In the next chapter, we'll make further use of triggers. We will create a collection game in which the player must find power cells in order to power a generator and unlock the outpost door, and write code to disallow entry to the outpost unless the generator is fully powered.

6
Collection, Inventory, and HUD

Working with a similar approach to the previous chapter, in this chapter we will be continuing our use of trigger collision detection, this time using it to pick up objects. We will then move on to look at creating parts of a 2D **Heads Up Display** (**HUD**) and how we can control these, as well as the environment, through code.

A **HUD** in video games varies between differing genres; in a racing game for example, the HUD would be elements such as your speed, position, remaining laps, and so on.

(Wipeout Pure © SCEE 2005)

In a first person shooter your HUD is more likely to be made up of elements such as health, ammunition, and inventory items.

(Half-Life 2: Episode Two © Valve Software 2007)

As we have already set up an outpost with an opening door, we will now restrict player access by making them find objects in order to open the door. By showing on-screen instructions when the player enters the outpost door's trigger zone, we will inform them that the door requires a power source to be opened. We will then add a 2D HUD of an empty power cell on the screen.

This will prompt the player to look for more power cells that we will scatter nearby, so as to charge up enough power to open the door. To signify charging within the 3D world, we will also add a model of a generator, positioned next to the door, with a meter displaying the current charge shown on it. Both this charge meter and the HUD will be controlled by an `Inventory` script containing arrays of different textures to show, depending upon how many power cells have been collected.

Finally, we will add a light above the door to the outpost, and switch this from red to green to signify unlocking to the player, when they have collected the amount of power cells required to charge the generator—and therefore power the door.

By creating this simple puzzle, you will learn how to:

- Collect objects with prefabs and triggers
- Count with integer variables
- Work with the `GUITexture` component to make a HUD
- Control on-screen text with the `GUIText` component
- Control in game textures and lights using scripting
- Create an inventory and controlling the HUD by using an array

Creating the power cell prefab

In this section, we will take the power cell model from the `Book Assets` folder that we imported previously, modify it in the **Scene** view, and turn it into a Unity prefab—a data template we can create instances or clones of. If you've worked with *Adobe Flash* before, then you might compare this idea to the *MovieClip* concept, wherein you can create many identical instances of a pre-built template during runtime, or modify individual instances post-creation.

Downloading, importing, and placing

To begin creating the puzzle, you'll need to locate the power cell assets within the `Book Assets` folder in the **Project** panel. You are provided with the following resources:

- A **powerCell** model in the `Models` folder
- Five texture files for the HUD of the power cell filling with charge, with names beginning **hud_charge,** in the **Book Assets** | **Textures** folder
- Five texture files to represent charging on a generator displayer panel, with names **meter_charge0** to **meter_charge4,** also in the **Book Assets** | **Textures** folder
- An audio clip named **cell_collected** to be played upon collection of a cell by the player, in the **Book Assets** | **Sounds** folder

Drag-and-drop the **powerCell** model from the `Models` folder in the **Project** panel onto the **Scene** view. Then hover your cursor over the **Scene** view and press *F* to focus the view on it. Your power cell may be placed at an arbitrary position—we will reposition it once we have finished making our prefab. Obviously, if you have dragged your **powerCell** into the scene and it is intersecting the floor, simply use the `Translate` tool (*W*) to move it to a position where you can see it well—remember you can always press *F* to re-focus the **Scene** view on your selected object.

Tagging the power cell

As we need to detect a collision with the `powerCell` object, we should give it a tag to help us identify the object in scripting that we will write shortly. Objects can be identified by their name in the **Hierarchy**, but tagging items of a similar type can be helpful for game mechanics such as collection. Click on the **Tag** drop-down menu, and at the bottom of the menu select **Add Tag**.

The **Inspector** panel then switches to display the **Tag Manager**. If you are not shown the list of tags immediately, simply expand this area by clicking the grey arrow to the left of the **Tags** title. In the next available **Element** slot, add a tag called **cell**, as shown in the following image:

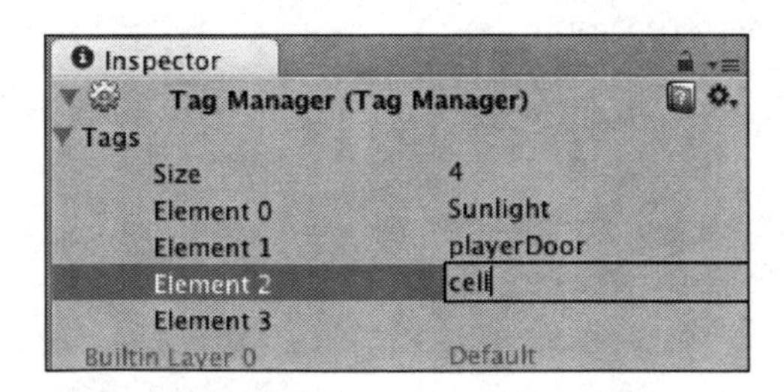

Press *Enter* to confirm the tag name, then reselect the **powerCell** object in the **Hierarchy** panel, and choose the new **cell** tag from the **Tag** drop-down menu at the top of the **Inspector** for that object.

Collider scaling and rotation

Now, we will prepare the **powerCell** as a prefab by applying components and settings that we'd like to feature on each instance of the **powerCell**.

Enlarging the power cell

We are creating something that the player is required to collect, so we should ensure that the object is of a reasonable size for the player to spot it in the game. As we have already looked at scaling objects in the **FBXImporter** for the asset, we'll take a look at simple resizing with the **Transform** component in the **Inspector**. With the **powerCell** object still selected in the **Hierarchy**, change all the **Scale** values in the **Transform** component of the **Inspector** to **1.6**.

Adding a trigger collider

Next, we should add a primitive collider to the **powerCell** to enable the player to interact with it. Go to **Component | Physics | Capsule Collider**. We have selected this type of collider as it is the closest shape to our **powerCell**. As we do not want the player to bump into this object while collecting it, we will set its collider to trigger mode. So, on the newly added **Capsule Collider** component, check the box to the right of the **Is Trigger** setting to enable it.

Collider scale

Any primitive collider placed onto an object in Unity needn't be of a particular size or position. Both of these properties can be adjusted using the *Shift* key with mouse-dragging of the boundary dots in the **Scene** view or through the **collider** component's settings on the **Inspector**. In the case of the **Capsule collider**, due to its shape, there are **Radius** and **Height** settings that will allow us to adjust the collider to better fit the **powerCell.** In the field for **Radius**, type in a value of **0.3**. This will still be larger than our **powerCell** but this is a good thing—it will allow the player to pick up this object more easily.

You'll likely notice that the orientation of this collider is wrong. To correct this, simply change the **Direction** value to be set to **X-axis**, as this is the direction that the model is oriented, length-wise. The other adjustable scale value in the case of a Capsule is the **Height**. The default value of **1** is longer than our **powerCell** but again this is fine as it will help us pick up the object—this is because the collider itself will intersect the player's collider before we are standing unnecessarily close to it. When you are done you should have a collider that looks like the following image:

Adding the Rigidbody

We will shortly be writing code to make our **powerCell** rotate. As such, we know that this object will not be static. As we learned with our animated door, moving objects in Unity should be given a **Rigidbody** component in order to save on performance, as the physics engine will be put in control of the object.

With the **powerCell** still selected in the **Hierarchy**, choose **Component | Physics | Rigidbody** from the top menu. In the **Rigidbody** component that is added, uncheck **Use Gravity** and check **Is Kinematic**.

Creating the power cell script

Now we will write a script to handle several actions we need to perform on our power cell during runtime:

- A rotation effect to make the power cell more noticeable to the player
- An `OnTriggerEnter()` function to detect the player collecting the power cell, which sends a message to update an `Inventory` script attached to the player

On the **Project** panel, select the **Scripts** folder to ensure that the script we are about to create gets created within that folder. Go to the **Create** button on the **Project** panel, and choose either **C#** or **JavaScript**. Rename the newly created file from **NewBehaviourScript** to **PowerCell**. Double-click its icon to launch it in the script editor.

Adding rotation

At the top of your new script above the opening of the `Update()` function, create a floating-point public variable called `rotationSpeed`, and set its value to `100.0` by adding the following line:

C#:

```
public float rotationSpeed = 100.0f;
```

Javascript:

```
var rotationSpeed : float = 100.0;
```

We will use this variable to define how quickly the **powerCell** object rotates. Because it is a public variable, we will also be able to adjust this value in the **Inspector** once the script is attached to the **powerCell**, so as a developer or if you are working with an artist, they can change this value after the script is written.

Within the `Update()` function, add the following command to rotate our **powerCell** around its **Y-axis** with a value equal to the `rotationSpeed` variable:

C#:

```
transform.Rotate(new Vector3(0,rotationSpeed * Time.deltaTime ,0));
```

Javascript:

```
transform.Rotate(Vector3(0,rotationSpeed * Time.deltaTime,0));
```

The `Rotate()` command expects a Vector3 (X, Y, Z) value, and we provide values of `0` for X and Z, feeding the `rotationSpeed` variable's value into the Y-axis. As we have written this command within the `Update()` function, it will be executed in every frame, and so the object would be rotated by 100 degrees in each frame. However, we have also multiplied by `Time.deltaTime`, which means that the rotation will not be frame rate specific—smoothing the motion to the way we need it to behave. In the script editor, go to **File | Save** in the script editor and then switch back to Unity.

To attach this script to our **powerCell** object, simply drag-and-drop the script from the **Project** panel onto the object's name in the **Hierarchy** panel, remembering to select the object to double-check it has been added in the **Inspector**.

Press the **Play** button at the top of the interface, and watch the **powerCell** in the **Scene** view (or Game view, if your **First Person Controller** camera is facing it) to make sure that the rotation works. If it does not work, then return to your script and check that you have not made any mistakes—double-check whether you have applied the script to the correct object. Remember to press **Play** again to end your testing before continuing.

Adding Trigger Collision Detection

Now we will detect whether this object's trigger collider is intersected by the **First Person Controller**'s collider. Return to your script, and beneath the closing right curly brace of the `Update()` function, add the following code:

C#:

```
void OnTriggerEnter(Collider col){
  if(col.gameObject.tag == "Player"){
    col.gameObject.SendMessage("CellPickup");
    Destroy(gameObject);
  }
}
```

Javascript:

```
function OnTriggerEnter(col : Collider){
  if(col.gameObject.tag == "Player"){
    col.gameObject.SendMessage("CellPickup");
    Destroy(gameObject);
  }
}
```

Here we see the familiar `OnTriggerEnter()` function that we used on the trigger zone for our outpost. We are establishing the function and then using an `if` statement to check for a collided with object tagged with the word `Player`.

If this condition is met, we send a message to the collided with object (the **First Person Controller**), calling a function we are yet to write called `CellPickup()`. We will write this into an `Inventory` script for the player in a moment.

Finally, the **powerCell** object is removed from the scene using the `Destroy()` command. Note here, that this is always the last command carried out in order to ensure that the object is not destroyed before other commands are carried out.

Save your script and switch back to Unity now. Press **Play** to test your game and walk the **First Person Controller** into the **powerCell**. You should be shown the following error in the Console bar at the bottom-left of the Unity editor interface:

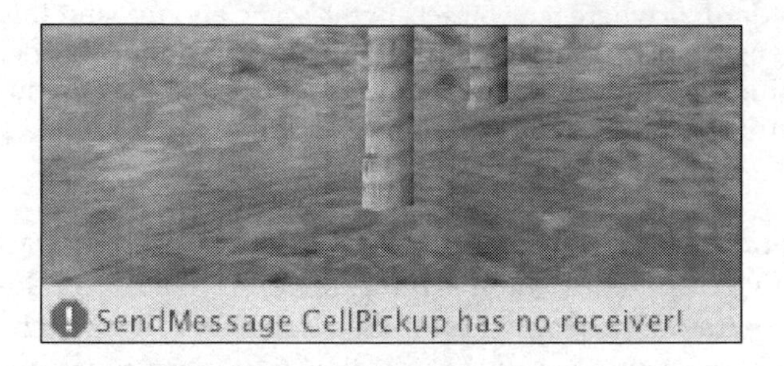

This is to be expected, as we have not written a script yet which contains a function named `CellPickup()` – so Unity warns us that although the code is correct, the sent message is not being received by any object. Now we will save this object as a prefab, before moving on to write an `Inventory` script, so that the player object has a place to store the information each time a new cell is collected.

Saving as a prefab

Now that the **powerCell** object is complete, we'll need to clone the object three times, giving us a total of four power cells. The best way to do this is with Unity's prefab system.

As we already have a folder named **Prefabs** to store our prefabs in, let's store it there. Drag-and-drop the **powerCell** object from the **Hierarchy** to the **Prefabs** folder in the **Project** panel now. This will save the object as a prefab and also means that the object in the **Hierarchy** is now an instance of that prefab. This means that any changes made to the prefab in the **Project** panel will be reflected in the instance in scene. Objects in the scene that are instances of prefabs or models in the project are shown in the **Hierarchy** panel with blue text, as opposed to the standard black text of scene-only objects.

Scattering power cells

Now that we have our power cell object stored as a prefab, when we duplicate the object in the scene, we are creating further instances of the prefab. Ensure that you still have the **powerCell** selected in the **Hierarchy** and then duplicate the object three times so that you have four in total; this can be done either by going to **Edit** | **Duplicate**, by using the keyboard shortcut *Command* + *D* (on Mac) or *Ctrl* + *D* (on PC), or by right-clicking the object in the **Hierarchy** and choosing **Duplicate** from the drop-down list.

When objects in the scene are duplicated, the duplicates are created at the same position—don't let this confuse you. Unity simply does this to standardize where new objects in the scene end up, and this is because when an object is duplicated, every setting is identical—including the position. Moreover, it is easier to remember that they are in the same position as the original and simply need moving from that position.

Now, select each of the four **powerCell** objects in the **Hierarchy** panel, and use the **Translate tool** (*W*) to reposition them around the `outPost` object. Remember that you can use the view gizmo in the top-right of the **Scene** view to switch from **Perspective** view to top, bottom, and side views. Ensure that you place the power cells at a height at which the player can pick them up; do not set them too high to reach or so low that it looks like the player's legs are collecting them!

Once you have placed the four power cells around the `outPost` object, your output should look similar to what's shown in the following image. Note that in the image, all four of the objects have been selected in the **Hierarchy** in order to help show their location and collider:

Writing the Player Inventory

In this next section, we will establish a script for the player that stores information on what the player has collected in the game. During the game we are creating, the player will need to collect power cells to power the door, and a box of matches to light a campfire.

The player is the best object upon which to store this information, as it will allow other objects to query this `Inventory` script for information—for example, later we will add a 3D model of a generator, which will display the current charge state of the door based upon information in this script.

Select the **Scripts** folder in the **Project** panel and click the **Create** button, then choose the relevant scripting language you have been working in. Rename your new script **Inventory**, and launch it in the script editor.

Saving the charge value

As we are establishing an inventory of collected items, we should make particular values of the inventory available to all scripts. The amount of power cells collected will be referred to as a variable called `charge` and to ensure it is easily available to other scripts, we will make it a `static` variable—a global variable easily accessible by other scripts. Begin by establishing the following public static variable in your script, as usual—for C# users this means after the opening of the class declaration, and for Javascript users this simply means at the top of your script:

C#:

```
public static int charge = 0;
```

Javascript:

```
static var charge : int = 0;
```

This integer (whole number) variable will be set by the script itself, and ordinarily we would not make variables set by the script `public` as this would show them in the **Inspector**. However, `static` variables are not shown in the **Inspector**, so this is not a concern. The advantage with using a `static` variable here is that the information stored in them is considered global, that is, globally accessible—this means that in other scripts we can refer to this value simply by stating, for example:

```
if(Inventory.charge == 4){
```

This will allow us to check the `charge` value in our **TriggerZone** script, as shown earlier, in order to deny entry to the `outpost` until the user has collected all four power cells. We will add this to the **TriggerZone** script once our basic `Inventory` script is completed.

Setting the variable start value

Ensure that when the scene loads, `charge` is set to `0` by setting it in a `Start()` function after your variables. When testing and reloading the same scene, variable values may be retained, and setting up a variable's default starting value in a `Start()` function such as the following will avoid that issue:

C#:

```
void Start () {
  charge = 0;
}
```

Javascript:

```
function Start () {
  charge = 0;
}
```

Audio feedback

In addition to the `charge` variable, also add the following public variable as a reference to a sound effect to play when the player collects a power cell:

C#:

```
public AudioClip collectSound;
```

Javascript:

```
var collectSound : AudioClip;
```

Adding the CellPickup() function

Now that our inventory has an integer to store how many power cells we have, we will write the `CellPickup()` function that is called through `SendMessage()` in our **PowerCell** script each time we pick up a new cell.

Add the following function to your script:

C#:

```
void CellPickup(){
  AudioSource.PlayClipAtPoint(collectSound, transform.position);
  charge++;
}
```

Javascript:

```
function CellPickup(){
  AudioSource.PlayClipAtPoint(collectSound, transform.position);
  charge++;
}
```

This function, called `SendMessage()` in the **PowerCell** script, will play our `collectSound` audio clip, and then add `1` to the value of charge. We are using `AudioSource.PlayClipAtPoint()` because there is no audio source on our player, and this command spawns a new temporary game object with an audio source on, plays the clip, and then removes itself. The second argument of `PlayClipAtPoint`—where we have stated `transform.position`—is the location at which we create this temporary sound object, and we are using `transform.position` (that is, the position of the player at that moment) as we simply need the sound to play near the player. This is also useful as it means the sound will fade if the player continues to walk away from the location of collection.

Save your script and switch back to Unity now.

Adding the Inventory to the player

Attach the script you have just written to the **First Person Controller** object by dragging it from the **Scripts** folder in the **Project** panel onto the object in the **Hierarchy**.

Your **First Person Controller** will now have an **Inventory (Script)** component, and you should notice that our public audio clip variable `collectSound` is shown in the **Inspector**. Expand the **Book Assets | Sounds** folder in the **Project** panel and drag-and-drop the **cell_collected** audio clip onto this variable to assign it.

Now let's test our script! As we have not set our trigger zone to be dependent upon the charge value yet, all you will see so far is that when collecting power cells, we no longer receive the **SendMessage has no receiver** error message, and you should also hear the power cell collection sound effect.

Press **Play** and make sure that this is working correctly; as always, press **Play** again to stop testing once you are done.

Restricting outpost access

Now that we have an inventory keeping track of the power cells that we have collected, let's set up a game mechanic that forces the player to collect all four power cells before they may be granted access to the `outpost`.

We will begin by achieving this in code, then add two visual indicators for the player.

Firstly, in the form of a 2D HUD—this will be in the form of a **GUITexture**, the texture which will be dependent upon the `charge` variable in the `Inventory` script:

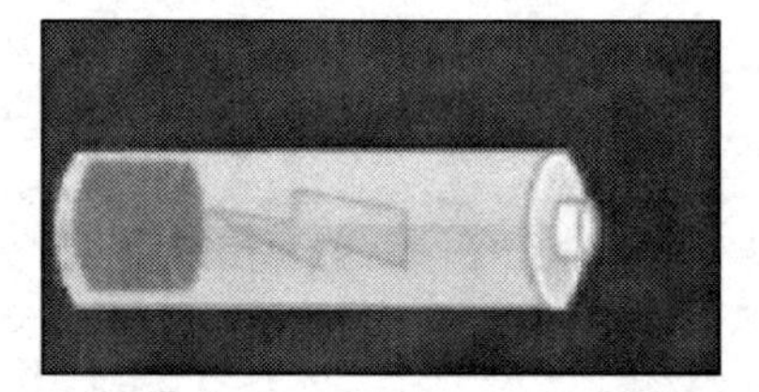

Secondly, in the form of a generator model that will be placed next to the `outPost` object's door, the texture of which will also be swapped depending upon the value of `charge`:

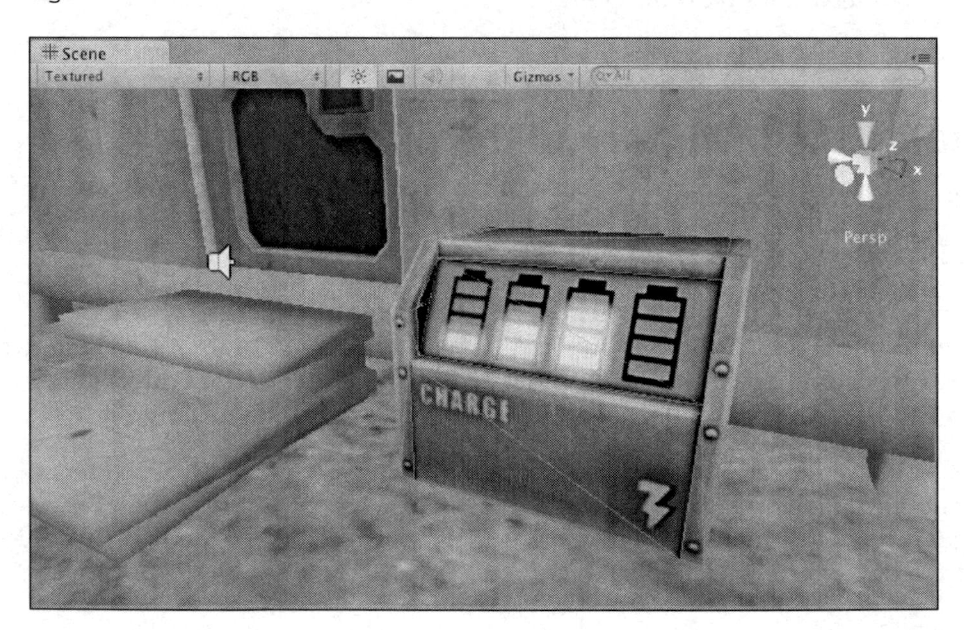

Restricting door access with a cell counter

In this section, we will write code into our inventory that checks that the player has enough power cells to open the door. We currently have a trigger zone in charge of opening the door, so we will amend this to query the value of charge in our new inventory, whenever the player enters the trigger.

First, let's ensure that our door only opens when the player has collected four power cells. Locate the **TriggerZone** script in the **Project** panel and launch it in MonoDevelop—or your chosen script editor.

In the `OnTriggerEnter()` function, add the following `if/else` statement inside the existing `if` statement that checks the current count in the `Inventory`, so that your code matches the one that is shown as follows:

C# and Javascript:

```
if(col.gameObject.tag == "Player"){
  if(Inventory.charge == 4){
    transform.FindChild("door").SendMessage("DoorCheck");
  }else{
  }
}
```

Here we are ensuring that our static `charge` variable in the `Inventory` class is equal to `4`—if it is, we call the same `DoorCheck()` as before, or if not, we prepare an `else` statement that we will use later to allow for warning the player that they do not have enough cells to power the door. We will add further code to this `else` statement later, once we have set up the visual HUD and GUItext objects we need to display such warnings.

Save your script now and return to Unity so that we can test this restriction. In Unity, press **Play** and ensure that the door does not open until you have collected all four power cells.

Displaying the power cell HUD

Now that we have our power cell collectables and inventory in place, we'll need to show the player a visual representation of what the player has collected. The textures imported with the `Book Assets` have been designed to clearly show that the player will need to collect four power cells to fully charge the door. By swapping an empty power cell texture image on-screen for one with `1` unit of charge, then for an image with `2` units of charge, and so on, we can create the illusion of a dynamic interface element. This is shown in the following image:

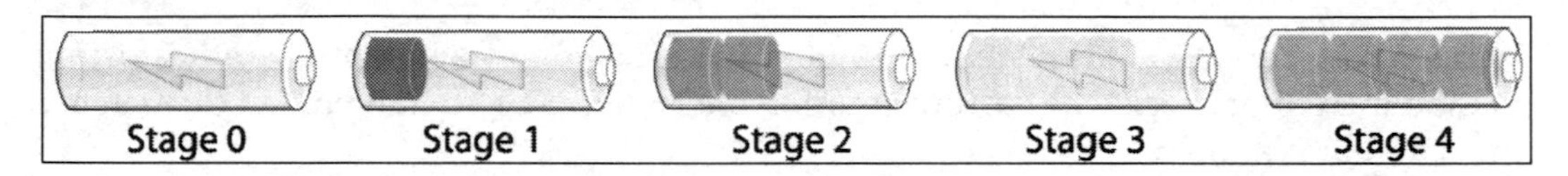

The **Book Assets | Textures** folder contains the five image files we need for this GUI Texture-based *HUD*—one of an empty power cell and the others of the four stages of charge. Created in Adobe Photoshop, these images have a transparent background, and are saved in a **PNG (Portable Network Graphics**) format. The PNG format was selected because it is compressed but still supports high quality **alpha channels**. Alpha channels are what many pieces of software refer to as the channel of the image (besides the usual red, green, and blue channels) that defines transparency in the image.

We will begin to create the GUI showing the progress of the cell charge, by adding the empty cell graphic to the scene using Unity's `GUITexture` component.

In the **Project** panel, expand the `Textures` folder within the `Book Assets` folder, and select the file named `hud_nocharge`.

In a differing approach to our normal method of dragging-and-dropping assets into the **Scene** view, we need to specifically create a new object with a `GUITexture` component and specify the **hud_nocharge** texture as the texture for that component to use.

Import settings for GUI textures

Before we set this texture file up as a `GUITexture` in our scene, we need to tell Unity how to interpret it. With the **hud_nocharge** texture selected in the **Project** panel, take a look at the import settings for this texture in the **Inspector** under the heading **Texture Importer**.

Begin by setting the **Texture Type** to **GUI**, instead of **Texture**. This will force Unity to display the texture at its original aspect when using it for a GUI element.

Creating the GUITexture object

While this is technically a three-step procedure, it can be done in a single step by selecting the texture to be used in the **Project** panel, and then going to **GameObject | Create Other | GUITexture** from the top menu. Do this now.

A new object will be created with a **GUITexture** component attached. In the **Inspector**, the **Pixel Inset Width** and **Height** fields will already be defined based on the chosen texture's dimensions.

Pixel Inset fields define the dimensions and display area of an object. Typically the `Width` and `Height` parameters should be specified to match the original dimensions of your texture file, and the **X** and **Y** values should be set to half of the dimensions. Again, this is set up for you when you create the object having selected the texture in the **Project** panel first. This approach will fill in the **X** and **Y** values of **Pixel Inset** and effectively create a centralized registration point to draw the texture from.

Setting a registration point

Using the standard centralized registration point is fine for the HUD element we are creating, as it does not need to be perfectly aligned with another element on the screen, but if you are used to working with 2D elements that position from a lower-left registration point this can be achieved by replacing **X** and **Y** values with **0**. However, it is important to understand that this affects the position of the **GUITexture** on screen. In the following example, the **GUITexture** is positioned in the same place, with differing registration points (**Pixel Inset X/Y** values):

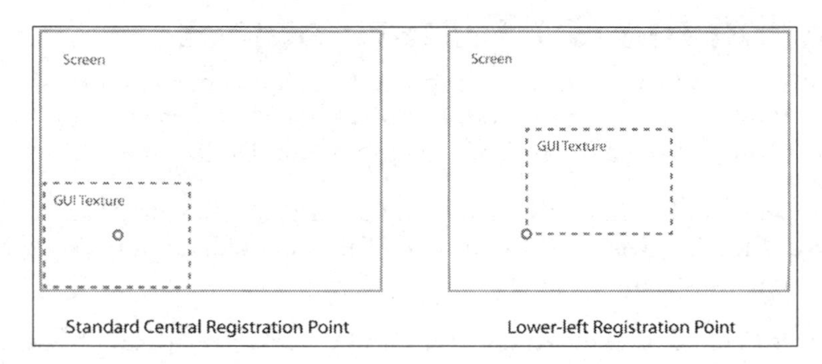

You should now see the Stage 0—empty power cell texture on screen, by default this is positioned at 0.5, 0.5 in the **Transform** position, so should be centered on the screen. Choose the object you have created in the **Hierarchy** panel by selecting **hud_nocharge**, and rename it to **PowerGUI** by pressing *Return* (Mac) or *F2* (PC).

By selecting the graphic you wish to use first, Unity knows that when it creates a new object with the **GUITexture** component, it should select that file as the texture and fill in dimensions of the texture also.

Also, when you select a graphic and create a **GUITexture** object using the top menu, the object created is named after your texture asset for the sake of convenience. Remember this, as it will help you find the object in the **Hierarchy** panel, post-creation.

Positioning the PowerGUI texture

When dealing with 2D elements, you will need to work in screen coordinates. Because they are 2D, these only operate in the X and Y axes—with the Z-axis used for layer priority between multiple GUITexture elements.

Screen coordinates go incrementally in decimals from 0 to 1, and in order to position the **PowerGUI** object where we want to see it (in the lower-left of the screen), we need to type values into the **X** and **Y** boxes of the **PowerGUI** object's **Transform** component. Fill in a value of **0.15** in **X** and **0.1** in **Y**.

You should now see the texture displayed on the **Game** view in the lower-left corner of the view.

You can also show 2D details in the **Scene** view by clicking on the **Game Overlay** button:

Scripting for texture swap

Now that we have several power cells to collect, and our inventory in place, we can use the `Inventory` script itself to control the texture property of the GUITexture HUD we just added.

To control this texture, along with the texture of the generator model shown previously, we can make use of an array in scripting.

Understanding arrays

Arrays are data containers that can contain many values. Try to think of them as a variable that contains many values or entries. The values in an array are organized by use of an **index**—a number of their entry into the array, much like the id of an entry in a database table. The number of items stored in an array is referred to as the **array length**. Basic arrays can be resized in the **Inspector**, using the `Size` parameter (we will make use of this shortly), but in code terms, they are read-only and cannot be resized through your script.

Declaring an array is similar to the declaration of a variable; it needs a name and a type. This is the same procedure as when declaring a variable, but in addition to the type, we also use square brackets to define it as an array. For example, if we wished to make an array of enemy game objects, we might write the following code snippet:

C#:

```
public GameObject[] enemies;
```

Javascript:

```
var enemies : GameObject[];
```

We could then set the size in the **Inspector**, and assign objects to the array. The following screenshot shows what it would look like in the **Inspector,** having filled in a **Size** (the length of the array) value of **3**:

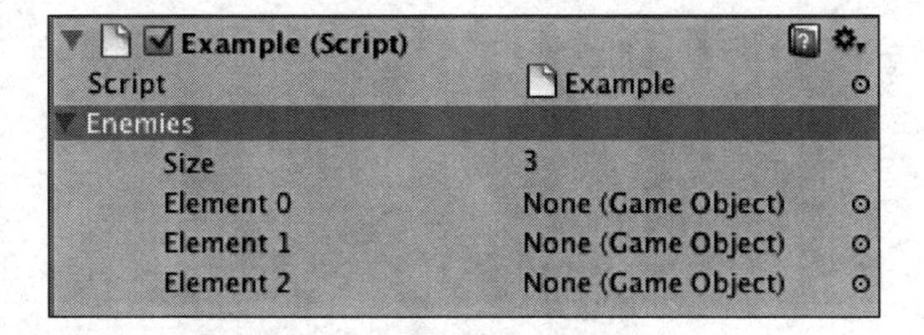

Drag-and-drop from the **Hierarchy** or **Project** panel could then be used to assign objects to these positions, but we can also use scripting to perform this task. Objects can be assigned to the array by stating a particular position within the array. For example if we wished to add a game object to the third position in the array, we would write something like this:

```
enemies[2] = gameObject;
```

Here, `gameObject` would ideally be a reference to a game object somewhere in the scene.

You should note that array indexes always begin at zero, so the third position is actually index number `2` in the previous example. If you attempt to add to an array an index that does not exist, Unity will give an error stating that the **Index is Out of Range**—meaning that it is not a number within the current length of the array.

Adding the HUD array

By creating an array of five textures—four states of charge, plus the original empty **hud_nocharge** texture—we can set the relevant texture on the HUD to a particular texture in our project depending on the current value of our `charge` variable. This means that whenever we pick up a power cell and increment `charge`, our HUD will automatically update!

Open the `Inventory` script now and place your cursor on a new line after the existing `collectSound` variable.

We will use an array for this task and a separate array to store the textures for our generator, so to keep these elements of our script separate, we'll add in comments to accompany them. Add the following code to your script:

C#:

```
// HUD
public Texture2D[] hudCharge;
public GUITexture chargeHudGUI;
```

Javascript:

```
// HUD
var hudCharge : Texture2D[];
var chargeHudGUI : GUITexture;
```

After our comment to remind us that this code handles the HUD, we have established a public array named `hudCharge` of type `Texture2D`, and then declared a public variable named `chargeHudGUI` of type `GUITexture`—we will use this to act as a reference to our **PowerGUI** object, so that our script can set the **texture** property of its **GUITexture** component to a different texture directly.

Save your script and return to Unity now.

Assigning textures to the array

Select the **First Person Controller** in the **Hierarchy**, in order to see the **Inventory (Script)** component in the **Inspector**. You will now see the **Hud Charge** and **Charge Hud GUI** listed beneath **Collect Sound**. Expand the **Hud Charge** array by clicking the grey arrow to the left of its name:

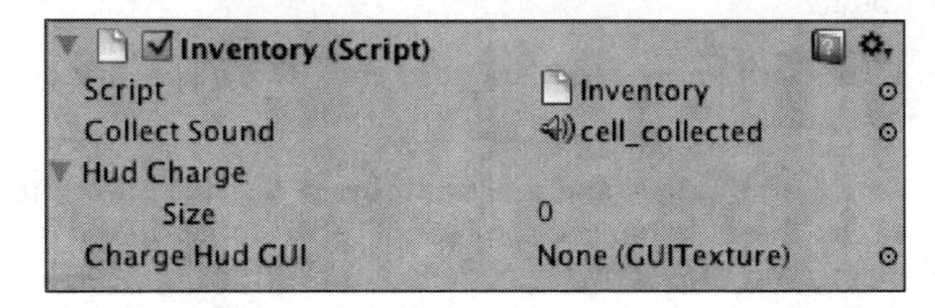

As the **Size** value defaults to **0**, no elements exist in the array. Set the **Size** value to **5** in the **Inspector**, and you will see **Element 0** to **Element 4** listed with their **Texture2D** type alongside them.

In the **Book Assets | Textures** folder you will find textures with names beginning **hud_charge**. Assign these textures to the array using drag-and-drop, remembering that **Element 0** should use **hud_nocharge** as its texture.

Next, assign the **PowerGUI** object in the **Hierachy** to the **Charge Hud GUI** variable so that your component looks like the screenshot shown as follows:

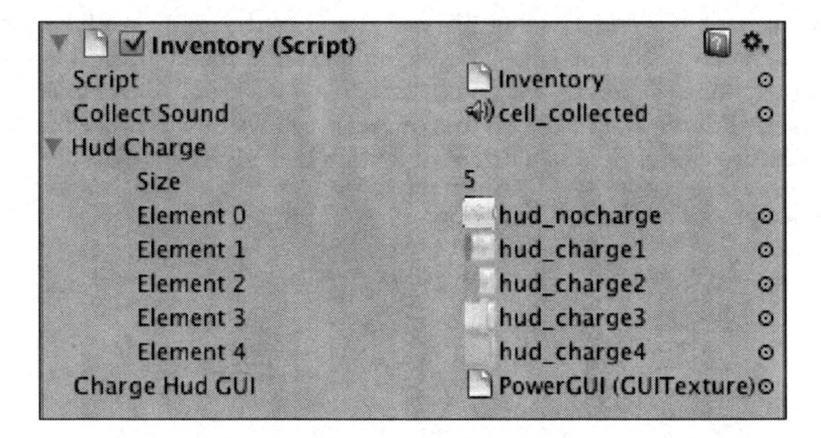

Now that our array is set up, let's return to the code and use the value of `charge` to choose a texture from the array for the **PowerGUI**.

Inside the `Inventory` script, add the following line to the existing `CellPickup()` function:

C# and Javascript:

```
chargeHudGUI.texture = hudCharge[charge];
```

Here we are addressing the GUITexture object (our **PowerGUI**) that is assigned to the `chargeHudGUI` variable, specifically its `texture` property. We are setting this to a particular texture in the `hudCharge` array. The particular index, and therefore the particular texture, is chosen by feeding in the value of the `charge` variable where we would ordinarily use a number—cool huh?

Save your script now and return to Unity.

Let's try it out! Press **Play** now and start collecting power cells you will see that your **PowerGUI** HUD now switches through each of the textures. Press **Play** again to stop testing.

Disabling the HUD for game start

Now that we have created the HUD, and have its increment based upon the Inventory, we should consider that when the game begins, we should not show the player the power cell HUD. This is too much of a clue as to what they need to do. Instead we should only display the HUD once the player attempts to enter the **outPost**.

Select the **PowerGUI** object in the **Hierarchy**, and disable the **GUITexture** component in the **Inspector** by un-checking the **checkbox** to the left of the component's title.

This disables the component, but we can use code to enable it again during the game. We should do this at two points during gameplay:

1. If the player walks into the trigger zone without having picked up any power cells.
2. When the player picks up a power cell without having entered the trigger zone.

We will work on the former situation first, where the player enters the trigger with no power cells. This is where the `else` statement of the `TriggerZone` script comes into play. Open the `TriggerZone` script now.

When the player first enters the trigger, but cannot open the door, they should be made aware that the door will not open without power. For this we will play a sound clip to show that door is currently locked without the generator to open it, and then enable the **PowerGUI** to show that there is an empty power cell to fill.

Above the opening of the `OnTriggerEnter()` function in your script, add a public variable for the door locked sound to be assigned to later:

C#:

```
public AudioClip lockedSound;
```

Javascript:

```
var lockedSound : AudioClip;
```

Next, place your cursor inside the `else` statement within the `OnTriggerEnter()` function that we created earlier, and place in the following line:

C# and Javascript:

```
transform.FindChild("door").audio.PlayOneShot(lockedSound);
col.gameObject.SendMessage("HUDon");
```

Here we are making use of two other objects—the `door` child object of the **outPost** parent object and the `Player` object (**First Person Controller**)—as this is the object stored in the `col.gameObject` reference. We make reference to the door using `FindChild()` as before and then use its `Audio Source` component to play our door locked sound. We then use `SendMessage()` to call a new function in the player object's **Inventory** that we will write shortly, called `HUDon()`.

This new function will simply check if the **PowerGUI** HUD is enabled, and if not, it will enable it by re-enabling the component. We are placing this function into the `Inventory` script because we already have a reference to the **PowerGUI** within that script.

Save your script now and re-open the `Inventory` script, or switch to the tab it is open in within the script editor.

Enabling the HUD during runtime

Within the Inventory, we should enable the HUD during runtime both when the player picks up their first power cell (if they have not tried to access the door) and when the player tries to enter the door without any power cells. We will deal with the latter first, as we have just created a call to a new function that we are calling from our **TriggerZone** script.

After the closing curly brace of the `CellPickup()` function, add the following function:

C#:

```
void HUDon(){
  if(!chargeHudGUI.enabled){
```

```
      chargeHudGUI.enabled = true;
    }
  }
```

Javascript:

```
  function HUDon(){
    if(!chargeHudGUI.enabled){
      chargeHudGUI.enabled = true;
    }
  }
```

This uses the reference to the **GUITexture** component on **PowerGUI** we have already set up, in the form of variable `chargeHudGUI`. The `if` statement here simply checks `if(!chargeHudGUI.enabled)`, the exclamation mark here meaning *not*. So we are checking if it is not enabled (or rather, if enabled is *false*), and then setting its enabled value to true.

Now let's take care of enabling the HUD when the player first picks up a power cell too. We know this is dealt with by our `CellPickup()` function, so we will simply call the new `HUDon()` function within `CellPickup()` too, rather than writing the same `if` statement again. Add the following function call to the start of your `CellPickup()` function:

C# and Javascript:

```
  HUDon();
```

By doing this, the same check is performed, when the player first picks up a power cell. Save your script now and switch back to Unity, so that we may test the toggling of the HUD in both of the aforementioned circumstances.

Before testing, select the **outPost** parent object, and assign the **door_locked** audio clip in the **Book Assets | Sounds** folder in the **Project** panel to the `Locked Sound` public variable in the **Trigger Zone (Script)** component.

Press **Play** to start testing and ensure that if you enter the trigger zone with no power cells, the HUD is enabled and locked door sound is played. Then restart testing (switch off **Play**, and press it once more) and this time, pick up a power cell without entering the trigger zone to ensure that the HUD is also enabled.

Once you have verified that this mechanic works properly, save your progress by choosing **File | Save Scene** from the top menu. Next we will visually link the HUD to the **outPost** model by adding a power generator to show the same charge.

Adding the power generator

In order to link the onscreen **PowerGUI** HUD with the **outpost** in the game, we will place a generator model into the game that displays its charge status to the player, in case they have not tried to enter the outpost and don't understand what the power cells they are collecting are intended for.

In the **Models** folder within **Book Assets** in the Project panel, find the **generator** model and drag it into the **Scene** view, placing it next to the **outPost**. Rotate this object by 180 degrees in the **Y** axis by typing **180** into the **Rotation Y** field of the **Transform** component on the **Inspector**.

Then use the **Translate** tool to position the generator to one side of the steps on the **outpost**, as if it is attached to the wall:

Now expand the parent **generator** object in the **Hierarchy** so that you can see the **chargeMeter** and **generator** child objects. Select the **generator** child object (see the following screenshot) and from the top menu go to **Component | Physics | Box Collider** in order to make sure that the player cannot walk through the generator:

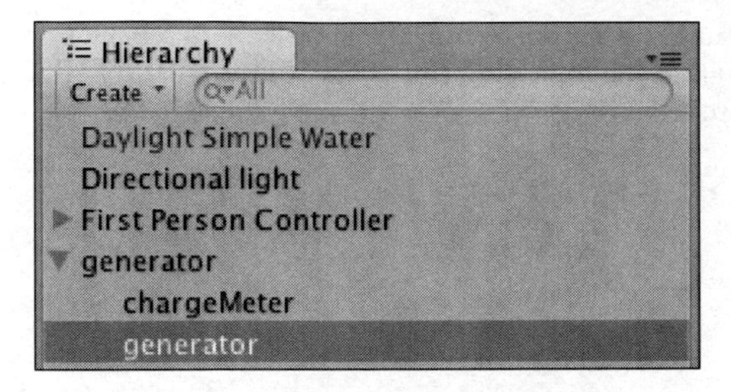

Now we will use the `Inventory` script to adjust the texture on the `chargeMeter` child object.

This object is a separate child object of the generator, as this will allow us to alter the texture applied to its material more easily:

We will begin by creating a reference to this **chargeMeter** in our `Inventory` script, and create another array in which to store the textures we will swap—again based upon the `charge` variable.

Launch the `Inventory` script once more or simply switch back to it if you still have it open, and add the following code beneath the existing HUD array and GUITexture reference:

C#:

```
// Generator
public Texture2D[] meterCharge;
public Renderer meter;
```

Javascript:

```
// Generator
var meterCharge : Texture2D[];
var meter : Renderer;
```

Here we have simply set up a new array of 2D textures and a `Renderer` component reference to which we will assign the **chargeMeter** child object, as it contains the `Mesh Renderer` component with the material to be swapped.

The 2D textures to be swapped will replace the entire **chargeMeter** panel, in a similar way to the PowerGUI, which replaces the entire texture to show a new status of charge:

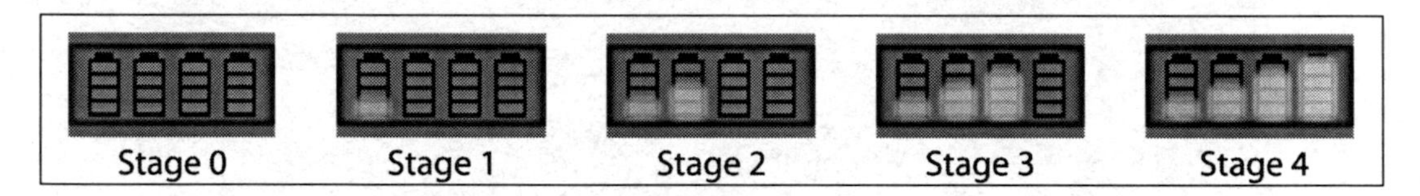

As before, we will resize the array to a length of **5** in the **Inspector**, and assign five textures from the **Book Assets | Textures** folder.

Before we assign these however, we will add the code that swaps the textures during runtime. In the `CellPickup()` function place the following line of code after the existing `chargeHudGUI.texture = hudCharge[charge];` line you already have:

C# and Javascript:

```
meter.material.mainTexture = meterCharge[charge];
```

Here we are using our reference to the **chargeMeter** object's renderer component, addressing the `material` applied to it, and that material's `mainTexture`.

We are setting the texture the material uses to a particular numbered texture assigned to the `meterCharge` array—which one depending again upon the number stored in the `charge` variable.

Save your script now and switch back to Unity. Select the **First Person Controller** to see the **Inventory(Script)** component in the **Inspector**.

Expand the newly added **Meter Charge** array by clicking the grey arrow to the left of its name and then resize the length of the array to a **Size** of **5**. You will then see **Element 0** to **4** as with the previous array we created.

Assign the five textures with names beginning **meter_charge** from the **Book Assets | Textures** folder in the **Project** panel to the array and then drag-and-drop the **chargeMeter** child object of the **generator** from the **Hierarchy** to the **Meter** variable, as shown in the following image:

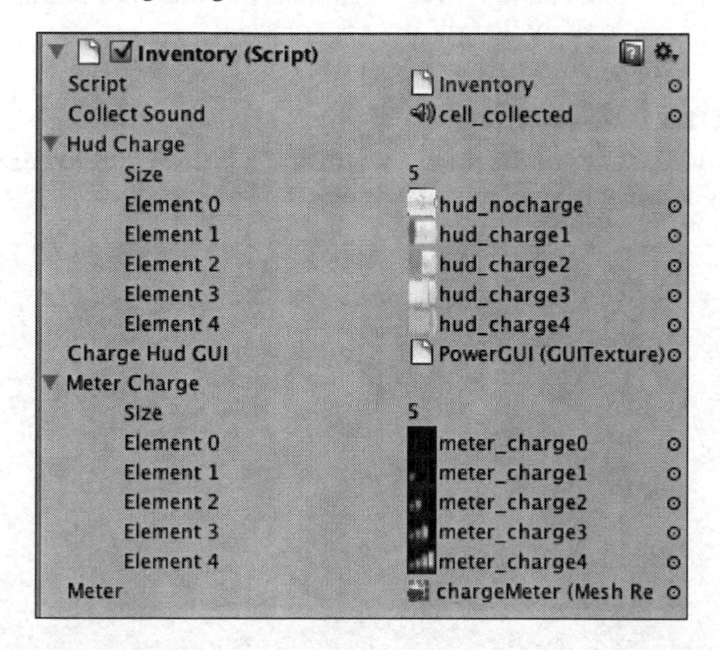

Now that our code is complete and the array and variables have been assigned, choose **File | Save Scene** from the top menu to save your progress.

Play test your game and observe that as you pick up power cells, the generator object's charge meter texture changes to display how many cells are currently held. Press **Play** again to finish testing.

Signifying door unlock

To complete the door generator charge game mechanic, we will signify to the player that they have unlocked the door. They will already know the door is unlocked as the door will open, but to add polish to this mechanic, we will perform the following tasks when the player enters the door trigger with all four power cells for the first time:

- Remove the PowerGUI HUD—as the player no longer needs to know that they picked up the power cells, and removing this will effectively seem like they have used the cells—a familiar gameplay response for the player.
- Change the color of a light. We will add to the door that changes color from red to green, to show that the door is unlocked.

Adding the locked light

To help display the status of the door, we will add a **Point Light** to our scene, beneath the light panel part of the **outPost** object, above its door:

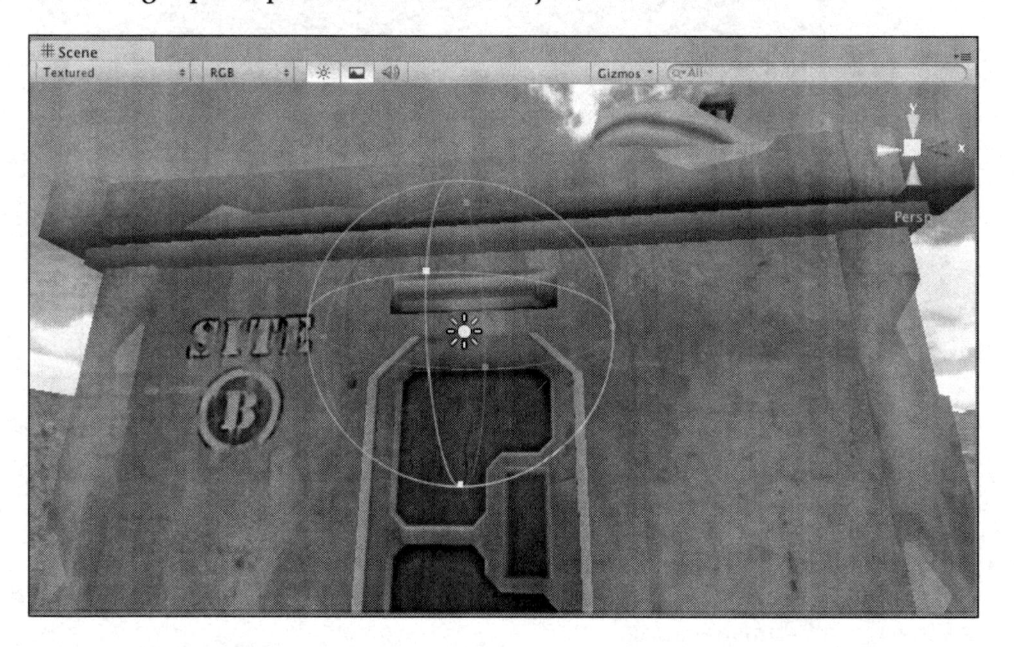

Before we add the light, position your view of the **Scene** view, so that it resembles the one shown in the following screenshot. This will assist you in positioning the light that we are about to add, as when introducing a new object from the **Create** menu, Unity will create it at the center of your view.

Begin by clicking the **Create** button on the **Hierarchy** panel, and choose **Point Light** from the drop-down list. Rename the **Point Light** in the **Hierarchy** to **Door Light**. Before you position the light, setting the intensity and range will help you see the light itself, so in the **Light** component of your new **Door Light**, set the **Range** value to **1.2**, and the **Color** to **red** by clicking the **Color** block and choosing a shade of red in the Color Picker that appears. Finally set the **Intensity** value to **3**, making this a light that's short range but bright.

Now make use of the **Translate** tool (*W*) to reposition the light as shown in the previous screenshot.

Switching lights and removing the HUD

Open the **TriggerZone** script now, and create a `Light` data type reference at the top of script:

C#:

```
public Light doorLight;
```

Javascript:

```
var doorLight : Light;
```

Now we have a reference we can use to address the light—we will assign our **Door Light** to this public variable later. Next, locate the `if` statement within the main `if` of the `OnTriggerEnter()` function:

```
if(Inventory.charge == 4){
  transform.FindChild("door").SendMessage("DoorCheck");
}
```

This is the part of the script where the door is opened, once the player has picked up four power cells. So it is here that we should check whether the player is opening the door for the first time and perform the two actions listed earlier.

After the following line of code:

```
transform.FindChild("door").SendMessage("DoorCheck");
```

Nest the following `if` statement:

C# and Javascript:

```
if(GameObject.Find("PowerGUI")){
  Destroy(GameObject.Find("PowerGUI"));
  doorLight.color = Color.green;
}
```

This `if` statement is within the main `if` statement that confirms that the player has picked up four power cells, so we can assume that this is the right time to remove the **PowerGUI** object.

Therefore, this `if` statement's condition is checking that the **PowerGUI** actually exists by using `GameObject.Find()` to check for its name within the **Hierarchy**. If it does not exist, then there is no need to perform its three commands. If it does exist, we remove it using the `Destroy()` command, again using `GameObject.Find()` to refer to it, and we then change the color of the light from red to green, by using our `doorLight` variable; we set it using the shortcut **green** of the `Color` class.

Shortcuts exist for all main colors, but you can also specify colors using RGB (Red, Green, Blue) values. For more information on this, see the Unity script reference at: `http://unity3d.com/support/documentation/ScriptReference/Color.html`.

Save your script now and switch back to Unity. As we have created a public variable to represent our **Door Light** object, we should assign this reference before continuing. Select the **outPost** object in the **Hierarchy** and check that your **Door Light** public variable has appeared on the **Trigger Zone (Script)** component in the **Inspector**. Drag-and-drop the **Door Light** object from the **Hierarchy** onto this exposed variable now.

Finally, press **Play** and play through the collection of all four power cells to charge the door generator. Once you have all four, approach the **outPost** door and it should now open, the **PowerGUI** HUD disappearing and the **Door Light** color changing to green:

Press **Play** again to stop testing, and then save your progress in Unity by choosing **File | Save Scene** from the top menu.

Next we will move on to give an additional hint to the player in the form of on-screen text. We will do this in the style of classic adventure games by using inner monologue, with which the player character effectively speaks to the player.

Hints for the player

What if the player, less intrigued by the scattered power cells than the outpost door itself, goes up to the door and tries to enter? It may seem a little cold to simply switch on the empty power cell by itself—having the player character speak to the player will be a much friendlier approach to the gameplay experience.

At this stage it is also important to think about phrasing; while we could easily say *Collect some power cells*! it is much better in gameplay terms to provide hints by using inner monologue, by having the player character's thoughts relayed to the player, for example, "The door's generator seems to be low on power..."

To show the text on screen we will use Unity's **GUI Text** component. There are various ways of displaying text on screen, but this is the simplest. We will go on to cover other methods, such as the Unity `GUI scripting` class later in this book.

Writing on screen with GUIText

Whenever you need to write text on the screen in 2D, the most straightforward way to do this is by using a **GUIText** component, though it can also be done by using the `GUI scripting` class.

By creating a new **GUIText** object from the top menus, you will get a new object with both Transform and **GUIText** components. Create one of these now by choosing **GUI Text** from the **Hierarchy Create** button, or by choosing **GameObject | Create Other | GUIText** from the top menu. You should now have a new object in the **Hierarchy** called **GUI Text** and some 2D text on the screen that says **Gui Text**.

Rename this object in the **Hierarchy** by selecting it and pressing *Return* (Mac) or *F2* (PC). Name it `TextHintGUI`.

With the object still selected in the **Hierarchy** panel, look at the **GUIText** component itself in the **Inspector**. As we want to inform the player, we'll leave the current position in the **Transform** component as **0.5** in **X** and **Y**—**GUIText** positioning works in screen coordinates also, so **0.5** in both axes places this in the middle of the screen, demanding the player's attention.

In addition to the positioning of the entire element, **GUIText** also features an **Alignment** parameter that works in a similar manner to justification settings in word processing software. Click the Up/Down arrows to the right of the **Anchor** parameter and choose **middle center,** then set the **Alignment** to **center**—this means that text will spread out from the center of the screen rather than starting in the center and then filling out to the right.

While you can easily type in what you wish this **GUIText** element to say into the **Text** property in the **Inspector**—we are instead going to control what it says dynamically, using scripting.

Scripting for GUIText control

Our first hint about the door needing more power should be displayed when the player attempts entry without enough power cells collected. For this reason, it makes sense to place our code into the `TriggerZone` script, and call a function within a script on the **TextHintGUI** object we just created. Open the `TriggerZone` script now, and add the following reference to the top of your script, beneath the `lockedSound` variable:

C#:

```
public GUIText textHints;
```

Javascript:

```
var textHints : GUIText;
```

The `GUIText` data type of this variable will allow us to drag-and-drop our **TextHintGUI** object onto this `public` variable to refer to the **GUIText** component directly. We have used this data type in order to save storing a reference to the entire game object.

Now, to make use of this reference, we will send this object a message. Add the following line to your `else` statement within the `OnTriggerEnter()` function:

C# and Javascript:

```
textHints.SendMessage("ShowHint", "This door seems locked.. maybe that
generator needs power...");
```

Here we are using `SendMessage()` yet again to call upon a function within our **TextHintGUI** object. This time we are calling a function with an argument; this is shown by the fact that not only the name of the function `ShowHint` is within the `SendMessage()` parentheses, but also additional information, separated by a comma. This additional information is an argument of the function we are calling. Declared as a string data type, we will use this in order to set what our **TextHintGUI** writes on the screen. Save your script now and return to Unity, and we will create the script that contains this function.

Before we write the receiver of this message, let's assign our new public reference to our `GUIText`—select the **outPost** object in the **Hierarchy** to view the **Trigger Zone (script)** component. Then drag-and-drop the **TextHintGUI** object from the **Hierarchy** to the `Text Hints` variable.

Now let's create the receiver of this message, a script to attach to the **TextHintGUI** object. Create a new script file by first selecting the **Scripts** folder in the **Project** panel. From the drop-down menu of the **Create** button, select your chosen script language as usual.

Rename the **NewBehaviourScript** this creates to **TextHints**, and then double-click its icon to launch it. We will begin by establishing the `ShowHint()` function that our `TriggerZone` script is calling. Add the following function to your new script now:

C#:

```
void ShowHint(string message){
  guiText.text = message;
  if(!guiText.enabled){ guiText.enabled = true; }
}
```

Javascript:

```
function ShowHint(message : String){
  guiText.text = message;
  if(!guiText.enabled){ guiText.enabled = true; }
}
```

Here we have added a function with a single argument (`message`) to receive the sentence from the `SendMessage()` function. We begin by setting the `text` parameter of this object's `guiText` component to the sentence string received by our argument.

We then perform a similar task to that which we did for the **PowerGUI**—checking if the component is enabled, and if not, enabling it.

So let's try this out. Save your script and return to Unity. Assign your new **TextHints** script to the **TextHintGUI** object in the **Hierarchy** using drag-and-drop from the **Project** panel, and then remove the default words **Gui Text** in the `text` parameter of the **GUIText** component for that object, so that nothing is written on the game view.

Now press **Play** at the top of the interface and you should notice that when you enter the trigger zone of the outpost, text appears on the screen with the sentence that we specified in the `SendMessage()` call to our `TextHints` script.

This is all well and good, but we need that text to go away too, right? Press **Play** to stop testing and return to your `TextHints` script.

Add the following variable to the top of your script:

C#:

```
float timer = 0.0f;
```

Javascript:

```
private var timer : float = 0.0;
```

This variable is exactly what it looks like—a timer. We will use the `Update()` function to increment this timer as soon as the **GUIText** component is enabled. When the timer reaches a certain value, we will disable it again, to stop the text obscuring the player's view.

Add the following code to your `Update()` function now:

C# and Javascript:

```
if(guiText.enabled){
  timer += Time.deltaTime;

  if(timer >=4){
    guiText.enabled = false;
    timer = 0.0f;
  }
}
```

Here we make use of the property `guiText.enabled` in order to check whether the component has been enabled by our `ShowHint()` function.

Another way of creating this would have been to establish a Boolean (true/false) variable and set this to true when `ShowHint()` enables the **GUIText** component and check its value in the first `if` statement we just added, but given that we can just as easily check the status of the component, it is best to keep things simple.

If the `guiText.enabled` property is true, we increment our `timer` variable by adding the value of `Time.deltaTime` to it—a property that counts time in a non-framerate specific manner.

After the timer increment, we have added a nested `if` statement that checks for our timer reaching `4` seconds. If it does, we disable the component by setting its `enabled` property to `false`, and reset our timer to `0.0` so that it may start counting again, the next time we use a hint.

Avoiding missed values

We always use the **more than or equal to** (>=) in an instance like the timer condition we just added because sometimes our `if` statement can miss the specific frame on which the value equals exactly `4.0`, and therefore, would not meet the condition. This is why you should not use `==` to check a value that is incrementing beyond a defined value in an `Update()` function.

Save your script and return to Unity now. Play your game and you should notice that when you enter the trigger zone of the **outPost**, the following sentence will appear on the screen:

"This door seems locked.. maybe that generator needs power..."

Now, thanks to our `timer`, the sentence should disappear after 4 seconds. Press **Play** again to stop testing. As usual, if you are receiving error messages at the bottom of the Unity interface, double-click on them and return to your script to fix them, checking it against the code in the book.

Save your scene in Unity now, by choosing **File | Save Scene** from the top menu.

Adjusting hints to show progress

Now that we have a hint shown on-screen, we should ensure that the player knows that if they have started collecting power cells, they are doing what the game requires of them. To do this, we should display a different message if they have begun to collect power cells, but do not have all four yet. Return to the `TriggerZone` script now to add this.

Place the following `else if` statement into the existing `if/else` statement within the `OnTriggerEnter()` function, remembering that any `else if` must be placed before the `else`:

C# and Javascript:

```
else if(Inventory.charge > 0 && Inventory.charge < 4){
  textHints.SendMessage("ShowHint",
    "This door won't budge..
     guess it needs fully charging
     - maybe more power cells will help...");
  transform.FindChild("door").audio.PlayOneShot(lockedSound);
}
```

Here we are checking if they have more than 0 cells, but less than all four. If these conditions are met, we are using `SendMessage()` to call the `ShowHint()` function on the **TextHintGUI** object, and playing the locked sound again as audial feedback.

Your full `if` / `else if` / `else` structure should now look as follows:

C# and Javascript:

```
if(Inventory.charge == 4){
  transform.FindChild("door").SendMessage("DoorCheck");
}else if(Inventory.charge > 0 && Inventory.charge < 4){
  textHints.SendMessage("ShowHint",
    "This door won't budge.. guess it needs fully charging
     - maybe more power cells will help...");
  transform.FindChild("door").audio.PlayOneShot(lockedSound);
}else{
  transform.FindChild("door").audio.PlayOneShot(lockedSound);
  col.gameObject.SendMessage("HUDon");
  textHints.SendMessage("ShowHint",
    "This door seems locked.. maybe that generator needs power...");
}
```

This gives variation to the feedback that the player is given and should help them feel as if they are progressing, that the game is responding to their actions. **Save** your script now and return to Unity. **Play** test your game and pick up a single power cell, then try to enter the door. You will be greeted with the sentence we just added!

To give our text hints a little more polish, we'll complete this mechanic by adding a font to the **GUIText** component on **TextHintGUI**.

Go to **File** | **Save** in Unity to update your progress.

Using fonts

When utilizing fonts in any Unity project, they must be imported as an asset in the same way as any other piece of media you include. This can be done by simply adding any **TTF (TrueType font)** or **OTF (OpenType font)** file to your project's `Assets` folder in Finder (Mac) or Windows Explorer (PC) or in Unity itself by going to **Assets** | **Import New Asset**.

For this example, we will download a commercially free-to-use font from `www.dafont.com`, which is a website of free-to-use fonts that is very useful when starting out in any kind of typographic design.

Be aware that some font websites provide fonts that are free to use, but have a restriction stating that you should not use them in projects that could make the font extractable. This is not a problem with Unity as all fonts are converted to textures in the exported build of the game.

Visit this site now and download a font whose look you like, and which is easy-to-read. Remember, you'll be using this font to give instructions, so anything overly complex will be counterintuitive to the player's experience. If you would like to use the same font as the examples in this book, then search for a font called `Sugo`. Download the font, unzip it, and then use the methods just outlined to import the `Sugo.otf` file as an asset in your project.

Once this is in your project, find the font inside the **Project** panel and select it. Fonts in Unity are represented by a capital letter `A` icon.

Next, to choose this as the font to use for the **TextHintGUI**, begin by selecting that object in the **Hierarchy** panel and then drag-and-drop your font from the **Project** panel onto the **Font** parameter of the **GUIText** component in the **Inspector**.

Finally, let's scale this **GUIText** component's **Font Size** to **25** by typing the value into the `Font Size` parameter on the component. If this is not set, Unity uses the default size of the font, you can check what this is by selecting the font in the **Project** panel and looking at the **True Type Font Importer** settings—usually this is set to `16`.

Now press the **Play** button, and test your game. Your text hints to the player will now display in your custom font—bear in mind that some fonts will look different in size at the same font size values, so if you are not happy with a size of 25 for your chosen font, feel free to return to the **Font Size** parameter of the **GUIText** component, and adjust to your preference.

Summary

In this chapter, we have successfully created and solved a game scenario. By assessing what your player will expect to see in the game you present to them—outside of your prior knowledge of its workings—you can best devise the approach you must take as a developer.

Try to consider each new element in your game from the player's perspective—play existing games, think about real-world scenarios, and most of all, assume no prior knowledge from the player (even of existing game traditions, as they may be new to gaming.) The most intuitive gameplay is always found in games that strike a balance between the difficulties in achieving the tasks set and properly equipping the player for the task in terms of information and familiarity with the intended approach. Appropriate feedback for the player is crucial here, be it visual or audio based—always consider what feedback the player has at all times when designing any game.

Now that we have explored a basic game scenario and looked at how we can build and control GUI elements, in the next chapter, we'll move on to solve another game scenario, a shooting gallery that will force the player to knock down all targets consecutively in order to win one of the power cells.

7
Instantiation and Rigidbodies

In this chapter, we'll expand upon the two crucial concepts in 3D game design that we looked at in *Chapter 2*. We will take the abstracted game mechanic of aiming and 'throwing' objects and put it into the context of our island game by creating a coconut shy (or coconut *shie*) game that the player can interact with.

When you first begin to build game scenes, you'll realize that not all of the objects required within any given scene would be present at the start of the game. This is true of a wide variety of game genres, like puzzle games; consider the blocks in *Tetris* for example. In *Tetris*, puzzle pieces of random shapes are created or *instantiated* at the top of the screen at set intervals because they cannot all be stored at the top of the screen infinitely.

Now take our island exploration game as another example. In this chapter, we'll be taking a look at instantiation and rigid body physics by creating a simple coconut shy game, but as with the prototype we made earlier, the coconut projectiles that will be thrown will not be present in the game scene when it begins. This is where instantiation comes in again. By specifying a game object stored as a prefab—as well as a position and rotation—objects can be created while the game is being played. This will allow us to create a new coconut whenever the player presses the fire button.

In order to tie this new part of our game into the game as it stands, we'll be removing one of the power cells from the game. We will give the player a chance to win the final power cell they require to enter the outpost by playing the coconut shy game. As part of this book's assets, you are provided with a model of the coconut shy shack and separate targets that we will place into it. You will need to create a prefab of a coconut and control the animation of the targets within the game through scripting—detecting collisions between the coconuts and the targets.

As the targets provided to you have a 'knocked down' and 'reset' animation, we will also write in script to ensure that the targets are reset after being knocked down for a defined number of seconds. This means that the player may win this mini-game only if all of the three targets are down at the same time. This adds an extra layer of difficulty for the player that can be adjusted by altering the number of seconds the targets need to stay down for.

In this chapter, you will learn about:

- Using Rigidbodies and prefabs in combination with the Instantiate command
- Providing feedback for the player
- Triggering animations as a result of collisions
- Counting scores with Integer variables
- Linking two separate game mechanics—the outpost and the coconut shy game

Utilizing instantiation

In this section, we will again make use of the `Instantiate()` command that we saw in our earlier prototype. This is a concept that is used in many games to create projectiles, collectable objects, and even characters, such as enemies.

Instantiation is simply a method of creating (also referred to as **spawning**) objects from a template (a prefab in Unity terms) during runtime—as opposed to those objects present in the scene when it loads.

The approach when using instantiation will usually take this form:

- Create the game object (that you wish to instantiate in your scene) manually, adding components as necessary
- Save this newly created game object as a prefab
- Delete the original object from the scene so that it is only stored as a prefab asset
- Write a script that involves the Instantiate() command, attach it to an active game object in the scene, and set the prefab you created as the object that the Instantiate() command creates by using a public variable to assign the prefab asset to the script

The prefab instance of our object—in this case a coconut—must be instantiated at a particular position within the 3D world, and when assigning the position of an object to be instantiated, you must consider where your object will be created and whether this position can be inherited from an existing object.

For example, when creating our coconut prefabs, we'll be creating them at a point in the world defined by an empty game object, which will be a child of our player character's **Main Camera** child object. As a result, we can say that it will be created in local space—not in the same place every time, but relative to where our player character is standing and facing, because it is the camera which defines where our character is effectively 'looking'.

This decision helps us to decide where to write our code, that is, which object to attach a script to. By attaching a script to the empty object that represents the position where the coconuts must be created, we can simply use dot syntax and reference `transform.position` as the position for the `Instantiate()` command. By doing this, the object created inherits the position of the empty object's **Transform** component because this is what the script is attached to. This can be done for rotation too—giving the newly spawned object a rotation that matches the empty parent object.

This would give us an `Instantiate()` command that looked like this:

```
Instantiate(myPrefab, transform.position, transform.rotation);
```

Where `myPrefab` is a reference to a game object stored as a prefab. We will put this into practice later in the chapter, but first let's take a look at rigid body physics and its importance in games.

Rigidbodies

Physics engines give games a means of simulating realism in physical terms, and they are a feature in almost all game engines either natively or as a plugin. Unity utilizes the **Nvidia PhysX** physics engine, a precise modern physics engine that is used in many commercial games in the industry. Having a physics engine means that not only are physical reactions such as weight and gravity possible, but realistic responses to friction, torque, and mass-based impact are also possible.

Forces

The influence of the physics engine on objects is known as **force**, and forces can be applied in a variety of ways through components or scripting. In order to apply physics forces, a game object must be what is known as a Rigidbody object.

The Rigidbody component

In order to invoke the physics engine on an object in Unity—making it a rigidbody object, you must give it a Rigidbody component. This simply tells Unity to apply the physics engine to a particular object—you need not apply it to an entire scene. It simply works in the background.

Having added a **Rigidbody** component, you would see settings for it in the **Inspector** in the same way as any other object, as shown here:

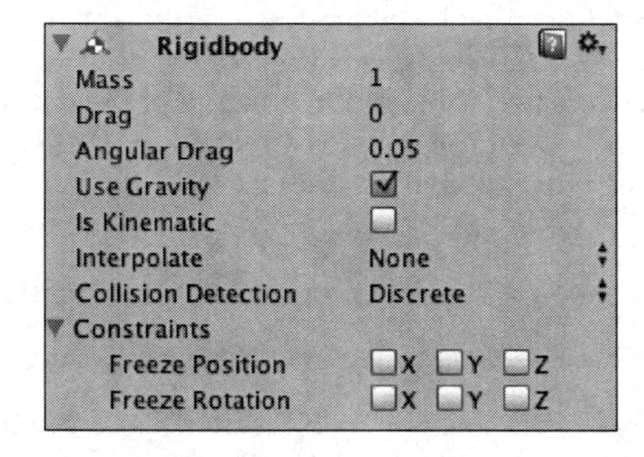

Rigidbody components have the following parameters to be adjusted or controlled through scripting:

- **Mass**: The weight of the object in kilograms. Bear in mind that setting mass on a variety of different Rigidbodies will make them behave realistically. For example, a heavy object hitting a lighter object will cause the light object to be repelled further.
- **Drag**: Drag, as in real terms, is the amount of air resistance affecting an object as it moves. The higher the value, the quicker the object will slow when simply affected by air.
- **Angular Drag**: Similar to the previous parameter, but angular drag affects the rotational velocity, defining how much air affects the object, slowing it to a rotational halt.
- **Use Gravity**: Does exactly as it states. It is a setting that determines whether the rigid body object will be affected by gravity or not. With this option disabled, the object will still be affected by forces and impacts from the physics engine and will react accordingly, but as if in zero gravity.

There are also global settings for gravity in Unity—simply choose **Edit | Project Settings | Physics** and expand the **Gravity** settings by clicking the grey arrow next to its title. This allows you to define the amount and direction—note that the default is **Y-9.81** as the acceleration of gravity is 9.81 m/s2.

- **Is Kinematic**: This option allows you to have a Rigidbody object that is not affected by the physics engine. For example, if you wished to have an object repel a Rigidbody with gravity on, such as the trigger in a pinball machine hitting the ball—but without the impact causing the trigger to be affected—then you might use this setting. This setting should be used for any moving object that you wish to control the movement of through scripting or animation, as it means that a) the physics engine is aware of the moving object and therefore will save on performance by not needing to compensate for its updated position and b) the object can still interact with other moving objects without being controlled by the forces of physics directly.
- **Interpolate/Extrapolate**: This setting can be used if your rigidbody objects are jittering. Interpolation and extrapolation can be chosen in order to smoothen the transform movement, based on the previous frame or predicted next frame respectively. Interpolate is useful when creating characters that use a Rigidbody and Extrapolate is useful for fast moving objects, to ensure that collisions are detectable with other objects.
- **Constraints**: This can be used to lock objects so that they do not move or rotate as a result of forces applied by the physics engine. This is particularly useful for objects that need to use physics but stay upright or in a certain position, such as objects in 2D games that must be locked in the Z (depth) axis for example.

Making the mini-game

To put into practice what we have just looked at, we'll create a coconut shy game that ties into our access to the outpost. By playing the game, the player will be rewarded with the final power cell they require to charge the outpost door.

As we have already set up the power charge element of the game, we simply need to remove one of the power cells from the existing scene, leaving the player with one less.

Select one of the objects called **powerCell** in the **Hierarchy** panel, and then remove it with *Command* + *Backspace* (Mac) or *Delete* (PC).

Creating the coconut prefab

Now let's begin our mini-game by creating the projectile object to be thrown, that is, the coconut.

Go to **GameObject** | **Create Other** | **Sphere**.

This creates a new sphere primitive object in the scene. While it may not be created close enough to the front of the editor viewport, you can easily zoom to it by hovering your cursor over the **Scene** view and pressing *F* (focus) on the keyboard. Rename this object from **Sphere** to **Coconut**, by selecting the object in the **Hierarchy** and pressing *Return* (Mac) or *F2* (PC) and retyping.

Next, we'll make this object a more appropriate size and shape for a coconut by scaling down and subtly extending its size in the Z-axis. In the **Transform** component of the **Inspector** for the **Coconut** object, change the **Scale** value for **X** and **Z** to **0.5** and **Y** to **0.6**.

The texture to be used on the coconut was downloaded with the rest of the book assets. Named **coconutTexture**, this asset can be found inside the **Book Assets** | **Textures** folder in the Project panel.

In addition to this file, you should also be able to find the following resources:

- A **crosshair** texture in **Book Assets** | **Textures**
- Two audio clips with names beginning with **target** in **Book Assets** | **Sounds** and one named **coconut_throw** also in this folder
- Two 3D models—one called **coconutShy**, and the other called **target** in **Book Assets** | **Models**

Creating the textured coconut

To apply the coconut texture, we'll need to make a new material to apply it to. On the **Project** panel, select the **Materials** folder we made earlier, and then click on the **Create** button, and from the drop-down menu that appears, select **Material**. Rename the new material you have made to **Coconut Skin** by pressing *Return* (Mac) or *F2* (PC), and retyping.

To apply the texture to this material, simply drag-and-drop the **coconutTexture** from the **Book Assets** | **Textures** folder in the **Project** panel over to the empty square to the right of the **Base (RGB)** setting for the new material in the **Inspector**. When this is done, you should see a preview of the material in the window in the lower half of the **Inspector**.

Remember that this preview simply demonstrates the material's appearance on a sphere; this is the default for Unity material previews and has nothing to do with the fact that we will be using this on a spherical object. You can change what primitive shape the preview window demonstrates the texture with by clicking on the first of the two buttons to the right of the **Preview** heading; the other button toggles lighting and shadow in the preview.

Next, we need to apply the **Coconut Skin** material to the **Coconut** game object that we have placed into our scene. In order to do this, simply drag-and-drop the material from the **Project** window to either the object's name in the **Hierarchy** or to the object itself in the **Scene** view now.

Adding physics

Now because our **Coconut** game object needs to behave realistically, we'll need to add a Rigidbody component in order to invoke the physics engine for this object. Select the object in the **Hierarchy** and go to **Component | Physics | Rigidbody**.

This adds the Rigidbody component that will apply gravity. As a result, when the player throws the object forward it will fall over time as we would expect it to in real life. The default settings of the Rigidbody component can be left unadjusted; you will not need to change them on this occasion.

We can test that the coconut falls and rolls (if you have created it over land! If not you can move it with the Translate tool) now by pressing the **Play** button and watching the object in the **Scene** or **Game** views. When you are satisfied, press the **Play** button again to stop testing.

Saving as a prefab

Now that our coconut game object is complete, we'll need to store it as a prefab in our project, in order to ensure that we can instantiate it using code as many times as we like, rather than simply having a single object.

To save your object as a prefab simply drag-and-drop an object from the Hierarchy panel anywhere into the Project panel. Drag the **Coconut** object we just made and drop it onto the **Prefabs** folder we made earlier to save it in there as a prefab.

Your prefab will be named the same as the originating object and you should see the text for the object in the Hierarchy turn blue, to signify that this is now linked to a prefab asset. The advantage of this is that any instance of a prefab can be adjusted by altering settings on the prefab version in the Project panel. For example, if your game scene had several buildings in it, all based on a prefab, changing a value for an attached script or swapping a material could be done to the prefab in order to effect all instances in the scene.

Now that your **Coconut** is stored as a prefab, delete the original instance from the scene by selecting it in the **Hierarchy** and pressing *Command* + *Backspace* (Mac) or *Delete* (PC).

Creating the Launcher object

As we are going to allow our player to throw the coconut prefab we have just created, we will need two things—a script to handle the instantiation and an empty game object to act as a reference point for the position to create the coconut objects in the world.

In real life when we throw a ball (over-arm style), it comes into view at the side of our head, as our arm comes forward to release the ball. Therefore, we should position an object just outside of our player's field of view and make sure it will follow wherever they look. As the player view is handled by the **Main Camera** child object of the **First Person Controller**, making an empty object a child of this will allow it to move with the camera, as its position and rotation will always be relative to its parent - so as the camera looks around, so will the launcher child object.

Begin by creating a new empty game object in your scene by going to **GameObject | Create Empty - shortcut** *Ctrl-Shift*-N (PC) or *Command-Shift-N* (Mac). Select this new object in the **Hierarchy** (by default, it will be called **GameObject**) and rename it **Launcher**. Next, expand the **First Person Controller** object by clicking on the gray arrow to the left of its name in the **Hierarchy**. Now drag-and-drop the **Launcher** object onto the **Main Camera** so that it becomes a child of it—you will know that you have done this correctly if a gray arrow appears next to the **Main Camera**, indicating that it can be expanded to show its child objects.

The **Launcher** object is indented beneath it, as shown here:

Making this object a child of the **Main Camera** will mean that it moves and rotates with its parent, but it still needs repositioning. Begin by resetting the position of the **Launcher** object in the **Transform** component in the **Inspector**. This can be done either by replacing all values with **0**, or to save time, you can use the Cog button to the right of the component in order to reset by selecting **Reset Position** from the pop-out menu.

The Cog button acts as a quick way of performing operations on components, and you'll see one next to each component in the Inspector. The Cog menu is also useful as it allows you to remove components that you no longer need or which have been added by mistake.

Setting the **Launcher** child object to a position of **0** means it is exactly in the center of - or in the same position as—its parent. Of course, this is not what we want, but it is a good starting point to go from. We must not leave the launcher in this position for two reasons:

- When coconuts are thrown, they would appear to be coming out of the player's head, and this would look rather odd.
- When you are instantiating objects, you must ensure that they are not created at a position where their collider will intersect with another collider, because this forces the physics engine to push the colliders apart and could interrupt the force applied when throwing the coconut; instantiating at the position of the camera would likely mean the coconut's sphere collider would overlap the **Character controller** collider of the **First Person Controller**.

To avoid this, we simply need to move the **Launcher** object forward and to the right of its current position. In the **Transform** component, set the **X** and **Z** positions to a value of **1**. Your **Launcher** object should now be positioned at the point where you would expect to release an object thrown by the player character's right arm, as shown in the following image. Remember that to see this object, you'll need the Translate tool selected (*W*) in order to see its axis handles. In the following image, the Main Camera object has also been selected in order to help show perspective:

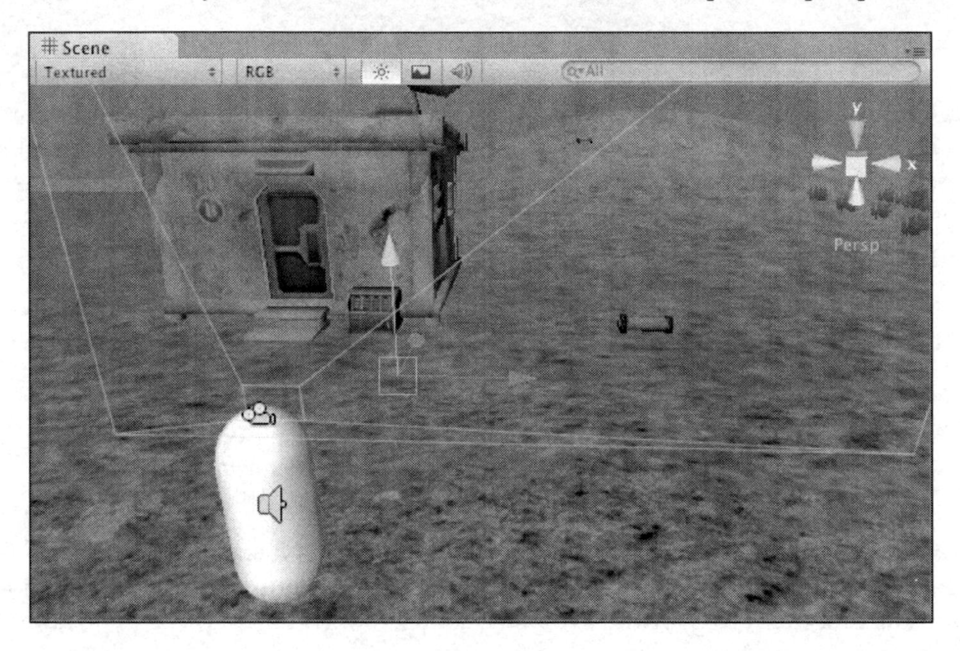

Finally, in order to make the thrown coconut head towards the center of our view, we need to rotate the launcher slightly around the Y-axis. Under **Y** axis **Rotation** in the **Transform** component, add a value of **352** to rotate it by 8 degrees.

Next, we'll need to script the instantiation of the coconut and its propulsion when the player presses the fire button.

Scripting to throw coconuts

As we need to launch coconuts when the player presses fire, we'll need to check whether a key is being pressed—tied to an input in Unity—each frame. Keys and mouse axes/buttons are tied to default named inputs in the Unity **Input Manager**, but these can be changed at your leisure by going to **Edit** | **Project Settings** | **Input**. Do this now, then expand the **Axes** by clicking the gray arrow to the left of it, and then finally expand the axis entry called **Fire1**.

The three crucial fields to observe here are the **Name** parameter, the **Positive** parameter, and the **Alt Positive** parameter. We will be addressing this axis by its name, and the **Positive** and **Alt Positive** are the actual keys themselves to look out for. New axes can be created by simply increasing the **Size** value at the top of the **Input Manager**—resulting in a new input being added, which you can then customize.

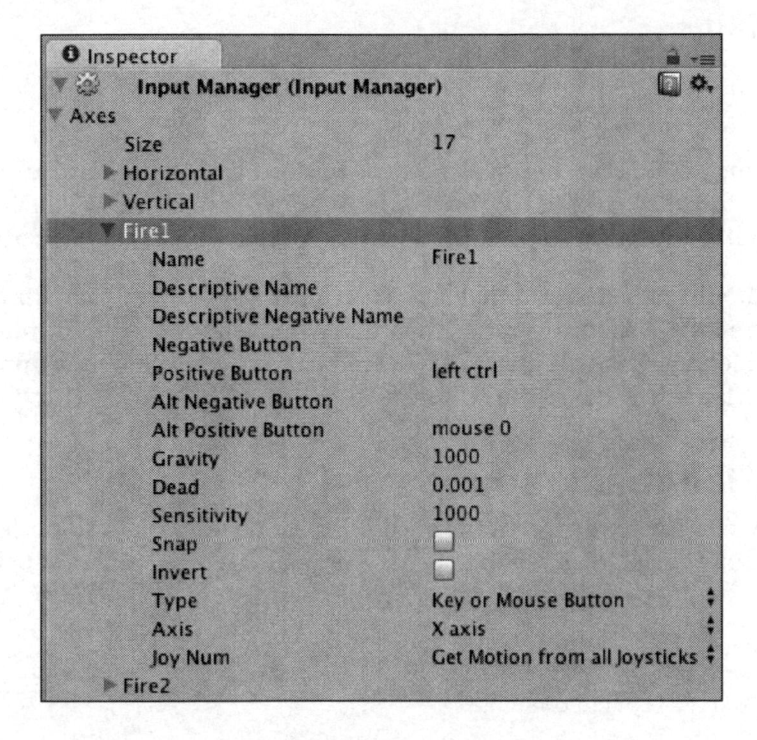

For the player to launch coconuts at the targets—which we'll place into our scene later—they must have a script that implements two key steps:

- Instantiation of the **Coconut** object to be thrown upon **Fire1** button press
- Assigning a velocity to the Rigidbody component to propel the coconut forward, as soon as it has been created

In order to achieve this, select the **Scripts** folder in the **Project** panel and then create a new C# or Javascript file from the **Create** button on the same panel. Rename the **New Behaviour Script** to **CoconutThrower** by pressing *Return* (Mac) or *F2* (PC), then launch this in the script editor by double-clicking its icon.

Checking for player input

Given that we need to listen for player key presses each frame, we need to write our code for the launcher inside the `Update()` function. Move the closing right curly brace } of this function down by a few lines, and then add the following `if` statement to listen for the `Fire1` key-press, just as we did in our prototype earlier:

C# and Javascript:

```
if(Input.GetButtonDown("Fire1")){
}
```

This checks the `Input` class and waits for the buttons tied to the **Fire1** input (*Left Ctrl* key and left mouse button) to be pressed. Into this `if` statement, we'll need to place actions we'd like the script to perform when the player presses either button.

Firstly, we should play a sound that acts as an audio-based feedback for throwing. If we were creating a shooting game, then this would likely be the sound of the gun being fired. However, in this instance, we simply have a subtle whooshing sound to represent the launch of the coconut.

Playing feedback sound

We'll need a variable to represent the audio clip we need to play, so place the following public variable above the opening of the `Update()` function before we continue:

C#:

```
public AudioClip throwSound;
```

Javascript:

```
var throwSound : AudioClip;
```

This creates a public variable, which means we will be able to assign the actual audio clip to this variable using the **Inspector** once we're finished writing this script.

Now, let's set up the playing of this audio clip inside our `if` statement. After the opening curly brace, add the following line:

C# and Javascript:

```
audio.PlayOneShot(throwSound);
```

This will play the sound as the player presses the **Fire1** button. Let's test this out now—save your script and return to Unity.

Assign this script to the **Launcher** child object in the Hierarchy by dragging it from the Project panel to this object.

Before we test, you will need to assign an audio clip to the exposed **Throw Sound** public variable—do this now by dragging the clip named **coconut_throw** from the **Book Assets | Sounds** to this variable in the newly added **Coconut Thrower (Script)** component of **Launcher**.

Finally, add an **Audio Source** component to the **Launcher** by selecting it in the Hierarchy and choosing **Component | Audio | Audio Source** from the top menu. Press Play now and tap the *Left Ctrl* key or click the *Left Mouse Button*—you should hear the throwing sound we have assigned.

Instantiating the coconut

Next, we need to instantiate (aka create, or spawn) the actual coconut itself, also within the current `if` statement. Switch back to the script editor now or re-launch the **CoconutThrower** script if you have closed it.

Given that we have created the coconut and saved it as a prefab, we should establish another public variable so that we can assign our prefab to a variable in the **Inspector** later. Below the last public variable we just placed in, add another:

C#:

```
public Rigidbody coconutPrefab;
```

Javascript:

```
var coconutPrefab: Rigidbody;
```

This adds a public variable with a data type of `Rigidbody`. Although our coconut is stored as a prefab asset, we'll be creating a game object with a Rigidbody component in our scene when we instantiate it, hence the data type. This ensures that we cannot drag a non-Rigidbody object to this variable in the **Inspector**. By strictly data typing to Rigidbody, this also means that if we wish to address the Rigidbody component of this object, then we wouldn't need to use the `GetComponent()` command to select the Rigidbody component first—we can simply write code that speaks directly to the Rigidbody class when referring to this variable name.

Now, inside the `if` statement in `Update()`, place the following line below the existing audio line:

C#:

```
Rigidbody newCoconut = Instantiate(coconutPrefab,
  transform.position, transform.rotation) as Rigidbody;
```

Javascript:

```
var newCoconut : Rigidbody = Instantiate(coconutPrefab,
  transform.position, transform.rotation);
```

Here, we establish a local variable called `newCoconut`—it is said to be local because it is declared within the `Update()` function, and so is not accessible outside of this function. Into this variable, we are passing the creation (Instantiation) of a new `Rigidbody` object—and therefore we set that as the data type.

Remember that the three parameters of an `Instantiate()` function are the object, position, and rotation-in that order. You'll see that we have used the public variable `coconutPrefab` in order to create an instance of our prefab and then inherited the position and rotation from the `transform` component of the object this script will be attached to—the **Launcher** object.

Let's check our progress now in Unity—save your script now and switch back. Select the **Launcher** child object of **Main Camera** in the Hierarchy and you will now see that there is a new public variable called **Coconut Prefab** that needs assigning. Drag-and-drop the **Coconut** prefab from the **Prefabs** folder to this variable now to assign it.

Press **Play** at the top of the interface now to test your game. Each time you press the *Fire1* button you should now be creating a new instance of your Coconut prefab—causing objects named **Coconut (Clone)** to appear in the Hierarchy.

However, the coconuts aren't going anywhere! At this point you will feel the need, the need for speed so let's add some **Velocity** to our coconuts! Press **Play** again to stop testing and return to your **CoconutThrower** script in the script editor.

Naming instances

Whenever you create objects during runtime with `Instantiate()`, Unity takes the name of the prefab and follows it with the text "(Clone)" when naming new instances. As this is rather a clunky name to reference in code—which we will need to do for our targets later—we can simply name the instances that are created by adding the following line beneath the one we just added:

C# and Javascript:

```
newCoconut.name = "coconut";
```

Here, we have simply used the variable name we created, which refers to the new instance of the prefab, used dot syntax to address the `name` parameter, and a single equals symbol to set it.

Assigning velocity

While this variable will create an instance of our coconut, our script is not yet complete, as we need to assign a velocity to the newly created coconut too. Otherwise, as we just saw, any coconuts will simply be created and fall to the ground. In general terms, velocity is regarded as a speed plus a direction; we will begin by addressing the former.

To allow us to adjust the speed of the thrown coconut, we can create another public variable above the `Update()` function. In order to give us precision, we'll make this variable a float data type, allowing us to type in a value with a decimal place if we wish. Place the following code below the last public variable named **coconutPrefab**, which we made earlier:

C#:

```
public float throwSpeed = 30.0f;
```

Javascript:

```
var throwSpeed: float = 30.0;
```

Now, beneath the `Instantiate()` and `name = "coconut";` lines in your `if` statement, add the following line:

C# and Javascript:

```
newCoconut.velocity = transform.forward * throwSpeed;
```

Here, we are referencing the newly instantiated Rigidbody object—`newCoconut` by its variable name, then using dot syntax to address the Rigidbody class's `velocity` property.

We have set the direction we need to throw by using `transform.forward`, as this command simply references the forward facing direction of the launcher's **transform** component, giving us its local direction without having to utilize the `transformDirection` command we looked at in our game prototype at the start of this book. Using `transform.forward` is a shortcut to saying `(0,0,1)`, so using this by itself would only repel our coconut by `1` in the Z axis. Instead this is multiplied by our `throwSpeed` to give our Rigidbody coconut a velocity.

Let's throw some coconuts! **Save** your script in the script editor now and switch back to Unity. Press **Play** and try firing coconuts again; this time they should be thrown forward in the direction you are facing, which is the direction **Launcher** inherits from the **Main Camera**.

Let's continue to improve our script by adding some development safeguards—once you are done playing with your new coconut throwing mechanic, stop Play mode and return to the script editor.

Adding development safeguards

In this section we will look at a few examples of ways we can ensure that our code does not cause problems for:

- Our development
- The game itself

We have just created a mechanic in which the player character can throw coconuts. However, we need to ensure a number of things in order for this mechanic to not cause any problems before we continue:

- We need to make sure that the coconut prefab we are throwing is a Rigidbody because the velocity we are setting refers to this class, so we will add a safeguard in the code for this.
- We should ensure that collisions never occur between the player character and the coconuts—we will look at two methods of doing this, through code and by using Layers and the Collision matrix in Unity.
- Finally, we have an audio clip that plays when the character throws, so we should ensure that the object this script is assigned to has an audio source component attached.

Ensuring component presence

When developing you will often need to ensure that an object has a component attached to it before addressing properties or commands relating to that component. In this instance, we are creating our coconut as a Rigidbody object—so we already know that the prefab assigned to the instantiate command will be a Rigidbody—otherwise this would have caused an exception (error) in the script when testing.

However, in order to show how to ensure that a component exists, we will briefly look at the following safeguard in order to help you learn how to add a component if it is not already present.

For example, with our instantiated coconut, we could check the new instance's variable `newCoconut` for a Rigidbody component by saying:

```
if(newCoconut.rigidbody == null) {
  newCoconut.AddComponent(Rigidbody);
}
```

Here we are saying that if there is no Rigidbody attached to this variable instance (if it is `null`), then add a component of that type.

> We would say "no Rigidbody" in this case by comparing with null, because simply placing an exclamation mark in front of the statement inside the `if` condition will not work outside of checking the status of objects. For example, this practice can be used to check if a String type variable has been assigned a value, which would not work when using an exclamation mark.
>
> As we have already prepared our prefab with a Rigidbody, we do not need to do it in this case, but it is a useful technique to be aware of.

Safeguarding collisions

While we have set up our **Launcher** in a position that is away from the player character's collider (the Controller Collider)—we should still ensure that the coconut itself never actually collides with the player. This can be done in two different ways in Unity: Using ignore collision code, or placing objects on layers that do not interact. We will look at both techniques to ensure that you are best equipped in your future development.

Using IgnoreCollision() code

To force objects in our game to not interact with one another via code, we can include the following piece of code in order to safeguard against instantiating new coconuts that accidentally intersect with our player's collider.

This can be done using the `IgnoreCollision()` command of the `Physics` class. This command typically takes three arguments:

```
IgnoreCollision(Collider A, Collider B, whether to ignore or not);
```

As a result, we simply need to feed it the two colliders that we do not want the physics engine to react to, and set the third parameter to `true`.

Add the following line to your CoconutThrower script, beneath the last line (newCoconut.velocity...) you added previously:

C# and Javascript:

```
Physics.IgnoreCollision(transform.root.collider,
  newCoconut.collider, true);
```

Here we are finding the player character's collider by using `transform.root`—this simply finds the ultimate parent object of any objects that the **Launcher** is attached to. While the **Launcher** is a child of the **Main Camera** object, the camera itself does not have a collider. So, we really want to find the object it is attached to—**First Person Controller**, which we find by using `transform.root`.

Then we simply pass in the variable name `newCoconut`, which represents our newly instantiated coconut. For both the parameters, we use the dot syntax to refer to the `collider` component.

Here we needed to find the ultimate parent of these objects, but if you are only referring to the parent of an object, you may address it using `transform.parent`.

Ignoring collisions with layers

In addition to the `Physics` class `IgnoreCollision()` command, we can also make use of the **Layers** built into Unity in order to tell the physics engine which objects should not collide with one another. By placing objects onto opposing layers and deselecting them within the **Physics** settings **Layer Collision Matrix**, we are telling Unity not to register collisions with objects added to those layers.

Let's begin by creating two new layers. Open the **Tag Manager** by going to **Edit | Project Settings | Tags**. Beneath the existing **Tags** in your project you will see the list of in-built layers, and beneath that **User Layers**:

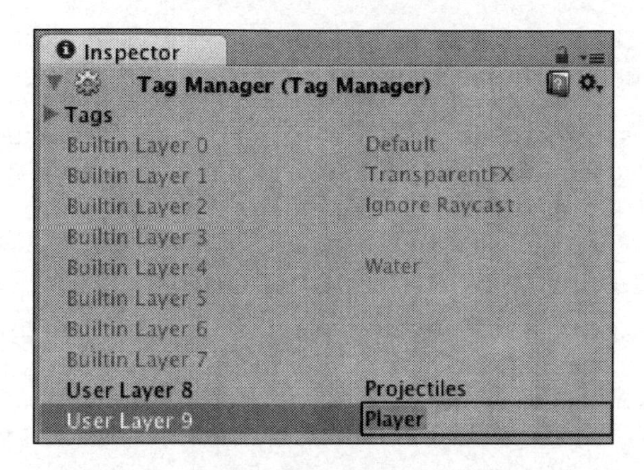

Add two new layers, one for **Projectiles** and another for **Player** as shown in the image. Simply press *Return* to confirm.

Next, to adjust the configuration of how these layers interact, go to **Edit | Project Settings | Physics**. Expand the settings for **Layer Collision Matrix** at the bottom, and deselect where your two new layers intersect:

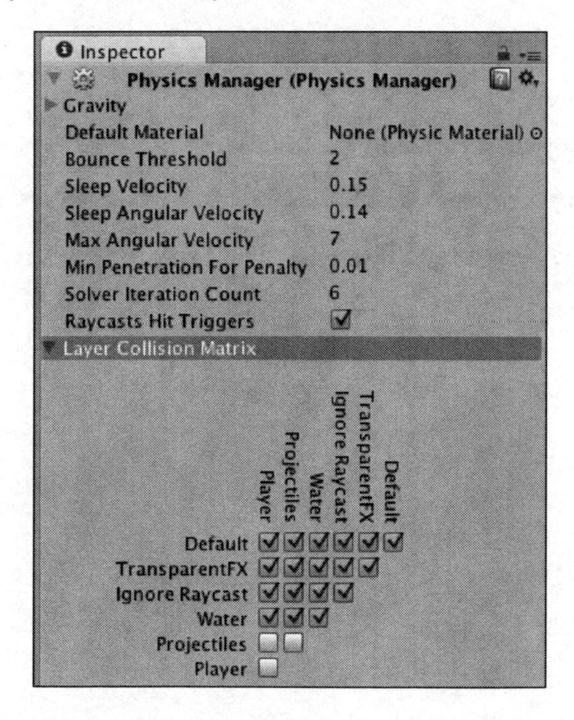

This sets up the layers to ignore collisions with one another—now we can simply assign our objects to these layers. Select the **First Person Controller** in the Hierarchy, and at the top of the **Inspector**, select **Player** from the **Layers** drop-down.

Now select the **Coconut** prefab in the **Prefabs** folder of the Project panel, and use the same approach to set this prefab's layer to **Projectiles**.

We now have two safeguards in place to stop our coconut projectile from interacting with the player itself—finding solutions such as this is an important part of minimizing bugs towards the end of your game's development.

Including the Audio Source component

Finally, as your throwing action involves playing audio, we can use the `RequireComponent` command to make Unity include an Audio Source component when this script is added to an object.

C#:

At the top of the script, below the lines:

```
using UnityEngine;
using System.Collections;
```

Add in:

```
[RequireComponent (typeof (AudioSource))]
```

Javascript:

At the very bottom of the script, add the following line:

```
@script RequireComponent(AudioSource)
```

Save your script now by going to **File | Save** and return to Unity.

Final checks

Although the code we have just added is more for safeguarding against bugs than it is functional—we should always test when adding new parts to our script. Press the **Play** button now, check the **Console** bar at the bottom of the Unity interface for errors, and either click the left mouse button, or press the left *Ctrl* key on the keyboard to throw coconuts! Press the **Play** button again to stop testing, once you are satisfied that this works correctly.

If anything does not work correctly, then return to your script and double-check that it matches the full script, which should be as follows:

C#:

Note that the `Start()` function and //comments have been removed.

```
using UnityEngine;
using System.Collections;
[RequireComponent (typeof (AudioSource))]

public class CoconutThrower : MonoBehaviour {
  public AudioClip throwSound;
  public Rigidbody coconutPrefab;
  public float throwSpeed;

  void Update () {
    if(Input.GetButtonDown("Fire1")){
      audio.PlayOneShot(throwSound);
      RigidbodynewCoconut =
        Instantiate(coconutPrefab,
          transform.position, transform.rotation) as Rigidbody;
      newCoconut.name = "coconut";
      newCoconut.rigidbody.velocity =
        transform.forward * throwSpeed;
      Physics.IgnoreCollision(transform.root.collider,
        newCoconut.collider, true);
    }
  }
}
```

Javascript:

```
var throwSound : AudioClip;
var coconutPrefab: Rigidbody;
var throwSpeed : float;
function Update () {
```

```
  if(Input.GetButtonDown("Fire1")){
       audio.PlayOneShot(throwSound);
       var newCoconut : Rigidbody = Instantiate(coconutPrefab,
transform.position, transform.rotation);
       newCoconut.name = "coconut";
       newCoconut.rigidbody.velocity = transform.forward * throwSpeed;
       Physics.IgnoreCollision(transform.root.collider, newCoconut.
collider, true);
  }
}
@scriptRequireComponent(AudioSource)
```

Instantiate restriction and object tidying

Instantiating objects in the manner in which we have done is an ideal use of Unity's prefab system, making it easy to construct any object in the scene and create many clones of it during runtime.

However, creating many clones of a Rigidbody object can prove costly, as each one invokes the physics engine and requires its own draw call from the GPU. In addition, as it negotiates its way around the 3D world—interacting with other objects—it will be using CPU cycles (processing power). Now imagine if you were to allow your player to create an infinite amount of physics-controlled objects, and you can appreciate that your game may slow down after a while. As your game uses too many CPU cycles and memory, the frame rate becomes lower, creating a jerky look to your previously smooth-motioned game. This will of course be a poor experience for the player, and in a commercial sense, would kill your game.

This is why games for PC and Mac have minimum system requirements—the developers will have looked at current existing hardware and created a reasonable specification to test their game on in order to guarantee a good experience for the player when their game is at its most intensive.

Rather than hoping that the player does not throw many coconuts, we will instead do two things to avoid too many objects slowing down the game's frame rate:

- Allow the player to throw coconuts only while in a defined spot in the game world
- Write a script to remove coconuts from the world after a defined time since their instantiation

If we were working on an instantiation of a larger scale, for example, a gun, then we would also add a time-based delay to ensure a 'reload' period. This is not necessary in this instance, as we avoid too many coconuts being thrown at once by using the `GetButtonDown()` command—although this is used within `Update()`, after the first firing it will not fire again until the player presses the button down anew—so holding the Fire button will do nothing.

Activating coconut throw

We will address the first point by simply having a switching Boolean variable that must be `true` for the player to throw coconuts, and we will only set this variable to `true` when the player character is standing on a part of the coconut shy model—which will be our coconut target arena.

Having the player randomly throwing coconuts around the level away from this mini-game would not really make sense, so it's a good thing to restrict this action in general regardless of our performance considerations.

Re-open the **CoconutThrower** script if you have closed it by double-clicking its icon in the **Project** panel. Otherwise, simply switch back to the script editor and continue working on it. Previously, we have looked at activating and deactivating scripts through the `enabled` parameter of a component. Similarly, in this instance, we could very well use a `GetComponent()` command, select this script, and disable it when we do not want the player to throw coconuts. However, as with all scripting issues, there are many solutions to any one problem, and in this instance, we'll take a look at using `static` variables to communicate across scripts.

When to use and when not to use Static variables

It is important to understand when to use static variables in your scripting. Because in this instance we are creating a single player game in which we have only one player—the static variable is fine because there will never be more than one instance of this script in the game. However, if working on a multiplayer game we can assume that there may be many instances of the script—this would cause a conflict as the game would need to address many thrower scripts, not just a single instance. For example it would be bad practice to add a static variable to a game that stored the health of an enemy, as there is likely to be more than one instance of an enemy in your game, so this information should not be global.

Add the following line before the opening of the `Update()` function in the **CoconutThrower** script.

C#:

```
public static bool canThrow = false;
```

Javascript:

```
static var canThrow : boolean = false;
```

This `static` prefix before our variable is one approach to creating a global—a value that can be accessed by other scripts. As a result of this, we'll be adding another condition to our existing `if` statement that allows us to throw, so find that line within the `Update()` function. It should look like this:

```
if(Input.GetButtonUp("Fire1")){
```

To add a second condition, simply add two ampersand symbols—`&&`—before the right closing bracket of the `if` statement along with the name of the static variable, as follows:

C# and Javascript:

```
if(Input.GetButtonUp("Fire1") && canThrow){
```

Bear in mind here that simply writing the name of the variable is a shorter way of stating:

```
if(Input.GetButtonUp("Fire1") && canThrow==true){
```

As we have set the `canThrow` variable in the script to `false` when it was declared, and because it is `static` (therefore not a public variable—so will not appear and therefore be overridden by the Inspector), we will need to use another piece of scripting to set this variable to `true`. Given that our player must be standing in a certain place, our best course of action for this is to use collision detection to check if the player is colliding with a particular object, and if so, set this static variable to `true`, allowing them to throw.

Because our coconut shy will feature a throwing mat upon which the player must stand, we will create another trigger area to act as a switch for the static variable in the **CoconutThrower** script.

The player must stand on the mat in order to throw, and we will use `OnTriggerEnter()` and `OnTriggerExit()` functions to activate and deactivate by setting `CoconutThrower.canThrow` to true or false.

Writing the throwing mat trigger script

Select the **Scripts** folder in the Project panel and then click on the **Create** button to make a new script of your chosen language. Name your new script **ThrowTrigger**. Launch the script in the script editor now and add the following functions:

C#:

```
void OnTriggerEnter(Collider col){
  if(col.gameObject.tag == "Player"){
    CoconutThrower.canThrow=true;
  }
}

void OnTriggerExit(Collider col){
  if(col.gameObject.tag == "Player"){
    CoconutThrower.canThrow=false;
  }
}
```

Javascript

```
function OnTriggerEnter(col : Collider){
  if(col.gameObject.tag == "Player"){
    CoconutThrower.canThrow=true;
  }
}

function OnTriggerExit(col : Collider){
  if(col.gameObject.tag == "Player"){
    CoconutThrower.canThrow=false;
  }
}
```

These two functions simply check whether the trigger colliding object is the player by checking its `tag`, and then switch the `static` variable `canThrow` in `CoconutThrower` to `true` if the player is entering the trigger, and `false` when they exit it. Save your script now and return to Unity. We will add the coconut shy next, and then apply this script to its **mat** child object.

Adding the coconut shy shack

By placing the coconut shy shack and three targets into the scene, we'll check for collisions between the coconuts and the targets, and write a script to check if all of the three targets are knocked down at once—the goal of the mini-game. Let's begin by adding the coconut shy shack model and ensure that the player can throw by adding a trigger-mode box collider and the **ThrowTrigger** script that we just wrote.

In the **Project** panel, locate the **Book Assets | Models** folder. Select the 3D model in this folder named **coconutShy** to see its properties in the **Inspector**.

Import settings

Before we place the shack into the scene, we will ensure that it is correctly scaled and can be walked on by the player by generating colliders for each part of the model.

In the **FBXImporter** component in the **Inspector**, set the **Scale Factor** to **1**, then check the box for **Generate Colliders** to ensure that Unity assigns a mesh collider to each part of the model, meaning that the player character will be able to walk into/on the shack as well as its mat and detect collisions with it.

To confirm this change, click on the **Apply** button at the bottom of the **Inspector** now.

Now drag the model from the **Project** panel to the **Scene** window, and use the **Translate tool** (*W*) to position it somewhere near to the outpost in order to ensure that the player understands that the two features are related. Rotate the **coconutShy** model by between **150** and **180** degrees in the **Y** axis using the Transform component so that it faces the same direction as the outpost. You may want to rotate this manually to make it look a little more organic—and not like the buildings have been built rigidly in exactly the same direction—this is an island after all!

Make sure that you lower the shack onto the surface of your terrain by dragging the **Y** (green) axis handle so that the feet of the beams that support the red and white tarpaulin rest on the ground. It may take some time and movement of your view (hold *Alt* and drag with the mouse) to get this right.

Remember that if the ground of your terrain at this location is not perfectly flat, it will intersect the floor—you may like the look of this as it could look like the foliage has grown through the floorboards, but if not, simply reselect the **Terrain** in the Hierarchy and use the second tool in the **Terrain (script)** component—**Paint Height**. Set the height to **30** as this was our basic ground level we established when creating the island earlier in the book. Paint the ground back to this level and then try lowering the shack onto the ground again—it should settle at a **Y** axis value of **30**.

Here is a suggested example position, using a **Y** rotation of **160** degrees, but feel free to try experimenting with different positioning if you like:

Creating the throwing mat trigger

Click the grey arrow to the left of the **coconutShy** title in the Hierarchy to expand it now. Select the **mat** child object, and from the top menu choose **Component | Physics | Box Collider**.

You will be prompted with a dialog window informing you that adding this child object will **Lose the prefab connection**. Simply click on the **Add** button here. This is simply informing you that changes made to components attached to the original model in the **Project** panel—for example, script parameters—will no longer apply to this copy in the scene because you are severing the connection between this instance and the original asset or prefab.

Unity will then prompt you, asking whether you wish to **Add** or **Replace** the existing collider. This is because we checked **Generate Colliders** earlier, which has assigned every mesh in this model's hierarchy a Mesh Collider. We will keep this **Mesh Collider** as we want the player to feel the step up onto the throwing mat as part of the game, so choose **Add** now.

You should now see that you have both a **Box Collider** and a **Mesh Collider** on the **mat** object in the Inspector. When adding a Box Collider to a cubic shape such as the mat, note that the collider adopts the scale of the mat—this is usually what we need but in this instance we will scale the height of the Box Collider up. Select the Hand Tool to hide the axis handles in the Scene view, and then hold **Shift** to show the collider boundary dots. Drag the dot on top of the mat up until it is roughly the same height as the player character:

Now that the collider is a useful scale, ensure that it is a trigger by checking the **Is Trigger** checkbox on the **Box Collider** component in the Inspector.

Finally, complete the function of the mat by adding the **ThrowTrigger** script we wrote earlier—drag the script from the **Scripts** folder in the Project panel onto the **mat** child object in the Inspector.

Let's test it out! Save your progress in Unity by choosing **File | Save Scene** from the top menu, and then press **Play** to test the game—you should now only be able to throw coconuts when standing on the throwing mat.

Removing coconuts

As mentioned earlier, too many physics-controlled objects in your scene can seriously affect performance. Therefore, in cases such as this, where your objects are simply throwaway objects (objects that need not be kept—no pun intended!), we can write a script to automatically remove them after a defined amount of time.

Select the **Scripts** folder inside the **Project** panel, click on the **Create** button, and choose your desired language to make a new script. Rename this script **TidyObject** by pressing *Return* (Mac) or *F2* (PC) and retyping. Then double-click the icon of the script to launch it in the script editor.

Remove the default `Update()` function from this script as we do not need it. To remove any object from a scene, we can simply use the **Destroy()** function and implement its second argument in order to establish a waiting period. `Destroy()` works as follows:

```
Destroy(which object or component to destroy,
  optional time delay number);
```

To make this script reusable we will establish a public variable to allow us to specify the time delay. This is because we may wish to use this to remove a different kind of spawned object after a defined time, but not the same amount of time as for our Coconut prefab. Above the `Start()` function add the following variable:

C#:

```
public float removeTime = 3.0f;
```

Javascript:

```
var removeTime: float = 3.0;
```

We will call the `Destroy()` function within the `Start()` function—C# users will already have a `Start()` function defined in their script, so will only need to add the command whereas Javascript users will need to add the function also. Make sure that your script matches what's given next:

C#:

```
  void Start () {
    Destroy(gameObject, removeTime);
  }
```

Javascript:

```
function Start(){
  Destroy(gameObject, removeTime);
}
```

By using the `Start()` command, we will call `Destroy()` as soon as this object appears in the world, that is, as soon as it is instantiated by the player pressing the fire button. By referring to `gameObject`, we are simply saying 'the object this script is attached to'. After the comma, we simply state a time in seconds to wait until activating this command by using our `removeTime` float variable.

As a result of this script—as soon as a coconut is thrown, it will stay in the world for three seconds, and then be removed. Go to **File** | **Save** in the script editor and return to Unity.

Previously, when we had written scripts, we had attached them to objects in the scene we had been working on. However, in this instance, we have already finished working on our coconut prefab, and we no longer have a copy in the scene.

There are two ways of applying the script we have just written to the prefab. To do this the easy way, you can:

- Drag-and-drop the **TidyObject** script from its position in the Project panel onto the prefab in the Project, or alternatively—select the **Coconut** prefab you made earlier in the **Project** panel, and go to **Component** | **Scripts** | **TidyObject**

Or to take a more long-winded route, you can modify the prefab in the **Scene** in the following way:

- Drag the **Coconut** prefab to the **Scene** window or the **Hierarchy** panel
- Go to **Component** | **Scripts** | **TidyObject**, click **Add** to confirm when told that '**Adding a component will lose the prefab parent**'
- Save this update to the original prefab by going to **GameObject** | **Apply Changes to prefab** or by pressing the **Apply** button at the top of the Inspector
- Delete the instance in the scene using the shortcut *Command* + *Backspace* (Mac) or *Delete* (PC)

In this instance, it is recommended to use the former, that is, the single step route, so let's do that now. But in some instances it can be useful to take a prefab back into the scene, and modify it before you apply changes to the prefab. For example, if you are working on something visual, such as a particle system, then you would need to see what effect your adjustments or newly added components will have. Therefore, taking a prefab of such an object into the scene to edit would be essential.

Go to **File** | **Save Project** in Unity now to update your progress so far. Press **Play** to test and you should now see that when standing on the mat and throwing coconuts that they only exist in the world for the default 3 seconds of the `Destroy()` command we have specified— meaning that the maximum amount of coconuts in the game at any time is limited.

Targets and coconut collisions

Locate the **target** model inside the **Book Assets | Models** folder in the **Project** panel, and select it in order to see the various import setting components in the **Inspector**.

In the **FBXImporter** component in the **Inspector**, select the box for **Generate Colliders** to ensure that any mesh part of the model that a coconut hits should cause it to repel—remember that with no colliders, 3D objects will pass through one another. Also, set the **Scale Factor** to a value of **1** here.

In the **Animations** component, we'll need to specify frames and give names for each animation we would like this model to have, in the same way as we did for the outpost door animations. By adding these animations, we can call upon them in our scripts if a collision between a coconut and the correct part of the target occurs.

Add three animations (as shown in the following image) by clicking on the plus (**+**) icon to the right-hand side of the animations table, then filling in a **Name** and the **Start** and **End** frames:

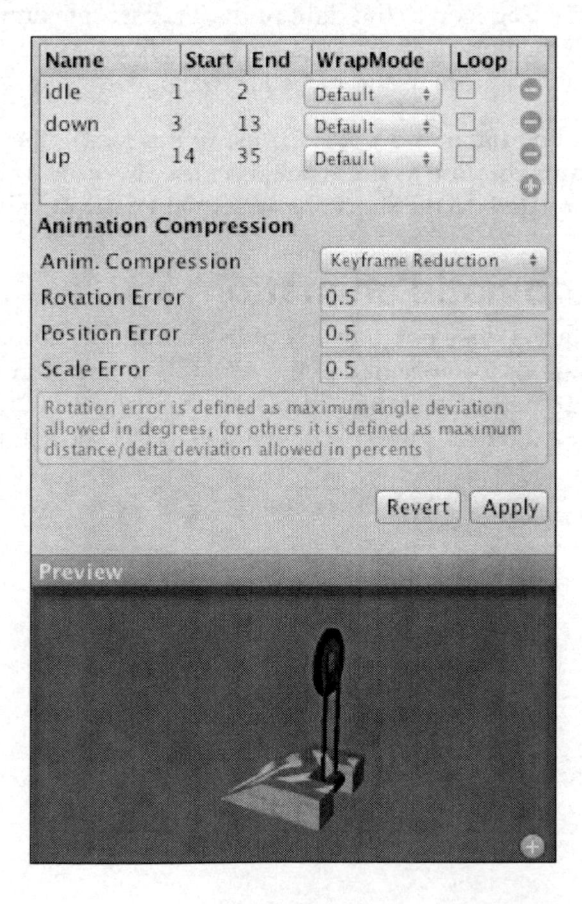

When you have completed the **Animations** table, remember to press the **Apply** button at the bottom to confirm the animations, as well as the other import changes you have made to the asset.

Placement

To place the targets easily inside the **coconutShy** shack, we will add them as children of the **platform** object already in our scene. To do this, simply drag the target model from the **Book Assets | Models** folder in the **Project** panel, and drop it onto the **coconutShy** parent object in the **Hierarchy** panel.

Adding the **target** as a child of the **coconutShy** will cause the title in the Hierarchy to expand and reveal its existing child objects along with the target you have just added.

Now that this is a child of the shack, we'll reset the position to place it in the center of the shack, as its makes it simple to start moving out from. With the **target** object still selected, click the **Cog** icon to the right of the **Transform** component, and choose **Reset position** from the pop-out menu. As the **target** is now in the center of the shack, lets position it in a more useful place for the player.

First rotate the target by **180** in the **Y** axis to ensure it is facing the player—remember it need not be the same rotation as the shack, because it is now a child object, and its coordinates will be relative to the shack. Now set the **Position** values to (0, 0, -2.4).

Disabling automatic animation

To ensure that our target does not play any of its animations automatically, and also that it has the animations we specified in the Animation importer earlier, uncheck the box for **Play Automatically** on the **Animation** component in the Inspector, and then ensure that the animations we specified are listed as shown in the image below:

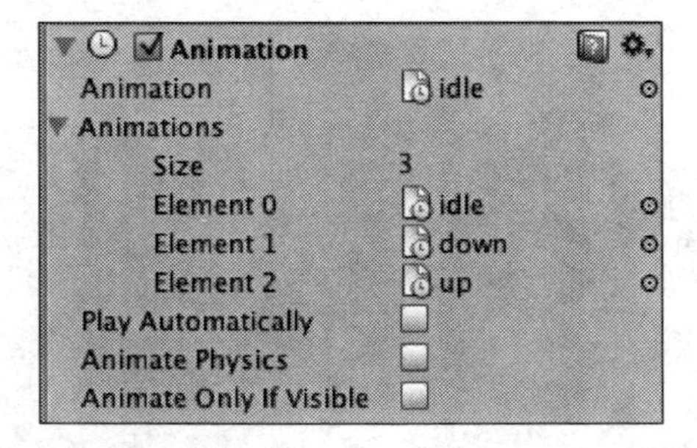

Adding Rigidbodies to moving parts

As certain parts of the target model will move via animation, we should ensure that they have a kinematic Rigidbody attached to allow the physics engine to track their movement and save on performance.

Expand the parent **target** object in the Hierarchy by clicking the gray arrow to the left of its title, and then expand the **target_pivot** child to reveal three further child objects.

These further three—**target**, **target_support_1,** and **target_support_2** will be animating during runtime, and so should have a non-gravitational kinematic Rigidbody component attached in order to allow them to interact with other Rigidbodies (our coconuts for example) but not be affected by their forces.

Begin by selecting the first of the three objects shown in the following image, and choose **Component | Physics | Rigidbody** from the top menu, and then uncheck **Use Gravity** and check **Is Kinematic**.

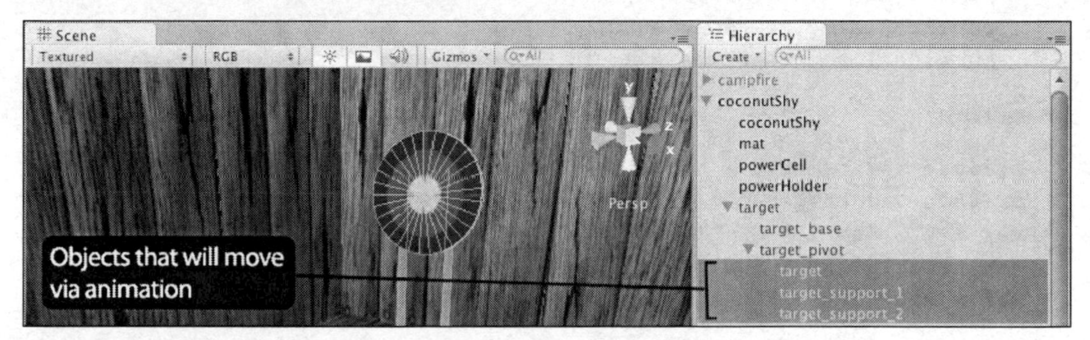

Now repeat this step for the other two objects, ensuring that all three have a non-gravitational kinematic Rigidbody component once you are done.

Writing the Coconut collision detection script

As we need to detect collisions between the child **target** part of the **target** parent model—as opposed to the supports or base, for example—we'll need to write a script with collision detection to be applied to the **target** child object only.

Select the **Scripts** folder in the **Project** panel, then click on the **Create** button, and select **C# Script** or **Javascript** from the drop-down menu. Rename this from **NewBehaviourScript** to **TargetCollision**, and then double-click its icon to open it in the script editor.

Establishing variables

Firstly, we need to establish five variables:

- A `beenHit` Boolean to check if the target is currently down
- A `targetRoot` private variable
- A `hitSound` audio public member variable
- A `resetSound` audio public member variable
- A `resetTime` float public member variable

To do this, add the following code to the script before the opening of the `Update()` function:

C#:

```
bool beenHit = false;
Animation targetRoot;
public AudioClip hitSound;
public AudioClip resetSound;
public float resetTime = 3.0f;
```

Javascript:

```
private var beenHit : boolean = false;
private var targetRoot : Animation;
var hit Sound : AudioClip;
var reset Sound : AudioClip;
var reset Time : float = 3.0;
```

Note here that `beenHit` and `targetRoot` are private variables, as they do not need to be assigned in the **Inspector**—their values are set and used only within the script.

We will use our `beenHit` variable as a toggle for each target to register its current status—if `beenHit` is set to true (this will be done through collision detection with the coconut), the target knows it is currently knocked down, and will not register another hit until it has been reset.

Then we have a private variable called `targetRoot`—this is of type `Animation`, and therefore will be used to represent an animation component on the object assigned to it within the script. Because our script will be placed on a child object of the **target** model, we will use this variable to store a reference to the overall parent, to which the animation component is attached.

We then have two audio clip variables for when the targets are hit and when they reset, and finally, a float variable that will define how long the target will wait before resetting.

Let's assign our `targetRoot` now in a `Start()` function. Add the following code to your script:

C#:

```
void Start(){
  targetRoot = transform.parent.transform.parent.animation;
}
```

Javascript:

```
function Start(){
    targetRoot = transform.parent.transform.parent.animation;
  }
```

Here we have assigned the Animation variable `targetRoot` to an animation component attached not to the parent of the target mesh, but to the parent's parent.

We cannot say simply `transform.parent` once because the primary parent object of the round target mesh is the **target_pivot** object—look at the Hierarchy and you will see this relationship:

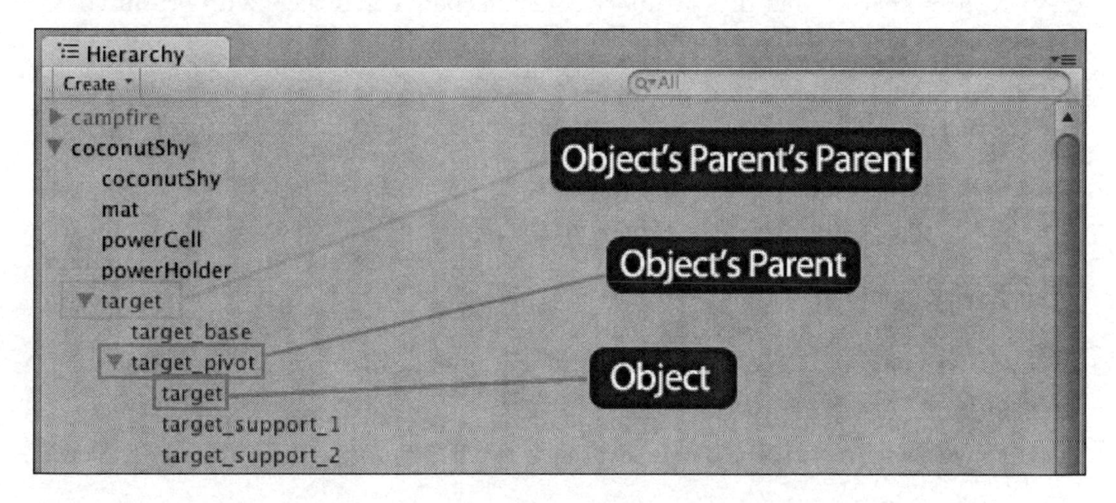

This is important because the round **target** child object itself does not have the animation component attached, so we use dot syntax to refer to its parent object (**target_pivot**), and finally that object's parent (**target**) that has the Animation component attached.

It is also important to store this reference in a variable, as we will be referring to the component within the script more than once, making it more efficient to use a variable than to address the same component manually several times.

Collision detection

Next, we need to check for the target mesh as being hit by the coconut. Write in the following collision detection function.

C#:

```
void OnCollisionEnter(Collision theObject) {
  if(beenHit==false && theObject.gameObject.name=="coconut"){

  }
}
```

Javascript:

```
function OnCollisionEnter(theObject : Collision) {
  if(beenHit==false && theObject.gameObject.name=="coconut"){
  }
}
```

Different from the `OnTriggerEnter()` functions that we've used previously, `OnCollisionEnter()` handles ordinary collisions between objects with primitive colliders, that is, not character controller colliders and not colliders in trigger mode.

In this function, the `theObject` argument is an instance of the `Collision` class, which stores information on velocities, rigidbodies, colliders, transform, `GameObjects`, and contact points involved in a collision. Therefore, here we simply check the information stored in this argument with an `if` statement, checking whether there is a stored `gameObject` with the name `coconut`. To ensure that the target cannot be hit many times, we have an additional condition in the `if` statement which checks that `beenHit` is set to `false`. This will be the case when the game starts, and as part of the function we are about to call when this collision occurs, `beenHit` will be set to `true` so that we cannot accidentally trigger it twice.

However, we are yet to call any commands when this collision occurs. This is because we are going to take a new approach to a problem we have already solved.

Using co-routines to time game elements

In our outpost door mechanic in *Chapter 6*, we used a trigger mode collider to detect the player's presence and open the door, and then set up a float-type timer variable in our **DoorManager** script that increments in an `Update()` function, counting up to a defined time before closing the door. We wrote:

```
if(doorIsOpen){
  doorTimer += Time.deltaTime;

  if(doorTimer>doorOpenTime){
      Door(doorShutSound, false, "doorshut");
      doorTimer = 0.0f;
  }
}
```

However, although the problem of resetting our targets is effectively the same as opening and closing a door—something happens, there is a timed delay, and then something else happens—in the case of our targets, we'll level up our programming knowledge and make use of something called a co-routine, instead of incrementing a timer.

Setting values in `Update()` is costly in terms of performance, and should be avoided if possible, but for the purpose of learning Unity we have opted to show you both the inefficient method of timing and resetting, and now, the more efficient method. Being able to write and increment timers is also useful in other contexts, so make sure you don't forget it; it'll come in handy when making a timed game later!

Co-routines to complement functions

As co-routines are a way of running commands in parallel to your currently executed code, they are often the best way to structure your game scripting.

Giving you an opportunity to carry out commands or pause until conditions are met, a co-routine can be very powerful, and our use of it to create a timed delay is only scratching the surface of what you can do with them.

A co-routine, although complex sounding, looks and behaves like a standard function, but can use yield to pause until a defined time or condition is met. The main visible difference is seen in C#, where the function begins with a return type called `IEnumerator`, instead of `void`.

Let's put this into practice without further delay; add the following to your **TargetCollision** script now:

C#:

```
IEnumerator targetHit(){
  audio.PlayOneShot(hitSound);
  targetRoot.Play("down");
  beenHit=true;

  yield return new WaitForSeconds(resetTime);

  audio.PlayOneShot(resetSound);
  targetRoot.Play("up");
  beenHit=false;
}
```

Javascript:

```
function targetHit(){
  audio.PlayOneShot(hitSound);
  targetRoot.Play("down");
  beenHit=true;

  yield new WaitForSeconds(resetTime);

  audio.PlayOneShot(resetSound);
  targetRoot.Play("up");
  beenHit=false;
}
```

This function handles both the knocking down, and resetting of our targets.

The first three lines of the co-routine carry out the following commands:

1. Play an audio clip assigned to the `hitSound` variable.
2. Play the `down` animation assigned to animation component stored in `targetRoot`.
3. Set the `beenHit` variable to `true` so that it cannot be called again by the collision detection function.

Then the co-routine uses a yield instruction called `WaitForSeconds`, passing in the value of the `resetTime` variable as the amount of time to pause for. After this pause, the final three lines reset the target by playing the `resetSound` and `up` animation, and set `beenHit` back to false so that the target may listen for a collision once more.

It's as simple as that—and we have removed the need for an `Update()` function listening for `beenHit` to change state, and any need for a float-type timer variable, which would also have required resetting.

Congratulations, you just wrote your first co-routine! But we still need to call it when our collision occurs. Return to your `OnCollisionEnter()` function and add the following line to call your co-routine when this function's if statement conditions are met:

C# and Javascript:

```
StartCoroutine("targetHit");
```

Your full function should look like this:

C#:

```
void OnCollisionEnter(Collision theObject) {
  if(beenHit==false && theObject.gameObject.name=="coconut"){
    StartCoroutine("targetHit");
  }
}
```

Javascript:

```
function OnCollisionEnter(theObject : Collision) {
  if(beenHit==false && theObject.gameObject.name=="coconut"){
    StartCoroutine("targetHit");
  }
}
```

This will call the co-routine by name, pretty easy right? And that's all we need to do. Our script manages itself because `beenHit` is set to true and false by the co-routine, so whatever we throw at it—literally! It will work.

Including the Audio Source component

As we are playing sounds, we'll need to add a `RequireComponent` command to our script in order to ensure that an audio source gets added to the object this script gets attached to.

C#:

At the top of the script, below the lines:

```
using UnityEngine;
using System.Collections;
```

And before the class declaration, add in:

```
[RequireComponent (typeof (AudioSource))]
```

Javascript:

Place the following line at the very bottom of the script:

```
@scriptRequireComponent(AudioSource)
```

Go to **File | Save** in the script editor, and switch back to Unity now.

Assigning the script

In the **Hierarchy** panel, expand the **target** model that you have added to the platform, in order to see its constituent parts, and then expand the **target_pivot** child group to reveal the **target** itself and its supports. They should look like this:

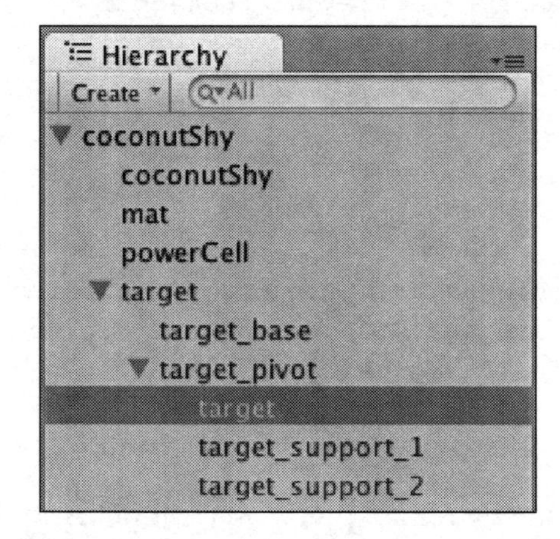

In the above image, the round visual target mesh itself is selected—select this yourself and hover your cursor over the Scene view and press *F* to focus on it. We need to check for collisions with this child part as we don't want collisions to be triggered if the player throws a coconut at the base or supports, for example.

With this object selected, go to **Component | Scripts | Target Collision**. The script we just wrote will be added, along with an **Audio Source** component. Now drag the **target_hit** and **target_reset** audio files from the **Book Assets | Sounds** folder in the **Project** panel to the relevant public variables in the Inspector.

Now go to **File | Save Scene** in Unity to update your progress. Press the **Play** button to test the game and walk over to the platform, making sure you stand on the throwing **mat** object to activate the trigger collider and allow you to throw—you should now be able to throw coconuts and knock down the target. Press **Play** again to stop testing.

To complete our mini-game setup, we'll make two more targets using the prefab system.

Creating more targets

To create more targets, we'll save our existing target as a prefab and then duplicate it. Collapse the target main parent in the Hierarchy so that you are hiding all of its child objects, then make a prefab out of this object by dragging it to the **Prefabs** folder inside the Project panel. Unity automatically converts this object into a prefab for you. Rename this from **target** to **TargetPrefab** to help differentiate it in the Project panel from the original model at a glance.

The text of the parent **target** object in the **Hierarchy** will turn blue, indicating that it is connected to a prefab in the project.

Now select the parent **target** in the **Hierarchy** panel, and press *Command* + *D* (Mac) or *Ctrl* + *D* (PC) to duplicate this object.

With the duplicate selected, set its **X Position** in the **Transform** component in the **Inspector** to **-1.6**. Repeat this duplicating step again now to make a third target, but this time, setting the **X** position to **1.6**. Your three targets within the shack should look something like this:

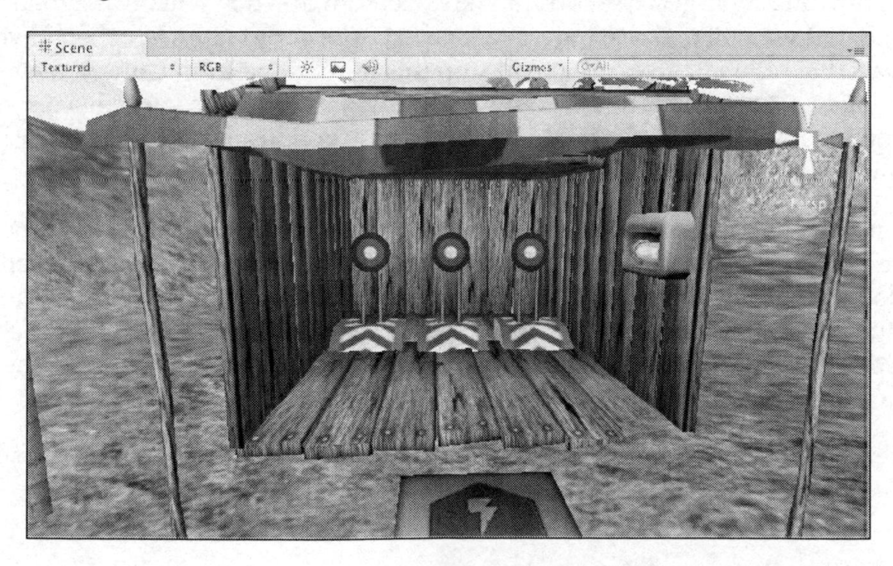

Winning the game

To complete the function of our mini-game—to give the player the final power cell that they need to charge the outpost door generator—we'll need to write a script that checks if all of the three targets are knocked down at once.

Select the **Scripts** folder in the **Project** panel, and use the **Create** button to make a new **C# Script** or **Javascript** file. Rename this script **CoconutWin**, and then double-click its icon to launch it in the script editor.

Setting up variables

Add the following four variables to the top of your script as usual:

C#:

```
public static int targets = 0;
public static bool haveWon = false;
public AudioClip winSound;
public GameObject cellPrefab;
```

Javascript:

```
static var targets : int = 0;
static var haveWon : boolean = false;
var winSound : AudioClip;
var cellPrefab : GameObject;
```

Here we begin with a static variable called `targets`, which is effectively a counter to store how many targets are currently knocked down—this will be assigned by a change that we will make to our `TargetCollision` script later. We then have a static variable called `haveWon` that will stop this mini-game from being replayed by simply being set to `true` after the first win. We will refer to this variable later, when checking whether the player should be shown instructions; if they have already won the game, instructions need not be shown.

We then have two public variables—one to store a winning audio clip, and the other to store a reference to a power cell game object. The reference to the power cell is provided so that this script can instantiate a new cell from the prefab we made earlier when the player has won—we will also remove the visible power cell that is part of the coconut shy at the same time so as to give the appearance that winning the game has caused the power cell to be released.

The prefab will be applied to this variable once we have finished writing the script.

Checking for a win

Now add the following code to the `Update()` function:

C#:

```
if(targets==3 && haveWon == false){
    targets=0;
    audio.PlayOneShot(winSound);
    GameObject winCell = transform.Find("powerCell").gameObject;
    winCell.transform.Translate(-1,0,0);
    Instantiate(cellPrefab, winCell.transform.position,
      transform.rotation);
    Destroy(winCell);
    haveWon = true;
  }
```

Javascript:

```
  if(targets==3 &&haveWon == false){
    targets=0;
    audio.PlayOneShot(winSound);
    winCell : GameObject = transform.Find("powerCell").gameObject;
    winCell.transform.Translate(-1,0,0);
    Instantiate(cellPrefab, winCell.transform.position,
      transform.rotation);
    Destroy(winCell);
    haveWon = true;
  }
```

This `if` statement has two conditions. It ensures that the `targets` integer count has reached `3`, meaning that they must all be knocked down, and also that the `haveWon` variable is `false`, ensuring that the player has not already completed the mini-game.

When these conditions are met, the following commands are carried out:

- The script resets the `targets` variable to `0` (this is simply another measure to ensure that the `if` statement does not re-trigger).
- The `win` audio clip is played as player feedback.
- A variable called `winCell` is created to represent the existing **powerCell** model that is part of the shack, visually embedded on the right inside the **powerHolder** object, and currently uncollectable.

- The `winCell` is then moved out of the **powerHolder** by a value of `1` in the `X` axis using the `Translate` command, so that it can then be used as a position to `Instantiate` an instance of the **powerCell** prefab, which we will later assign to the `cellPrefab` variable.
- The aforementioned instance is then created using the `Instantiate` command, using the position of `winCell` as its own position, but the rotation of the shack as its rotation, hence the use of simply `transform.rotation` instead of `winCell.transform.rotation`.
- The original **powerCell** assigned to the `winCell` variable is then removed from the scene using the `Destroy()` command to ensure that there is no longer the original fake cell inside the power holder.
- We set the `haveWon` variable to `true`, which means that the game cannot be won again, and stops the player from generating more power cells.

Finally, as we are playing sound, follow the instructions under **Including the Audio Source component** above to add a `RequireComponent` command for an audio source to your script—or why not test yourself and see if you can remember how to first?

Your finished **CoconutWin** script should look like this:

C#:

```
using UnityEngine;
using System.Collections;
[RequireComponent (typeof (AudioSource))]

public class CoconutWin : MonoBehaviour {
  public static int targets = 0;
  public static bool haveWon = false;
  public AudioClip winSound;
  public GameObject cellPrefab;

  void Update () {
    if(targets==3 && haveWon == false){
      targets=0;
      audio.PlayOneShot(winSound);
      GameObject winCell = transform.Find("powerCell").gameObject;
      winCell.transform.Translate(-1,0,0);
      Instantiate(cellPrefab, winCell.transform.position,
        transform.rotation);
      Destroy(winCell);
      haveWon = true;
    }
  }
}
```

Javascript:

```
static var targets : int  = 0;
static var haveWon : boolean = false;
var winSound : AudioClip;
var cellPrefab : GameObject;

function Update () {
  if(targets==3 &&haveWon == false){
    targets=0;
    audio.PlayOneShot(winSound);
    var winCell : GameObject =
      transform.Find("powerCell").gameObject;
    winCell.transform.Translate(-1,0,0);
    Instantiate(cellPrefab, winCell.transform.position,
      transform.rotation);
    Destroy(winCell);
    haveWon = true;
  }
}
@scriptRequireComponent(AudioSource)
```

Now go to **File** | **Save** in the script editor, and switch back to Unity.

Script assignment

Select the **coconutShy** parent object in the **Hierarchy** panel and go to **Component** | **Scripts** | **Coconut Win**.

To complete this, assign the **powerCell** prefab from the **Prefabs** folder in the **Project** panel to the **Cell Prefab** public variable on the **Coconut Win (Script)** component, and the **win_cell** sound effect from the **Book Assets** | **Sounds** folder to the **Win Sound** public variable. When done, the script component should look like this:

Incrementing and decrementing target count

Finally, to make the game work, we must return to our **TargetCollision** script, and add one to the static variable `targets` in `CoconutWin` when we knock down a target, and subtract one when the target resets.

This is simple to do, as our script is already set up to handle those two events within the co-routine. If you still have it open, switch back to the **TargetCollision** script now or if not, double-click on the icon of the script in the **Scripts** folder to launch it in the script editor.

Adding to the target count

In the co-routine there are two stages—the knocking down of the target, and its reset. These are easy to spot as they reside either side of the yield that marks the pause in the routine whilst the targets are down.

Find the following line:

```
beenHit=true;
```

After it, add the following line:

```
CoconutWin.targets++;
```

Subtracting from the target count

After the `yield`, we reset the target, and allow them to be hit again by resetting the `beenHit` variable to false. This is where we should subtract from the number of targets currently knocked down. Find the following line:

```
beenHit=false;
```

...and then add the following line after it:

```
CoconutWin.targets--;
```

In both addition and subtraction, we are using dot syntax to address the script (or Class name), followed by the name of the static variable targets, then using ++ and - - to add and subtract. These are shortcuts for plus one and minus one, which can also be written as +=1 and -=1.

Go to **File | Save** in the script editor, and return to Unity.

Press the **Play** button now and test the game. Throwing coconuts and knocking down all of the three targets at once should cause the platform to instantiate a power cell for you to collect. When it does, simply walk into it to collect it as you would for any other instance of the power cell prefab. Press **Play** again to stop testing the game, and go to **File | Save Scene** in Unity to update your progress.

Finishing touches

To make this mini-game feel a little more polished, we'll add a crosshair to the heads-up display when the player is standing on the throwing mat, and use our existing **TextHintGUI** object to give the player instructions on what to do to win the coconut shy game.

Adding the crosshair

To add the crosshair to the screen, do the following:

- Open the **Book Assets | Textures** folder in the **Project** panel.
- Select the **Crosshair** texture file.
- In the **Texture Importer** in the Inspector, set the **Texture Type** to **GUI** in order to tell Unity we will use this texture as part of our 2D display.
- With the texture still selected, choose **GameObject | Create Other | GUI Texture** from the top menu or click the **Create** button on the Hierarchy and choose **GUI Texture** there. This will take dimensions of the texture file and assign them for you while creating a new GUI Texture object named after the **Crosshair** texture.

This will automatically get selected in the **Hierarchy** panel, so you can see its **GUI Texture** component in the **Inspector**. The crosshair graphic should have become visible in the **Game** view and also in the **Scene** view if you have the **Game Overlay** button toggled. As this is centered by default, it works perfectly with our small 64 x 64 texture file.

When we created the texture file for this example, it was important that we used light and dark edges so that the cross is easy to see regardless of whether the player is looking at something light or dark.

Bear in mind that when not selecting the texture file and simply creating the GUI Texture, you will be presented with a Unity logo. You then have to swap this for your texture in the Inspector, as well as fill in the dimensions manually. For this reason, it is always best to select the texture you wish to form your GUI Texture object first.

Toggling the crosshair GUI Texture

Open the **ThrowTrigger** script from the `Scripts` folder of the **Project** panel. In the `OnTriggerEnter()` function, you'll notice that we already have scripting that checks if we are on the throwing mat. As we want the crosshair to be visible only when we are on this mat, we will add more code to these `if` statements.

Firstly, create a reference to our new crosshair above the functions in your script.

C#:

```
public GUITexture crosshair;
```

Javascript:

```
var crosshair : GUITexture;
```

Now, inside our `OnTriggerEnter()` and `OnTriggerExit()` functions we can enable and disable this object easily.

In the if statement of `OnTriggerEnter()` add the following line:

C# and Javascript:

```
crosshair.enabled=true;
```

In the if statement of `OnTriggerExit()` add this line:

```
crosshair.enabled=false;
```

Save your script now and return to Unity. Select the **mat** child object of the **coconutShy**, and you will notice that the **Crosshair** public variable we just added has appeared on the **Throw Trigger (script)** component. Drag-and-drop the **Crosshair** object from the Hierarchy to this variable to assign it now.

Finally, ensure that the crosshair is disabled by default by selecting the **Crosshair** object in the Hierarchy, and un-checking the box next to the **GUI Texture** component in the Inspector. Save your progress now by choosing **File | Save scene** and press **Play** to test your game. The crosshair should not appear onscreen until you step onto the throwing mat of the coconut shy, it should also then disappear as soon as you step away.

Informing the player

To help the player understand what they need to do, we'll use our **TextHintGUI** object from *Chapter 6, Collection, Inventory, and HUD* to show a message on screen when the player stands on the throwing mat.

Open the `ThrowTrigger` script, and above the `OnTriggerEnter()` function create a public reference we can assign the `TextHintGUI` to:

C#:

```
public GUIText textHints;
```

Javascript:

```
var textHints : GUIText;
```

Now into the `if` statement of `OnTriggerEnter()` add the following lines:

C# and Javascript:

```
if(!CoconutWin.haveWon){
  textHints.SendMessage("ShowHint",
    "\n\n\n\n\n There's a power cell attached to this game, \n
    maybe I'll win it if I can knock down all the targets...");
}
```

Here we are switching on the **TextHintGUI** only if the static variable `haveWon` in the `CoconutWin` script is false—this is denoted by the exclamation mark at the start of the condition—we are effectively saying if this is not true. If `haveWon` is indeed false, then we switch on the **TextHintGUI** by using `SendMessage()` as we did in our **TriggerZone** for the outpost door.

We are calling the `ShowHint()` function as before and sending the string of text:

```
"\n\n\n\n\n There's a power cell attached to this game, \n
maybe I'll win it if I can knock down all the targets...");
```

You will note there are a number of instances of `\n` within this string—this is an instruction to create a new line. So why are we doing five of these at the start of our hint? Can you guess?

This is because at the same time we are showing a hint, we are also displaying the crosshair to the player—and in order to avoid these two elements overlapping, and to avoid having to move the **TextHintGUI** object's position, we are cheating and inserting five empty lines at the start of the string to move it down.

We are also making using of the newline command to create a new line half way through the sentence, to make it easier to read.

Save your script now and return to Unity. We will need to assign our public reference to **TextHintGUI** in the **ThrowTrigger (Script)** component—select the **mat** child object of the coconutShy in the Hierarchy and then drag-and-drop the **TextHintGUI** object from the Hierarchy to the **Text Hints** variable.

Press the **Play** button and test the game. Now when standing on the throwing mat, you should see a crosshair and the onscreen text hint that we added.

Leave the mat and the crosshair should disappear from the screen, followed by the message after a few seconds. Press **Play** again to stop testing the game, and go to **File | Save Project** to update your progress so far.

Summary

In this chapter, we have covered various topics that you will find crucial when creating any game scenario. We have looked at implementing rigid body objects both for animated dynamic elements and instantiated projectiles. This is something you'll likely expand upon in many other game scenarios while working with Unity. We have also continued our use of Instantiation from our Prototype scene at the start of this book, and effectively created a game mechanic that ties in with the rest of our game, forcing the player to interact with another element in order to gain access to our outpost, adding depth to the game and creating a simple puzzle for the player to solve—win the coconut shy to release the last power cell they need to charge the door generator.

We also gave the player further feedback by reusing our **TextHintGUI** object made in *Chapter 6, Collection, Inventory, and HUD* and worked across scripts in order to send the information to this object. We also took a look at how co-routines can be used to provide structure and added functionality to your scripting, something that you'll definitely need to use again in your future development.

These are all concepts you will continue to use in the rest of this book and in your future Unity projects. In the next chapter, we'll take a break from coding and take a look at more of Unity's aesthetic effects. We'll explore the use of particle systems to create a campfire outside the outpost cabin. We will use this as the end goal of our game—the player will find collectable matches in the outpost that they can use to light the campfire and signal for help to escape the island.

8 Particle Systems

In this chapter, we will look at more versatile rendering effects that can be achieved by using particle systems within your 3D world. Games use particle effects to achieve a vast range of effects from fog and smoke to sparks, lasers, and simple patterns. In this chapter, we will look at how we can use two particle systems to simulate fire.

In this chapter, you will learn:

- What makes up a particle system—its components and settings
- Building particle systems to simulate fire and smoke
- Further work with on-screen player instructions and feedback
- Using scripting to activate particle systems during runtime

What is a particle system?

A particle system is referred to in Unity as a system—rather than a component—as it requires these components working together in order to function properly:

- A Particle Emitter—this defines the creation of particles, their lifespan, velocities, and range
- A Particle Animator—this defines the behavior of the particle throughout its lifespan
- A Particle Renderer—this defines the appearance of the particles rendered

Before we begin to work with these systems themselves, we need to understand these three component parts in more depth.

Particle Emitter

Within any particle system, the emitter component is in charge of instantiating individual particles. In Unity, there is an **Ellipsoid Particle Emitter** and a **Mesh Particle Emitter** available.

The ellipsoid emitter is most commonly used for effects such as smoke, dust, and other such environmental elements that can be created in a defined space. It is referred to as the ellipsoid because it creates particles within an ellipsoid shaped 3D space—though they may go beyond this space during their lifetime.

The mesh emitter creates particles that are tied directly to a 3D mesh and can either be animated along the surface of a mesh or simply emitted upon the vertices of the mesh. This is more commonly used when there is a need for direct control over particle position—giving the developer the ability to follow vertices of a mesh means that they can design precise particle systems in whatever 3D shape they desire.

In component terms, both emitters have the following settings in common:

- **Size:** the visible size of an individual particle
- **Energy:** the amount of time in seconds that a particle exists in the game before auto-destructing
- **Emission:** the number of particles emitted at a time
- **Velocities:** the speed and direction with which particles travel

We will look at some of the more detailed settings specific to either kind of emitter as we go further in the chapter. For the task of creating a fire, we'll be using the ellipsoid emitter—this will allow a more random effect as it is not tied to a mesh shape.

Particle Animator

The **Particle Animator** is in charge of how individual particles behave over time. In order to appear dynamic and maintain performance, particles have a lifespan, after which they will auto-destruct. In the case of creating a fire, particles should ideally be animated so that each individual particle's appearance changes during its lifespan in the world.

As flames burst and fade in real fire, we can use the animator component to apply color and visibility variance, as well as apply forces to the particles themselves for movement variation.

Particle Renderer

Particle renderers define the visual appearance of individual particles. Particles are effectively square sprites (2D graphics), and in most instances are rendered in the same manner as the grass we added to our terrain in *Chapter 3*—by using the billboarding technique to give the appearance of always facing the camera. Particle renderers in Unity can display particles in other ways, but billboarding is appropriate for most uses.

The Particle Renderer component also handles the materials applied to the particle system. As particles are rendered simply as sprites, applying particle shaders to materials in the renderer component means you can create the illusion of non-square sprites by using alpha channel (transparency) surrounded textures. Here is an example that we'll be using shortly on our fire material—the dark area here is the transparent part:

As a result of using transparency for particles, they no longer have a square appearance, as rendered 2D sprites would ordinarily. By combining the render of only the visible part of this texture with higher emission values of the emitter, the effect of density can be achieved.

Particle renderers can also animate particles using UV animation, by using a grid of images to effectively swap textures during a particle's lifespan, but this is slightly more advanced than the scope of this book, so it is recommended that you refer to the Unity manual for more information on this:

```
http://unity3d.com/support/documentation/Components/class-
ParticleRenderer.html
```

A particle system works because it has a series of components that work together, namely, the emitter creating the particles, the animator defining their behavior or variation over time, and the renderer defining their aesthetic using materials and display parameters.

Now, we'll take a look at creating the next part of our tutorial game, which will culminate in lighting a fire made of two particle systems, one for flames and the other creating a smoke plume.

Creating the task

Our existing game consists of a task for the player to complete in order to enter the outpost—they must collect four power cells to power the door, one of which has to be won by winning the coconut shy game that we added in the previous chapter.

Currently, having entered the outpost, the player is met with a sense of disappointment, as there is nothing to be found inside except for the abandoned desk. In this chapter, we will change that by adding a box of matches to be picked up by the player when they enter the outpost. We will then create a campfire outside, which can only be lit if the player is carrying the box of matches. In this way, we can show the player the campfire logs waiting to be lit, leading them to attempt to find matches by completing the tasks laid out (that is, opening the door).

To create this game, we will need to implement the following in Unity:

- Introduce the campfire model to our scene near to the outpost.
- Create the particle systems for fire and smoke for when the fire is lit. Then disable the emitter components so that the systems do not emit until they are enabled again by a script.
- Set up collision detection between the player character and the campfire object in order to light the fire by enabling the emitter components of the two particle systems.
- Add the matches model to the outpost and set up trigger collision detection to allow collection of the object, and make this restrict whether the fire can be lit.
- Use our `TextHintGUI` object to show the player a hint if they approach the fire without having found the matches.

Assets involved

This exercise will involve several files you will have already imported as part of the Book Assets:

- A 3D model of a campfire—in **Book Assets | Models**
- A Flame texture for our fire particle system material in **Book Assets | Textures**

- A Smoke texture for our smoke particle system material in **Book Assets | Textures**
- An audio clip of the fire crackling in **Book Assets | Sounds**
- Textures for the 3D campfire model in **Book Assets | Textures**

Adding the log pile

In the **Book Assets | Models** folder in the Project panel, you'll find a model called **campfire**. Select it, and change the **Scale factor** to **0.5** in the **FBX Importer** component of the **Inspector**.

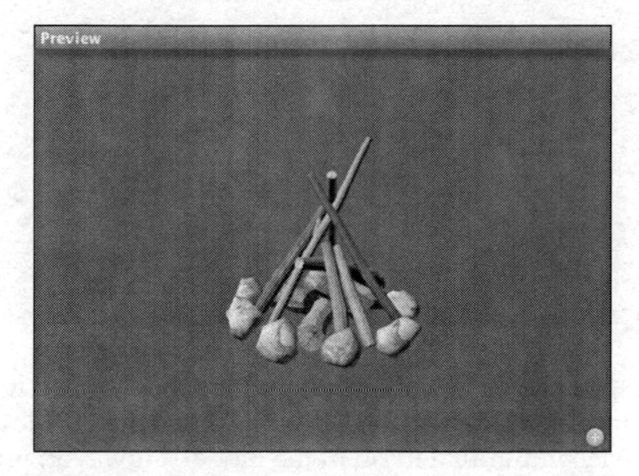

This will ensure that the model is imported into our scene at a reasonable size compared to the other objects already present. Press the **Apply** button at the bottom of the components in the **Inspector** to confirm this change.

You may have to rescale models when using them in Unity, but if modeling for a game yourself, take time to test the scale of imported objects and ensure that an imported cube of size (1, 1, 1) matches the scale of the cube primitive created in Unity—this will differ between modeling packages.

Now drag the campfire model over to the **Scene**, and use the **Transform tool** to position it near the outpost and coconut shy that are already present, as seen in the following image:

As we do not want our player to walk through this model, it needs to have a collider. Ordinarily, with complex models such as this, we'd use the FBX Importer to generate mesh colliders for each individual mesh in the model. However, given that we only need to ensure that the player bumps into this object, we can simply use a capsule collider instead. This will work just as well for our purposes and save on processing power because the processor will not have to build a collider for every mesh within the model.

Select the **campfire** object in the **Hierarchy** and go to **Component | Physics | Capsule Collider**. You will be prompted to confirm that you wish to disconnect this instance from the original model with a dialog window saying **Losing Prefab**—simply click on **Add** to continue as usual.

This will give you a small spherical looking collider at the base of the fire model. We need to increase the size of this to cover the boundary of the fire—now either make use of the Hand Tool (*Q*) by holding the *Shift* key to use the draggable collider boundary dots, or in the newly added **Capsule Collider** component in the **Inspector**, set the **Radius** to **2**, **Height** to **5**, and in the values for **Center**, set **Y** to a value of **1**. Your collider should now look something like the next image, and upon play testing, should cause the player to bump into the object:

Creating the campfire particle systems

In this section, we'll create two different particle systems, one for the fire and the other for smoke emanating from it. By using two separate systems, we will have more control over the animation of the particles over time, as we will not need to animate from fire to smoke in a single system.

Creating fire

To begin building our fire particle systems, we can add a game object with all three essential particle components. On the **Hierarchy** panel, click the **Create** button and choose **Particle System**, or alternatively, you may choose **GameObject | Create Other | Particle System** from the top menu. This creates a new game object in the **Scene/Hierarchy** named **Particle System**. Press *Return* (Mac) or *F2* (PC) and type to rename this to **FireSystem**, ensuring that there is no space in the name—this is crucial as it will help us keep a consistent naming convention for scripting later.

Bear in mind that at this stage, we needn't position the fire particle system until we have finished making it. Therefore, it can be designed at the arbitrary point in the 3D world that the Unity editor has placed it at—unless it has been placed underground, in which case you may use the **Translate** tool (*W*) to move it up to where you can see it in the **Scene** view. You may wish to move this object to within the campfire object to help you visualize what it will look like in context. To do this simply select the **campfire** object in the Hierarchy, hover your mouse over the scene view and press *F* to focus, and then reselect the **FireSystem** object in the Hierarchy and from the top menu go to **GameObject | Move to View**.

By default, your particle system has the default particle appearance of white softened dots in a cluster that resemble simple fireflies. This simply demonstrates the most generic settings for each component—the particle emitter is emitting and has a modest number of particles, the animator is simply making particles fade in and out, and the renderer has no material set up yet.

Let's go through each component now and set them up individually. You'll be able to see a preview of the particle system in the **Scene** view, so watch as you adjust each setting in the **Inspector**.

Ellipsoid Particle Emitter settings

Begin by setting the **Min Size** value to **0.5** and **Max Size** value to **2**; this is because our flames will need to be considerably larger than the firefly-like dots seen in the default settings. As with all Min and Max settings, the emitter will spawn particles of a size between these two values.

Now set **Min Energy** to **1** and **Max Energy** to **1.5**—this is the lifespan of the particles, and as a result, particles will last between 1 and 1.5 seconds before auto destructing. Set the **Min Emission** value to **15** and **Max Emission** value to **20**. This is the value defining how many particles are in the scene at any given time. The higher these values go, the more particles will be on screen, giving more density to the fire. However, particles can be expensive to render for the GPU. So, generally speaking, it is best to keep emission values like these to the lowest possible setting that you can aesthetically afford.

Set the **Y** value of **World Velocity** to **0.1**. This will cause the particles to rise during their lifespan, as flames would due to natural heat.

We do this using **World Velocity** with objects that must always go up in the game world. If this was done with **Local Velocity** on an object that was movable and that object rotated during the game, then its local Y axis would no longer face the World Y.

For example, a flaming barrel with physics may fall over, causing the axes of the attached particle system to rotate around, but its fire should still rise in World coordinates. While our campfire is not movable, it is a good practice to understand the difference between Local and World here.

Then set the **Y** value of **Rnd Velocity** (Random) to **0.2**—this will cause occasional random flames to leap a little higher than others.

Tangent Velocity should be set to **0.1** in the **X** and **Z** axes, leaving the **Y** axis on **0**. **Tangent Velocity** defines the initial speed and direction of individual particles relative to the ellipsoid space they are emitted within. So by setting a small value in **X** and **Z**, we are giving the flames of the fire a boost out horizontally.

Emitter Velocity Scale can be set to **0**, as this is only relevant to moving particle systems as it controls how quickly the particles themselves move if the system's parent object is moved. As our fire will remain static, it can be left at **0**.

Simulate in Worldspace handles whether particles follow the game object they are created on, or stay in their world positions when the system is moved. Our campfire object will not move in the game so it is irrelevant in this instance but if creating a moveable flaming torch, you would want to have this option enabled to make the flames flow in world space but still emit from the position of the particle emitting game object so as to appear to be following or trailing.

One Shot can be left unchecked, as we need our particles to flow continuously. **One Shot** would be more useful in something such as a single puff of smoke from a cannon for example.

Ellipsoid values can be set to **0.5** for all axes—this is a small value, but our particle system should emit on a small scale—the ellipsoid value for the smoke plume particle system, for example, will need to be much taller, allowing smoke particles to be created higher above the campfire, for the appearance of density.

Particle Animator settings

Next we need to set up the Particle Animator component, which will define behavior of our particles over the course of their lifespan. Here we will need to make the particles fade in and out, and animate through colors (shades of red/orange), as well as apply forces to them, which will cause the flames to leap and billow at the sides more realistically.

Begin by ensuring that **Does Animate Color** is checked, which will cause the five **Color Animation** boxes to come into play. Now go through each box by clicking on the color block to the right, and in the color picker that appears, set colors that fade from white in **Color Animation [0]** through to dark orange in **Color Animation [4]**.

As you do this, also set the A (alpha) value at the bottom of the color picker to a value so that **Color Animation [0]** and **Color Animation [4]** have an alpha of around 0 to 5 percent of the full bar, and the states in between fade up and back. Alpha is illustrated in the **Inspector** by the white/black line beneath each color block.

See the following image for a visual representation of what you need to do here:

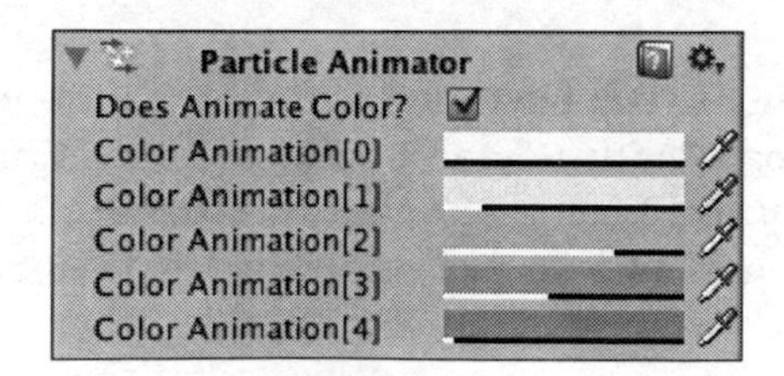

If you are reading this book in its printed edition, you will need a reference to the colors used as you will be viewing images in grayscale. See the RGB numerical values below for each **Color Animation** block in order to match the settings shown in the previous image:

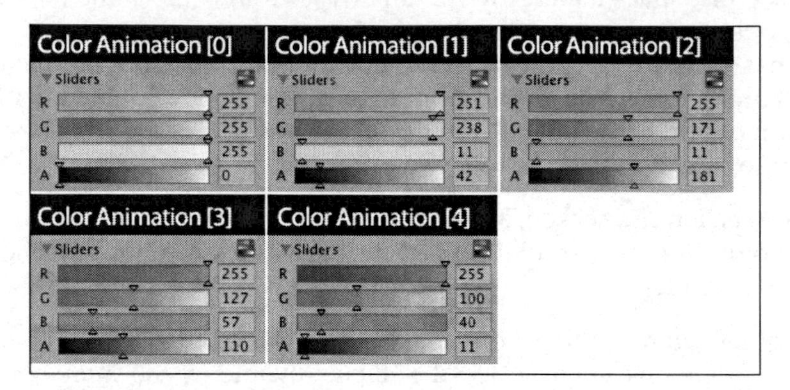

Your particle system in the **Scene** view should now be billowing more naturally and animating through the colors and alpha values that you have specified.

> The effect of the **Color Animation** system may look more or less effective depending upon whether materials applied to your particle system use particular **Shaders**—some show color more so than others. For example, shaders with transparency may appear to show colors less effectively.

After leaving the **Rotation Axis** settings at their default of **0** in all axes, set **Size Grow** to a value of **-0.3**. We set this to a minus value in order to cause particles to shrink during their lifespan, giving a more dynamic look to the fire.

Next we'll add forces to give a more realistic motion to the fire. Forces are different to the velocities added in the **Emitter** settings, as forces are applied when the particles are instantiated—causing a boost of speed following by deceleration and then continuation at the speed defined within velocity settings. Expand the **Rnd Force** parameter by clicking on the gray arrow to the left of it and place a value of **1** into the **X** and **Z** axes. Then expand the **Force** parameter in the same way, and set the **Y** axis value to **1**.

Set the value for **Damping** to **0.8**. Damping defines the amount that particles slow down during their lifespan. With a default value of 1 meaning that no damping occurs, values between 0 and 1 cause slow down, 0 being the most intensive slowing. We are setting a mild value of 0.8 so that our particles do not slow too unnaturally.

The final setting, **Autodestruct,** can be left unchecked. All particles themselves naturally autodestruct at the end of their lifespan, but the autodestruct setting here relates to the parent game object itself—if selected, and all particles in the system have auto-destructed, then the game object will be destroyed. This only comes into play when using the **One Shot** setting in the emitter component; in the example of a cannon blast, the developer would likely instantiate an instance of a one-shot particle system with autodestruct selected. This means that as soon as it had been created, once all the particles had died, the game object would be destroyed, thus improving performance.

Particle Renderer settings

In our fire particle system, we simply need to apply a particle-shaded material containing the fire graphic you downloaded and imported. But before we do that, we'll ensure that the **Particle Renderer** is set up correctly for our purposes.

As the particles or flames of a fire should technically emit light, we'll deselect both **Cast Shadows** and **Receive Shadows** to ensure that no shadow is cast on or by the fire—bear in mind that this is only valid for users of Unity Pro version, as the standard free version does not feature dynamic shadows.

Currently there are no materials applied to this particle system, so there are no entries in the **Materials** area; we will rectify this shortly. Next, ensure that **Camera Velocity Scale** is set to **0**—this would only be used if we were not billboard rendering our particles. If we planned to stretch particles, then we would use this setting to define how much of an effect camera movement had on particle stretching.

Stretch Particles should be set to **Billboard** as discussed earlier, ensuring that no matter where the player views the fire from, particles are drawn facing them. As **Length** and **Velocity** scale are only used in stretched particles, we can happily leave these two settings at **0**—altering these values will not affect billboarded particles.

The final setting to consider, bearing in mind that we are not using UV Animation, is **Max Particle Size**. This setting controls how large a particle can be in relation to the height of the screen. For example if set to **1**, particles can be of a size up to the height of the screen, at **0.5** they can be up to half the height of the screen, and so on. As our fire particles will never need to be of a size as large as the screen height, we can leave this setting on its default of **0.25**.

Adding a material

Now that our particle system is set up, all that is left to do is to create a material for it using our fire texture. Select the **Materials** folder in the **Project** panel, and click on the **Create** button at the top of the panel, and choose **Material**. This will make a new asset called **New Material** in the folder—simply rename this **Flame**, and keep it selected in order to see its properties in the **Inspector**.

From the **Shader** drop-down menu, choose **Particles | Additive (soft)**. This will give us a transparency-based particle with a soft render of the texture we apply. Now, drag the texture called **flame** from the **Book Assets | Textures** folder in the **Project** panel, and drop it onto the empty square to the right of **Particle Texture** where it currently says **None (Texture)**.

To apply this material, simply drag the material from the **Materials** folder in the **Project** panel and drop it onto the **FireSystem** object in the **Hierarchy** panel. It will now appear listed in the Particle Renderer component in the Inspector for this object and thus can be modified from there.

Positioning the FireSystem

In order to position the fire particle system more easily, we'll need to make it a child of the **campfire** object already in our scene. In the **Hierarchy** panel, drag the **FireSystem** object, and drop it onto the game object named **campfire** to make it a child object. Then reset its position by clicking on the **Cog** icon to the right of the **Transform** component of **FireSystem**, and choose **Reset.**

Now that you have reset the position, your particle system will be directly in the center of its parent object; as you'll notice, this is too low down. If you cannot see this, then select the object in the **Hierarchy** and hover your mouse cursor over the **Scene** view and press *F* to focus your view on it. Still in the **Transform** component, set the **Y** axis position to **0.8** to raise it slightly.

Time to Test!

Press the **Play** button to test the game now and admire your handiwork! Remember to press **Play** again to stop testing before you continue.

Blowing smoke!

As the saying goes, "There's no smoke without fire", and vice versa. With this in mind, we'll need a smoke plume emerging from above our campfire, if it is to look realistic at all.

Begin by adding a new particle system to the Scene; click the **Create** button on the Hierarchy panel and choose **Particle System** or choose **GameObject | Create Other | Particle System** from the top menu. Rename the **Particle System** that you have just made in the Hierarchy to **SmokeSystem** (again, note that we are not using a space in this object name for ease of scripting later).

Ellipsoid Particle Emitter settings

As we have already discussed the implications of settings in the previous step, now you can simply use the following list and observe the changes as you make them. Any settings not listed should be left at their default setting:

- **Min Size: 0.8**
- **Max Size: 2.5**
- **Min Energy: 8**
- **Max Energy: 10**
- **Min Emission: 10**
- **Max Emission: 15**
- **World Velocity Y: 1.5**
- **Rnd Velocity Y: 0.2**
- **Emitter Velocity Scale: 0.1**

Particle Animator settings

Set up your Particle Animator to animate through shades of gray, as shown in the following image:

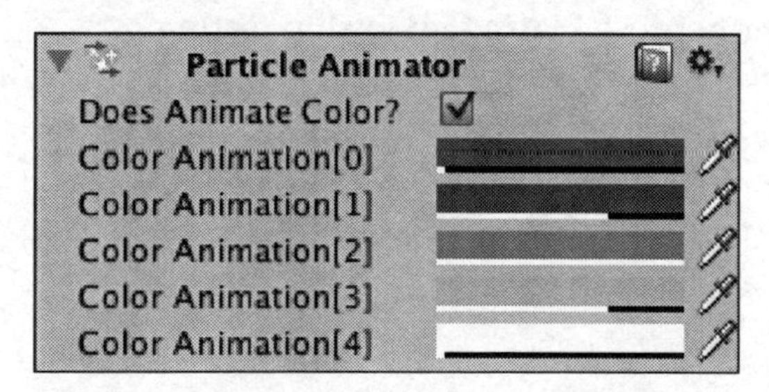

Again, here you should notice that particles should be animated between two near zero-alphas so that they start and end close to invisibly. This will avoid a visual "pop" as the particles are removed—if they are visible when they are removed, the removal is a lot more noticeable, and less natural.

Now alter the following settings:

- **Size Grow**: **0.2**
- **Rnd Force**: **(1.2, 0.8, 1.2)**
- **Force**: **(0.1, 0, 0.1)**
- **Autodestruct**: Not selected

Particle Renderer settings

We will create a material to apply to the smoke shortly, but first, ensure that the following settings are applied to the particle renderer component:

- **Cast/Receive Shadows**: both unchecked
- **Stretch Particles**: **Billboard**
- **Camera Velocity Scale, Length Scale, Velocity Scale**: **0**
- **Max Particle Size**: **0.25**

Now, follow the step titled **Adding a Material** under the section **Creating fire** above. However, this time, name your material **Smoke** and assign the texture file called **smoke** located in the **Book Assets | Textures** folder, and drop the material you make onto the **SmokeSystem** game object in the Hierarchy.

Positioning

Repeat the step for positioning of the fire for the smoke system by dragging and dropping the **SmokeSystem** object onto the **campfire** parent in the **Hierarchy**. Then using the **Cog** icon to the right of the **Transform** component, choose **Reset**, and set the **Y** position value to **1.5**. Press the **Play** button now and your campfire should light, and the smoke plume should rise, looking something like the following image. As always, remember to press **Play** again to stop testing.

Adding audio to the fire

Now that our fire looks aesthetically pleasing, we'll need to add atmospheric sound of the fire crackling. In the **Book Assets | Sounds** folder you have imported, you are provided with a sound file called `fire_atmosphere`. Select this file and in the Audio Importer in the Project panel, ensure that **3D Sound** is checked; this will mean that when we apply this file to an audio source, walking away from the fire will mean the audio will fade away with distance, which should make sense to the player.

Select the **campfire** object in the **Hierarchy**, and go to **Component | Audio | Audio Source**. This adds an Audio Source component to the object, so now simply drag the **fire_atmosphere** audio clip from the **Book Assets | Sounds** folder in the **Project** panel, and drop it onto the **Audio Clip** parameter of the **Audio Source** component in the **Inspector**. To ensure that this sound continues to play, simply check the box next to the **Loop** parameter.

Press the **Play** button and approach the fire while listening for the sound of the fire crackling; then walk away, and listen to the fading effect. Press **Play** again to stop once you have finished testing.

3D Audio

To adjust the **Rolloff** value of the fire crackling—how the sound fades as the distance of the **Audio Listener** (usually attached to the player's camera) increases—we can adjust the roll off curve of the Audio Source component.

By expanding the **3D Sound Settings** in the **Audio Source** component, you will be able to view and adjust the **Rolloff** curve settings:

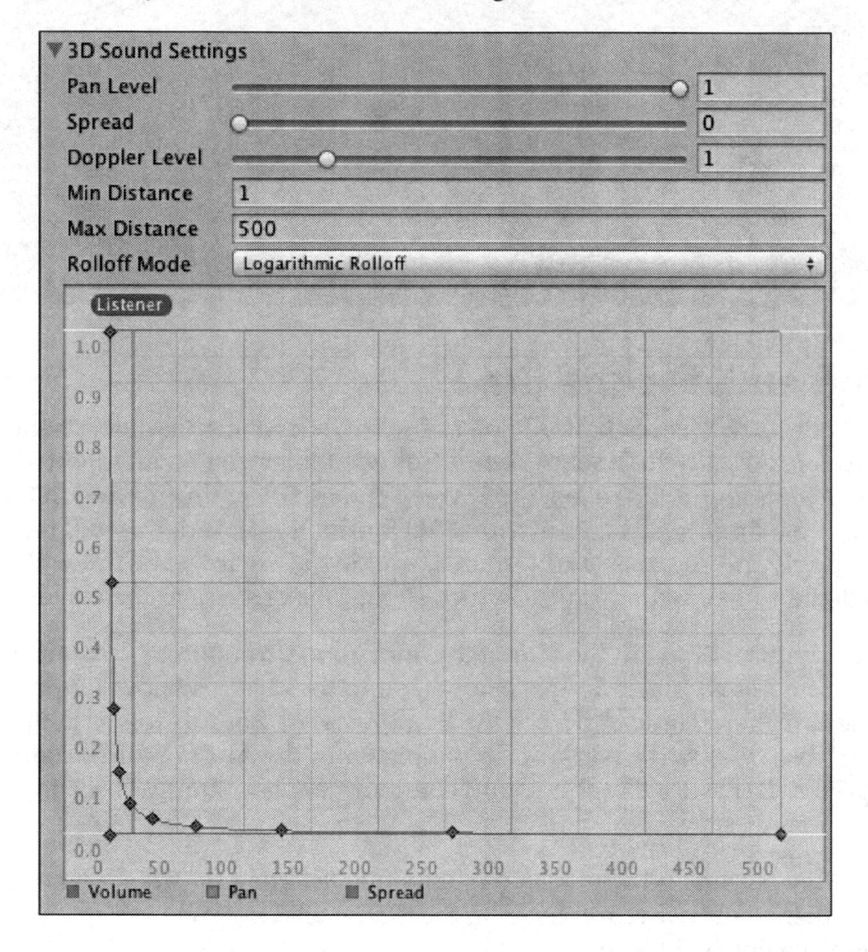

Here you can create a custom curve by changing the **Rolloff Mode** to **Custom** and dragging the Bezier points to adjust the curve, and even change the **Rolloff Mode** to a linear curve if making less realistic game environments.

The standard logarithmic curve is an appropriate Rolloff setting for this fire, but if you wish to edit the fading of the campfire's audio to experiment, do so now.

Lighting the fire

Now that our fire is prepared, let's make it function within the game, creating the mechanics for the player to collect matches, and then light the fire once it is collected.

First we need to disable the fire, so that it is not lit when the game begins. To achieve this, we must switch off the particle systems and audio:

- Select the **campfire** object in the **Hierarchy**, and in the **Audio Source** component in the **Inspector**, uncheck the **Play On Awake** parameter so that the sound does not play before we enable it via script.
- Select the **FireSystem** child object of the campfire, and in the **Particle Emitter** component, uncheck the **Emit** parameter.
- Select the **SmokeSystem** child object of the campfire, and in the **Particle Emitter** component, uncheck the **Emit** parameter.

Now we need to create the collection of matches and a HUD display of the fact we have matches. To do this, we'll need to do the following:

- Add the **matchbox** model to the outpost, making it the reward of gaining entry.
- Make a HUD element using a GUI Texture of a box of matches, and save this as a prefab.
- Write a Trigger script to allow collection of the matches, which will register this collection in the Inventory script on the player, and display the HUD element.

Adding the matches

Select the **matchbox** model in the **Book Assets | Models** folder of the **Project** panel, drag this over to the **Hierarchy**, and drop it onto the **outPost** object, making it a child object. This will make it easier to position.

In the **Transform** component for the matchbox in the **Inspector**, click the **Cog** icon to the right of the **Transform** component and then choose **Reset Position**, then set Y axis for **Position** values to **2.5**. Now that the matchbox is at a position in the outpost you can spot it at, use the Translate tool (*W*) to position it on top of the table, so that it is easy enough to spot for the player, and it makes sense that this is the object they should collect when entering the building.

As we need to collect this object, it will need a collider in order to detect collisions between it and the player. With the **matchbox** still selected, go to **Component | Physics | Box Collider**, and click on **Add** when presented with the **Losing Prefab** dialog window. To avoid the player bumping into the object, and to allow the player to collect with `OnTriggerEnter()`, we'll put this collider into trigger mode. To do this, simply check the box next to the **Is Trigger** parameter in the **Box Collider** component in the **Inspector**.

As this object is not placed overlapping the edge of the desk it is likely that the player's collider will hit the desk before they can interact with the Box Collider we just placed onto the matchbox. To help with this, we can simply make the collider itself bigger, rather than having to move the matchbox close to the edge. Locate the **Size** parameters on the **Box Collider** component, and set **X**, **Y** and **Z** to a value of **1**. Your collider outline should now look like the following image in the Scene panel:

Your matchbox will now be much easier to interact with—considering that ultimately when the player sees it and walks up to grab it, they won't be thinking about the position of the player's collider; they just know there is an object they likely need to grab, and must walk toward it to collect it.

Writing the Match Collection script

To allow the player to pick up the matches, we will write a script that checks the trigger for the player, and calls upon a new function we will add to the Inventory script later.

Select the **Scripts** folder in the Project panel, click the **Create** button and choose your preferred language, then rename your new script **Matches**. Launch the script in the script editor and add the following function:

C#:

```
void OnTriggerEnter(Collider col){
  if(col.gameObject.tag == "Player"){
    col.gameObject.SendMessage("MatchPickup");
    Destroy(gameObject);
  }
}
```

Javascript:

```
function OnTriggerEnter(col : Collider){
  if(col.gameObject.tag == "Player"){
    col.gameObject.SendMessage("MatchPickup");
    Destroy(gameObject);
  }
}
```

Here we are checking for the `Player` through tag, in a similar style to how our **powerCell** script works. If the player is detected, we send them a message to call a function named `MatchPickup`, which we will add to our Inventory shortly. Finally, the `gameObject` itself—the matches—is removed from the game using `Destroy()`.

Save your script and return to Unity. Apply this script by dragging and dropping the **Matches** script from the **Scripts** folder onto the **matchbox** object in the Hierarchy. Play testing the game now would give us a **Send Message has no receiver** error, because there is currently no function to receive that message in any of the scripts on the player, so we will continue to work on our scripts until we have established the `MatchPickup()` function to complete this collection mechanic.

Now let's move on to create a GUI element to represent the collection of this item, before amending our Inventory to accommodate the collection of this object.

Creating the matches GUI

Select the **MatchGUI** texture file in the **Book Assets | Textures** folder in the **Project** panel. In the **Texture Importer** settings on the Inspector, set the **Texture Type** drop-down menu to **GUI**. This better prepares the asset to display in 2D. Press **Apply** at the bottom of the Import settings now to confirm.

With this texture still selected in the Project panel, go to **GameObject | Create Other | GUI Texture**. We needn't position this texture on screen now as this can be done when we instantiate it from a prefab. Currently it will look like the following:

To save this object as a prefab, open the **Prefabs** folder in the Project panel, and drag the **MatchGUI** object from the Hierarchy and drop it into the **Prefabs** folder to save it as a prefab.

Finally, select the original **MatchGUI** object in the **Hierarchy** again, and remove it from the scene by pressing *Command* + *Backspace* (Mac) or *Delete* (PC).

Collecting the matches

From the **Scripts** folder in the Project panel, open the script called **Inventory**. To remember whether we have collected the matches or not, we'll add a Boolean variable to the script, which will be set to `true` once the matches are collected. We will also add a reference to the **MatchGUI** prefab that we just created so we can instantiate it once the player has picked up the matches. Add the following lines after the last variables for the generator that we added previously:

C#:

```
// Matches
bool haveMatches = false;
public GUITexture matchGUIprefab;
```

Javascript:

```
// Matches
private var haveMatches : boolean = false;
var matchGUIprefab : GUITexture;
```

Our `matchGUIprefab` reference is `public`, so we will assign our new **MatchGUI** prefab to this variable in the **Inspector** once we have finished our script.

In addition to the reference to the prefab, we will also add a private GUI Texture reference next that we can use to store a reference to the MatchGUI game object once it is created. We can use this reference to remove the MatchGUI later once the player uses the matches. Add the following private variable below the two you just added:

C#:

```
GUITexture matchGUI;
```

Javascript:

```
private var matchGUI : GUITexture;
```

The next function we will add is named `MatchPickup()` — you should recall that this is the function being called by our `SendMessage()` within the **Matches** script if the Player is detected walking into the trigger collider of the matches.

Add the following function to the **Inventory** now:

C#:

```
void MatchPickup(){
        haveMatches = true;
        AudioSource.PlayClipAtPoint(collectSound, transform.position);
        GUITexture matchHUD = Instantiate(matchGUIprefab,
          new Vector3(0.15f, 0.1f, 0),transform.rotation) as
GUITexture;
        matchGUI = matchHUD;
}
```

Javascript:

```
function MatchPickup(){
  haveMatches = true;
  AudioSource.PlayClipAtPoint(collectSound, transform.position);
  var matchHUD : GUITexture =
    Instantiate(matchGUIprefab, Vector3(0.15, 0.1, 0),
      transform.rotation);
  matchGUI = matchHUD;
}
```

Here we are setting our `haveMatches` variable to true—we will query this later when we add a function to use the matches.

We then play the collect sound we used earlier; this could be altered to a differing clip by adding a further variable at the top of the script to allow for a different sound for collecting matches from collecting power cells. For simplicity and continuity we will make use of the same audio clip.

In the third line of the function, we are instantiating an instance of the `matchGUIprefab`, and simultaneously saving it into a local variable named `matchHUD`. For its position we are passing in a screen position using a `Vector3` that is (0.15, 0.1, 0)—the lower left-hand side of the screen.

Finally, we are setting the our `matchGUI` private reference to the newly created instance by setting it equal to `matchHUD` local variable—we can make use of this when we need to remove the MatchGUI object later when the player uses the matches on the campfire.

Save your **Inventory** script now and switch back to Unity.

Select the **First Person Controller** to see the **Inventory (Script)** component. You will notice the public variable **MatchGUI** prefab is exposed and expecting a **GUI Texture** object to be assigned to it. Drag and drop the **MatchGUI** prefab from the **Prefabs** folder in the Project panel onto this variable.

Save your progress in Unity now by choosing **File | Save Scene** from the top menu. Press the **Play** button and ensure that upon entering the outpost, you can pick up the matches by walking into them. The texture of the matches should then appear in the lower left of the screen. Now we will use the `haveMatches` variable to decide whether the fire can be lit or not.

Starting the fire

In order to light the fire, we need to check for collisions between the player and the campfire object. For this, return to the script editor to edit the **Inventory** script, or if you have closed it, re-open it from the **Scripts** folder of the **Project** panel.

Next we will check for a collision between the player and the campfire. However, we are using a physical collider rather than a trigger mode collider so we need to make use of a collision detection function for character controller collisions —`OnControllerColliderHit()`. We looked at this earlier in our first attempt at opening the outpost door but abandoned it as the use of triggers was more appropriate.

Add the following function to the Inventory script now:

C#:

```
void OnControllerColliderHit(ControllerColliderHit col){
  if(col.gameObject.name == "campfire"){
    LightFire(col.gameObject);
  }
}
```

Javascript:

```
function OnControllerColliderHit(col : ControllerColliderHit){
  if(col.gameObject.name == "campfire"){
    LightFire(col.gameObject);
  }
}
```

In this function, we are establishing a variable as usual to store the interactions that the function detects. As with other instances of collision detection we are calling this variable `col` for simplicity, but unlike other collision functions, `OnControllerColliderHit()` stores a `ControllerColliderHit` type of variable. However, we can still access the `gameObject` we have hit within this, and we do so in the `if` statement within this function.

If this condition is met then we call a custom function called `LightFire()` and pass the collided with game object to it as an argument. Let's establish this function now.

Using arrays and loops for commands on multiple objects

Here we will make use of an array and a **for loop** in order to carry out the same set of commands on multiple objects. This technique is useful in many game development scenarios. For example in a puzzle game a player may select corresponding pieces of a puzzle in a particular column that must all fall away, so finding these objects and applying commands to them in a loop is the most efficient method of achieving this.

After the closing right curly brace of the `OnControllerColliderHit()` function, establish the following function:

C#:

```
void LightFire(GameObject campfire){
}
```

Javascript:

```
function LightFire(campfire : GameObject){
}
```

In the parentheses of this function we have created a `GameObject` type argument named `campfire`, which the `OnControllerColliderHit()` function is sending the collided with object to.

This function needs to light the campfire by enabling the `emit` property of both the **FireSystem** and **SmokeSystem**'s **Particle Emitter** components. For this we can make use of an array to collect both of the emitter components, and then iterate through this array, switching on both emitters. Begin by establishing the following local array inside your `LightFire()` function:

C#:

```
ParticleEmitter[] fireEmitters;
```

Javascript:

```
var fireEmitters : ParticleEmitter[];
```

Now we need to populate this array with both of the particle emitter components. For this we can make use of the `GetComponentsInChildren` command that will find components in any child objects of a stated game object. For this reason we will use the `campfire` argument as it is a reference to the parent game object of the FireSystem and SmokeSystem objects. Add the following line to your `LightFire()` function:

C#:

```
fireEmitters = campfire.GetComponentsInChildren<ParticleEmitter>();
```

Javascript:

```
fireEmitters = campfire.GetComponentsInChildren(ParticleEmitter);
```

Here we are sending the Particle Emitter components found in child objects of the `campfire` object to our `fireEmitters` array. Now we simply need to use a `for` loop to iterate through this array and perform a command on the emitters in the array. Add the following code after the line you have just added:

C#:

```
foreach(ParticleEmitter emitter in fireEmitters){
  emitter.emit = true;
}
```

Javascript:

```
for(var emitter : ParticleEmitter in fireEmitters){
  emitter.emit = true;
}
```

The syntax of the for loop between C# and Javascript may vary but they achieve the same task. Within the condition of the loop we establish a variable named `emitter`, which is passed each entry `in` the `fireEmitters` array each time the loop runs.

This is then used to address the `emit` parameter of the Particle Emitter component, setting it to true.

Finally, let's re-enable the audio of the campfire too. After the closing right curly brace of the for loop, add the following line of code:

C# and Javascript:

```
campfire.audio.Play();
```

Signifying Inventory usage

In a typical hallmark of videogames, we need to signal to the player that they have used the matches by removing the **MatchGUI** HUD element from the player's screen.

We must also set our `haveMatches` Boolean variable to false, in order to register that we no longer have matches to use. After the closing right curly brace of the `for` loop we just added, but before the closing right brace of the `LightFire()` function, add the following lines:

C# and Javascript:

```
Destroy(matchGUI);
haveMatches=false;
```

The `Destroy()` command removes the **MatchGUI** game object as we stored it in this variable in the `OnControllerColliderHit()` function. Lastly, `haveMatches` is set to false—we will use this now to ensure that our collision detection does two different things depending upon whether the player has approached the fire with or without matches:

- With matches—`LightFire()` function will be called
- Without matches—the player will be shown a hint using our existing **TextHintGUI** object

Return to the top of the script, and add another public variable to allow us to refer to the **TextHintGUI** object:

C#:

```
public GUIText textHints;
```

Javascript:

```
var textHints : GUIText;
```

We will assign our **TextHintGUI** object to this variable in the Inspector once we have finished the script. Now we simply need to create an if/else statement within our `OnControllerColliderHit()` function's existing `if` statement. Amend your existing if statement:

```
if(col.gameObject.name == "campfire"){
  LightFire(col.gameObject);
}
```

So that it now features a check to see whether the player has picked up the matches:

```
if(col.gameObject.name == "campfire"){
  if(haveMatches){
    LightFire(col.gameObject);
  }else{
    textHints.SendMessage("ShowHint",
      "I could use this campfire to signal for help..
        if only I could light it..");
  }
}
```

Now our collision with the fire will light it if the player has the matches, and if not, it will show them a hint.

Save your script and return to Unity now. We need to assign our **TextHintGUI** object to our **Text Hints** variable that we just added to the Inventory script.

Select the **First Person Controller** in the Hierarchy, and in the **Inventory (script)** component in the Inspector, drag-and-drop to assign **TextHintGUI** from the Hierarchy to the **Text Hints** public variable.

Play test your game once more and ensure that if you approach the fire without matches you are shown a hint, but once you have collected the matches, the fire is lit.

This will work, but there is one last problem to counteract—can you spot it? Or had you already guessed what this might be? We will reveal and fix this shortly, but first let's update our progress. When you have finished play testing, press **Play** to stop. Save your progress so far by choosing **File | Save Project** from the top menu.

Testing and confirming

As with any new feature of your game, testing is crucial. In *Chapter 10* and *Chapter 11*, we will look at optimizing your game and ensuring that test builds work as they are expected to, along with various options for delivering your game.

For now, you should ensure that your game functions properly so far. Even if you have no errors showing in the Unity console (*Command* + *Shift* + *C* shows this panel on Mac, *Ctrl* + *Shift* + *C* on PC), you should still make sure that as you play through the game, no errors occur as the player uses each part of the game.

If you encounter errors while testing, the **Pause** button at the top of the Unity editor will allow you to pause, play, and look at the error listed in the **Console** window. When encountering an error, simply double-click on it in the Console, and you'll be taken to the line of the script which contains the error, or at least to where the script encounters a problem. You can also select the Error Pause button on the Console window to force Unity to pause the game as soon as errors occur.

From here, you can diagnose the error or check your script against the Unity scripting reference to make sure that you have the correct approach. If you are still stuck with errors, ask for help on the Unity community forums or in the IRC channel. For more information, visit the following page: `http://unity3d.com/support/community`

So, what's the problem?

If there are no errors with the code, there is still a slight problem with our current approach to lighting the fire—did you spot it yet?

What you should have noticed when play testing the game is that when colliding with the fire whilst carrying the matches, the fire is lit, but the text hint still appears, because it is within the `else` statement, that is, when `haveMatches` is false. To correct this, we should add a further Boolean variable to check whether the fire has been lit.

If you think you can solve this yourself, close the book now and try writing the code yourself.

However, if you aren't too sure, worry not—read on for what you need to do.

Safeguarding with additional conditions

Re-launch the **Inventory** script in the script editor, and add the following private variable at the top:

C#:

```
bool fireIsLit = false;
```

Javascript:

```
private var fireIsLit : boolean = false;
```

Now at the bottom of the `LightFire()` function, after the line `haveMatches=false;` add the following to toggle `fireIsLit`:

C# and Javascript:

```
fireIsLit=true;
```

Now return to the `OnControllerColliderHit()` function's `if` statements, and amend them as follows:

C# and Javascript:

```
if(haveMatches&& !fireIsLit){
  LightFire(col.gameObject);
}else if(!haveMatches&& !fireIsLit){
  textHints.SendMessage("ShowHint",
    "I could use this campfire to signal for help..
      if only I could light it..");
}
```

Here we are ensuring that if the player approaches with the matches, but the fire has not been lit, then it will be lit by the `LightFire()` function, but if they approach without matches and before the fire has been lit, they will be shown a hint. This means that if they are lighting the fire, then the hint will not be shown, as the `else if` condition requires `fireIsLit` to be false (hence the use of the preceding exclamation mark to say 'not'). Save your script and return to Unity now.

Play test your game once more and you will see this in action! Once you are satisfied, save your Scene and Project progress using the **File** menu in Unity.

Summary

In this chapter, we have looked at the use of particles to give a more dynamic feel to our game. Particles are used in a wide array of different game situations, from car and spaceship exhausts to guns and air-vent steam, and the best way to reinforce what we have just learned is to experiment. There are a lot of parameters to play with and, as such, the best results are found by taking some time out of a project just to see what kind of effects you can achieve. We have also looked at one method for triggering particles as part of the game—something that in most kinds of games, you will likely do quite often.

In the next chapter, we will take a look at making menus for your game, and this will involve scripting with Unity's GUI class, as well as using GUI Skin assets to style and create behaviors for your interfaces. The GUI class is a specific part of the Unity engine, which is used specifically for making menus, HUDs (Heads Up Displays), and when used in conjunction with GUI Skin assets, becomes completely visually customizable and re-usable. This is because Skin assets can be applied to as many GUI class scripts as you like, creating a consistent design style throughout your Unity projects.

9
Designing Menus

In order to create a rounded example game in this chapter, we will look at creating a separate scene to our existing island scene to act as a menu. Menu design in Unity can be achieved in a number of ways using a combination of built-in behaviors and 2D texture rendering.

Game titles can be added using GUITextures, GUI class scripting, or by adding textures to a flat plane primitive; these may be used to create for example a splash screen with developer logos, parts of a game's GUI or loading screens. In this chapter, you will learn:

- Two different approaches to interface design
- Controlling GUITexture components with scripted mouse events
- Writing a basic Unity GUI script
- Defining 2D spaces with Rect values
- Styling GUI code and using GUI skin assets
- Loading scenes to navigate menus and loading the game level

When adding interactive menus, you may wish to consider two different approaches, one using Unity's simple, component based GUITextures—an area we've already explored when implementing our Match GUI in the previous chapter and the crosshair in *Chapter 7*, and the other utilizing Unity GUI classes, and incorporating GUI skin assets.

We will learn two approaches for adding interactive menus:

1. **GUI Textures and mouse event scripting**

   The first approach will involve creating GUITexture objects, and with scripting based on mouse events—mouse over, mouse down, and mouse up—for example, swapping the textures used by these objects. With this approach, less scripting is required to create the buttons themselves, but all actions must be controlled and listened to through scripts.

2. **Unity GUI class scripting and GUI skins**

   The second approach will take a more script-intensive methodology and involve generating our entire menu using scripts, as opposed to creating individual game objects for menu items in the first approach.

   With this approach, more scripting is required to create menu elements initially, but GUI skin assets can be created to style the appearance and assign behavior through the Inspector for mouse events. This approach also saves on Draw Calls to the GPU, as there is usually only one object with the script attached, rather than many objects representing a part of the menu each.

The latter approach is generally the more accepted method of creating full game menus, as it gives the developer more flexibility. The menu items themselves are established in the script, but styled using GUI skins in an approach comparable to HTML and CSS development in web design—the **CSS** (**Cascading Style Sheets**) controlling the form with the HTML providing the content—in this example the GUI is the HTML and the GUI skin is the CSS.

Interfaces and menus

Menus are most commonly used to set up controls and to adjust game settings, such as graphics and sound, or to load saved game states. In any given game, it is crucial that the accompanying menu does not get in the way of the player diving straight into the game or any of its settings. When we think of a great game, we always remember it for the actual game itself, rather than the menus—unless they were especially entertaining, or especially badly designed.

Many games seek to tie the menu of their game with the game's design or themes. For example, in 2D Boy's excellent *World Of Goo*, the cursor is changed to the form of a goo ball with a trail that follows it in the menus and game, tying the game's visual concept with its interface:

This is a good example, as the game itself is already giving the player something akin to its core mechanics to toy with as they navigate through the opening menu.

In Media Molecule's *LittleBigPlanet*, this concept is taken to another level by giving the player a menu that requires them to learn how to control the player character before they can navigate through the game menu.

As with any design, consistency is the key, and in our example, we'll be ensuring that we maintain a set of house colors and consistent use of typography. You may have encountered poorly designed games in the past and noticed that they use too many fonts, or clashing colors, which—given that the game menu is the first thing a player will see—is a terribly off-putting factor in making the game enjoyable and commercially viable.

The textures to be used in the menu creation are available inside the **Book Assets | Textures** folder, where you will find the following:

- Textures for a main game title and three buttons—**Play**, **Instructions**, and **Quit** all beginning with the word **menu_**
- An audio clip of an interface **beep** for the buttons

Creating the scene

In this section, we'll take our existing design work of the island itself and use it as a backdrop for our menus. This gives players a sneak preview of the kind of environment they'll be exploring and sets a visual context for the game.

By duplicating our existing island, viewed from a distance using a remote camera, we'll overlay 2D interface elements using the two previously mentioned approaches.

For our menu, we'll aim to make use of the island environment we've already created. By placing the island in the background of our menu, we're effectively teasing the player with the environment they can explore, if they start playing the game. Visual incentives such as these might seem minor, but they can work well as a way of subliminally encouraging the player, and getting them into the mood of the game.

Duplicating the island

To begin, we'll reuse our **Island** scene that we have already created. To make things easier to manage, we'll group together the essential environment assets—the terrain itself, water, and directional light to keep them separate from objects we don't need, such as the outpost, coconut shy, and power cells. This way, when it comes to duplicating the level, we can simply remove everything but the group we are about to make.

Grouping the environment objects

Grouping in Unity is as easy as nesting objects as children under an empty parent object. Follow these steps now:

1. Go to **GameObject** | **Create Empty**– shortcut *Ctrl* + *Shift* + *N* (*Command* + *Shift* + *N* on Mac).

2. This makes a new object called simply **GameObject**, so rename this as **Environment**.
3. In the **Hierarchy** panel, drag-and-drop the **Directional Light, Daylight Simple Water**, and **Terrain** objects onto the **Environment** empty object. Now we are ready to duplicate this level to create our menu in a separate scene.

Duplicating the scene

Follow these steps to duplicate the scene:

1. Ensure that the **Island** scene is saved by going to **File | Save Scene**, and then select the **Island** scene asset in the **Project** panel.
2. Go to **Edit | Duplicate,** or use the keyboard shortcut *Command* + *D* (Mac) or *Ctrl* + *D* (PC). When duplicating, Unity simply increments object/asset names with a number, so your duplicate will be named **Island 1**—. Ensure that the duplicate is selected in the **Project** panel and rename this to **Menu** now.
3. Load this **Menu** scene to begin working on it by double-clicking on its icon in the **Project** panel.
4. With the **Menu** scene open, we can now remove any objects we do not need. If you are on a Mac, hold down the *Command* key, or if on a PC, hold down the *Ctrl* key, and select all objects in the **Hierarchy** except for the **Environment** group by clicking on them one-by-one.
5. Now delete them from this scene by using keyboard shortcuts *Command* + *Backspace* on Mac, or *Delete* on PC.

Framing the shot

As shown in the previous image, our menu screen comprises of a shot of the island from afar—positioned in the lower-right of the screen, with the title and menu superimposed over the top in empty space, such as the sky and the sea. To achieve this, we will need to introduce a new camera to the scene, as previously the only camera was the one attached to the **First Person Controller**. As there is currently no camera in the scene, the **Game** view should now be completely blank, as there is no viewport on our 3D world.

To create a camera, click the **Create** button on the Hierarchy and choose **Camera** from the drop-down menu, or choose **GameObject | Create Other | Camera** from the top menu.

Now position your view in the Scene view so that you are looking at the island from afar, as shown in the following image:

Now align your camera with this view by selecting the **Camera** object in the Hierarchy and choosing **GameObject | Align with view**. If the game view seems to cut off any detail, simply increase the **Far** value under **Clipping Planes** in the **Camera** component in the Inspector; increase the value until a far view into the horizon is shown with neither the island nor water cut off.

If you are not happy with this view you can always move the scene view and repeat the above step. This is a simple and quite flexible way of positioning cameras that avoids the need to use the axis handles and game view to position your camera.

Preparing textures for GUI usage

There are various import settings to be aware of when introducing assets into Unity, and textures are no exception. In this section, we'll ensure that the textures we are about to use for our menu are all prepared to be used as 2D GUI graphics, rather than textures placed on 3D meshes.

Begin by selecting the **menu_mainTitle** texture file inside the **Book Assets | Textures** folder in the **Project** panel. You will now see the **Import** settings for this texture in the **Inspector**; to set this up to work as a GUI element rather than a texture, simply select **GUI** in the drop-down menu for **Texture Type**. Click the **Apply** button to confirm this change.

We need to select this setting for all of the textures we'll use in our menu in the **Import** settings for each asset.

Repeat this step for the following textures inside the **Book Assets | Textures** folder:

- **menu_instructionsBtn**
- **menu_instructionsBtnOver**
- **menu_playBtn**
- **menu_playBtnOver**
- **menu_quitBtn**
- **menu_quitBtnOver**

As we are dealing with 2D, we needn't alter settings for Aniso Level, Filter Mode, and Wrap Mode, as these are settings that handle the rendering of textures in 3D.

Other settings in this import dialog you should be aware of immediately are:

- **Max Size**: This can be set to a smaller dimension than the original file—often artists will work with high resolution graphics and then use this setting in Unity to compress their file down to a smaller resolution, saving them a step in their graphics package.
- **Format**: Generally speaking this should be kept set to Compressed, as it will allow Unity to control compression for textures, but if necessary this can be used to display full quality true color.

Adding the game title

Next we need to add the logo for our game to the menu scene. The easiest way to do this is with a texture you have designed, which is set up in Unity as a GUI Texture, in the same way as we created HUD elements for other parts of our game.

GUITexture formats

In the **Project** panel's **Book Assets | Textures** folder, select the texture named **menu_mainTitle**. This texture, designed in Photoshop, is saved as a **PNG** file (**Portable Network Graphics**). This is a good format to use for any textures that you intend to use as a GUITexture. It provides high quality, uncompressed transparency and can avoid some problems with white outlines, which you may see when using other formats, such as **GIF** (**Graphics Interchange Format**).

Creating the GUITexture object

With this texture selected, create a new GUITexture object by going to **GameObject** | **Create Other** | **GUITexture** from the top menu or by clicking the **Create** button on the Hierarchy panel and choosing **GUITexture** from the drop-down menu that appears. This automatically reads the dimensions of the selected texture and sets it as the texture to use in the new object, as discussed previously. You will now find an object called **menu_mainTitle** in the **Hierarchy**, as the object would have taken the name from the file you had selected during its creation.

Positioning

As most computers nowadays can handle resolutions at or above 1024 x 768 pixels, we'll choose this as a standard to test our menu and ensure that it works in other resolutions by using the `Screen` class to ascertain dynamic positions. In the upper-left of the **Game** view, you'll see a drop-down menu. This menu will allow you to specify different screen ratios or resolutions. From this drop-down menu, select **Standalone (1024x768)** to switch to a preview of that size.

Bear in mind that if your own computer's resolution is running close to this size, then the **Game** view will not show an accurate representation of this, as it may make up a smaller part of the Unity interface.

To toggle the **Game** view (and any of the interface panels) into fullscreen mode, you can hover over it with the mouse and tap the *Space* bar. As we position GUI elements in this chapter, use this method to preview what the interface will look like in the finished game. Be aware that you can toggle the interface spaces more easily when not in Play mode as Unity assumes by default that the **Space** bar may be used in the game, forcing you to click away from the game view if wishing to maximize or minimize other panels. For this reason, there is a toggle for **Maximize on Play** at the top of the game view.

By default, all GUITextures begin with their position at (0.5, 0.5, 0), which—given that 2D GUI Text and GUITexture components work in screen coordinates from 0 to 1—is in the middle of the screen.

In the **Transform** component for the **menu_mainTitle** object in the **Hierarchy**, set the position to (**0.2**, **0.8**, **0**). This places the logo in the upper-left of the screen. Remember that this may seem as if it is off the screen unless you maximize (press *Space* bar) the game view to see its position and the **Standalone** size—see the information box above for details.

Now that we have added the main title logo of the game, we'll need to add three buttons using further GUITexture objects.

Creating the menu with GUITextures and mouse events

In this first approach, we'll create a menu that uses a texture with a transparent background presented as a GUITexture, in the same way as we have just done with our main title logo.

We will then need to write a script in order to make the texture receive mouse events for mouse enter, mouse exit, and mouse down/up actions.

Adding the play button

In the **Book Assets | Textures** folder in the **Project** panel, select the texture called **menu_playBtn**. Go to **GameObject | Create Other | GUITexture** or select **GUITexture** from the Hierarchy **Create** button menu as before. Select the **menu_playBtn** object in the **Hierarchy** that you have just made and in the **Inspector**, set its **Transform Position** values to (**0.3, 0.55, 0**).

GUITexture button script

This is the first of our three buttons, and because they all have common functions, we will now write a script that can be used on all of the three buttons, using public variables to adjust settings. For example, each button will:

- Play a sound when clicked
- Perform an action such as loading another scene or quitting the game
- Swap textures when the mouse is over them to highlight them

Select the **Scripts** folder in the **Project** panel, and from the **Create** button drop-down menu, select **C#** or **Javascript**. Rename the **NewBehaviorScript** to **MainMenuBtns**, and then double-click its icon to launch it in the script editor—C# users may also remove the entire `Start()` function.

Begin by establishing four public variables above the `Update()` function, as shown in the following code snippet.

C#:

```
public string levelToLoad;
public Texture2D normalTexture;
public Texture2D rollOverTexture;
public AudioClip beep;
```

Javascript:

```
var levelToLoad : String;
var normalTexture : Texture2D;
var rollOverTexture : Texture2D;
var beep : AudioClip;
```

The first variable we will use to store the name of the level to be loaded when the button this script is applied to is clicked. By placing this information into a variable, we are able to apply this script to all three buttons, and simply use the variable name to load the level.

The second and third variables are declared as `Texture2D` type variables, but not set to a specific asset so that the textures can be assigned using drag-and-drop in the **Inspector**.

Finally, an `AudioClip` type variable is established, which will be played when the mouse is clicked.

Now after the variables you have just added, add the following function to set the texture used by the GUITexture component when the mouse enters the area that the texture occupies. This is usually referred to as a hover or rollover state.

C#:

```
void OnMouseEnter(){
  guiTexture.texture = rollOverTexture;
}
```

Javascript:

```
function OnMouseEnter(){
  guiTexture.texture = rollOverTexture;
}
```

In the **Book Assets | Textures** folder that you imported, you are provided with a normal and hover state for each button texture. This first `OnMouseEnter()` function simply sets the **texture** property of the component to whatever has been assigned to the public variable `rollOverTexture` in the **Inspector**. In order to detect when the mouse moves away or exits the boundary of this texture, add the following function:

C#:

```
void OnMouseExit(){
  guiTexture.texture = normalTexture;
}
```

Javascript:

```
function OnMouseExit(){
  guiTexture.texture = normalTexture;
}
```

If this was not present, the `rollOverTexture` would simply stay on, appearing to the player as if that specific menu option was still highlighted.

Now, to handle the sound and loading of the appropriate scene, add the following function:

C#:

```
IEnumerator OnMouseUp(){
  audio.PlayOneShot(beep);
  yield return new WaitForSeconds(0.35f);
  Application.LoadLevel(levelToLoad);
}
```

Javascript:

```
function OnMouseUp(){
  audio.PlayOneShot(beep);
  yield new WaitForSeconds(0.35);
  Application.LoadLevel(levelToLoad);
}
```

Note that in C# this function has a differing return type called `IEnumerator`—meaning that it has support for yields, which ordinarily cannot be done with the standard void return type that we use for functions. Specifying `IEnumerator` as the return type makes this function into what is called a **Co-routine**, as **routine** is a blanket term for the instructions being carried out in programming terms.

Co-routines can be used to hold instructions that only occur when certain conditions are met, whilst the rest of the script continues, or they can be used to halt a script until conditions are met. This is useful if you wish to create a pause in the script as we have done here. This is not necessary in the Javascript equivalent here as the yield can be done within a standard `OnMouseUp()` function.

With these functions, we are playing the sound as the first command to ensure that it plays before the next scene is loaded, and that it is not cut off. By placing a `yield` command in between the script for playing the sound and loading the next scene, we are able to halt the execution of the script for the defined number of seconds.

Using yields in scripting is a quick way of creating a delay without having to write further code for a timer.

Loading scenes

After the yield, our game will load the scene using the `Application.LoadLevel()` command, taking whatever string of text we write into the `levelToLoad` public variable in the **Inspector** and using that to find the relevant scene file.

To address the project you are working, you can make use of the Application class. Here we have used the `LoadLevel()` function, and there are various functions and properties of this class. In our final tweaks we will make use of it to dynamically choose whether to render the Quit button, as we will not need a quit button in our web player build. For more information on the `Application` class, see the following page of the Unity script reference:

`http://unity3d.com/support/documentation/ScriptReference/Application.html`

User experience for buttons

When creating interfaces, it is usually advised to place actions into a mouse up event, rather than a mouse down event. This gives the player a chance to move their cursor away if they have selected the wrong item.

Finally, as we are playing a sound, ensure that your object has an `AudioSource` component by adding a `RequireComponent` line to your script. In case you have forgotten how to do this, let's review it now:

C#:

To be placed after `using System.Collections;` and right before the `Class` declaration, at the top of the script.

```
[RequireComponent (typeof (AudioSource))]
```

Javascript:

To be placed at the very bottom of the script.

```
@script RequireComponent(AudioSource)
```

Go to **File** | **Save** in the script editor and return to Unity now. Select the **menu_playBtn** object in the **Hierarchy**, and go to **Component** | **Scripts** | **Main Menu Btns** to apply the script you have just written, or drag and drop the script from the Project panel onto the **menu_playBtn** object in the Hierarchy. The **Main Menu Btns (Script)** component should then appear in the **Inspector** list of components for the **menu_playBtn** object. As a result of the `RequireComponent` line, you will also have an **AudioSource** component on your object.

Assigning public variables

As you will see, the public variables will need to be assigned before this script can function. In the **LevelToLoad** variable, type in the name **Island,** in order to ensure that it is loaded when the button is clicked on. Then drag the **menu_playBtn** and **menu_playBtnOver** textures from the **Book Assets** | **Textures** folder in the **Project** panel to the **Normal Texture** and **Roll Over Texture** variables respectively.

Now, before we assign our **menu_beep** sound, we need to select it in the **Book Assets** | **Sounds** and uncheck the box for 3D Sound in the Audio Importer in the Inspector, remembering to click the **Apply** button at the bottom to confirm this change. This means that the sound is simply played at normal volume, as its volume is not based on distance from the audio listener component on the camera.

Finally, drag the **menu_beep** audio clip from the **Book Assets** | **Sounds** folder to the **Beep** variable. When finished, your component should look like this:

Testing the button

To ensure that we're seeing a valid representation of where the button is located on the screen, locate and highlight the button titled **Maximize on Play** on the game view—this will mean that when we test, the game view is maximized, and depending on your screen resolution, should show you the default Standalone screen size. To ensure that it does so, make sure that **Standalone (1024x768)** is selected on the first drop-down menu on the game view; if you do not see this option, ensure your **Build Settings (File** | **Build Settings)** are set to **Standalone**. If they are not, you can select **PC and Mac Standalone** as a platform from the list and hit **Switch Platform** at the bottom of the window.

Now press the **Play** button to test the scene. When you move your mouse cursor over the **Play Game** button, it should swap texture to the **PlayBtnOver** texture, which is colored red and has a flame motif to the right. When moving the cursor away from the texture, it should switch back.

Now try clicking the button. At the bottom of the screen, you will see an error in the console, which is previewed in the bar at the bottom of the Unity editor interface. The error will state that:

Level 'Island' (-1) couldn't be loaded because it has not been added to the build settings.

This is Unity's way of ensuring that you do not forget to add all included levels to the Build Settings. **Build Settings** are effectively the export settings of your game (in game development terms, a finished or test product is referred to as a build). The build settings in Unity must list all scenes included in your game. To rectify this, make sure you press **Play** to stop testing the game, and then go to **File | Build Settings**.

With the **Build Settings** panel open, beneath the **Scenes to build** section, click on the **Add Current** button to add the Menu scene we are working on. Scenes in the build settings list have an order, represented by the number to the right-hand side of the scene name, and you should make sure that the first scene you need to load is always in position **0**.

Drag-and-drop the **Island** scene from the **Project** panel, and drop it onto the current list of scenes so that it is listed beneath **Menu.unity**.

Be aware that there is no confirmation or save settings button on the **Build Settings** dialog, so simply close it and then retest the game. Press **Play** in Unity and then try clicking on your **Play Game** button—the **Island Level** should load after the **menu_beep** sound effect is played. Now press **Play** again to stop testing, and you will automatically return to the **Menu** scene.

Adding the instructions button

To add the second button in our menu, simply select the **menu_instructionsBtn** texture in the **Book Assets | Textures** folder in the **Project** panel, and go to **GameObject | Create Other | GUITexture** or click the **Create** button on the Hierarchy panel, and choose **GUITexture** from the drop-down menu. This creates an object in the Hierarchy called **menu_instructionsBtn**. In the **Transform** component of this object, set the **Position** values to **(0.3, 0.45, 0)**.

As the scripting is already done, simply go to **Component | Scripts | Main Menu Btns**, or drag and drop the script onto the object in the Hierarchy, and then assign the appropriate textures and **menu_beep** in the same manner as we did in the *Assigning public variables* section. As we have not made the instructions area of the menu yet, simply leave the `levelToLoad` variable unassigned for now.

Adding the quit button

This button works in a similar manner to the first two, but does not load a scene. Instead it calls upon the build's **Application** class, using the **Quit()** command to terminate the game as an application so that your operating system closes it down.

This means that we'll need to modify our `MainMenuBtns` script to account for this change. If you do not still have the script open, double-click this script in the **Scripts** folder of the **Project** panel to launch it in the script editor.

Begin by adding the following Boolean public variable to the script, after the last public variable—`beep`—we added earlier:

C#:

```
public bool quitButton = false;
```

Javascript:

```
var quitButton : boolean = false;
```

This we will use as a toggle, if it is set to `true`, then it will cause the click of the button —the `OnMouseUp()` function—to run the `quit()` command. If it is `false` (that is, its default state), then it will load the level applied to the `levelToLoad` variable as normal.

To implement this, restructure your `OnMouseUp()` actions with an `if/ else` statement, as shown in the following code snippet:

C#:

```
IEnumerator OnMouseUp(){
  audio.PlayOneShot(beep);
  yield return new WaitForSeconds(0.35f);
  if(quitButton){
    Application.Quit();
  }
  else{
    Application.LoadLevel(levelToLoad);
  }
}
```

Javascript:

```
function OnMouseUp(){
  audio.PlayOneShot(beep);
  yield new WaitForSeconds(0.35);
  if(quitButton){
    Application.Quit();
  }
  else{
    Application.LoadLevel(levelToLoad);
  }
}
```

Here we have simply modified the function to play the sound and pause (`yield`), regardless of what kind of button this is. However, we have to choose between two options—if `quitButton` is `true`, then the `Application.Quit()` command is called; otherwise (`else`), the level is loaded as normal.

Go to **File | Save** in the script editor, and switch back to Unity.

Select the **menu_quitBtn** texture in the **Book Assets | Textures** folder in the **Project** panel, and go to **GameObject | Create Other | GUITexture**, or use the **Create** button on the Hierarchy panel as before. This creates an object called **menu_quitBtn** in the **Hierarchy**. In the **Transform** component for this object, set the **Position** values to **(0.3, 0.35, 0)**.

With **menu_quitBtn** still selected in the **Hierarchy**, go to **Component | Scripts | Main Menu Btns** or drag-and-drop from the Project panel to the Hierarchy object to add the script. In the **Inspector**, fill in the public variables as before, but this time leave **Level To Load** blank, and check the box next to the newly added **Quit Button** variable to enable it.

To double-check your script, here it is in full:

C#:

```
using UnityEngine;
using System.Collections;
[RequireComponent (typeof (AudioSource))]

public class MainMenuBtns : MonoBehaviour {

  public string levelToLoad;
  public Texture2D normalTexture;
  public Texture2D rollOverTexture;
  public AudioClip beep;
```

```
  public bool quitButton = false;

  void OnMouseEnter(){
    guiTexture.texture = rollOverTexture;
  }
  void OnMouseExit(){
    guiTexture.texture = normalTexture;
  }
  IEnumerator OnMouseUp(){
    audio.PlayOneShot(beep);
    yield return new WaitForSeconds(0.35f);
    if(quitButton){
      Application.Quit();
    }
    else{
      Application.LoadLevel(levelToLoad);
    }
  }
}
```

Javascript:

```
var levelToLoad : String;
var normalTexture : Texture2D;
var rollOverTexture : Texture2D;
var beep : AudioClip;
var quitButton : boolean = false;
function OnMouseEnter(){
  guiTexture.texture = rollOverTexture;
}
function OnMouseExit(){
  guiTexture.texture = normalTexture;
}
function OnMouseUp(){
  audio.PlayOneShot(beep);
  yield new WaitForSeconds(0.35);
  if(quitButton){
    Application.Quit();
  }
  else{
    Application.LoadLevel(levelToLoad);
  }
}
@script RequireComponent(AudioSource)
```

Now go to **File** | **Save Scene** to update the project, and then press **Play** to test the menu. Pressing the **Play** menu button should load the Island Level. The **Instructions** button will cause the 'level could not be loaded' error we saw previously, as we have not assigned the name of any scene in the build settings to the Level to Load variable in our script component. The **Quit** button will not cause an error but will also not preview in the Unity editor (naturally—we don't want the testing process to quit the editor itself!), so we would not be able to test this until we create a build.

Remember to press **Play** again to finish testing. As the first approach at making a menu creation is now complete, we'll now take a look at another method of creating a functional menu in Unity, using scripting to render buttons as part of the `GUI` class in Unity.

Checking scripts with Debug commands

Despite the `Application.Quit()` command not previewing in the Unity Editor, we should ensure that the **Quit** button does work, rather than assuming that this is the case. In order to test any part of a script, you can simply place in a **Debug** command. Debugging is ordinarily used to do what it sounds like—remove bugs from your script, but it can also be used to simply send information at particular points in the script. The command we are about to add will send a message to the console part of Unity, which is previewed at the bottom of the interface.

Let's try this out now. Return to your **MainMenuBtns** script in the script editor, and locate the `quitButton` part of the code:

```
if(quitButton){
  Application.Quit();
}
```

A debug read-out can be logged in a list with others of its kind along with errors in the console. They normally look like this:

```
Debug.Log("This part works!");
```

By writing this line of code to where you expect the script to execute, you can discover whether or not particular parts of your script are working. In our example, we would place this command after the `Application.Quit()`, as this would prove that the command had been executed without a problem. Add this in so that it looks like the next code snippet:

C# and Javascript:

```
if(quitButton){
  Application.Quit();
  Debug.Log("This part works!");
}
```

Save the script by going to **File | Save** in the script editor, and return to Unity. Now test your menu scene again by pressing the **Play** button, and by clicking the Quit button on the menu, you will see the debug command printing at the bottom of the Unity interface. If you open the **Console** part of Unity—**Window | Console** or *Command* + *Shift* + *C* on Mac, *Ctrl* + *Shift* + *C* on PC, then you'll see this listed there also, as shown in the following image:

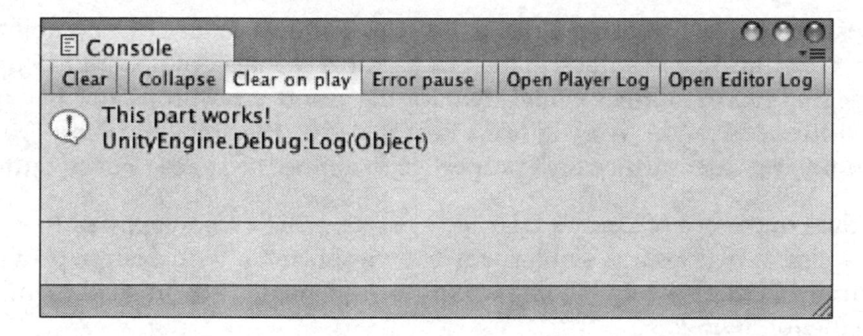

This technique can prove very useful when diagnosing script issues or even when designing parts of a theoretical script for which you don't have commands to fill out yet.

As well as writing simple String messages to yourself in the parentheses of `Debug.Log()`, you can also add variables and functions in order to check their values during runtime; this can be invaluable when testing and it is recommended that you use them when encountering any kind of unexpected behavior within your scripts.

Creating the menu with the Unity GUI class and GUI skins

As we already have a working menu, rather than removing it from our scene, we will temporarily disable the objects that make it up.

Disabling game objects

One at a time, select the **menu_playBtn**, the **menu_instructionsBtn**, and the **menu_quitBtn** in the **Hierarchy**, and deactivate them by doing the following:

- In the **Inspector**, uncheck the checkbox to the left-hand side of the name of the object at the top
- Ensure that this has turned the text of the object to light gray in the **Hierarchy** and that the element itself has disappeared from the **Game** view preview—you should now be left with only the game title logo texture visible

Creating the menu

For this example, we'll be using Unity's `GUI` class, and make use of a combination of public `float` and `Rect` values. A `Rect` is a property that contains four floating point (decimal place) number values, two for the X and Y positions and two more for the Width and Height. We will use a Rect to define the area our menu group exists within and then further Rect properties to define the space of each button.

We will then make use of Unity's **GUI Skin** assets, which when applied to an `OnGUI()` script, functions in a similar way to stylesheets for web design, providing a coherent set of themes for GUI items that can be reused. Our finished menu will look like the following:

To begin, create a new empty object by going to **GameObject | Create Empty**. This makes a new object in the **Hierarchy** called **GameObject** with only a **Transform** component attached. This will be the holder object for our `GUI` scripted menu. This is because the script we are going to write will need to be attached as a component in order to function. It makes sense to have an object dedicated to it for the sake of organization.

As the position of GUI elements is handled through scripting, the transform position of this object is irrelevant, so we will not need to adjust this. Simply rename the object from its default name to **Menu2** in the usual manner.

Select the **Scripts** folder in the **Project** panel and click on the **Create** button, choosing **C# Script** or **Javascript** from the drop-down menu. Rename this script to **MainMenuGUI** and then double-click its icon to launch it in the script editor.

Creating public variables

Begin your script by establishing the following six public variables above the `Update()` function:

C#:

```
public AudioClip beep;
public GUISkin menuSkin;
public Rect menuArea;
public Rect playButton;
public Rect instructionsButton;
public Rect quitButton;
```

Javascript:

```
var beep : AudioClip;
var GUISkin : GUISkin;
var menuArea : Rect;
var playButton : Rect;
var instructionsButton : Rect;
var quitButton : Rect;
```

Here we're creating the same beep audio clip variable as seen in our first approach script, then a slot for a GUI skin to be applied to our menu, as well as four `Rect` values to store the on-screen positions and dimensions of our menu group area and its buttons.

The OnGUI() function

Next, below these variables, establish the following function in your script:

C#:

```
void OnGUI(){
  GUI.skin = menuSkin;
}
```

Javascript:

```
function OnGUI(){
  GUI.skin = menuSkin;
}
```

This establishes the `OnGUI()` function, and sets up the first crucial element—to apply the skin asset represented by the `menuSkin` variable. This means that any GUI elements placed into this function, such as buttons, forms, and so on will be governed by the style of the skin applied to this variable. This makes it easy to swap out skins, and thus completely restyle your GUIs in one go.

Positioning for GUIs

Next we need to establish an area for the buttons to be drawn in. We already have a `menuArea` Rect variable waiting to be used, and as part of learning about positioning, we will try positioning this rectangular space in a specific location on-screen and also in a centralized position that will work for differing screen resolutions.

Pixel-specific positioning

For the first part approach to positioning our GUI, we will place our menu at a defined point on the screen. After the `GUI.skin` line you just added, but still within the `OnGUI()` function, establish the space for our GUI to exist within by opening a new GUI group.

C# and Javascript:

```
GUI.BeginGroup (menuArea);
```

The `BeginGroup()` function needs to be given a `Rect` within its parentheses. As a result, we have placed the `menuArea` Rect public variable that we can assign dimensions and positions to shortly. Whenever you open a group in a GUI script, it should be closed also. So that we do not neglect to do this, press return a few times to move your cursor down, creating empty lines where our GUI code will reside, then add the corresponding closing line.

C# and Javascript:

```
GUI.EndGroup();
```

This closes the group and means that we will not receive errors from Unity.

As GUI Groups are essentially empty holders for your GUI, rendering them without any visible interface elements—buttons, sliders, textfields, and so on—will mean you literally see nothing onscreen. As a result, let's continue writing our script to add three buttons, and then test the script.

After the opening `GUI.BeginGroup()` line but before the `EndGroup()`, add the following lines of code to establish three buttons:

C#:

```
if(GUI.Button(new Rect(playButton), "Play")){

}
if(GUI.Button(new Rect(instructionsButton), "Instructions")){

}
if(GUI.Button(new Rect(quitButton), "Quit")){

}
```

Javascript:

```
if(GUI.Button(Rect(playButton), "Play")){

}
if(GUI.Button(Rect(instructionsButton), "Instructions")){

}
if(GUI.Button(Rect(quitButton), "Quit")){

}
```

Here we are making use of the GUI class, this time—the `Button` function, which expects a Rect and also a String, Texture, or piece of GUI Content as its arguments.

We are using a String to simply write text onto the button itself. For more on this function see the script reference at:

`http://unity3d.com/support/documentation/ScriptReference/GUI.Button.html`

We place buttons such as these into `if` statements in order to allow the actual click of the button to carry out commands—otherwise the buttons would simply be rendered!

By feeding in the value of our public Rect variables, we are able to specify the dimensions and position of each button in the Inspector, but before we save the script and assign these values, let's make our buttons do something in order to get feedback and ensure that the click works. In our first approach, we utilized `Debug.Log()` to write a message into the Unity console, but this time we'll do something we will actually use in the menu itself. You'll recall that we just added a variable for an audio clip, so lets play this clip when the player clicks our buttons. Place the following line into each of our `if` statements:

C# and Javascript:

```
audio.PlayOneShot(beep);
```

As we are playing an audio clip here directly with this object's Audio Source component (hence the use of lowercase `audio` in our script) we should ensure that this component is present on the object this script is added to. To do this, we'll use our old friend—the `RequireComponent()` command. If you remember how, add this in now, but if you've forgotten how, follow the next step to add it now:

C#:

Place the following line before your class declaration:

```
[RequireComponent(typeof(AudioSource))]
```

Javascript:

At the very bottom of the script, add the following line:

```
@script RequireComponent(AudioSource)
```

Now we can save and try this script out. Save your script and return to Unity now. To enable this script, we must add it to our empty **Menu2** object. Drag the **MainMenuGUI** script from the Project panel to this object in the Hierarchy now. Select the object and you should now see that you have a **Main Menu GUI (Script)** component as well as the **Audio Source** component that our script requires. Expand all four public Rect variables (**Menu Area**, and the three buttons) by clicking the grey arrows to the left-hand side of their name.

GUI scripts only render when the game is played, but as our **Menu Area Rect** (that defines the GUI group dimensions) is currently set to 0, we need to scale it, as well as our buttons, in order to see anything rendered. Fill in the properties of these variables as follows, keeping in mind that you can use the *Tab* key on the keyboard to move through inspector fields to speed up entering many values:

Main Menu GUIjs (Script)	
Script	MainMenuGUIjs
Beep	None (Audio Clip)
Menu Skin	None (GUISkin)
Menu Area	
X	100
Y	300
Width	200
Height	150
Play Button	
X	0
Y	0
Width	200
Height	40
Instructions Button	
X	0
Y	50
Width	200
Height	40
Quit Button	
X	0
Y	100
Width	200
Height	40

Here we have defined a **Menu Area** group that is **100**px (pixels) from the left edge of the screen and **300**px down from the top of the screen. It is **200**px wide and **150**px tall. As you can tell from this, the GUI is rendered to the top left corner of the screen itself—and this relativity is also true for buttons inside the GUI group—their X and Y positions relate to the top left corner of the group, rather than the screen.

For this reason, positioning the **Play Button** at **0,0** places it in the top left corner of the group, whilst the others are positioned so that their height of 40px is factored in, with a gap of 10px in between, placing the Instructions button at 50px from the top of the group, and the **Quit Button** at **100**px from the top—taking into account two other buttons and a 10px gap for each.

Before testing, assign the **menu_beep** file from the **Book Assets | Sounds** folder in the Project panel to the **Beep** public variable on this script component—we will create and style our menu with a GUI skin once we have tested its functionality. Save your scene by choosing **File | Save scene** from the top menu, then press **Play** to test.

When testing, ensure that **Maximize on Play** on the game view is still highlighted in order to preview at the Standalone resolution of 1024x768. You should see your menu rendered with the default look of a Unity GUI.

Ensure that when you click each button, you hear the menu beep audio clip—if so, the buttons work as expected! If not, as usual, double check your script and look at the console at the bottom of the screen for any errors.

As you will agree, this doesn't look too good; the textures of the buttons don't fit into our game's style, and the font is basic and small. Let's jazz it up with a GUI skin!

Styling GUI buttons with a GUI skin

Press **Play** to stop testing, and the click the **Create** button on the Project panel, and choose **GUI Skin** from the drop-down menu.

Rename the newly created asset **Main Menu**, and then select it in the Project to see its properties in the Inspector. You will see a number of potential GUI elements that you can make with GUI code and style with this skin—if you have experience in web design, think of a GUI skin as a stylesheet. Begin styling by dragging our existing game font, **Sugo**— or the one you chose yourself—from the Project panel onto the **Font** property of the skin at the top of the Inspector. You can set fonts for individual GUI elements too by expanding them and setting their own font property, but this font simply acts as the core font for all GUI elements until individual elements are told to use a different font.

Now expand the section for a **Button** by clicking the grey arrow to the left of its name, so that you can see its properties in the Inspector.

Expand the **Normal, Hover** and the **Active** state also here, as the player may see this when using our menu. The Active state is appearance of the button whilst it is held down, which may be brief but we should ensure that its design is considered also.

Using textures for GUI button backgrounds

When rendering a GUI button we should use the skin to style the button itself; you have three textures provided for this in the **Book Assets | Textures** folder—**guiBtnNormal**, **guiBtnHover**, and **guiBtnActive**. Select each of these textures in the Project panel in turn and in the Inspector panel, set their **Texture Importer** Texture Type property to **GUI** instead of **Texture**, and click **Apply** at the bottom of the window in order to prepare these textures for use with GUIs.

As the GUI button stretches a texture to fill its rectangular dimensions, backgrounds such as the ones we are using here are designed as rounded boxes that will therefore scale well at differing widths:

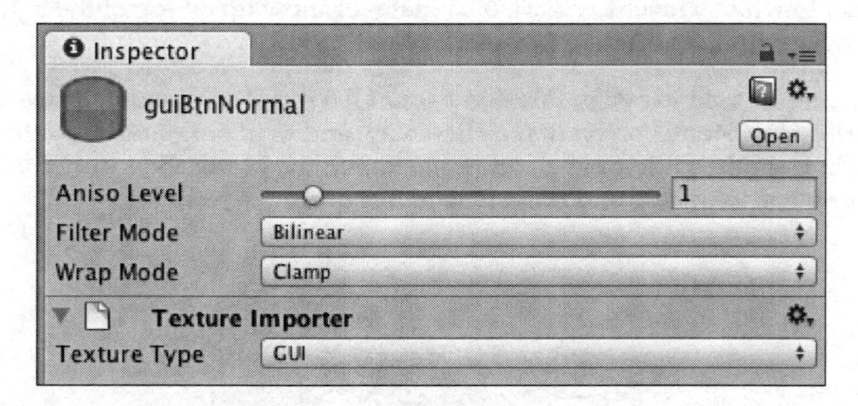

If you wish to design your own button backgrounds, you can simply design at the intended dimensions of a button—or you can design in the style of the assets used here, creating rounded graphics to suit varied widths.

Now reselect the **Main Menu** GUI skin in the Project panel, and drag-and-drop **guiBtnNormal**, **guiBtnHover**, and **guiBtnActive** from the Project panel, dropping them onto the **Button** | **Normal**, **Hover**, and **Active** | **Background** properties as shown:

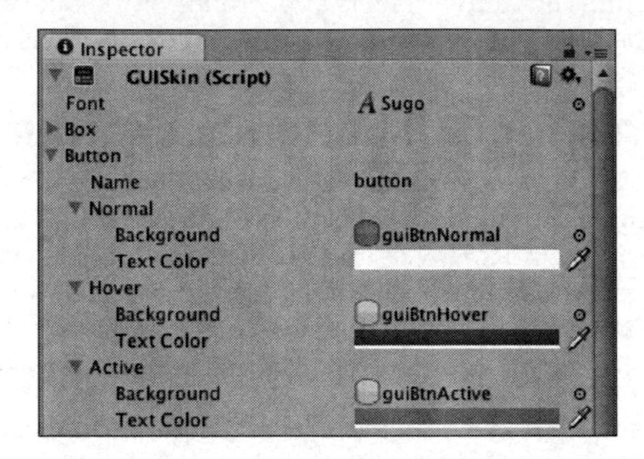

Finally, change the **Text Color** values to suit the background textures—set the color of **Normal** to white, **Hover** to a dark blue that will show up on top of the light blue button background, and **Active** to a shade of red.

Now we simply need to assign this skin to our GUI script component to see it in action. Select the **Menu2** object in the Hierarchy, and then drag-and-drop the **Main Menu** skin from the Project panel, dropping it onto the **Menu Skin** public variable. Save your scene to update and press **Play** to test to see the results!

Choosing font size for GUI buttons

So it's looking good, but the text on the buttons is still pretty small! Instead of setting the size on the font we are using, the GUI skin allows us to define a font size for buttons. Select the **Main Menu** skin in the Project panel, and in the properties of a **Button** you will see **Font Size** toward the bottom of the list. Set this to **26**, and then play test again; you should now see your buttons looking even cooler! Make sure to test the Hover state by moving your cursor over them, and click them to ensure that you hear the menu beep audio clip.

Resolution-independent positioning

This looks good, but what if we want to make sure this GUI is positioned properly with our title at other resolutions? Leaving pixel values in the X and Y coordinates of our **Menu Area** Rect would mean that whilst the **menu_mainTitle** texture is at (**0.2**, **0.8**) in Screen coordinates, the menu itself would stay precisely at (100px, 300px) from the top left corner of the screen. For example, we have been testing our game with the default Standalone resolution of 1024 x 768, which gives us this desired menu position:

However, when playing our game as a standalone, the player will be given the option to choose a higher resolution, which will mean that the position of 100px from the left and 300px from the top will become out of sync with the relatively positioned title graphic; for example, the menu would appear as shown below when playing the game at 1680 x 1050:

Note that here, the screen position of **0.2** in X for the title texture is keeping it in the desired top left corner relative to the current screen width, so we should find a way of positioning our menu that isn't specific to just 1024 x 768, but will reposition itself relatively too.

For this reason, we will now create an additional private Rect that will allow us to type values from 0 to 1 into the X and Y positions of the Menu Area public Rect variable in the Inspector, and have it display relative to the current screen size—in the same way that Unity handles the rendering of our GUITexture based title.

Return to your **MainMenuGUI** script now, and add the following variable beneath the existing variables at the top of the script:

C#:

```
Rect menuAreaNormalized;
```

Javascript:

```
private var menuAreaNormalized : Rect;
```

This creates a private `Rect` variable that we can use in the actual definition of the Group in the `BeginGroup()` function we have already established. But we need to convert the values within the existing `menuArea`, and assign them to this variable, otherwise it is worthless. We will do this inside a `Start()` function so that it is only done when the scene loads—detecting the current resolution and assigning the group a position should be done here, rather than with a local variable inside `OnGUI()` as we do not want to repeat this action.

Establish a `Start()` function above your `OnGUI()` function:

C#:

```
void Start(){

}
```

Javascript:

```
function Start(){

}
```

Next we will add a line that will convert the values for X and Y position in the `menuArea` Rect into what we will refer to as **Normalized** values. In Vector terms, a normalized vector is one that has a direction, but has had its length scaled to a value of 1; this is useful for resetting velocities for example, as we can maintain a direction, but get a value that can be easily multiplied by.

In this instance we are referring to the position of our GUI as normalized because we are converting values in such a way that we will be able to type values into the Inspector for X and Y that run from 0 to 1.

Add the following line to your `Start()` function now:

C#:

```
menuAreaNormalized =
  new Rect(menuArea.x * Screen.width - (menuArea.width * 0.5f),
    menuArea.y * Screen.height - (menuArea.height * 0.5f),
    menuArea.width, menuArea.height);
```

Javascript:

```
menuAreaNormalized =
  Rect(menuArea.x * Screen.width - (menuArea.width * 0.5),
    menuArea.y * Screen.height - (menuArea.height * 0.5),
    menuArea.width, menuArea.height);
```

This looks complex on first inspection, but we will break it down one step at a time. As we are performing the same calculation for the Y axis as the X, let's just take a simple overview of how we are assigning this Rect its X position value.

Let's imagine we type a value of 0.2 into our **MenuArea** Rect's X position property in the Inspector. We begin by multiplying this by `Screen.width`:

```
menuArea.x * Screen.width
```

`Screen.width` is the exact width of the screen in pixels, so by multiplying by 0.2, we should be getting the same position as we did by typing 0.2 into the X position of the Transform component of our GUITexture **menu_mainTitle**.

However, at our current resolution of 1024px wide, multiplying by 0.2 places our X position at 204.8px—but as we need to recreate our previous approach, we know this calculation is not yet complete because previously our X position was a value of 100px in from the left of the screen.

This is because we need to take into account the fact that when you position a GUI Texture, it is rendered from its center, the Pixel Inset X value being a minus value of half of the width of the texture. For example, if we multiplied by 0.5 to try and place our GUI group into the center of the screen we would see this:

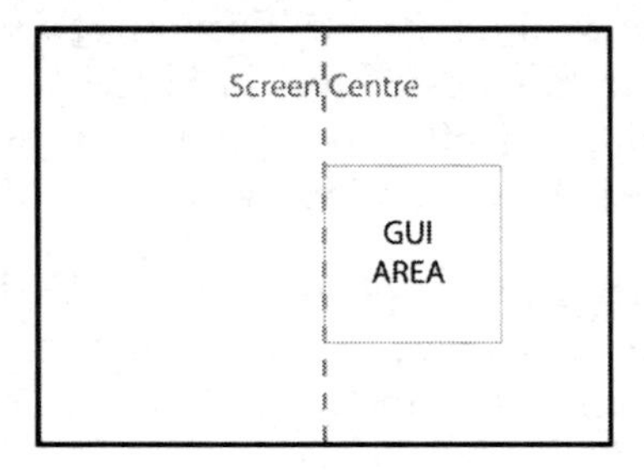

In the example above, a GUI group is positioned at half of the screen's width, but problematically appears to one side because it is rendered from the left-hand edge of the group. This is corrected by subtracting half of the group's width as part of the equation:

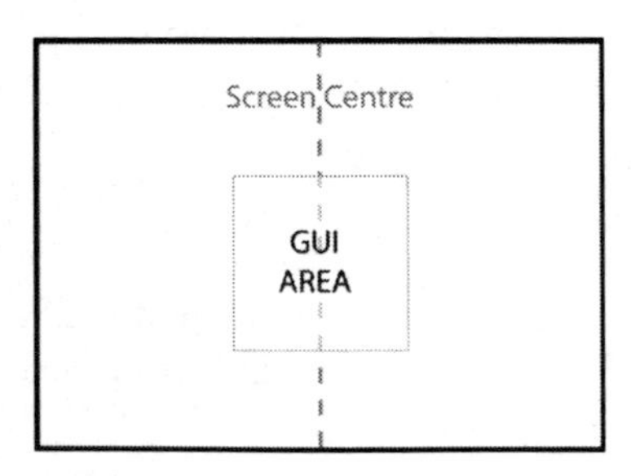

Although we are not creating a centralized menu, we also need to subtract half of the width of the `menuArea` Rect, which we do by subtracting (`menuArea.width * 0.5`). We are multiplying by 0.5 because it requires less CPU cycles than dividing by `2`. So now we have:

```
menuArea.x * Screen.width - (menuArea.width * 0.5)
```

This leaves us with a value of `104.8` for the `X` value of the `menuNormalized` Rect. You should note that whilst the calculation does not give us exactly the 100px from the left we saw previously, it renders almost identically, and will scale to other resolutions—our main goal. As for the rest of this command, we do a similar calculation for the Y position:

```
menuArea.y * Screen.height - (menuArea.height * 0.5)
```

...substituting `Screen.width` for `Screen.height`, and subtracting half of `menuArea.height`. To fill in the last two properties of the `menuNormalized` Rect we simply copy the values of `menuArea.width` and `menuArea.height` for the dimension values, and this completes our `menuNormalized` Rect variable's properties.

To make use of this new variable, simply locate the following line in your `OnGUI()` function:

```
GUI.BeginGroup (menuArea);
```

And change it to the following:

C# and Javascript:

```
GUI.BeginGroup (menuAreaNormalized);
```

This means that your GUI group will now be drawn with the normalized equivalents of the values in the **Menu Area** public Rect. Now save your script and return to Unity, and select the **Menu2** object in order to see the **Main Menu GUI (Script)** component. No difference will be noticeable as the variable we just added was private, and simply performs the conversion behind the scenes.

However, given that the normalized Rect is based on the values of **Menu Area** in the Inspector, we need to amend them to be based on a value between 0 and 1. Set X to **0.2** and Y to **0.45** now, then press **Play** to test. Your menu should be positioned as shown in the original image showing 1024x768 resolution.

Now that our positioning code is in place, and will scale for differing resolutions, we'll return to our menu, and add in the actual functionality of the menu! Save your scene in Unity now and then return to your **MainMenuGUI** script in the script editor.

Scripting button actions

In our first menu approach, we wrote a script that would be applied to each button and as such we made use of a public string variable to pass in a particular scene to load. However, as we have an if statement to render each button, we will write a custom function that will play our menu beep sound, pause briefly, and then perform an action—be it loading a scene or quitting the game.

After the closing right curly brace of the `OnGUI()` function, establish the following function:

C#:

```
IEnumerator ButtonAction(string levelName){
  audio.PlayOneShot(beep);
  yield return new WaitForSeconds(0.35f);

  if(levelName != "quit"){
    Application.LoadLevel(levelName);
  }else{
    Application.Quit();
    Debug.Log("Have Quit");
  }
}
```

Javascript:

```
function ButtonAction(levelName : String){
  audio.PlayOneShot(beep);
  yield new WaitForSeconds(0.35);
  if(levelName != "quit"){
    Application.LoadLevel(levelName);
  }else{
    Application.Quit();
    Debug.Log("Have Quit");
  }
}
```

Note that in C# we have used the return type `IEnumerator` to denote a co-routine, rather than a standard function, as this function needs to use a yield to create a pause as seen in our first menu design approach.

Here we have established a function that has a single string argument named `levelName`; with this we can send the function instructions as to which scene to load, using its name from the Project panel. To accommodate our **Quit** button, we have built in detection for the word quit in order to perform the `Quit()` command.

Our function begins by immediately giving the player audio feedback by playing our menu beep audio clip, then yields for `0.35` seconds—long enough to play the audio clip, and then continues with its commands. The function then decides whether to load a scene using `Application.LoadLevel()` but only does this if the string sent to this function—that is, the value of `levelName` does not equal the word `quit`, otherwise (if it does equal `quit`) the `Application.Quit()` function is called to exit the game.

Because the `Application.Quit()` command does not have an effect in the Unity editor, we have also added a `Debug.Log("Have Quit");` after the `Quit()` command, to ensure that this part of the script is called. This saves us the effort of building the game as a Standalone application in order to test that the **Quit** button `else` statement is being called correctly.

Now let's call this function within our `OnGUI()` button if statements. Place your cursor inside the if statement for the Play button, and remove the existing `audio.PlayOneShot(beep);` line, as our new function features that already.

Now add the following code:

C#:

Because in C# we have used a co-routine, we must use the `StartCoroutine()` command:

```
StartCoroutine("ButtonAction", "Island");
```

Here we state the name of the function we are calling as a string, then a comma, and its argument's value as a string—in a similar way to calling a function with an argument in a `SendMessage()` as we do in the **TriggerZone** script when calling our text hint GUI.

Javascript:

```
ButtonAction("Island");
```

Here we are simply calling our `ButtonAction()` function, and sending the string `Island` to its `levelName` argument; this will be detected as not equaling the word `quit`, and open the Island scene.

We will leave the Instructions button for now, and create the instructions part of the menu within the next section of this chapter. So finally, place your cursor inside the `if` statement for the Quit button, remove the `audio.PlayOneShot(beep);` line already there, and then add the following:

C#:

```
StartCoroutine("ButtonAction", "quit");
```

Javascript:

```
ButtonAction("quit");
```

As you can guess, this calls our `ButtonAction()` function again, this time sending the word `quit` to the `levelName` argument of the function, which will be detected by its if statement and call the `Application.Quit()` command to exit the game.

Save your script now and return to Unity. Play test the game once more by pressing the Play button. In your new menu, press the **Quit** button to test that your `Debug.Log()` command prints the Have Quit message into the console—see the bottom of the Unity interface. Then press the **Play** menu button and you should hear a beep before being taken to the Island scene, success!

To check over your script so far, compare it to the full scripts shown next:

C#:

```
using UnityEngine;
using System.Collections;
[RequireComponent(typeof(AudioSource))]

public class MainMenuGUI : MonoBehaviour {

  public AudioClip beep;
  public GUISkin menuSkin;
  public Rect menuArea;
  public Rect playButton;
  public Rect instructionsButton;
  public Rect quitButton;

  Rect menuAreaNormalized;

  void Start(){
    menuAreaNormalized =
      new Rect(menuArea.x * Screen.width - (menuArea.width * 0.5f),
        menuArea.y * Screen.height - (menuArea.height * 0.5f),
        menuArea.width, menuArea.height);
  }

  void OnGUI(){
    GUI.skin = menuSkin;
```

```
      GUI.BeginGroup (menuAreaNormalized);

        if(GUI.Button(new Rect(playButton), "Play")){
          StartCoroutine("ButtonAction", "Island");
        }
        if(GUI.Button(new Rect(instructionsButton), "Instructions")){
          audio.PlayOneShot(beep);
        }
        if(GUI.Button(new Rect(quitButton), "Quit")){
          StartCoroutine("ButtonAction", "quit");
        }
      GUI.EndGroup();
    }

    IEnumerator ButtonAction(string levelName){
      audio.PlayOneShot(beep);
      yield return new WaitForSeconds(0.35f);

      if(levelName != "quit"){
        Application.LoadLevel(levelName);
      }else{
        Application.Quit();
        Debug.Log("Have Quit");
      }
    }
  }
```


Javascript:

```
var beep : AudioClip;
var menuSkin : GUISkin;
var menuArea : Rect;
private var menuAreaNormalized : Rect;
var playButton : Rect;
var instructionsButton : Rect;
var quitButton :  Rect;

function Start(){
  menuAreaNormalized =
    Rect(menuArea.x * Screen.width - (menuArea.width * 0.5f),
      menuArea.y * Screen.height - (menuArea.height * 0.5f),
      menuArea.width, menuArea.height);
}

function OnGUI(){
```

```
    GUI.skin = menuSkin;
    GUI.BeginGroup (menuAreaNormalized);

      if(GUI.Button(Rect(playButton), "Play")){
        ButtonAction("Island");
      }
      if(GUI.Button(Rect(instructionsButton), "Instructions")){
        audio.PlayOneShot(beep);
      }
      if(GUI.Button(Rect(quitButton), "Quit")){
        ButtonAction("quit");
      }

    GUI.EndGroup();
  }

  function ButtonAction(levelName : String){
    audio.PlayOneShot(beep);
    yield new WaitForSeconds(0.35f);

    if(levelName != "quit"){
      Application.LoadLevel(levelName);
    }else{
      Application.Quit();
      Debug.Log("Have Quit");
    }
  }
```

Now let's complete our menu by building in the page of instructions for the player.

Adding the Instructions page

To finish our menu, we will look at making GUI scripting that is dynamic, allowing us to change the part of the menu that is rendered, rather than having many scripts that are enabled or disabled.

As our **Instructions** menu page should mimic the rest of the menu, we'll modify our GUI scripting in the **Menu** scene so that the background behind the menu remains the same when navigating through it.

Creating menu pages

Ensure that the **MainMenuGUI** script is still open or launch it by double-clicking its icon in the **Scripts** folder in the Project panel. In this script we left the Instructions button calling only the beep audio clip to ensure that the button worked.

Now we will use this button to switch between what we will call the main page of the menu—the existing **Play**, **Instructions**, and **Quit** button layout—and a new page that shows the player the aim of the game, as well as a **Back** button to return to the main menu.

To achieve this we will create a string variable that stores the current page of the menu we should be on. Our GUI code will then include an additional `if/else` structure that checks the current status of this `menuPage` variable string and render different buttons or GUI elements as appropriate. We are using a string for ease of readability, but this could also be done with an integer, perhaps using 0 to represent the main menu, and 1 for the instructions page.

Let's begin by adding a new private `string` variable, which we will use to choose which page we are on—and therefore what is rendered in our menu—by setting the value of this variable to differing words. Beneath the last variable we added, `menuAreaNormalized`, add the following private variable:

C#:

```
string menuPage = "main";
```

Javascript:

```
private var menuPage : String = "main";
```

Next, locate the existing set of IF statements:

C#:

```
  if(GUI.Button(new Rect(playButton), "Play")){
    StartCoroutine("ButtonAction", "Island");
  }
  if(GUI.Button(new Rect(instructionsButton), "Instructions")){
    audio.PlayOneShot(beep);
  }
  if(GUI.Button(new Rect(quitButton), "Quit")){
    StartCoroutine("ButtonAction", "quit");
  }
```

Javascript:

```
if(GUI.Button(Rect(playButton), "Play")){
  ButtonAction("Island");
}
if(GUI.Button(Rect(instructionsButton), "Instructions")){
  audio.PlayOneShot(beep);
}
```

```
if(GUI.Button(Rect(quitButton), "Quit")){
  ButtonAction("quit");
}
```

Now create a new empty line above these three `if` statements, and place in the opening of an `if` statement.

C# and Javascript:

```
if(menuPage == "main"){
```

Then close this if statement with a right curly brace } after the three `if` statements below it, in order to make sure that they are within this new if statement. This checks if the `menuPage` variable is currently set to the word `main`, which it is by default, so the three buttons already making up our main menu will be rendered when the scene loads.

To aid readability, you should make use of the *Tab* key to indent your code. This can be done in MonoDevelop by simply selecting a chunk of code that you wish to indent, and pressing *Tab* on the keyboard. So select the three `if` statements that form our main menu and press *Tab* to indent them from your newly added parent `if` statement as shown below (C# shown):

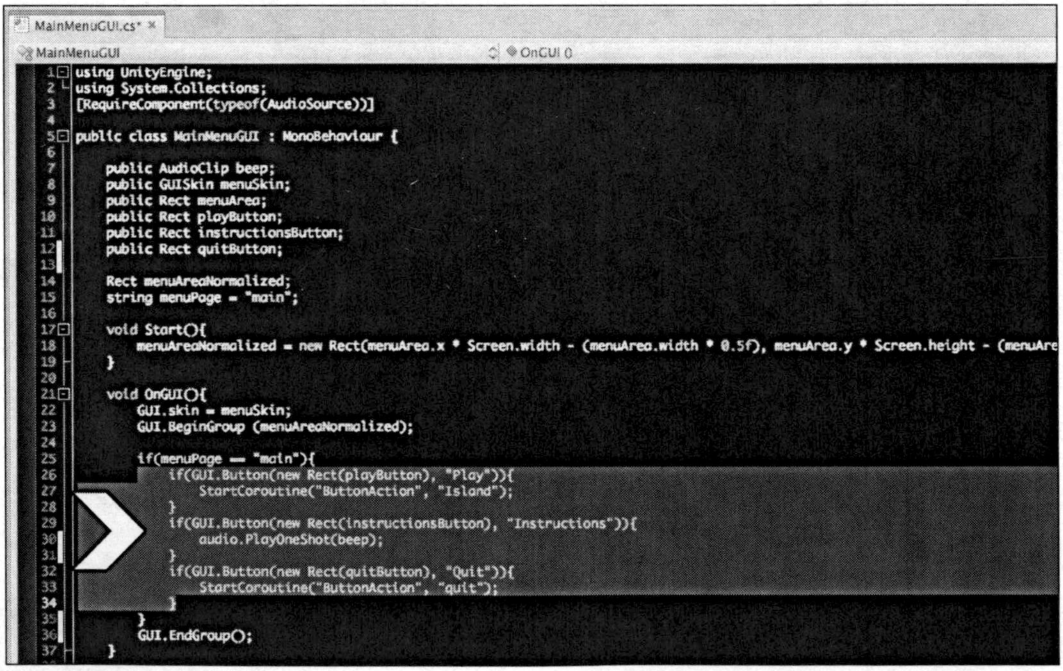

```
MainMenuGUI.cs* ×
MainMenuGUI                                    OnGUI ()
1  using UnityEngine;
2  using System.Collections;
3  [RequireComponent(typeof(AudioSource))]
4
5  public class MainMenuGUI : MonoBehaviour {
6
7      public AudioClip beep;
8      public GUISkin menuSkin;
9      public Rect menuArea;
10     public Rect playButton;
11     public Rect instructionsButton;
12     public Rect quitButton;
13
14     Rect menuAreaNormalized;
15     string menuPage = "main";
16
17     void Start(){
18         menuAreaNormalized = new Rect(menuArea.x * Screen.width - (menuArea.width * 0.5f), menuArea.y * Screen.height - (menuAre
19     }
20
21     void OnGUI(){
22         GUI.skin = menuSkin;
23         GUI.BeginGroup (menuAreaNormalized);
24
25         if(menuPage == "main"){
26             if(GUI.Button(new Rect(playButton), "Play")){
27                 StartCoroutine("ButtonAction", "Island");
28             }
29             if(GUI.Button(new Rect(instructionsButton), "Instructions")){
30                 audio.PlayOneShot(beep);
31             }
32             if(GUI.Button(new Rect(quitButton), "Quit")){
33                 StartCoroutine("ButtonAction", "quit");
34             }
35         }
36         GUI.EndGroup();
37     }
```

This allows you to see at a glance that those three `if` statements are within the `if(menuPage == "main"){` statement. Next, to allow our menu to switch to the instructions page, move down a line from the `audio.PlayOneShot(beep);` inside the `Instructions` button if statement (the second of the three), and add the following code:

C# and Javascript:

```
menuPage="instructions";
```

This invalidates the rendering of our main page of the menu, and will stop it from rendering—so we need an `else if` statement of the parent if to add another part of the menu if the `menuPage` variable is set to the word `instructions`.

Place your cursor after the closing right curly brace of the parent if statement that is checking for `menuPage` being equal to main, and add an else if with the following code inside it:

C#:

```
else if(menuPage == "instructions"){
  GUI.Label(new Rect(instructions),
    "You awake on a mysterious island...
      Find a way to signal for help or face certain doom!");
  if(GUI.Button(new Rect(quitButton), "Back")){
    audio.PlayOneShot(beep);
    menuPage="main";
  }
}
```

Javascript:

```
else if(menuPage == "instructions"){
  GUI.Label(Rect(instructions),
    "You awake on a mysterious island...
      Find a way to signal for help or face certain doom!");

  if(GUI.Button(Rect(quitButton), "Back")){
  audio.PlayOneShot(beep);
    menuPage="main";
  }
}
```

Here we are checking for the `menuPage` variable being equal to the word `instructions`, so as soon as the user clicks the **Instructions** button that sets it to that, the GUI will switch to rendering what is inside this newly added `if` statement.

We have added a new GUI element—a `Label`—and used a yet to be defined Rect variable called `instructions` to define its space on the screen. Let's add this variable now so that we can define it in the Inspector shortly. At the top of your script, beneath your existing Rect public variables, add the following:

C#:

```
public Rect instructions;
```

Javascript:

```
var instructions : Rect;
```

The `Label` contains text that simply explains what the player needs to do to win the game, keeping it nice and simple for them! This is followed by an `if` statement into we which pass the creation of another button, using the existing `quitButton` rect in order to use the same position and dimensions as the **Quit** button. This means that when the user goes to this part of the menu, the **Quit** button will be instantly replaced by a **Back** button. The `Back` button `if` statement contains two commands—it resets our `menuPage` string back to the word `main`, which will cause the GUI code to switch to rendering our main page of menu buttons, and it also plays the `beep` audio clip that other buttons do, in order to maintain consistency.

Let's try this out, Save your script and return to Unity now.

Select the **Menu2** object in the Hierarchy in order to see the **Main Menu GUI (Script)** component in the Inspector. You'll note that our new public Rect **instructions** has been added and needs defining—click the grey arrow next to its name to expand its properties now and fill in its values. Leaving **X** and **Y** at **0**, give this Rect a **Width** of **200** and a **Height** of **150**.

Press the **Play** button now, and click the **Instructions** button on the menu. You will be taken to a new page of the menu, but there's a problem—by default, a GUI Label has light grey text, which doesn't show up too well against our clouds!

We can easily rectify this by using our existing GUI Skin to style this label. Ensure that you have switched off Play mode, and then select the **Main Menu** GUI Skin asset in the Project panel—you can find this immediately by clicking on its name next to the **Menu Skin** variable in the **Main Menu GUI (Script)** component. Unity will highlight its position in the Project panel, and you can simply select it there.

Formatting the GUI label with the GUI skin asset

Expand the settings for a **Label** and you will see our problem immediately—the **Normal** state of this element has a light grey **Text Color** property. Change this to a dark grey now by clicking on its color block and choosing from the Color picker window that appears.

Now, set the following other properties of the **Label** style:

- **Font**—drag-and-drop your chosen font to this setting to assign it
- **Alignment**—choose **Upper Center** in order to render the text center aligned from the top of the Rect space it is in
- **Font Size**—set to **21**

Save your Menu scene in Unity now to update your progress. As our GUI skin is already assigned, we needn't do any more work to apply the changes we just made to our menu, so simply press **Play** now and check out the new part of the menu.

Your new menu instructions area should look like the next image—if not, return to your GUI skin and ensure you have filled in the settings as described above.

Congratulations! Your menu is now complete. You should be able to switch between the main page and instructions pages of the menu. As we have added a variable to define the section of the menu we are working with, you should also be able to add other parts of the menu. Whenever writing code to add a particular behavior to something, always try and write in this scalable manner—just in case you wish to add further behavior in the future.

A note on optimizing the loading process

Now that we have finished our menu in its separate scene, you may be wondering why we have a separate menu scene from our Island scene at all. This is to help optimize loading times for the game. By creating a less detailed scene that loads first, we are effectively stalling the player from requiring the game to load the main Island scene—something which when deployed on the web will take time to buffer, but could be loaded whilst the menu scene is being viewed by using **Web Player Streaming**.

We will add support for this in *Chapter 12*. Having a scene that will load whilst the rest of the game loads is a common practice, and gives the player something to do (read the instructions) whilst the rest of the game's content is downloaded or *streamed* behind the scenes.

You can read more about using Web Player Streaming in the Unity manual here:

`http://unity3d.com/support/documentation/Manual/Publishing%20Builds.html`

Summary

In this chapter, we have looked at the two core ways of creating interface elements in Unity—GUITextures and GUI scripting. By now you should have enough knowledge to get started in implementing either approach to build interfaces. While there are many more things you can do with GUI scripting, the techniques for establishing elements that we have covered here are the essentials you'll need each time you write a GUI script. We have also looked at how you can alter what is being rendered by a piece of GUI code, a crucial element of creating navigation in Unity game menus.

In the next chapter on Animation Basics, we will finish the game by adding a sequence of congratulatory messages once the player lights the campfire to signal for help.

10 Animation Basics

In this chapter, we will polish our game by adding a win sequence. When the player completes all the tasks that they need to in order to win the game, we would like to show them a sequence of congratulatory messages. In a more detailed game, this might be a cut-scene as a way to another part of the game, but as we are simply learning, we'll take this opportunity to learn some animation using both scripting—with linear interpolation, and also through the Animation tool that is built into Unity.

You will learn about:

- Fading the screen using GUITextures and scripting
- Transitioning between values using linear interpolation
- Animating using curves in the Animation window
- Layering 2D o bjects

Game win sequence

We will create a sequence of GUI elements that occur when the player wins the game. This win sequence will consist of three stages.

Firstly, animated text informing the player that lighting the fire has won them the game will appear:

We will animate these messages onto the screen using a script technique called **linear interpolation**—a method of transition from one value to another, over a defined period of time. Abbreviated to **Lerp** in code, linear interpolation is useful for many scripting tasks and as such is important to learn.

After making use of Lerp to animate through code, we will then dive into the Unity Animation window, and look at how we can use that to visually design animations for objects.

Using the Animation window we will create the second part of the win sequence in which the screen fades to black and further animated text will appear to tell the player the game is loading, before returning to the main menu:

The fader and **Loading..** text will be created as GUITextures, and we will add a script to the fader to scale it to the current screen resolution. We will then use the Animation window to design animations for the fader—by animating its transparency or *alpha* value to create the fade itself, and then animate the position of the **Loading..** text, making it pop-up from the bottom of the screen.

Win sequence approach

But how will these elements be created within the scene? Let's take an overview of how this will work before we start:

- The Player character (First Person Controller) collides with the campfire, having picked up the matches in the outpost.
- The Inventory script on the Player then sends a message to the Win Object to call function `GameOver()`.
- The `GameOver()` function is a co-routine that begins by instantiating a prefab called `WinSequence`, containing three Lerp animated pieces of text in the form of GUITextures that inform the player they have won the game.
- The `GameOver()` co-routine then uses a yield to pause for eight seconds whilst the player reads the text.
- The `GameOver()` co-routine then instantiates a prefab called fade—a GUI Texture of solid black color.
- The fade has a script called Fader attached that scales it to fill the screen, and an Animation component with an animation that fades it from invisible to visible to create the fade.
- During the animation of the fade, an animation event calls a function in the Fader script that instantiates the final element, loading GUI; this is another GUI Texture with the phrase **Loading..** which is animated to pop up onto the screen, and then fall back down.
- The animation of loading GUI finishes with an animation event that calls a function called `Reload()` in an attached script called Reloader. This function uses `Application.LoadLevel()` to load the Menu scene.

Now that we know the order of things, let's get started with making our final sequence and learning about animation.

Ensure that you are no longer working on the Menu scene - load the **Island** scene now by double clicking its icon in the Project panel.

Triggering the win

We have already set up a winning condition within our **Inventory** script—the `LightFire()` function. This marks the winning goal of the game, so it makes sense for us to use this as a trigger point to inform the player that they have won.

Locate and launch the **Inventory** script in the **Scripts** folder of the **Project** panel. In this script we need to place a reference to an object we will create to manage the instantiation of our game over sequence.

Begin by adding the following public variable beneath the existing variables at the top of the script:

C#:

```
public GameObject winObj;
```

Javascript:

```
var winObject : GameObject;
```

Now let's make use of this Win Object by using the `SendMessage()` function to call a function on an external game object. When the player has lit the fire, the win sequence should begin, so we will call a function on the managing win object. Add the following line to the bottom of `LightFire()` after the `fireIsLit=true;` line:

C# and Javascript:

```
winObj.SendMessage("GameOver");
```

This command sends a message to the win object we will create, asking it to call a function called `GameOver()` in a script attached to it. Note here that the name of the script is not necessary, as this command searches the object we have specified for the function name, regardless of the script that function is inside.

After creating our animated GUI elements we will create the win object, and write a script with the `GameOver()` function inside to attach to it. For now, make sure that you save your **Inventory** script and then return to Unity.

Creating the game win messages

In the **Book Assets | Textures** folder in the Project panel you will find three textures with names beginning with `win`:

- **win_message**
- **win_survival**
- **win_youWin**

These textures are designed to be used as GUITextures, which we will animate onto the screen. As such, select each one in turn—and in the **Texture Importer** in the Inspector, set **Texture Type** to **GUI**, remembering to click **Apply** to confirm.

Positioning win sequence GUI elements

Next, select the **win_message** texture and click the **Create** button on the Hierarchy panel, and choose **GUITexture**. Now repeat this step for **win_survival** and **win_youWin**. By default these textures will be positioned at (0.5, 0.5, 0) in the Transform component, therefore centered on the screen, so change their positions to the following to space them apart appropriately:

- win_message—(0.5, 0.4, 0)
- win_survival—(0.5, 0.8, 0)
- win_youWin—(0.5, 0.7, 0)

Remember that you will only see them spaced correctly when you maximize the game view (unless you are running your computer at a very high screen resolution)-hover your mouse cursor over it and tap the space bar to maximize and minimize.

Grouping GUITextures for optimized instantiation

Because we will instantiate these objects later using our **winObj**, we should group them under a parent object now so that we can create a single prefab, rather than three individual prefabs. This saves us using three instantiate commands later, and is therefore more efficient.

Choose **Game Object | Create Empty** from the top menu, and then rename your new game object **WinSequence**. Reset its **Position** values by clicking the **Cog** icon to the right of the its Transform component and choosing **Reset Position** from the pop-out menu. Now select all three **win_** objects, and drag-and-drop them onto the **WinSequence** object so that they are nested beneath it as child objects.

Now that our messages are in place, let's look at a simple use of scripted position animation using linear interpolation.

Animating with linear interpolation (Lerp)

To create this animation using Lerp, we will create a new script, so select the **Scripts** folder in the **Project** panel and click on **Create**, selecting your preferred language from the drop-down menu. Rename this new script **Animator**.

In the script we are about to write, we have already learned many of the elements; only the concept of using a Lerp is new, so with this in mind let's complete the script, and then take a look at the part which we're focusing on. Copy out the script in full, then read on.

C#:

```
using UnityEngine;
using System.Collections;

public class Animator : MonoBehaviour {

  public float xStartPosition  = -1.0f;
  public float xEndPosition = 0.5f;
  public float speed = 1.0f;
  float startTime;

  void Start () {
    startTime = Time.time;
  }

  void Update () {
    Vector3 pos =
      new Vector3(Mathf.Lerp(xStartPosition, xEndPosition,
        (Time.time-startTime)*speed),
        transform.position.y,transform.position.z);
    transform.position = pos;
  }
}
```

Javascript:

```
var xStartPosition : float = -1.0;
var xEndPosition : float = 0.5;
var speed : float = 1.0;
private var startTime : float;

function Start(){
  startTime = Time.time;
}

function Update () {
  transform.position.x =
    Mathf.Lerp(xStartPosition, xEndPosition,
      (Time.time-startTime)*speed);
}
```

Note here that the approach taken in C# differs slightly from Javascript, as we must modify the entire position parameter by temporarily storing it as a Vector3 variable. In Javascript, we can modify the X coordinate property directly, and so set it to be equal to our Lerp. This is the main part of this script and what we will focus on now—as it is used in C# to modify the X coordinate by being placed as the first coordinate of a Vector3.

Here is the crucial part of the script, the `Lerp` itself:

```
Mathf.Lerp(xStartPosition, xEndPosition,
  (Time.time-StartTime)*speed)
```

This command contains three arguments, a starting value (in our case, it is being used as a position—though it can be used for any purpose), an end value, and the time over which to complete the transition or *interpolation* between values.

Here we are simply referring to interpolation as a transition between two differing values. If you would like to read more about this concept, you can refer to Wikipedia—`http://en.wikipedia.org/wiki/Interpolation`.

For our timing, we are setting a value of `Time.time`—which registers the time since the game began but is reset by subtracting our custom value `StartTime`, that is assigned the value of `Time.time` when the object is instantiated. This value is, as a result, a timer counting upwards from zero, rather than an arbitrary time—and finally, we are altering this time by multiplying by our `speed` variable. Currently the `speed` variable is set to `1.0`, so no change will be made, but any value over `1` will increase the speed, and values lower than `1` will decrease it.

Go to **File | Save** in the script editor now, and switch back to Unity.

As our new **Animator** script has public variables exposed to allow us to alter the start and end position of an object, we can create different animations for whatever we attach it to without diving back into the script. This means we can use it on all three of our GUITexture win sequence messages, and create a different animation for each.

Attach the **Animator** script to all three child objects of the **WinSequence-win_message, win_survival**, and **win_youWin**—drag the script from the Scripts folder in the Project panel onto each of the three objects in the Hierarchy.

Adjusting animations

Our script is only a simple implementation of `Lerp`, being used to control the X axis position of our objects, as such we will only achieve horizontal animation—but we can control from which direction our animation occurs, simply by setting the **XStart Position** variable in the Inspector. Select each of our three GUITexture objects and set up the following values for the **XStart Position** variable in the **Animator (Script)** component in the Inspector:

- win_message: 1
- win_survival: 1
- win_youWin: -1

Here, writing a value of -1 will cause the texture to animate from off-screen left, whilst positive 1 will cause animation from the right, so our **Survival!** title and message paragraph will enter from the right, whilst the **You win** texture will emerge from the left. You can also slow down this effect—try selecting **win_message** and setting **XStart Position** to **2** and **Speed** to **0.5**.

Save your scene in Unity now by choosing **File | Save** from the top menu and press **Play** take a look at the effect.

Storing the win sequence

If you are happy with the animation effect you have achieved, expand the Prefabs folder in the Inspector, and then select the parent **WinSequence** object in the Hierarchy and drag it to the **Prefabs** folder in the Project panel in order to store it and its child objects as a single prefab—we do not want the sequence to be in our game by default, so we will create the aforementioned win object to instantiate it for us.

Now that this object is stored as a prefab, delete it from the Hierarchy by selecting the **WinSequence** parent object and using shortcut *Command* + *Backspace* (Mac) or *Delete* (PC) to remove it from the Island scene.

Creating the win object

To manage the instantiation of the GUI objects we have just made, we will create the win object that we referred to in our **Inventory** script earlier. We have already set up a reference to this object, so we will create it now, and then assign it to our public variable on the **Inventory(Script)** component on the **First Person Controller**.

Choose **Game Object | Create Empty** from the top menu and then rename the new empty object **winObj**. Select the **Scripts** folder in the Project panel and click the **Create** button on this panel and choose your preferred scripting language.

Name the script **WinGame** and then drag-and-drop to assign it to the new empty object named **winObj** in the Hierarchy. Launch this script now by double-clicking its icon in the Project panel.

Begin by establishing three public variables:

C#:

```
public GameObject winSequence;
public GUITexture fader;
public AudioClip winClip;
```

Javascript:

```
var winSequence: GameObject;
var fader : GUITexture;
var winClip : AudioClip;
```

The `winSequence` variable creates a reference for our **WinSequence** prefab that contains child objects of the animating `GUITextures`. The fader variable is a reference to a screen `fader` we will create shortly and the `winClip` variable is a reference to an audio clip to be played when the player wins the game.

Next, establish a new custom function called `GameOver()` in your **WinGame** script—this name is essential as we are calling this function using `SendMessage()` from our **Inventory** script.

C#:

```
IEnumerator GameOver () {
}
```

Javascript:

```
function GameOver () {
}
```

Note that in C# it is necessary to use the prefix `IEnumerator` rather than `void` in order to allow this function to behave as a co-routine, meaning that we will be able to implement a pause within it, by using the `yield` command.

Next, place a `PlayClipAtPoint()` command into this function, and an `Instantiate()` function for our `winSequence` variable.

C# and Javascript:

```
AudioSource.PlayClipAtPoint(winClip, transform.position);
Instantiate(winSequence);
```

Note here that we are using `Instantiate()` with only one argument—a reference to the asset to be created. By doing this, the instantiated prefab will inherit its position and rotation from its originating game object; remember that the Transform values are stored as part of the prefab. Therefore our `winSequence` object will be created at (0,0,0) exactly as it was previously. This is especially important to remember when Instantiating objects that need to be positioned using screen coordinates from 0 to 1.

Next we will add a pause in the script using the yield command we have seen previously, then begin a fade out by instantiating the `fader` GUITexture object we will create shortly. Add the following two lines to your `GameOver()` function:

C#:

```
yield return new WaitForSeconds(8.0f);
Instantiate(fader);
```

Javascript:

```
yield WaitForSeconds(8.0);
Instantiate(fader);
```

We now have a script set up to instantiate our game winning messages, wait for eight seconds, and then instantiate another GUITexture object that will fade in and trigger a loading message.

Save your script now and return to Unity; we will return to the **Win Game (Script)** component and assign the public variables that make up the sequence at the end of the chapter, once we have created them!

Creating the Fader and using the Animation panel

Our fader object will consist of a GUITexture object, with animation applied through the Unity Animation panel, which when instantiated will play its animation, and then trigger a further object to be created and animated—another GUITexture to tell the player the game is loading, before returning them back to the menu.

In **Book Assets | Textures** locate the texture file called **fade**. This is simply a 2 x 2 pixel black square texture that we will stretch to the dimensions of the screen and animate to fade in from 0 opacity. With this texture selected in the Project panel, set the **Texture Type** parameter in the **Texture Importer** in the Inspector to **GUI**, and press **Apply**.

With this texture still selected, click the **Create** button on the Hierarchy and choose **GUI Texture**. Now because we need our texture to cover the screen, alter the settings of the GUITexture component to match those shown here:

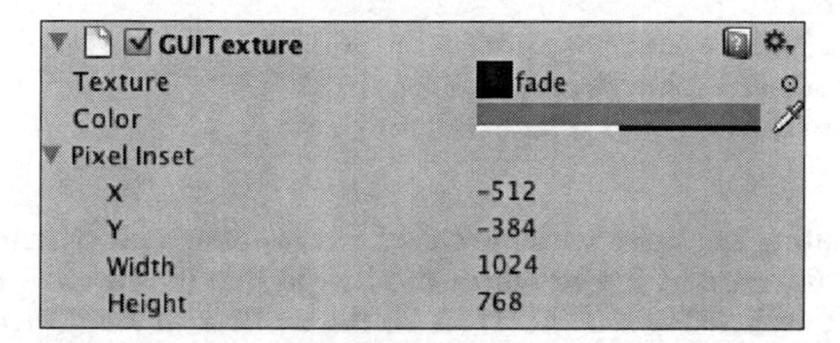

This prepares the texture to work for the default standalone size of 1024 x 768 pixels we are testing with—but we will build in support for scaling to the current resolution when we write for this object now.

Scaling for various resolutions

In order to ensure that our fader will work at any resolution, we can write a script that will check what its Pixel Inset values should be when the object is instantiated— making use of a `Start()` function to perform this operation. To continue our developmental approach of creating individual scripts to perform tasks on the object they relate to, we will write a script that checks the system value `Screen.width` and `Screen.height`—in a similar way to how we positioned our menu in the previous chapter.

Select the **Scripts** folder in the Project panel and click the **Create** button there, choosing your preferred scripting language. Rename your script **Fader** and then double-click its icon to launch it in the script editor.

Pixel Inset values are a similar type of data to what we have seen before—a Rect, and as such we can simply create a new Rect value in `Start()` and assign it to the GUITexture's `pixelInset` property there. To do this, add the following function to your script now:

C#:

```
void Start(){
  Rect currentRes = new Rect(-Screen.width * 0.5f, -Screen.height *
     0.5f, Screen.width, Screen.height);
  guiTexture.pixelInset = currentRes;
}
```

Javascript:

```
function Start(){
  var currentRes : Rect = Rect(-Screen.width * 0.5, -Screen.height *
    0.5, Screen.width, Screen.height);
  guiTexture.pixelInset = currentRes;
}
```

Here we are creating our `Rect` variable called `currentRes` and passing negative X and Y values of the current screen width and height into its `x` and `y` properties and then dividing by two (using `* 0.5`). Then for the width and height we simply make use of the full `Screen.width` and `Screen.height` values.

This guarantees that the fade will work at any resolution! Save your script now and then return to Unity. Select the **Fader** script in the Project panel and drag-and-drop to assign it to the **fade** object in the Hierarchy.

Now test this by maximizing the game view (hover over it and press *Space*) and Play testing the game—the script will scale the Fader to whatever size the game view happens to be. Stop play testing now.

Starting the Fader from invisibility

We will need to ensure that the Fader does not obscure the screen for a frame when instantiated because it is possible that its default visible state could be shown before the animation from 0 to visible occurs. To avoid this, we should set the GUITexture to be invisible by default by setting its Color alpha value to 0.

Click the **Color** block on the GUITexture component and in the **Color Picker** that appears, drag the **A** (alpha) slider to **0** to make it invisible. Close the Color Picker and you should now see only a black line beneath the **Color** block, indicating an alpha value of 0.

Now, launch the Animation panel by choosing **Window | Animation** from the top menu.

Animation panel overview

Before we use this panel to fade our GUITexture over time, let's look at a brief overview of how this works.

This is the **Animation** window, with our fade object selected:

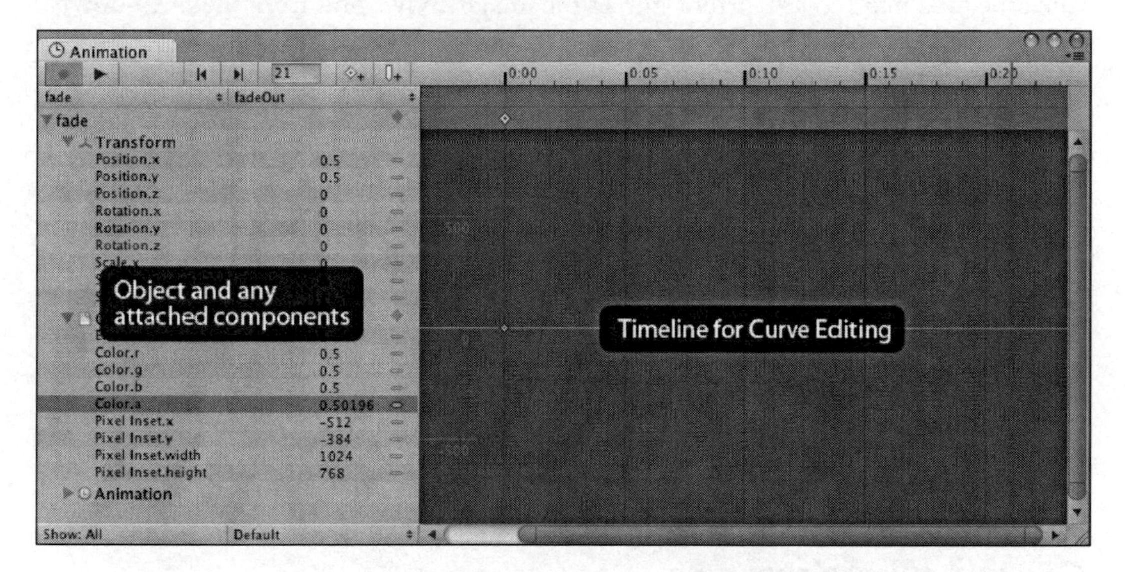

In this example a new clip named **fadeOut** has already been created. When you first create an animation on an object using this window, Unity adds an Animation component to your object automatically, as it requires this component in order to apply the clip to it.

The core controls of the Animation window are shown here:

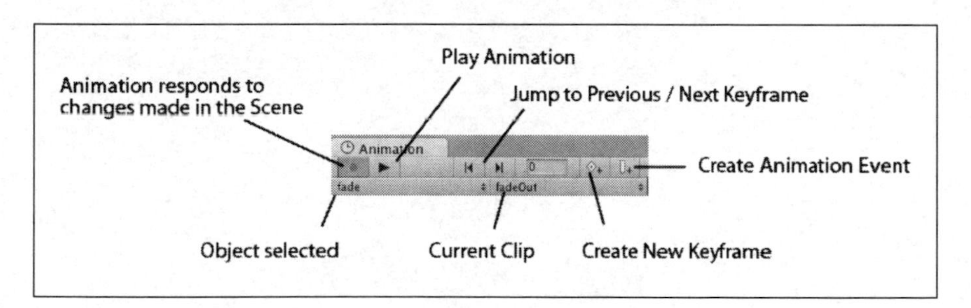

These are the main elements of the Animation window, but let's learn by doing and start animating our fade GUITexture.

Creating an animation clip

Click the area marked as Current Clip in the image above, and from the drop-down menu, select **Create New Clip**:

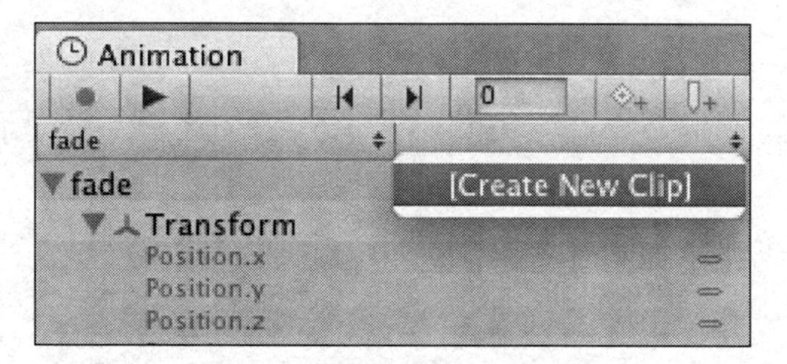

Unity will then ask you to name your new clip—name this **fadeOut** and save it inside your main Assets folder in order to store this in the root of the Project, or make an **Animations** folder if you wish and store it there.

Creating keyframes

Once you have made a clip, its name is selected in the Current clip area, and once you have several animations on a single object, you can easily switch between them using the same drop-down, or create new ones.

To animate any of the available parameters of your components, you need simply to add a curve. To do this, locate the parameter you wish to animate—in this instance we need to animate the **Color.a** (alpha) parameter of our GUITexture—click the icon to the right-hand side of this parameter, and choose **Add Curve**, as shown below:

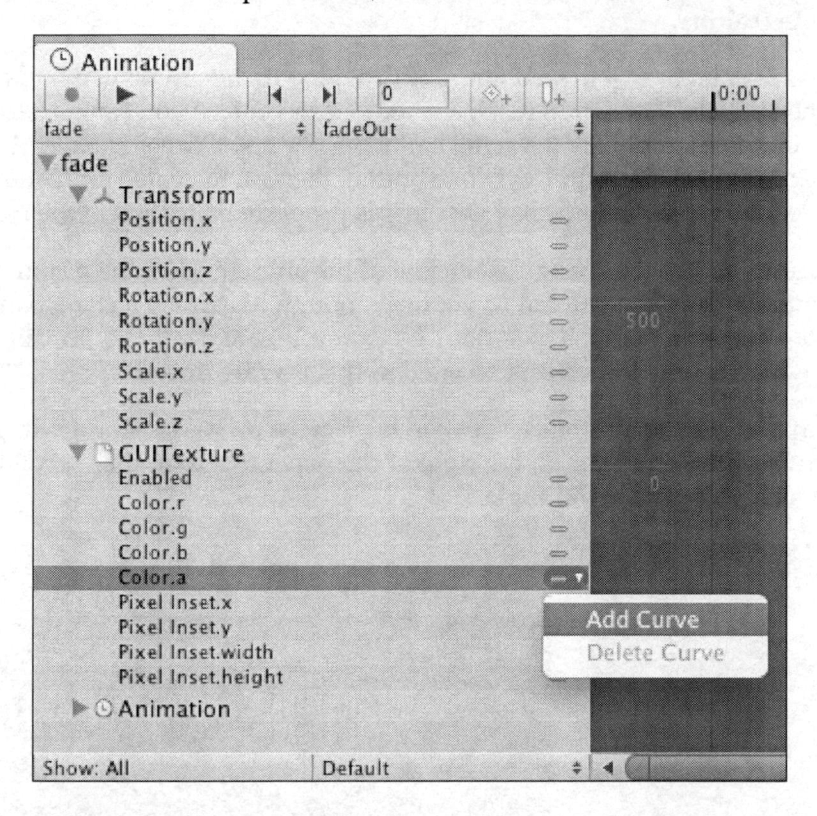

This creates the first keyframe at 0 in the timeline. If you are new to animation, keyframes are a way of establishing points in time that a particular property has a certain value. Because games work in the same way—they are simply frame by frame renderings—we expect a progression. Instead of establishing a value each frame, software is there to help you animate more easily by simply allowing you to state what values should be at a specific frame in time. The software package then estimates what the values for each frame in between will be. This is called **Tweening**, and this is what Unity will do in between the values set for your keyframes.

For this reason, we will set a keyframe at the start of our animation that sees a 0 value for the GUITexture's alpha, and a value of 1 at the end of our animation. This means that at the end of our animation, our GUITexture will be completely visible—and because GUITextures are rendered in front of the 3D view of the game camera, the game will be obscured by this black texture, as if the screen has faded out.

Keyframes are represented by a small diamond shape—and when the playhead, represented by a red line—is over a keyframe you can alter the value of it by clicking on its current value and retyping. As we have already set it, you should note that the first keyframe value for **Color.a** is set to **0** so that our animation will fade in this texture from 0 alpha.

Now, move the playhead—the red line—by dragging it along with your cursor over the timeline scale itself until you reach a value of 2 seconds; if you cannot see that far down the timeline, simply use the scroll bar at the bottom. Once you have placed the playhead at **2:00**, click the **Add Keyframe** button, then set the value for **Color.a** for the keyframe to 1 by typing into the box next to this property on the left of the panel.

You will barely notice the change in the line of the animation on the graph itself because initially the view will not be zoomed enough to display a change in value from 0 to 1—some animations (positions for example) are dealing with values from 0 to 100s, which is why the view is zoomed in this way by default.

To zoom in and see the difference between keyframes properly, simply drag the notched ends of the scroll bar on the right of the panel together, then scroll to the point at which you can see the angle:

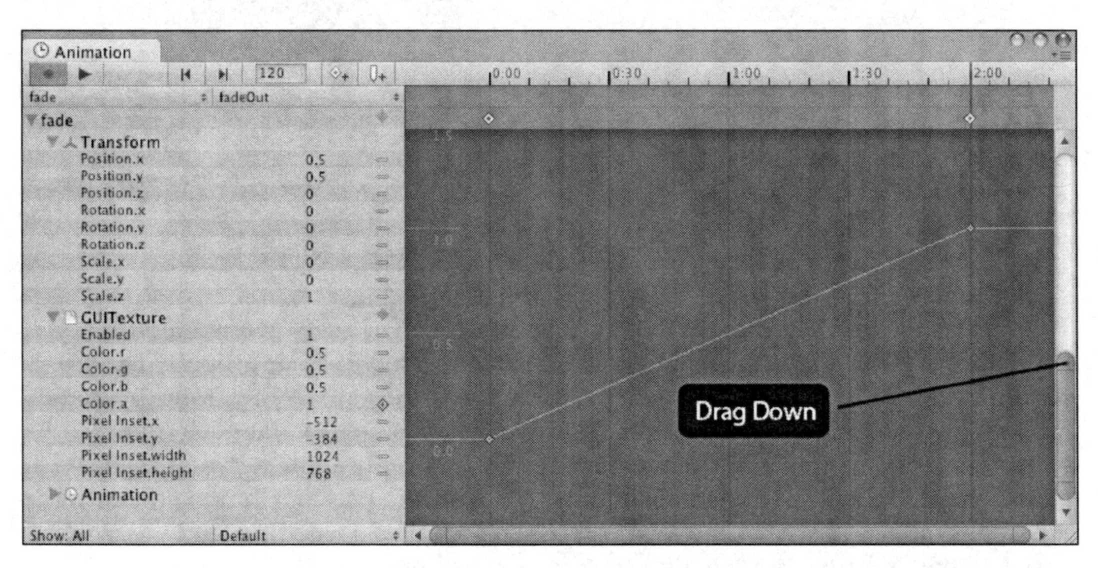

Alternatively, you can make use of Unity's Focus in order to scale the animation view's current zoom to the animation you have made. Simply hover your cursor over the Animation view, and press *F* to focus.

Using animation curves

To create a smoother fade, we can add curvature to our keyframes. This allows you to animate smoothly using Bezier curves to control motion. Right-click the first keyframe you have made on the graph editor (as opposed to the representation of the keyframe at the top, beneath the timeline), and from the drop-down menu that appears, choose **Flat**:

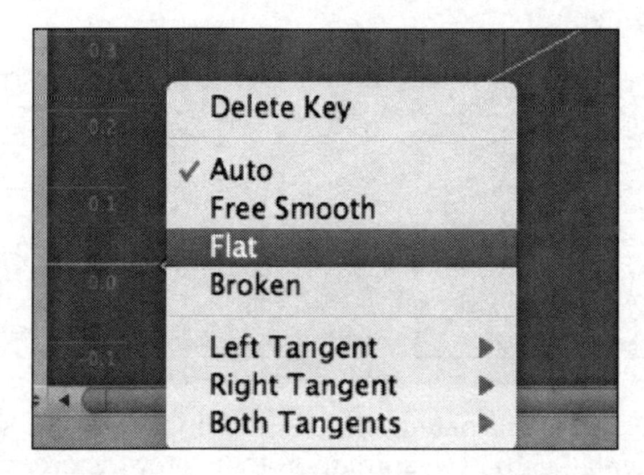

Repeat this step for the second keyframe and your animation curve should now look like this:

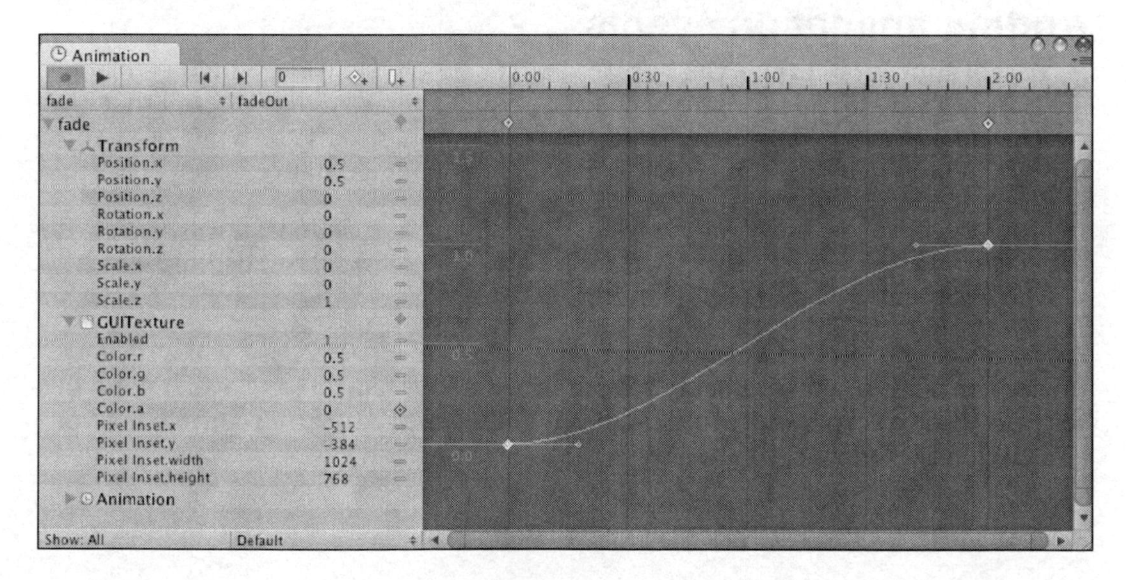

Note that in the above image, both keyframes have been selected to demonstrate the handles.

Our first animation is now complete! Close the Animation panel for now, or dock it as part of the Unity interface, and then press **Play** in Unity to see the effect of the animation fading in our GUITexture.

Press **Play** again to stop testing, or you'll be walking around in the dark! You should notice that the fade object now has an **Animation** component shown in the Inspector, and lists **fadeout** as its current animation, which will **Play Automatically** as this option is checked by default:

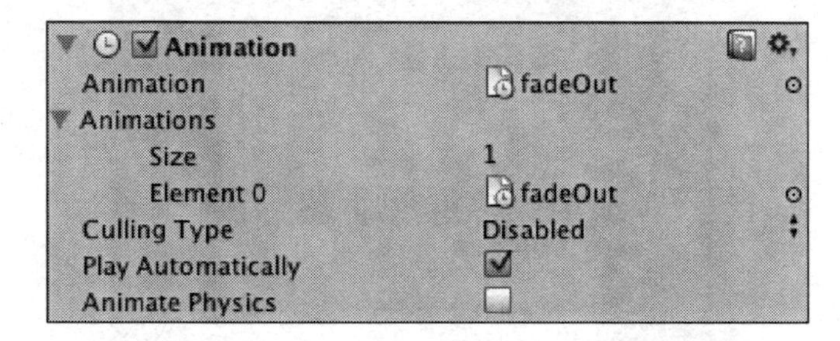

Now that our fade object is animated, there is one final step to complete before we save this as a prefab—using the animation to trigger the creation of a further GUI element.

Adding animation events

As part of animation, **Events** can be placed on the timeline. Events within animation are simply a way to call functions at specific points in time. Writing a script that attaches to the object you are animating, you can simply specify the name of a function within that script and call it at any point in your animation.

In order to inform the player about what is happening as they have finished the game, we will animate a further GUITexture object with the word Loading, which will be instantiated as the **fadeOut** occurs.

As events refer to script functions in scripts attached to an object, we will write a function into the script we already have attached to our **fade** object—**Fader**. Find this script in the Project panel now and launch it in the script editor, or return to it if you already have it open.

Write in the following public variable and function to simply instantiate the **Loading** GUITexture that we will create shortly.

C#:

```
public GUITexture loadGUI;

void LoadAnim(){
  Instantiate(loadGUI);
}
```

Javascript:

```
var loadGUI : GUITexture;

function LoadAnim(){
  Instantiate(loadGUI);
}
```

Save this script and return to Unity now. As this is complete and attached to our **fade** object already, we are now ready to call it using an animation event.

Open the Animation window once more—choose **Window | Animation** from the top menu or make use of the shortcut *Command + 6* (Mac) or *Ctrl + 6* (PC).

Select the **Color.a** property of the **GUITexture** component on the left-hand side of the panel, and then move the timeline to halfway through the animation to **1:00**.

Click the **Add Event** button:

An event will be placed and the **Edit Animation Event** window should appear. This can also be opened by clicking on the event in the timeline. Here you can select from a list of any functions in scripts attached to the object whose animation you are currently working on. Click on the drop-down where it currently reads **No Function Selected**, and select the function we just wrote-LoadAnim**()**, instead:

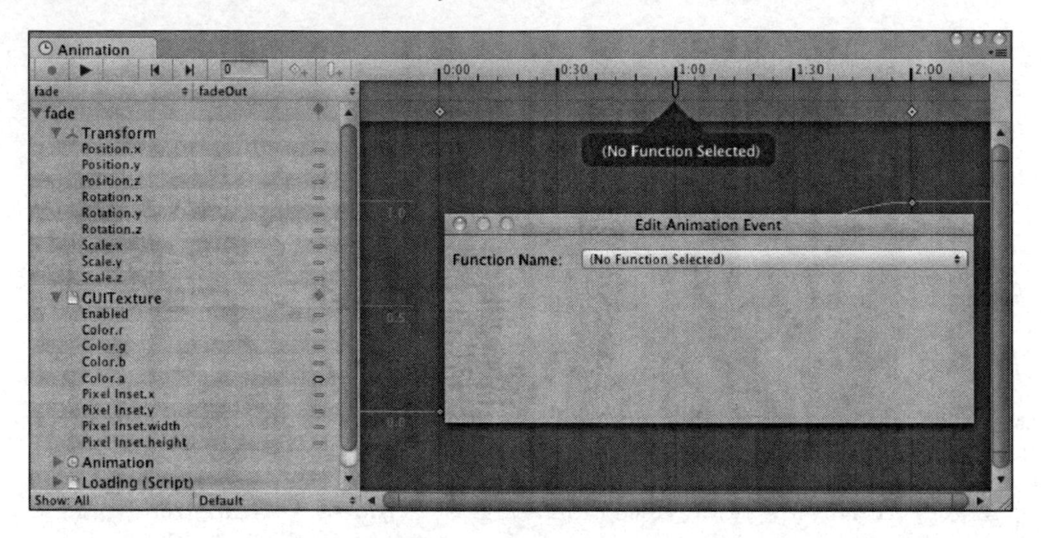

This function will be called at this point in the timeline, and can be moved at any time by simply revisiting this animation and adjusting its position in the timeline. Save your progress now by choosing **File | Save Scene** from the top menu.

To complete our win sequence, the fade out is followed by the word **Loading..** popping up onto the screen—we have prepared our Fader with a method to instantiate this as it is fading out, so now we simply need to create it, and assign it to our **Fader** script. The **Loading..** GUI will complete the sequence by reloading the main menu after a defined period of time.

Creating and animating the Loading GUI

In the **Book Assets | Textures** folder, select **loadingGUI** and on the **Texture Importer** component in the Inspector, choose **GUI** as the **Texture Type**, and hit **Apply** to confirm.

With this texture still selected, click the **Create** button on the Hierarchy and choose **GUI Texture**. You will now have a game object in the Hierarchy called **loadingGUI**—to ensure that this object begins off-screen, set the **Y** Position value to **-1**.

Open the Animation panel once more and click the Add Clip button, naming it **showHide**—saved in the **Assets** folder or your own **Animations** folder as before.

Right-click on the **Position.y** property of the **Transform** component in the section on the left and select **Add Curves**, then select the **Position.y** property so that it highlights in blue and you only see a green keyframe on the graph. Ensure that the value of this keyframe is set to -1 so that the GUI element is off screen vertically.

Now, by moving the timeline and placing keyframes, add the following keyframes and values for the **Position.y** property:

- 1:00 second : 0.5
- 4:00 seconds : 0.5
- 5:00 seconds : -1

This will animate the GUITexture to the center of the screen (0.5), pause until 4 seconds into the animation, then animate out again by 5 seconds.

Your curve should look like this:

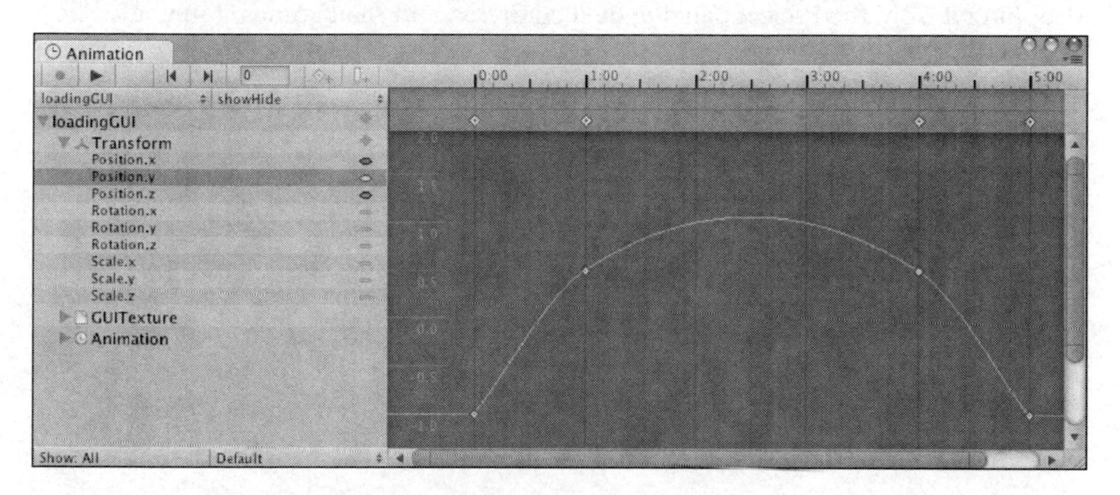

However, this means that the **loadingGUI** will animate up in a smooth curve to a higher point than the center, and then fall back down as if it were an object being thrown upward and then effected by gravity—test this for yourself by pressing play on the Animation panel and watching the scene or game view.

To correct this, simply right-click on the keyframes at **1:00** and **4:00** and choose **Flat** from the menu that appears.

Once both are set to **Flat**, press Play on the Animation panel once more and in the scene or game view you should see your **loadingGUI** animate up, stay centered, then fall back down.

The animation of our Loading screen is complete, so it's about time we reloaded the game! As we have just learned to use Animation Events, let's make use of these once more in order to reload the Menu scene of the game, letting the player play again if they wish or quit (for standalone versions).

Loading scenes with animation events

Before we add an event to an animation, we should write the script and function for the event to call. Select the **Scripts** folder in the Project panel, then click the **Create** button and choose **C#** or **Javascript,** and rename your new script **Reloader**.

Attach this script to the **loadingGUI** object in the Hierarchy by dragging and dropping it from the Project panel to the Hierarchy, and then launch it in your script editor.

This script is simply to be used to reload the menu scene, so just write in the following function:

C#:

```
void Reload(){
  Application.LoadLevel("Menu");
}
```

Javascript:

```
function Reload(){
  Application.LoadLevel("Menu");
}
```

Save your script now and return to Unity. Attach the **Reloader** script you have just written to the **loadingGUI** object, and then re-select the **loadingGUI** object in the Hierarchy and switch to the **Animation** panel once more if it is not already open.

We need to continue to work on our **showHide** animation, so the **loadingGUI** object must be selected in the Hierarchy, as this is one of its animations. Remember you can tell which object and animation you are working on as they are shown in the top left of the panel.

Place the play head at **6:00** seconds on the timeline—this is one second after our Loading text animates back down and off of the screen. Click the **Add Event** button. Click on the new Event marker in order to show the **Edit Animation Event** window and choose the **Reload()** function from the drop-down menu, then close the window.

Congratulations, our animations are now complete! But remember that we do not want the **loadingGUI** in our Island scene by default, as we are relying on the **Fader** script to instantiate it for us, as a result of the first animation event we created.

Storing and instantiating the Loading GUI

Save **loadingGUI** as a prefab by dragging it from the Hierarchy to the **Prefabs** folder in the Inspector. Delete the instance of **loadingGUI** from the Hierarchy now that it is stored using shortcut *Command* + *Backspace* (Mac) or *Delete* (PC).

Remember that our **Fader** script has an Instantiate command intended for use with our **loadingGUI** prefab, which is called when its `LoadAnim()` function is called by our animation event. Therefore, we need to assign the prefab we have made to our **Fader** script so that it can create an instance of the **loadingGUI**. Select the **fade** object in the Hierarchy so that you can see the **Fader (Script)** component in the Inspector. You should see the public variable **Load GUI** is awaiting a GUITexture to be assigned to it—so drag-and-drop the **loadingGUI** prefab from the **Prefabs** folder onto this variable to assign it.

Your **Fader (Script)** component should look like this:

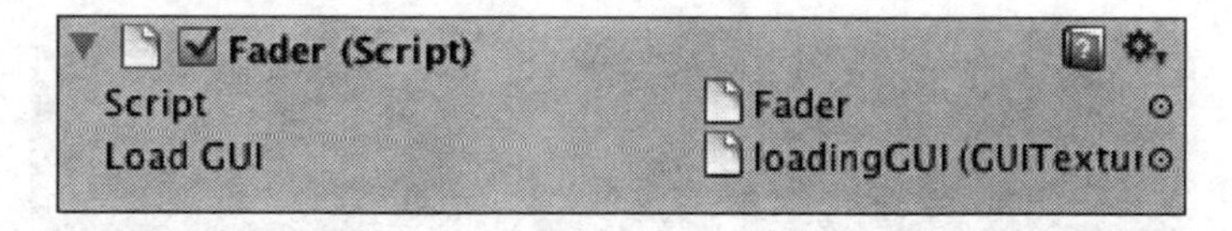

As usual, we do not need this object in the Hierarchy during the game, so we will store the **fade** as a prefab also. Drag and drop **fade** from the Hierarchy to the **Prefabs** folder in the Project panel to store it there, and then delete it from the Hierarchy in the usual manner.

Loading the win sequence

Now that our **fade** prefab is set up to instantiate the **loadingGUI** prefab once it begins to fade to black, and our **loadingGUI** is set up to reload our **Menu** scene, the last thing to do is to make sure that when the player wins the game, our win object's (winObj) **Win Game** script will instantiate the two stages of the win sequence.

Select the **winObj** in the Hierarchy to see the **Win Game (Script)** component.

From the **Prefabs** folder in the Project panel, drag-and-drop the **fade** prefab to the **Fader** public variable, and drop the **WinSequence** prefab onto the **Win Sequence** variable to assign them. Also assign **win_clip** from the **Book Assets | Sounds** folder to the Win Clip variable:

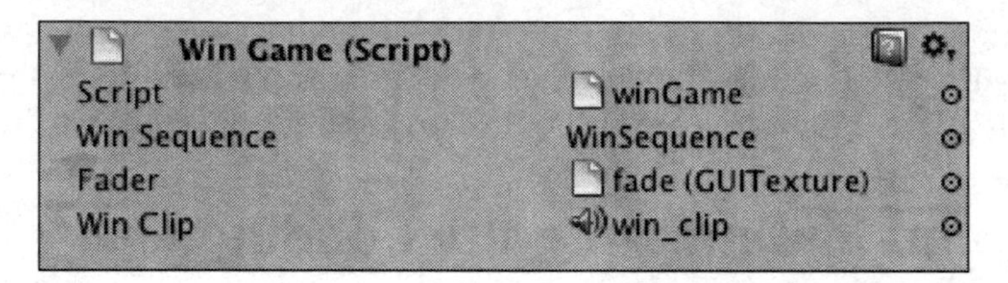

Finally, select the **First Person Controller** in the Hierarchy, and in the **Inventory (script)** component in the Inspector, drag and drop the **winObj** object from the Hierarchy to the **Win Obj** public variable. This assigns **winObj** as the object to call the `GameOver()` function on, when the player lights the fire.

Now that we have assigned our game win sequence elements, let's see this in action! Press the **Play** button and play through the game. Upon lighting the campfire, the screen should show you the congratulatory messages, followed after 8 seconds by the fade to black, and **Loading..** text—this will then load the Menu scene after it animates off screen.

But wait! There's a bug to fix! Our GUITexture messages are still visible when the fade in begins and the **Loading..** message is nowhere to be seen, but why?

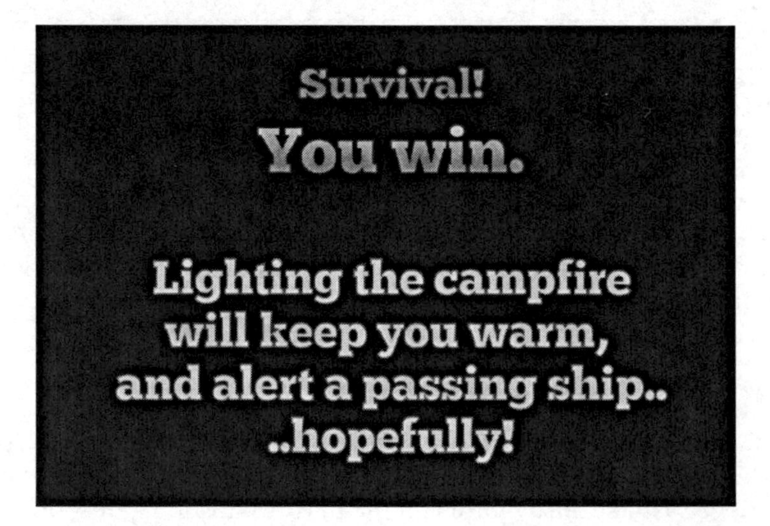

This is because when placing GUITextures onscreen, the Transform position Z property is used for layering, or ordering—think of it as depth, as you would expect for 3D objects. Because all of our elements currently have the same Z position, they are not rendering in the order we need them to; ideally the messages, followed by the fade to hide them, and finally the **Loading...** message on top. Let's fix this now.

Layering GUITextures

To ensure that our **fade** appears in front of our game win messages, but behind the **loadingGUI**, we can make use of the Z axis to effectively order layers of 2D objects.

Because our game win messages need to be below the **fade** and **loadingGUI**, select each child object of the **WinSequence** prefab in the **Prefabs** folder, and set its **Z** position value to **-2** in the Transform component in the Inspector.

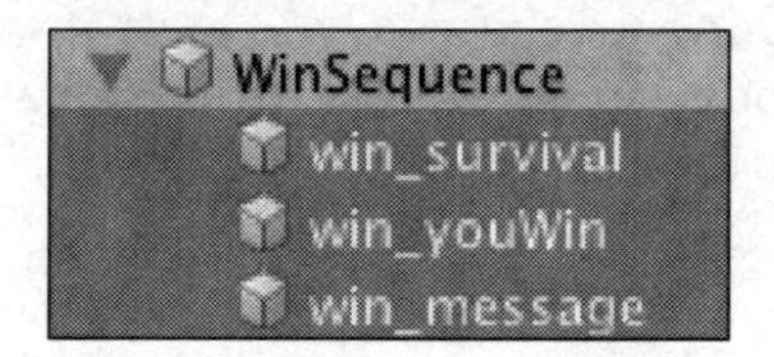

Now, leaving the **Transform Z** position of the **loadingGUI** prefab at 0 (highest, or *in front of* the rest), set the **Z** position for the **fade** prefab to **-1**.

All done! Save your scene and then play test the game, and enjoy our newly added game win sequence! Press Play to test now, remembering to press it again once you are finished testing.

Challenge—fading in the Island scene

As a final finishing touch, let's reuse what we have just learned, and create a fade-in from white for the start of the Island level.

As this is not a functional part of the game—we won't discuss exactly what to do here, it's a challenge for you to complete! Instead, let's take a look at an overview of what you need to do, and we'll leave you to fill in the finer details, based on what you have just learned:

- Use the **fadeWhite** texture in **Book Assets | Textures** to make GUITexture
- Attach a script with code to make it display at the current resolution
- Set its Color alpha to 1 (fully visible)

- Create a new animation for this object to tween from 1 to 0 over time to make it fade out
- Add an animation event at the end of the fade out to destroy the game object to remove it from the scene

Good luck!

Summary

In this chapter, we have looked at two different ways to animate in Unity. Remember that both the Lerp and Animation feature in Unity can be used to animate almost any property of your game, by addressing a particular property of a component. This gives you almost infinite control of the action happening in your game scenes.

In the next chapter on finishing touches, we will look at some new techniques such as Lightmapping to give your game the more professional, polished look that it needs to stand out from the crowd.

11

Performance Tweaks and Finishing Touches

In this chapter, we will take our game from a simple example to something we can deploy by adding some finishing touches to the island. As we have looked at various new skills throughout this book, we have added a single example at a time. In this chapter, we'll reinforce some of the skills that we have learned so far, and also look in more detail at some final effects that we can add that aren't crucial to the gameplay, but add a professional quality to your work—which is why it is best to leave them until the end of the development cycle.

When building any game, mechanics are crucial; the physical working elements of the game must be in place before additional artwork and environmental flair should be introduced. As in most cases, when building a game, deadlines will be set either by yourself, as part of an independent developer discipline, or by a publisher you are working with. By keeping the finishing touches at the end of the development cycle, you'll ensure that you have made the most of your development time working on getting gameplay—the most important factor, just right.

For the purposes of the book, we will assume that our game mechanics are complete and working as expected. Now, let's turn our focus to what we can add to our island environment and game in general to add some finishing flair.

For this, we'll add the following to our game in this chapter:

- Terrain tweaks and player start position
- Fog to add realism to the line of sight
- Lightmapping for the Island environment
- A particle system inside the volcano part of the terrain
- Proximity-based sound of the volcano rumbling
- Light trails for our coconut shy mini-game to show coconut trajectory

Terrain tweaks and player position

To make our game appealing to the player when they begin, let's take some time now to go around the environment, improving the detail on the terrain, and then choose a position to place the First Person Controller so that the player character begins the game at a position on the island that does not immediately give away the existence of the buildings and the end goal of the game.

Tweaking the terrain

We will now return to the Terrain tools and improve the detail of our island. This will be done to the terrain in our Island scene, so ensure that you have the Island scene open in Unity now.

In this section, we will look at the following three ways to add detail to the terrain:

- Tree positioning
- Hills, troughs, and texture blending
- Player path

Positioning trees

To get a natural look to the trees that are placed on the island, you should attempt to think logically about where they may grow. In simple terms, a tree spreads seeds that cause other to grow around it over many years, where man-made planted forests may be created in a uniform order of rows of trees that are spaced apart. Our island is supposed to be a relatively untouched environment, so let's take time to place some more trees onto the island in small groups.

Select the **Environment** parent object in the Hierarchy and click its grey arrow to expand it. Select the **Terrain** object and then in the Inspector, click the **Place Trees** button on the **Terrain (Script)** component in the Inspector.

Set the following settings for the tool:

- Brush Size: 1
- Tree Width / Height : 60
- Variation: 5

Then go around the environment placing trees in groups and also try to create a tree-line just before the edge of the coast, to make the environment feel dense. As you do this, bear in mind that afterward we will add some hills and further texturing to help the placement of the trees seem more natural.

Hills, troughs, and texture blending

Now let's take some time to experiment with the **Raise / Lower Terrain** tool to create a more interesting landscape with some hills and troughs. Select this tool now and then set the **Brush size** to **35** and **Opacity** to **10**. We will begin with a low opacity to allow us to click this tool many times and create a more varied effect over time.

Here is an example island before adding additional hill and troughs:

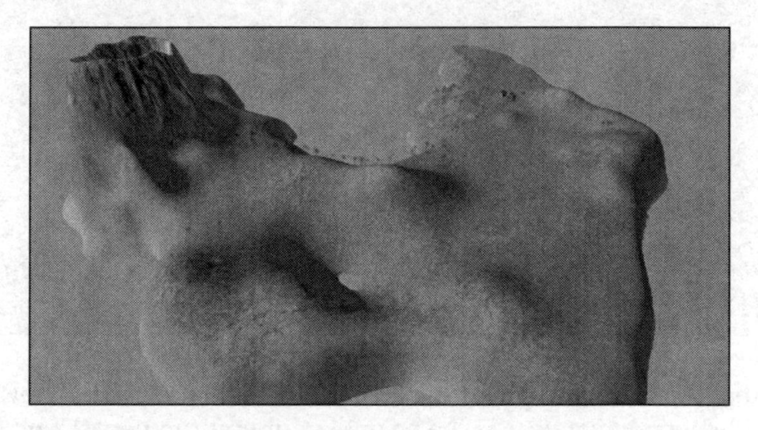

Now go around the island and add detail; vary the brush size as you work to create hills with smaller details. It may also benefit you to try different brushes also. Keep the opacity low and work slowly, remembering that if you wish to lower the terrain, simply hold down *Shift*, and if you make a mistake, simply use Undo (*Command* + Z on Mac, *Ctrl* + Z on PC).

As you make additional detail around the terrain, try and ensure that you add texture detail using the **Paint Texture** tool. Keep the opacity low, and then draw details onto the terrain where you have raised and lowered the terrain. Remember that different foliage will appear naturally as the landscape changes—higher areas may show rock instead of grass, and there may be a sandy transition in between; why not use the rock texture to create a path across the island with sandy hills either side?

Life's a beach

Try and make use of the **Smooth Height** and **Paint Height** tools, for example you could create a beach by making a plateau on one edge of the island. To achieve this, try using the **Paint Height tool** with **Height** set to **9**, then use Smooth Height to round the transition between beach, sea, and land. Finally, add some trees, and paint texture details to polish the transition of differing topography:

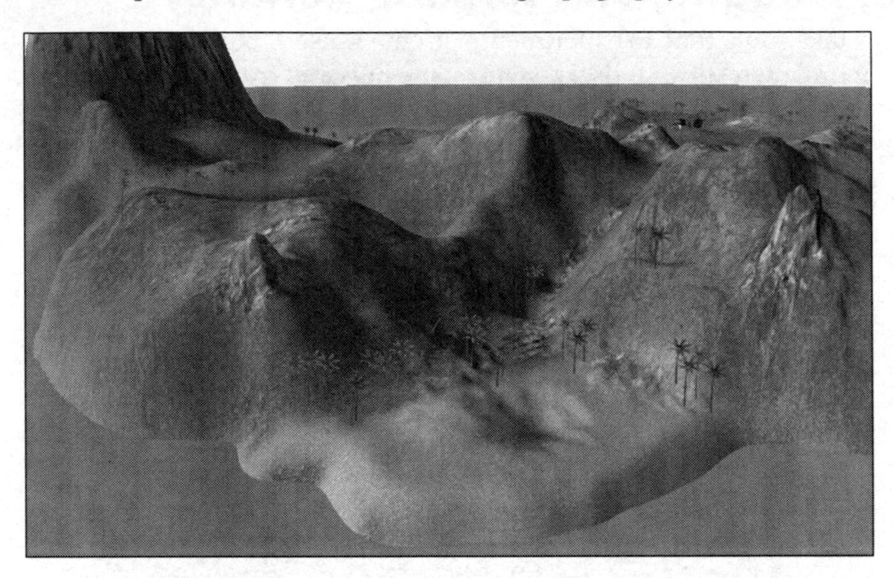

Remember that the more you practice, the more you will get used to how the brushes behave, and the more creative you can be with your environment. Don't be afraid to try things out; there's always undo!

Keep on the right path

In order to let us place the player on a part of the island that will lead them to our buildings, create a path going from the beach you have just created that leads across the island to where the buildings are located. This will encourage the player to explore the island, ultimately leading them to where they need to go.

For this, try using the **Paint Height** tool, starting at a height of **12**, and slowly increasing this height as your path leads from the beach to the location of your buildings. To avoid harsh inclines leading down to the path, use the **Smooth Height** tool to create a smooth transition. Paint over this with the Rock and Sandy textures, to create a path that looks something like this:

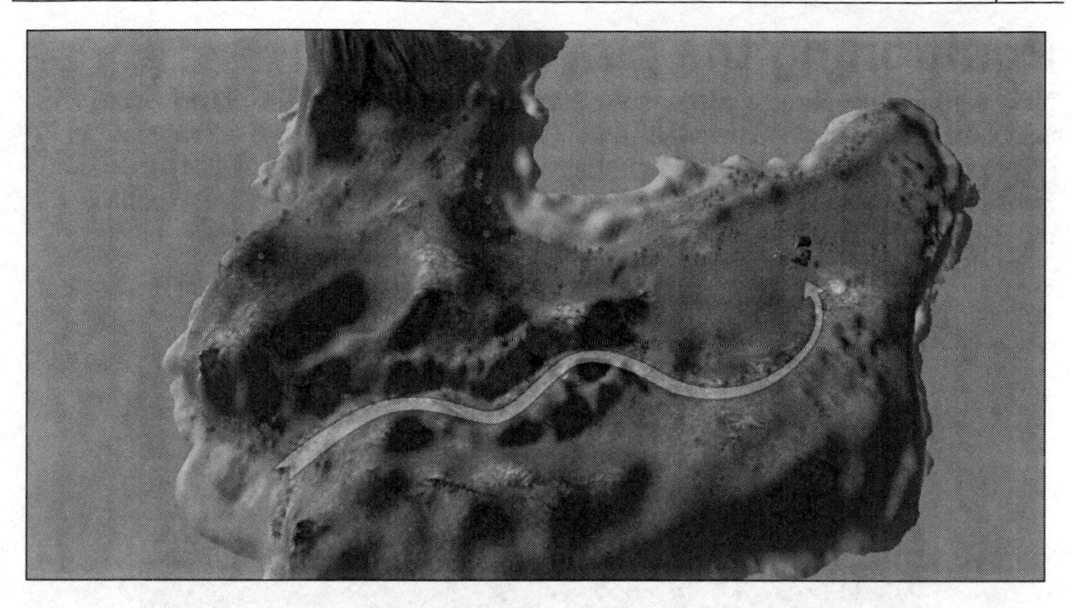

Go around the island and keep working on it as much as you like to create interesting features, just remember to try and maintain the path so that the player makes their way to the buildings intuitively.

Toward the end of the path, create a hilled area around the buildings so that the player takes the hint that they have arrived at the desired point:

Positioning the player

Now we have prepared a path on our Terrain, let's reposition the player character. Select the **First Person Controller** in the Hierarchy and then use the **Translate** tool (*W*) to move this object to the beach that we have created at the edge of the island. It may be useful to make use of the top and side views using the View Gizmo in the top-right of the Scene view. It should end up somewhere like this:

Now that our environment is looking polished, let's take a look at how we can improve it even more!

Optimizing performance

In this section we will look at ways in which you can boost the performance of your game as an end-product. Also known as optimization, this process is crucial to do once you have ensured that your game works as expected—ensuring that your player has the best possible experience from your game. Covered here are some of the basics you should be aware of, but you should also understand that Optimization is a broad topic that you will need to dig deeper into once you have more experience with Unity.

Camera Clip Planes and Fog

To add a nicer visual appearance to our island, we will enable fog. In Unity, fog can be enabled very simply and can be used in conjunction with the Camera's **Far Clip Plane** setting to adjust draw distance, causing objects beyond a certain distance to not be rendered. This will improve performance. By including fog, you will be able to mask the cut-off of rendering distant objects, giving a less clunky feel to exploring the island. This means that we are able to boost the performance by reducing the draw distance, whilst still appearing to the player as if it is an effect intended by the game developer.

We discussed **Far Clip Plane** settings in *Chapter 4* when we deconstructed the **First Person Controller** object. Now, let's adjust the value of the far plane to improve performance by cutting down the distance at which objects are still rendered by the camera:

- Expand the **First Person Controller** parent group by clicking its gray arrow to the left-hand side of its name in the **Hierarchy** panel.
- Select the child object called **Main Camera**.
- In the **Inspector**, find the **Camera** component, and set the **Far Clip Plane** value to **400**. This is a shorter distance, described in meters, and although it cuts down the visual distance of our player's view, this will be masked by the fog we are about to add.

Next, choose **Edit | Render Settings** from the top menu. This brings up **Render Settings** in place of the **Inspector**. Simply check the box for **Fog** here, and then click on the **Color** block to the right of **Fog Color** to open the settings for Color and Alpha. Set the Alpha value (*A*) to 155, around 60% of the slider.

Now close the Color Picker and in the Inspector for **Render Settings**, set the **Fog Density** value to **0.005**.

We are setting the **Fog Color** alpha and **Fog Density** to a lower value, as the default and higher values mask the view so well that the particles from the volcano would contrast with the fog too much—until the player stands quite close to the volcano.

Lightmapping

Lightmapping is the method of baking, rendering to a texture file—the lighting that happens to be affecting a rendered 3D object. This can be done in modeling applications, but Unity also allows you to lightmap all of your lights and environment elements in one, alter lighting, and lightmap again—a crucial working style that fits with the experimental nature of Unity itself. For this reason many Unity developers choose to use the Unity lightmapper instead of those in third party art packages.

Why do we need to lightmap? Well firstly lighting placed in your game scenes makes your Graphics Processing Unit (GPU) work harder, and by saving the effect of lighting into a texture, rather than having lights affect parts of our game dynamically, we can boost performance and improve the look of our game environments at the same time.

It is also worth noting that in the free edition of Unity, dynamic shadows are not supported, so baking shadows onto your environments is an essential process.

Lightmapping is typically only to be done to objects that will never move within the game; this is why Unity includes a **Static** checkbox next to every game object name at the top of the Inspector. Take a look now and you'll see it!

To prepare 3D objects for lightmapping, we typically have to carry out two preparatory steps:

1. Ensure that the 3D asset that the in-game object originates from has **Generate Lightmap UVs** checked in the **FBXImporter** component in the Inspector.
2. Check the **Static** checkbox in the Inspector on the game object once it is in a scene to tell Unity to include this in our lightmapping.

Lighting and baking the island

Before we bake our scene, we will setup our outpost, the coconut shy and campfire objects to be enabled for baking.

Preparing for lightmapping

The first object we will set up will be the **outPost** object. As we expect to see differing lighting indoors compared to outdoors, we need to light the interior of the building. But, instead of casting light onto the lamp to make it appear lit, we will use a **Self Illuminated** shader on the Material component of the **lamp** part of the model, to give the illusion that it is lighting the room; the actual lighting will be done by a baked point light.

Note that in Unity Pro, Self Illuminated shaders will light their surroundings as part of lightmapping. This is part of the **Global Illumination** feature of Unity Pro.

The outpost and generator

Before we adjust the instance of the **outpost** game object we have already placed, select the **outPost** model asset inside the **Book Assets | Models** folder in the Project panel. In the **FBXImporter** component, check the box named **Generate Lightmap UVs**, and then click **Apply** at the bottom of the Inspector. This allows Unity to prepare a secondary UV channel in the model's asset file.

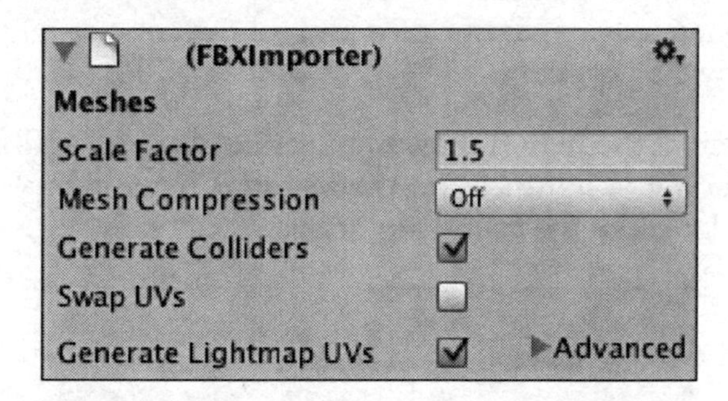

Now select the **outPost** object in the Hierarchy once more, and look at its settings in the Inspector. You will notice the **Static** checkbox at the top of the Inspector is unchecked—check this box now. You will be asked if you wish to apply this setting to the object's children, or just the parent object; here you should choose **Yes, change children**, as the model has several child objects such as the table, ceiling lamp, and so on, that should all be lightmapped along with the actual walls of the structure itself.

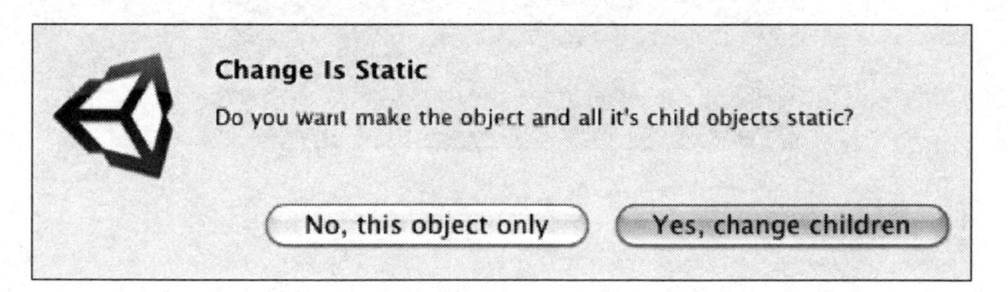

Now repeat both of these steps for the **generator**, in order to ensure that it too is prepared for lightmapping.

Lighting inside the outpost

As we are setting up our outpost to be baked, we'll need to light the inside of it - otherwise it will be dark inside when the player enters. Inside the model, there is a lamp hanging from the ceiling that we can illuminate the mesh of, by using an Self Illuminated shader on its material; but this alone will not illuminate the room, only the mesh it is applied to.

Lighting a mesh with a Self Illuminated shader

Collapse the **outPost** parent object to show its children, and select the child object named **lamp**. Locate the **lamp** material in the Inspector, and from the drop-down menu to the right-hand side of **Shader**, choose **Self-Illum / Diffuse**. Click the color block to the right-hand side of **Main Color** and set the color to a light yellow in the color picker window that appears.

Finally, at the bottom of the material settings, set **Emission (Lightmapper)** to a value of **80**. This is the amount of lightness for the material. Your completed lamp material component should look like the following image:

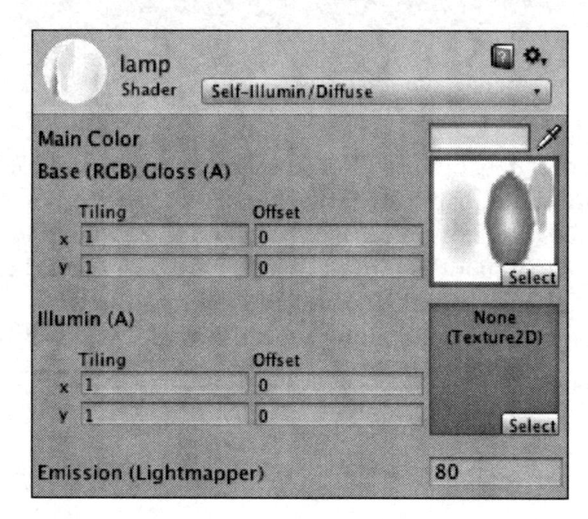

Lighting inside with Baked-Only Point Lights

When lighting indoor scenes for baking, you can often save on performance by ensuring that the lights you use are set to Baked Only. This means that they will not illuminate dynamic objects, and decrease performance. Instead, the light they cast on the world will only be used by the Lightmapping tool in order to illuminate the lightmap texture created during the baking process.

Now let's add such a light to represent the lamp inside the outpost. Click the **Create** button on the Hierarchy and choose **Point Light**. To position this quickly and easily, drag the new **Point Light** object you have created and drop it onto the **lamp** child object of the **outPost** parent, so that it becomes a child of **lamp**. Now simply click the **Cog** icon to the right-hand side of the Point Light's **Transform** component in the Inspector and choose **Reset**. This places the Point Light at the origin point of the lamp, which is a great starting point, but does not give us an illuminated ceiling, as the light is intersecting the mesh that features the ceiling.

As the lamp itself is rotated within the design, we will need to move the Point Light down from its parent using the Z-axis instead of the usual Y-axis. This is a common problem when working with external models, and something you should get used to spotting, just in case. Place in a value of **-1** in the **Z**-axis position for the Point Light, to move it down just below the lamp:

Now, to ensure that this Point Light is only part of our lightmapping—and does not attempt to try and light objects dynamically, on the light component of the Point Light object, choose **BakedOnly** for the `Lightmapping` setting:

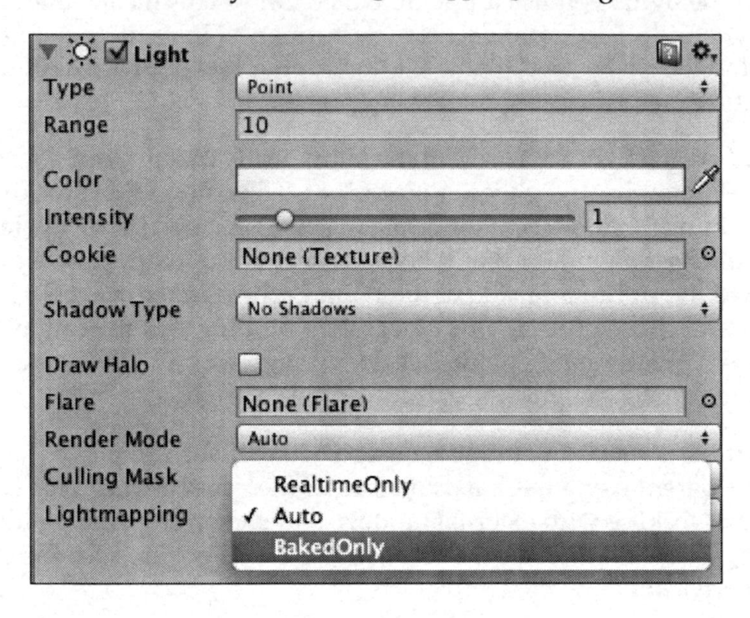

And that's it! Our **outpost** and **generator** objects are prepared for lightmapping, so let's move on to our other objects, the **coconutShy** and the **campfire**.

The coconut shy

As with the outpost, we must first ensure that the model has UVs generated for lightmapping, so select the original **coconutShy** model in the **Book Assets | Models** folder, check the box for **Generate Lightmap UVs** in the **FBXImporter** component of the Inspector, and then click **Apply** at the bottom. Now, because the target objects inside the shy originate from a separate model, repeat this step for the **target** model asset, also in **Book Assets | Models**.

Given that our coconut shy has no inherent lighting as part of the model, we will place a Point light inside to give it a better look, and draw the player to—otherwise when baking, it will look too dark inside.

Click the **Create** button on the Hierarchy and choose **Point Light** from the drop-down menu. Now make the **Point Light** a child of the **coconutShy** object by dragging it and dropping it onto the **coconutShy** parent object's title in the Hierarchy. Next, center this light within the shy by clicking on the **Cog** icon in the top-right of the **Transform** component and choosing **Reset**.

This will place the light at the origin of this model, which is at its base—to correct this, simply set the **Y** Position value to **1.5**. Finally set **Intensity** to **2** and the **Color** for the light to an off-white color such as a light yellow, in order to give the coconut shy a warm feel to it:

Now we need to set the coconut shy to be included in our lightmap bake—select the **coconutShy** parent object and check the **Static** checkbox next to its name in the Inspector—again choose **Yes, change children** when prompted.

The campfire

Finally, as we would like our **campfire** to cast a shadow on the terrain and receive light from our Directional Light in the bake, select the campfire object in the Hierarchy, and check the **Static** checkbox next to its name in the Inspector. As before, confirm that child objects should also be made static when prompted.

Baking the lightmap

Now that our **outPost** ,**coconutShy**, and **campfire** objects are prepared for the lightmapper, it's time to get to grips with the tool itself. Open the **Lightmapping** window by choosing **Window** | **Lightmapping** from the top menu.

[You may wish to dock this window with part of the Unity interface, for example in the same position as the Inspector. To do this, simply drag the title tab of the window and drop it to the right of the Inspector title tab—the window will snap into place and you may switch back to the Inspector at any time using the title tabs.]

Lightmapping overview

The Lightmapping tool has three main sections—**Object**, **Bake**, and **Maps**:

- **Object**—The first section deals with settings for the Object you are about to bake, and often these can be left at their defaults when baking.
- **Bake**—This section allows you to specify settings for the Bake itself. In the free version of Unity, you can simply adjust quality settings and resolution, and in Unity Pro you have more control over how the lightmaps are created.
- **Maps**—This section gives you access to the created lightmap files once they are made and stored, allowing you to locate the texture files and edit them using an application such as Photoshop if you wish.

Ambient lighting

In **Render Settings**, you can also set the **Ambient Light** of the scene. While our **Directional Light** handles the main lighting—acting as the sun in this example—the ambient light will allow you to set a general overall brightness, meaning you can create scenes that look like a certain time of night or day. Try adjusting this setting now by clicking on the color block to the right of the setting and experimenting with the color picker's color and alpha settings.

Note that if you choose to adjust ambient lighting after a bake, in order for this change to affect static objects, you will need to re-bake your scene by switching to the **Lightmapping** window, and choosing **Bake**.

Including lights

Before we continue with our Bake, we will set two of the lights in our scene—our **Directional Light** (aka, the Sun) and our **Point Light** in the coconut shy, also to be static. Our Door Light cannot be static, as we do not wish to bake its default red color onto the outpost, as this will remain there even when it changes to green when the player unlocks the door. This is because the lightmap is stored as a texture that, once baked, remains unchanged at runtime.

Whilst it is not necessary to include their light in the bake, marking these objects as static makes our game run more efficiently. Remember that lights can also be forced to only function as part of lightmapping by setting them to **Baked Only** as we did for the Point Light earlier.

Another advantage of making these objects static is that it will help to remind you not to move these objects.

Select the **Directional Light** in the Hierarchy now—you should recall it is set as a child of the **Environment** empty parent object, so expand that parent object to reveal the **Directional Light** object if necessary. Check the **Static** checkbox in the Inspector and then switch to the Lightmapping window if it is not already open.

In the **Object** section of the Lightmapping window, set **Baked Shadows** to **On (Realtime: Soft Shadows)** using the drop-down menu, leaving the other settings that appear at their defaults.

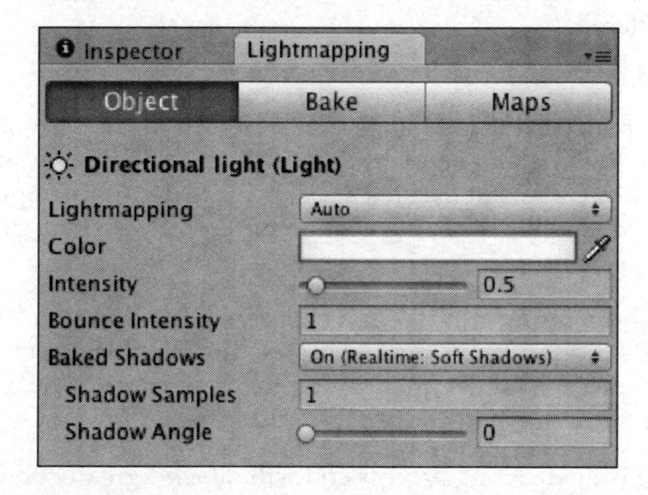

Excluding from the bake

Whilst lightmapping will make our scene look a lot better, and improve performance, we must take care to exclude certain objects from being baked. For example we must not set our Point Light inside the coconut shy to cast shadows in our baked texture, as otherwise when the targets animate their shadow would remain on the back wall!

For this reason, we must not include the matchbox object as a static object, because if this object was included and cast a shadow on the table, this shadow would remain after the player had picked them up. Expand the **outPost** object now to show the **matchbox** as a child, select the matchbox object and then uncheck **Static** for this object at the top of the Inspector

Select the **Point Light** child object of the **coconutShy**, and in the Inspector, check the **Static** checkbox. Then to ensure no shadows are cast, in the **Lightmapping** panel under **Object**, set **Baked Shadows** to **Off**.

Baking the scene

Now that our scene is prepared—note that the **Terrain** object itself is marked as static by default—we are ready to bake! At the bottom of the **Lightmapping** panel, there are three buttons:

- **Clear**—This option deletes any currently stored lightmaps, allowing you to see only dynamic lighting and the original lightness of an object's materials and textures.
- **Bake Selected**—This option will only bake the object you have selected in the Hierarchy, and will clear a previously baked scene. This is useful as it allows you to focus on a single object's lighting, without waiting for the entire scene to be rendered.
- **Bake**—This option bakes the entire scene.

At this stage you may wish to take some time to return to the Terrain editor to add further detail to the island and perhaps also add a few trees around the **outPost** and **coconutShy** objects so that the area appears more naturally populated, and when baked, the trees will cast shadows upon the scenery making them fit in more naturally.

Switch to the **Lightmapping** window and choose the **Bake** section from the tabs at the top. Set the **Resolution** value to **50**— this sets the overall quality for the bake, and if you decide you prefer a higher quality after the bake is complete, you can always return to this value and increase it, then re-bake.

Lightmap baking is often a long process and will depend greatly on the speed of the computer Unity is running on; as many calculations are performed, baking may take anywhere from a few seconds to hours, depending upon the complexity of a scene. In this instance, we do not have many objects to include in the bake, and as such it should not take too long, but maybe prepare something else to do whilst you wait! The great thing about the Lightmapping tool in Unity is that you can continue to view your open scene whilst baking is completed in the background—naturally you cannot change the scene as this would invalidate the bake.

Press the **Bake** button at the bottom of the **Lightmapping** window now to start. A blue progress bar will appear, showing you calculations of the various parts of the lightmapping process. Be patient! It will be worthwhile once the bake is finished!

Here are some example results—as you can see the addition of calculated lighting and projected shadows really makes all the difference.

Before Lightmapping:

After Lightmapping:

For more information on Lightmapping, refer to the Unity manual page at:

`http://www.unity3d.com/support/documentation/Manual/LightmappingInDepth.html`

Restoring dynamic objects

Because we allowed Unity to set all of the child objects of the **outPost**, **coconutShy**, and **campfire** to **Static**—crucial for them to be included in the baking we just did—we must now return to some of the objects and make them dynamic once more in order to allow for animation.

Locate the following child objects and uncheck the **Static** checkbox at the top of the Inspector for them:

- **door**—A child of the outPost parent object
- **target** (three instances)—Children of the coconutShy parent object
- **SmokeSystem** and **FireSystem**—Both child objects of the campfire object

Remember that if you choose to re-bake your scene at any time, you'll need to temporarily re-mark these objects as **Static** once more.

Finishing touches

In this section we will add some final polish to our game in order to make sure the player feels like they are playing a finished game. These extra flourishes may not be essential to gameplay, but will help to flesh out the game as a product.

We will look at:

- Adding particles to the volcano in our Island scene
- Adding a visual trail to the thrown coconuts in our Island scene

Volcano!

In *Chapter 3*, we built an island terrain with the terrain editor, including a corner of the island dedicated to a volcano mouth. To make this volcano seem a little more realistic, we'll add a plume of smoke and an audio source using a 3D sound in order to create a proximity-based sound of the volcano bubbling with molten lava. By adding both the audio and visual elements, we'll hopefully achieve a more dynamic and realistic feel to the island and maintain player immersion in our game.

Begin by creating a new particle system in Unity by clicking the **Create** button on the Hierarchy and choosing **Particle System** from the drop-down menu or by choosing **GameObject | Create Other | Particle System** from the top menu. This creates a new game object called **Particle System** in the **Hierarchy**. Ensure that this is selected now, and rename it **Volcano Smoke**.

Positioning the particle system

As our volcano is simply part of the terrain object itself and not an independent game object in the Hierarchy, positioning our particles in relative terms by using parenting is not possible. Ordinarily, to relatively position an object, we might make the new object a child of the object we wish it to be within and reset its relative position to (0, 0, 0).

In this instance however, we'll need to take advantage of the **Scene** panel's **View Gizmo**. Begin by clicking on the **Y**-axis (green handle) of the gizmo to change from a perspective view to a top-down or *bird's eye* view of the island. If done correctly, the gizmo then shows the word **Top** beneath it:

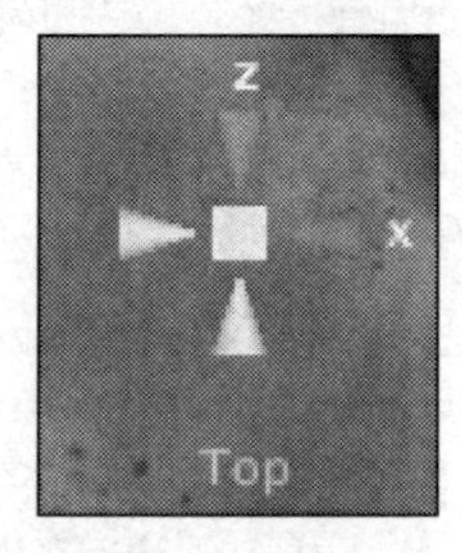

Then to see where your **Volcano Smoke** object is located, ensure that it is selected in the **Hierarchy** panel, and then select the **Translate** tool (Shortcut key: *W*) to see its axes in the scene.

Using this Top view, we can position the particle system in the **X** and **Z** axes by dragging the handles in the Scene view until the object is located inside the volcano mouth. To make sure you can see both the particle system's axes and the volcano itself, you may simply need to zoom out to see both on screen. To do this, switch to the Hand tool (*Q*), and holding the *Alt* key, drag with the *right mouse button* (Mac & PC) to the left to zoom out, then switch back to the Translate tool (*W*) to see your object's axis handles again.

Now using the **Translate** tool, drag the **X** (red) and **Z** (blue) axis handles independently until you have positioned your particle system in the center of the volcano's mouth from this perspective, as shown in the following image:

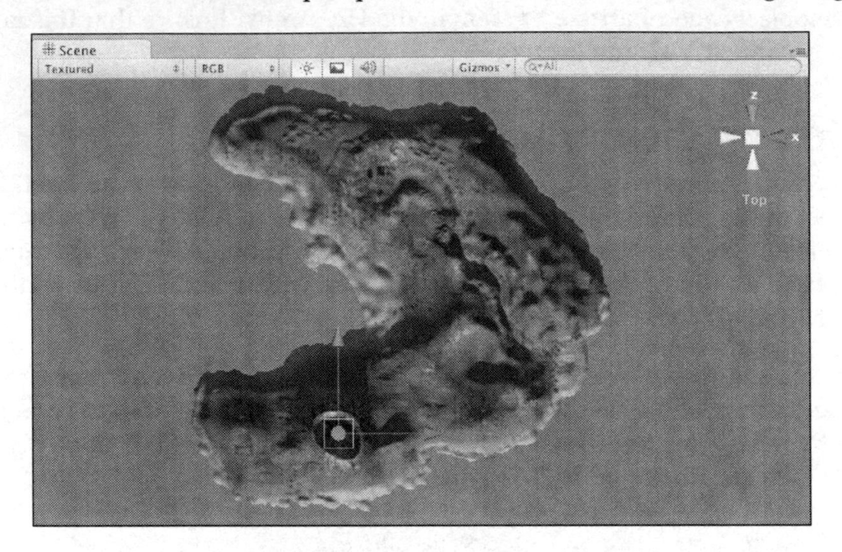

Do not be confused by the handles highlighting in yellow when you have them selected—you still have the correct handle!

Now click on the red **X**-axis handle of the **View Gizmo**, in order to give you a side-on view of the island. Use this view, along with the **Translate** tool, to drag the **Y-**axis handle (green) of your particle system, in order to get it to a position in the centre of the volcano, as shown in the following image:

Finally, switch back to Perspective view by clicking on the **white cube** in the center of the **View Gizmo** in the upper right-hand side of the Scene view.

Required assets

In the **Book Assets** folder, you will find:

- A **Smoke** texture for the smoke of the volcano in the **Textures** folder
- A **volcanoRumble** audio clip to represent the rumbling lava of the volcano in the **Sounds** folder

Making the smoke material

Now we will need to make a material for our volcano smoke texture. To keep things neat, we'll create this inside the existing **Materials** folder within the main project—*not* the one within **Book Assets**. Select the **Materials** folder in the **Project** panel, and then click on the **Create** button, selecting **Material** from the drop-down menu.

Rename this new material **Volcano Smoke Material**, and ensure that it is selected in the **Project** panel to see its settings in the **Inspector**. From the **Shader** drop-down menu, choose **Particles | Alpha Blended**. This will set the rendering style for the material to one suitable for particles—**Alpha Blended** will show the particle textures' transparent background (known as an Alpha Channel) and softened edges. Drag-and-drop the **volcanoSmoke** texture file from the **Book Assets | Textures** folder onto the empty slot to the right-hand side of the **Particle Texture** setting, leaving the **Tiling** and **Offset** parameters at their defaults.

Now drag the **Volcano Smoke Material** from the **Materials** folder in the **Project** panel, and drop it onto the **Volcano Smoke** particle system object in the **Hierarchy** to apply it.

Particle system settings

As with any visual effect, especially regarding particle systems, a lot of experimentation is necessary to achieve an effect that you feel looks good. With this in mind, it is recommended that you simply use the settings suggested here as a guide, and then take some time out to try adjusting a few settings by yourself to achieve an effect that:

- You like the look of
- Works well with the style of volcano mouth that you have created on your own terrain

Note that settings listed here are only the ones that have been adjusted from the defaults that Unity already sets, so you need not adjust other settings.

Ellipsoid Particle Emitter settings

- **MinSize**: **40**
- **MaxSize**: **60**
- **Min Energy**: **10**
- **Max Energy**: **30**
- **Min Emission**: **2**
- **Max Emission**: **8**
- **World Velocity Y-axis**: **30**

Particle Animator settings

- **Color Animation[0]**: **Dark Orange color, 75% Alpha**
- **Color Animation[1]**: **Red / Grey color, 50% Alpha**
- **Color Animation[2]**: **Mid Grey color, 40% Alpha**
- **Color Animation[3]**: **Darker Grey color, 25% Alpha**
- **Color Animation[4]**: **Black color, 5% Alpha**
- **Size Grow**: **0.05**
- **Rnd Force**: **(10, 0, 10)**

Now take some time to adjust these settings to make the particles suit your terrain a little better if you need to.

For more information on Particle systems, see the Unity Manual page at:

`http://www.unity3d.com/support/documentation/Manual/Particle%20 Systems.html`

Adding audio to the volcano

To complete the effect of a genuine volcano, we'll add an Audio Source component now with a volcanic audio loop playing on it.

As noted previously, our volcano is not an actual game object, so in this instance also, we cannot add a component to it because of this fact. However, we do now have an object at the center point of our volcano—the particle system. This means that we can use that object as the one to add our audio component to.

Ensure that the **Volcano Smoke** object is selected in the **Hierarchy** and then choose **Component | Audio | Audio Source** from the top menu.

This adds an **Audio Source** component to the bottom of the list of components in the **Inspector**. As the particle system already has several components making it work, you may need to scroll down in the **Inspector** panel to find the **Audio Source**.

Assign the **volcanoRumble** audio clip from the **Book Assets | Sounds** folder to the **Audio Clip** parameter by dragging and dropping from the Project panel, then make sure that **Play On Awake** is selected; this ensures that the sound will not need triggering, but simply plays when the scene is loaded. Expand the **3D Sound Settings**, and then set the following settings for the rest of the component, leaving other settings at their default:

- **Min Distance**: **50**—To ensure that volume is loud outside of the volcano, and at its maximum volume when up to 50 meters away from the position of the particle system.
- **Max Distance**: **500**—This default ensures that on all parts of the island the volcano will be heard, so it does not fade out at the furthest point of the island; as our island is 500 x 500, the rumbling sound of the volcano should be inescapable! Finally, check the box for **Loop** to ensure that the sound continues to play indefinitely.

Volcano testing

Now that our volcano is complete, we should test its effectiveness. Firstly, go to **File | Save Scene** to ensure that we do not lose any unsaved progress. Then press the **Play** button, and try walking from the current location of your player, towards the volcano. The particles should be rising into the air. As you approach the volcano, the volume of the volcano's sound should become louder.

Remember that any changes made using the **Inspector** during play testing will be undone as soon as you hit the **Play** button again to stop testing. Simply use this as a literal testing period, and ensure that you place the values you settle upon into the relevant component in the **Inspector** again when you have stopped testing the game.

Also be aware that this does not apply to changes made in the Inspector to assets in your Project, for example Materials, as you are modifying an asset rather than a property of your object in the scene.

It is worth noting that for testing purposes, you may wish to increase the speed of the **First Person Controller** to allow you to walk around your island more quickly.

To do this, while you are play testing, select the **First Person Controller** object in the **Hierarchy**. Set the **Max Forward Speed** public member variable of the **Character Motor(Script)** component to your desired value—remember this is simply for testing, so unrealistic speeds are fine! Because you are doing this during testing, this property will revert once you press the **Play** button again to stop the test, meaning that you will not lose your originally intended speed.

Coconut trails

Next we'll add some flair to our coconut shy game by adding light trails to our coconut prefabs. By doing this, when the player throws them, they'll see a trail of light following the trajectory of the projectile, which should give a nice visual effect. For this we will make use of the **Trail Renderer** component in Unity, an effect that can really add to the style of moving objects.

Editing the Prefab

To implement this change, we'll need to return to our coconut prefab from *Chapter 7*, as the **Trail Renderer** component we will use must be attached to this object. Open the **Prefabs** folder in the **Project** panel, and locate the **Coconut** prefab asset.

Drag it into the scene so that we can work on it; assets can be worked on directly from their location in the **Project** panel, but in order to preview and test the effect we're creating, it is best to drag the coconut prefab to the scene, and see what we're doing "in action". Remember that by pressing *F* with your cursor over the **Scene** view, you can zoom straight to the location of the selected object you have just placed, so do this now if you cannot see the object.

Trail Renderer component

To add the component, ensure that the **Coconut** prefab is still selected in the **Hierarchy** panel, and choose **Component | Particles | Trail Renderer** from the top menu. You will be prompted, explaining that you are losing the connection with the prefab, simply click **Add** to continue at this point—we will update the prefab once we have finished making our trail.

This component simply draws an arcing vector line by plotting a series of points behind an object, as it moves through the 3D world. By specifying the length (time), material, and start/end widths of the line, we'll be able to achieve the effect we want. To see the default setting of the trail renderer, press the **Play** button now, and watch the coconut fall to the ground, leaving a trail behind it. You should see an un-textured pink line being rendered—not good!

Firstly we'll address some performance issues—for Unity Pro version users, the ability to use dynamic shadows comes as standard; however, as we do not need the line to cast or receive any shadows, uncheck the first two parameters on the component in the **Inspector**. Shadows are generally expensive, and as the trail renderer itself is adding to the strain put on the processing power of the player's computer, anything we can do to reduce the strain is definitely a good idea.

Next expand the **Materials** parameter to see the **Size** and **Element 0** settings. Here we can assign a texture to use for the trail. As we have already made a flame material, we'll re-use that because it uses an appropriate shader type for a trail—Additive (soft). Open the **Materials** folder in the **Project** panel, and locate the **Flame** material, then drag-and-drop it onto the **Element 0** setting for the **Trail Renderer** component in the **Inspector** where it currently reads **None (Material)**.

Now, to ensure the trail is not overly long, set the **Time** parameter to a value of **0.25**. This means that the trail is one second long—points at the end of the trail are deleted after they have existed for this amount of time.

Now set the **Start Width** to **0.25** and the **End Width** to **0.1**—these define the width of the rendered material at either end of the trail, and generally it makes sense to make the start width value wider than the end in order to taper the trail.

Finally, expand the **Colors** parameter so that you can see each box for color. With this, we can animate the appearance of the trail through color and also visibility, using the alpha settings. As we have color in our flame texture, we'll leave the colors of these settings, but simply make the trail fade towards its end. Click on each **Color** block in turn. By using the **A** (Alpha) value, set value from 80 percent down to 0 percent over the course of each of them:

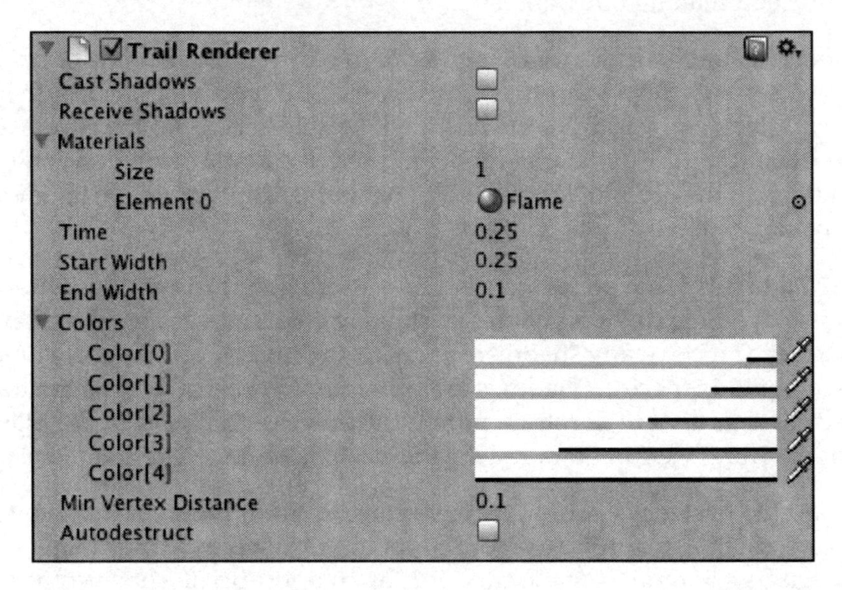

The remaining settings can be left to their defaults. **Min Vertex Distance** simply defines what the shortest distance between two points in the line can be—the more points present, the more detailed the line is, but also the more costly it is processing wise. **Autodestruct** needn't be enabled either, as the object itself has a script handling removal of these prefabs from the world—the **Object Tidy** script we wrote in *Chapter 7*.

Updating the prefab

As we are effectively working on an instance of the prefab that has lost its connection with the original asset—hence the warning when we added the trail renderer—we'll need to apply the changes we've made to the original prefab asset in order to have all new instances of the prefab feature this trail.

To do this, you have two options: either select the **Coconut** object in the **Hierarchy** and go to **GameObject | Apply Changes to Prefab**, or use the **Apply** button at the top of the **Inspector** for this object:

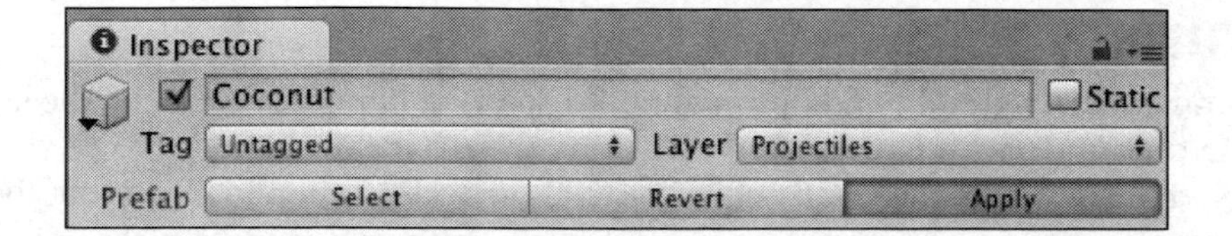

Now that you have updated the original prefab asset, we no longer need the instance in the scene. Simply select it in the Hierarchy and remove it using the keyboard shortcut *Command* + *Backspace* (Mac) or *Delete* (PC).

To see the effect, play test the game now, and try out the coconut shy mini-game we made earlier.

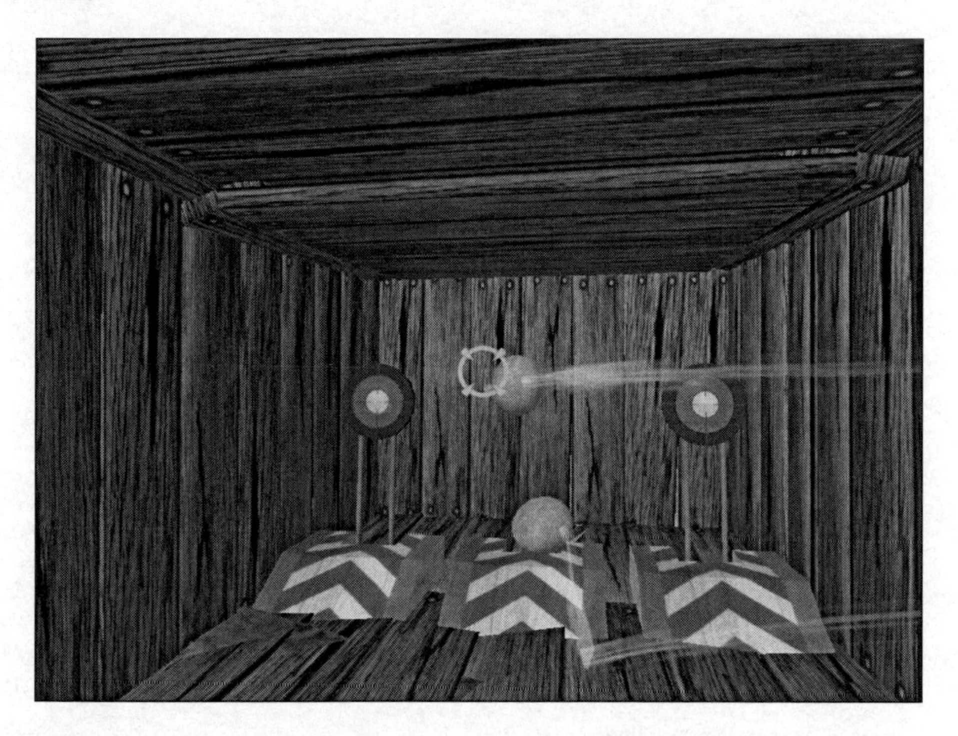

You should see flaming trails following each coconut you throw! When you are finished, remember to stop the game to finish testing and then choose **File | Save Scene** to update your progress.

Summary

The visual effects, lighting, and optimization discussed here only scratche the surface of what you can do with Unity, but while Unity makes it easy to add these polishing features to make your game really stand out, it is crucial to keep in mind that they should only be considered once your project's gameplay is honed—finishing touches are a great way to complete your project, but the playability should always come first.

Now that we have completed the game, we'll spend the next chapter looking at building, testing, and rebuilding, and the implications of deploying your game. We'll also take a look at further optimizations for your game and discuss getting your game seen as an independent developer.

12
Building and Sharing

In order to take our game from a simple example to something that we can share with play testers, we need to consider various platforms of deployment and how we can adapt the game to be exported to the Web versus exporting as a standalone desktop game. The best way to start working in a fashion that will help you grow as a developer is to share your work; one of the most important elements of creativity is being able to accept other viewpoints and allow this to enrich you as a creative developer. This is why Unity's ability to export to the web is so important, and why we will look at how to export for both platforms in this chapter.

Unity allows for various scaled qualities of the final build of your game and will compress textures and various other assets as appropriate for you. You should also be aware of platform detection for web builds as you may wish to alter your game slightly when deploying online, as opposed to a full standalone desktop build or mobile build if you have purchased one of the Unity add-ons such as iOS or Android.

The standard free version of Unity offers you the opportunity to build your game for:

- PC and Mac standalone
- Mac OSX Dashboard widget
- Web Player

The Pro version of Unity and its console and mobile add-ons can be used to build to all of the above, and are required to add support for console or mobile development to current generation consoles. The addition of mobile add-ons allows you to also build for hardware that runs either iOS or Android OS.

For professional developers, the add-ons of development for consoles will also require use of hardware development kits from console manufacturers.

In this final chapter, we'll look at how to customize assets to create a Web Player and a standalone desktop build. We will cover the following topics:

- Build options
- Working with **Build Settings** to include scenes and choose a platform
- Choosing **Player Settings** to prepare for building Web Player and standalone versions of your game
- Platform detection to remove un-required elements from web builds
- Ways in which you can share your games with others and get further help with your Unity development

Build options

Unity offers you an array of differing build platforms to choose from, and when considering your work as a Unity developer, you should rest assured that as a product, Unity will continue to add new build options as different hardware and software platforms emerge.

The current build options are contained in Unity's **Build Settings** window, which looks like this:

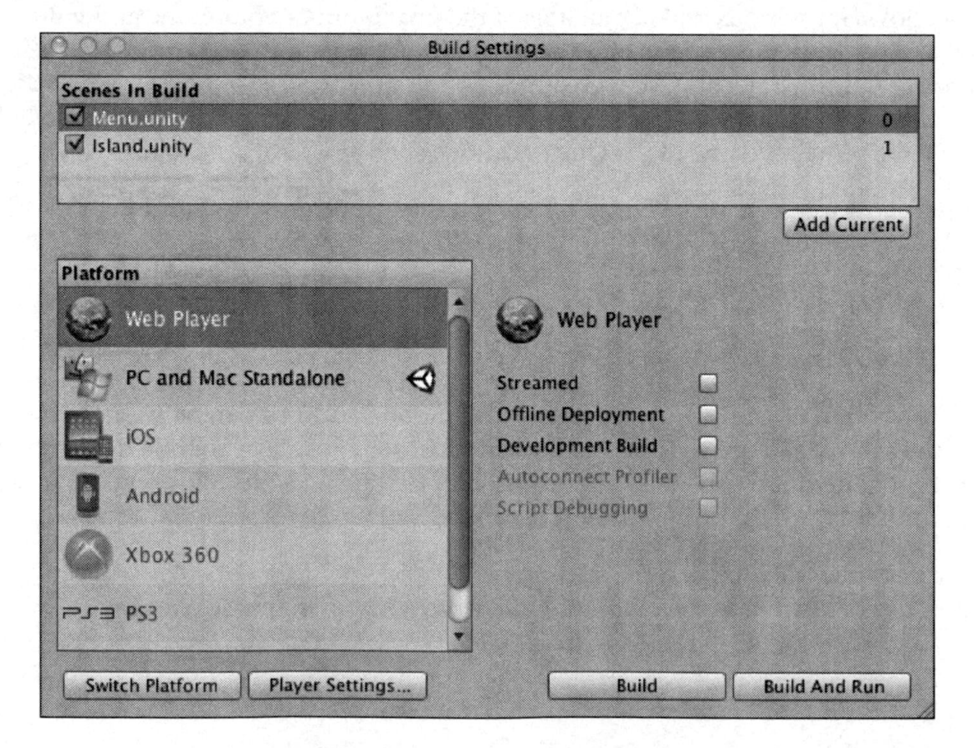

Let's take an overview of what these different options are, before looking at the parameters available for building to them.

Web Player

When placing any plugin-based content onto the Web, it must be uploaded as a bundled file which calls the installed plugin. Viewers of Unity's web builds will be required to download the Unity Web Player plugin for their browser in much the same way as, for example, Adobe Flash content requires users to download Flash Player. The Unity Web Player is available for download at `http://www.unity3d.com/webplayer`.

But if your player attempts to load your game without it installed, they will be prompted to install the web player directly so that they may play, so it is unlikely that the user will need to visit this URL.

Web player builds create a game file with the extension `.unity3d`, which calls the Unity Web Player plugin, along with an accompanying HTML file containing the necessary embedding code. This embedding HTML can then be taken along with the game file and embedded into a web page of your own design.

As web players rely on the web browser to load the HTML page that calls the Unity plugin, any computer running your game as a web player is already using up processing power on the browser and some of the intensity of this cost is caused by the dimensions of the web player embedded on the page.

With this in mind, it can help to provide your game at a lower resolution than you would for a desktop build. We designed our game to an entry-level desktop resolution of 1024x768 pixels. However, when deploying into a web build, the screen size should be reduced to something smaller, such as 800x600. This makes the load on the GPU less intensive as lower resolution frames are being drawn, thus giving better performance. We will look at building your game at this resolution, and how to alter settings for the player later in the chapter.

Web Player Streamed

Web Player Streamed—a separate build option on the list—allows you to build a web deployment that does not force the player to wait too long for a loading bar to complete.

When encountering any wait online, it is characteristic for users to be impatient, and it is important that you restrict waiting times as much as possible when creating web builds of your game. Using **Web Player Streamed** means that you can start playing your game before the entirety of its assets are loaded—then as the player interacts with the first scene, the rest of the game's assets continue to load. This is comparable to the way that streaming video sites such as YouTube offer you the ability to start watching a video before it is completely loaded, by streaming in the data in small packets.

This factor is absolutely crucial when submitting your game to games portal sites, such as `www.kongregate.com`, `www.miniclip.com`, or `www.indiepubgames.com`. Sites such as these expect your game to be launchable after around 1 MB of data has been downloaded (conditions vary from site to site), and by adhering to these guidelines, you're more likely to be able to get your game onto such sites, giving you exposure for your work. For more information on web streaming, please read the Unity manual page on this topic: `http://unity3d.com/support/documentation/Manual/Web%20Player%20Streaming.html`.

PC or Mac standalone

Standalone or desktop builds are fully-fledged applications that are delivered as a self-contained executable.

Building your game for Mac OS X standalone will build a single application file with all required assets bundled inside, while building for Windows PC standalone will create a folder containing an `.exe` (executable) and the associated assets required to run the game in folders alongside it.

Building a standalone is the best way to ensure maximum performance from your game as the files are stored locally and your user is unlikely to have other applications open whilst running the game, an instance that may be the case with a web player deployment. That said, due to Unity's efficiency, most Unity developed games will run as well in the Web Player as they do as a standalone executable.

OSX Dashboard Widget

Mac operating systems (version 10.4 onwards) have a feature called the Dashboard. It is a set of simple tools and applications known as **Widgets**, which can be brought up at any time as an overlay on the screen. Unity can publish your game as a Widget, and this is simply another way for you to provide your game to people. If you're making a simple puzzle or timewaster game, this could be appropriate as a deployment method. However, with something such as our first person game, the Dashboard is less appropriate.

Ideally, games deployed as Widgets should be basic because it is best to avoid loading masses of data into a Dashboard Widget, as this has to stay resident in the computer's memory so that the game can continue when the Dashboard is activated and deactivated.

Build Settings

In Unity, choose **File | Build Settings** from the top menu, and take a look at the options you have. You should see the various options mentioned previously.

In the **Build Settings** window, each platform gives additional options in the form of checkboxes to the right when selecting it on the left. Whilst you can export a build of your project by selecting (highlighting in blue) your desired target and choosing **Build**, in order for Unity to be best setup for your intended platform, you should select it and then click the **Switch Platform** button in the bottom left of the Build Settings.

This effectively sets up Unity to work best for your intended target platform. This is especially important when working with mobile development, as Unity will reinterpret the assets you are working with to suit the chosen mobile platform, automatically choosing compression settings in the Inspector for assets already in your project.

The other key advantage of selecting your platform is that it causes the **Game View** to show the chosen platform and resolution as a setting. This allows you to test your game with the correct resolution, which helps to show you realistic positions for 2D elements.

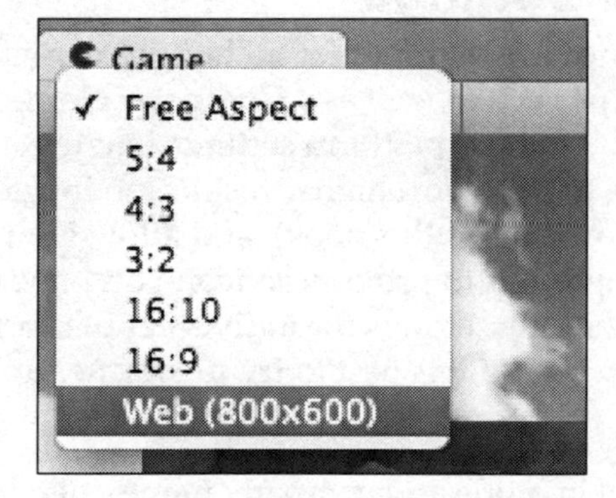

At the top of the **Build Settings**, you are shown a list of scenes added to our project so far, beginning with the **Menu** scene. It is important to have the first scene you would like your player to see as the first item in the **Scenes In Build** list. If your menu or first scene is not first in the list, then you can simply drag-and-drop the names of the scenes to reorder them. Note also here that scenes are indexed—given a specific number starting at 0—shown to the right-hand side of the scene name in the list. These index numbers can be useful when loading scenes, but you may also refer to scenes by name (using a string) as we have done in this book.

Let's look at customizing our build further by adjusting **Player Settings** to suit our Survival Island project.

Player Settings

In software development terms, an exported version of your project is known as a **build**. In Unity, when exporting a build you are effectively placing your content into what is known as the Unity player. On the Web, the **.unity3d** file that Unity exports exists to call the player that is contained inside the installed Unity plugin itself. As a standalone build, the player is part of the packaged executable PC or Mac game. In **Player Settings**, you can specify certain elements, such as resolution, icons and rendering settings, for the player to use.

To adjust settings such as these, we'll need to look at the **Player Settings**. Go to **Edit | Project Settings | Player** now. The **Player Settings** in Unity are divided into two core separations—**Cross-Platform Settings** and **Per Platform Settings**.

Cross-Platform Settings

The cross-platform settings are required for all builds, and simply ask you to provide a **Product Name** for the project, as well as a **Company Name** and **Default Icon**. This icon can be overridden by the per platform settings where required, but otherwise it is generally acceptable to provide a higher resolution image for this setting (such as the 128x128 image provided for this book), and allow Unity to scale where appropriate. The other option is to provide an icon you have designed yourself for each icon resolution within the settings for individual platforms - this approach ensures total control for you but it is best to try the former approach in case it *just works* for you.

Take a second now to fill in a title and company name, then locate the **icon_large** texture inside the **Book Assets | Textures** folder. Select this and then in the **Texture Importer** component of the Inspector, set **Texture Type** to **GUI,** and click **Apply**. Now return to the **Player Settings** (**Edit | Project Settings | Player**) and drag it onto the **Default Icon** setting :

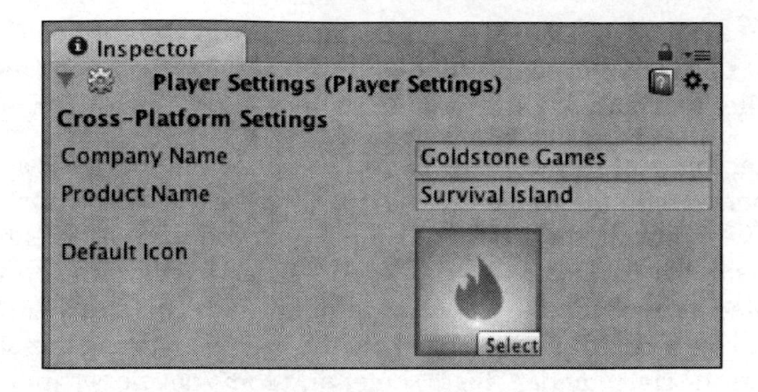

Per-Platform Settings

These further settings for your chosen platform are divided up into four categories:

- Resolution and Presentation
- Icon
- Splash Image
- Other Settings

As both the Web Player and Standalone builds feature these categories, let's look at each of them for both platforms.

Resolution and Presentation

The settings in this section of the menu allow you to customize what the player will see when they experience your game, and are especially crucial for setting up the resolution that the game is exported at.

Web Player Settings

The Web Player should be at a smaller resolution than a standalone build for performance reasons, as the smaller the screen real estate you are rendering, the better performance you can expect. Despite this smaller scale, it is possible for the user to right-click games deployed in the web player in-browser to switch to full-screen mode.

Set the **Default Screen Width** to **800** and **Default Screen Height** to **600**. At the time of writing, 800 x 600 is a reasonable high-end web player resolution, and is seen on many portal sites that feature Unity games, such as `Kongregate.com`.

The **Web Player Template** selection gives you an option of three basic styles of HTML page to be exported with the web build. As it is always presented within a web page, like any other web content, these options simply give you three differently styled HTML pages with the `.unity3d` file embedded—**Black Background** and **White Background**, and a page with the **Context Menu Locked**. This stops the user from right-clicking to see a pop-out menu. Blocking the user from doing this stops them from accessing full-screen mode. This is something some developers may wish to do in order to ensure that users only play their game as an embedded window, perhaps to ensure that the user also sees the surrounding website.

These simple templates are useful to allow you to simply upload the HTML and `.unity3d` file to a server to get feedback without having to style your own page. They also act as an example of how to embed the `.unity3d` file in HTML and how to lock the context menu if you need to do so.

If you have web design skills you will likely wish to simply take the embedding of the .unity3d file on to a new page of your own design or if not you may upload your game onto a portal site, removing the need for an accompanying HTML page of your own. Choose which of the three styles you like the look of now.

Standalone Settings

When loading a standalone copy of your game, the player can be presented with the **Resolution Dialog**—a window showing them options for resolution, control input, and quality settings at which to play your game. However, you have the choice to disable this option from being shown—the setting titled **Display Resolution Config** (Enabled by default) toggles this. The Resolution Dialog will look like this (Mac version):

Therefore, the **Default Screen Width** and **Height** settings here simply define a default resolution if this dialog window is not enabled, so set these settings to 1024 and 768 respectively as this is the lowest likely resolution you should expect to cater for on a desktop or laptop computer.

All other settings can be left at their defaults for **Resolution and Presentation**.

Icon

This setting is not applicable for Web Player deployment, as the only icon in web terms is that seen as the HTML page fav icon, which is defined by the site on which your game content is embedded.

Standalone

The Icon settings shown here for the standalone have been taken from our Default Icon and are scaled appropriately. This shows the benefit of creating a Default Icon larger than 48x48—the one provided as part of this book's assets is designed at 128x128.

As you can see from these settings you are able to provide different textures for various scales of texture, allowing you to create a simpler design for smaller scales if you wish.

Splash Image

This is also not applicable to the Web Player, as splash images for your game would be designed as part of the first scene you load into the game, perhaps making use of animation to introduce the developer's logo, as you've likely seen in commercial games.

Standalone

For standalone deployed games, the Splash Image setting gives you a slot to assign the **Config Dialog banner** to. This banner is shown in the previous image as part of the Resolution Dialog window that loads when the player first launches your game, if this has not been disabled under **Resolution and Presentation** as discussed above.

A splash image for Survival Island has been designed for you. Simply select the texture called **splash_image** in the **Book Assets | Textures** folder in the Project panel, and set its **Texture Type** to **GUI** in the **Texture Importer** component of the Inspector; click **Apply** to confirm. Return to the **Player Settings** (**Edit | Project Settings | Player**) and drag the **splash_image** texture onto the empty **Config Dialog Banner** slot where it currently shows **None (Texture 2D)**.

[If you wish to design your own Config Dialog Banner texture for your games, you should create a file in your preferred art package at a resolution of 432 x 163 pixels.]

Other Settings

The other settings focus on **Rendering** and **Optimization**, and in the case of Web Players, streaming.

Web Player

These settings should be left at their default for the Web Player, but it is worth being aware that the **Rendering Path** can be switched to **Forward** or **Vertex Lit** if you are working on a project that is designed with older hardware in mind. Ideally, **Deferred Lighting** should always be used to get the best visual performance, although it does not support anti-aliasing (softening of harsh edges in your game), so it is best to try out these two options to balance performance and quality.

The **First Streamed Level** setting allows you to specify an index number of a scene that you want to be loaded first through streaming if your game is setup to work that way. If this is anything other than your first level (index number 0), you may specify the index number of the scene—this can be found to the right-hand side of the list of scenes in the Build Settings.

Standalone

Note that most projects will be fine using the Default settings for **Rendering and Optimisation** when building a standalone game.

A note on batching

Unity free edition utilizes Dynamic batching, a technique that batches objects together (grouping the render) with a shared material and low mesh detail into single draw calls. This means far better performance when creating multiples of the same object, for example multiples of props such as buildings. Dynamic batching is done automatically, provided that the object's mesh does not exceed a vertex count of 300. The addition of static batching is a feature that does the same function for non-moving objects that you have marked as static, but is only available as part of the Unity Pro edition.

Quality Settings

When exporting from Unity, you are not restricted to any single level of quality. You have a lot of control over the quality of your output, which comes in the form of the **Quality Settings**. Open this now in the **Inspector** part of the interface by choosing **Edit | Project Settings | Quality** from the top menu.

Here you'll find the ability to set your three different builds to one of the six different quality presets—**Fastest**, **Fast**, **Simple**, **Good**, **Beautiful**, and **Fantastic**. You can then edit these presets yourself to achieve precise results as you need to. To understand the range of potential quality that Unity can produce, let's take a look at the opposite ends of the scale, comparing **Fastest** with **Fantastic**:

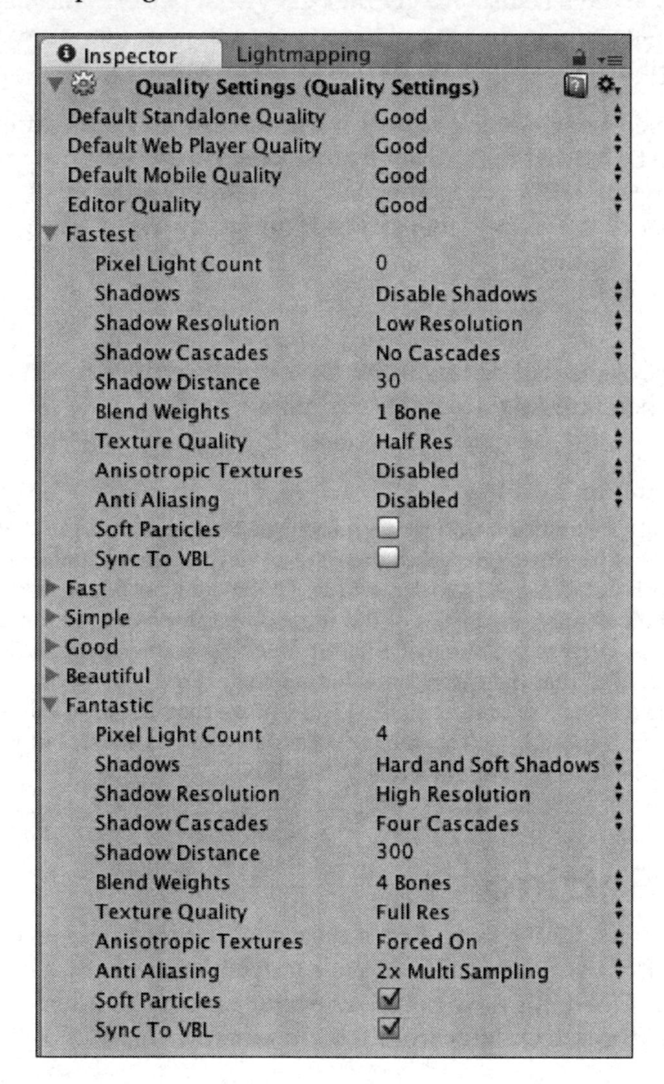

As you can see, these settings are vastly different at each end of the scale, so let's take a look at what the individual settings do:

- **Pixel Light Count**: The number of pixel lights that can be used in your scene. Lights in Unity are rendered as a pixel or vertex; pixel lights look better but are more expensive processing-wise. With this setting, you can allow a certain number of pixel lights, with the rest being rendered as vertex lights. This is why the low end of the scale **Fastest** preset has the **Pixel Light Count** set to **0** by default.
- **Shadows**: This feature is available only in the Unity Pro version and allows you to specify no dynamic shadows, hard shadows only, or hard and soft shadows. However, as we have seen, shadows can be baked as part of the lightmapping process in the free version of Unity.
- **Shadow Resolution**: Again this applies to Unity Pro only, and this setting allows you to choose a quality setting specifically for the shadows being rendered. This can be useful to save performance when having multiple objects with dynamic shadows in your scene—setting them to a low resolution could mean the difference between switching them off and keeping shadows entirely during optimization.
- **Shadow Cascades**: Unity Pro can take advantage of **Cascaded Shadow Maps**, which can improve the appearance of shadows on directional lights in your scene. By drawing the same shadow map over progressively larger expanses dependent upon proximity, closer to the player's camera gets more shadow map pixel detail, improving quality.
- **Shadow Distance**: Similar to the optimization of restricting the camera's far clip plane, this is another level of detail tweak. It can be used to simply set a distance after which shadows are not rendered.
- **Blend Weights**: This setting is used for rigged characters with a boned skeleton, and controls the number of weights (levels) of animation that can be blended between. Unity Technologies recommend two bones as a good trade-off between performance and appearance.
- **Texture Quality**: Exactly as it sounds, the amount to which Unity will compress your textures.
- **Anisotropic Textures**: **Anisotropic filtering** can help improve the appearance of textures when viewed at a steep angle, like hills, but is costly in terms of performance. Bear in mind that you can also set up this filtering on an individual-texture basis in the **Import Settings** for assets.
- **Anti Aliasing**: This setting softens the edges of 3D elements, making your game look a lot better. However, as with other filters, it comes at a cost of performance.

- **Soft Vegetation**: This allows Unity terrain elements, such as vegetation and trees to use **alpha blending**, which vastly improves the appearance of transparent areas of textures used to create the vegetation.
- **Sync to VBL**: This forces your game to be synchronized to the refresh rate of the player's monitor. This generally degrades the performance, but will avoid 'tearing' of elements in your game—the appearance of a misalignment of vertices where textures appear 'torn' from each other.

You should use these presets to set options that will benefit the player, as they will have the ability to choose from them in the **Resolution Dialog** window (see the *Player Settings* section) when launching your game as a standalone, unless you have disabled this. However, it is fairly safe in most instances to use Unity's own presets as a guide, and simply tweak specific settings when you need to. The settings at the top of the Quality settings that offer defaults are also useful as they will allow you to set the Editor itself to a particular quality, giving you a more realistic representation of your game's final look as you work.

Player Input settings

While the **Resolution Dialog** window gives the standalone build player the ability to adjust the input controls of your game in the **Input** tab (see the following image), it is important to know that you can specify your own defaults for the control of your game in the **Player Input** settings. This is especially useful for web builds, as the player has no ability to change control settings when they load the game. Therefore, it is best that you set them up sensibly and provide information to the player through your in-game GUI.

In Unity, go to **Edit | Project Settings | Input** to open the **Input Manager** in the **Inspector** part of the interface. You will then be presented with the existing axes of control in Unity. The **Size** value simply states how many controls exist. By increasing this value, you can build in your own controls, or alternatively you can simply expand any of the existing ones by clicking on the gray arrow to the left of their name and adjusting the values therein. Click the arrow to the left of the **Fire1** entry now to expand it.

Looking at this setting, you can see how this ties together with the code we wrote earlier; when looking at the `CoconutThrower` script we wrote:

```
if(Input.GetButtonUp("Fire1")){
```

Here, the `Fire1` axis is referenced by its name. By changing the **Name** parameter in the input settings, you can define what needs to be written in scripting. For more information on the keys you can bind to in these settings, refer to the **Input** page of the Unity manual at the following address:

`http://unity3d.com/support/documentation/Manual/Input.html`

Building the game

Now that we are nearly ready to build the game, you need to consider the varying deployment methods discussed previously, and adapt the project to be built for the Web Player as well as a standalone game.

Adapting for web build

In Unity, the 3D world you work with is fully scaled by the engine to be presented in whatever resolution you specify in the **Player Settings**. We have also designed the menus in this book to be scalable in different resolutions by utilizing the `Screen` class to position GUIs based on current resolution. However, in order to learn about platform detection we will remove an element that we don't want to be seen in our web version—the **Quit** button. In the `Scripts` folder in the **Project** panel, double-click the icon for the `MainMenuGUI` script in order to launch it in the script editor now.

Quit button platform automation

When deploying as a web build, having a **Quit** button as part of the menu is meaningless. This is because `Application.Quit()` commands do not function when a Unity game is played through a browser—instead, players simply close the tab or window containing the game or navigate away when they are finished playing. We need to exclude this button from our web menu, but we do not want to delete it from our script because we still want the script to render the **Quit** button in a standalone build.

To solve this problem, we'll utilize another property of the `Application` class called `platform`, which we can use to detect what kind of deployment (desktop, web, mobile, console, and so on) the game is being built as.

We will do this by writing the following `if` statement:

```
if(Application.platform != RuntimePlatform.OSXWebPlayer
  && Application.platform != RuntimePlatform.WindowsWebPlayer){
```

Here we are simply checking the `platform` property of `Application`, using `!=` to say 'not equal' to `OSXWebPlayer` (Mac) or `WindowsWebPlayer` (PC). So here we are saying, if this is not being run on either Mac OR PC Web player, then do something! Now we simply need to combine this with the existing IF statement that renders the **Quit** button.

In the `OnGUI()` function, locate the `if` statement in charge of creating the **Quit** button; it should look like this:

C#:

```
if(GUI.Button(new Rect(quitButton), "Quit")){
  StartCoroutine("ButtonAction", "quit");
}
```

Javascript:

```
if(GUI.Button(Rect(quitButton), "Quit")){
  ButtonAction("quit");
}
```

Now add in the following `if` statement, placing the original **Quit** button's `if` statement into it. It should now look like this:

C#:

```
if(Application.platform != RuntimePlatform.OSXWebPlayer
  && Application.platform != RuntimePlatform.WindowsWebPlayer){
    if(GUI.Button(new Rect(quitButton), "Quit")){
      StartCoroutine("ButtonAction", "quit");
    }
}
```

Javascript:

```
if(Application.platform != RuntimePlatform.OSXWebPlayer
  &&Application.platform != RuntimePlatform.WindowsWebPlayer){
    if(GUI.Button(Rect(quitButton), "Quit")){
      ButtonAction("quit");
    }
}
```

This means that when deployed as a standalone player, the quit button will be rendered but if the platform is detected as being Mac or PC Web Player, it will be skipped.

Thanks to the `Application` class automation we've implemented, we now have a **Menu** scene that can be placed in the **Build Settings** list, along with the **Island** scene and deployed as a **Web Player** or **Standalone**, without the need to alter code when exporting builds. This technique can be very useful when creating more detailed menus, and various other features when designing with Unity to maximize its cross-platform capabilities.

Preparing for streaming

In order to help our **Island** level load as a streamed asset, we can arrange our code to only allow the player to access the Play button from the menu if the scene is downloaded in full—this avoids having to load the entire game before the menu is presented. Instead, we can show the menu, with a **Loading..xx% Loaded** message whilst the Island scene is being downloaded.

Ordinarily, all Unity content loaded as a Web Player will display the default Unity web player progress bar, unless a custom one has been created.

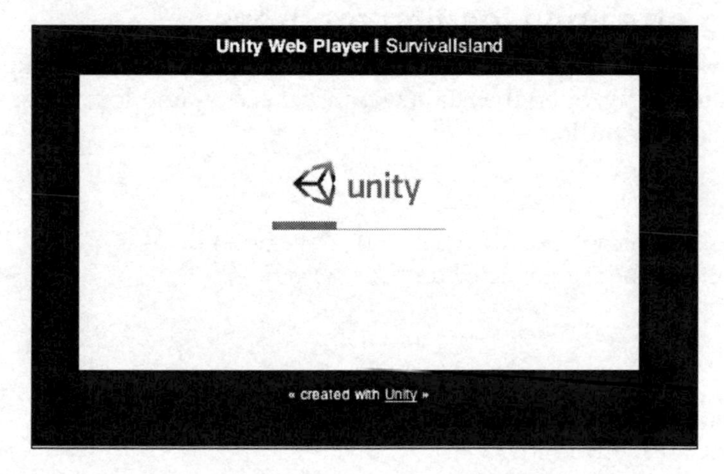

We will complement this by showing additional loading information on the Menu scene whilst the Island scene loads by replacing the Play button with loading information, until the Island scene is ready:

Displaying streamed loading progress

As we are working on the menu, open the Menu scene by double-clicking its icon in the Project panel. Now, open the **MainMenuGUI** script, and locate the existing code that renders the **Play** button –

C#:

```
if(GUI.Button(new Rect(playButton), "Play")){
  StartCoroutine("ButtonAction", "Island");
}
```

Javascript:

```
if(GUI.Button(Rect(playButton), "Play")){
  ButtonAction("Island");
}
```

Surround this with a further `if` statement to check if the Island scene can be loaded, as shown below:

C#:

```
if(Application.CanStreamedLevelBeLoaded("Island")){
  if(GUI.Button(new Rect(playButton), "Play")){
    StartCoroutine("ButtonAction", "Island");
```

```
    }
}
```

Javascript:

```
if(Application.CanStreamedLevelBeLoaded("Island")){
  if(GUI.Button(Rect(playButton), "Play")){
    ButtonAction("Island");
  }
}
```

This checks whether the `Island` scene is ready to be loaded, and if so, renders the Play button. We can then accompany this with an `else` statement that will display the progress of loading the Island level through streaming, if it is not yet ready.

Add the following `else` statement to the above `if` statement:

C#:

```
else{
  float percentLoaded =
    Application.GetStreamProgressForLevel(1) * 100;
  GUI.Box(new Rect(playButton),
    "Loading.. " + percentLoaded.ToString("f0") + "% Loaded");
}
```

Javascript:

```
else{
  var percentLoaded : float =
    Application.GetStreamProgressForLevel(1) * 100;
  GUI.Box(new Rect(playButton),
    "Loading.." + percentLoaded.ToString("f0") + "% Loaded");
}
```

Here we begin by creating a variable called `percentLoaded` that checks the `GetStreamProgressForLevel` command and uses `1` as an argument—the number 1 here is a reference to the Island scene's index number from the Build Settings.

This value is multiplied by `100` to create a percentage, before being visually displayed in a `GUI.Box`, which we give a position and scale by reusing the `Rect` for the `playButton`. This is useful as it means that until the Island is ready to be played, the loading info will display in its place.

The actual text displayed in this `Box` is the important part; we have written the following:

```
"Loading.." + percentLoaded.ToString("f0") + "% Loaded"
```

The beginning and end of this are simply strings of written text - `"Loading.."` and `"% Loaded"`, but we are using the plus symbol to add in a command to display the value of our `percentLoaded` variable between these two pieces of text. This is formatted with the `ToString("f0")` command which removes any decimal places from the value stored in the variable. The end result means that this box will display the following text for example:

Loading.. 86% Loaded

> Using the plus symbol to add together the result of variables and functions to a string is called concatenation (the verb therefore is 'to concatenate'). This may be useful to know when discussing your code in future with other developers.

Styling the loading info box

Before we are finished with our loading info box, we'll need to return to our GUI skin once more and give it a style. Because this functionality is only viewable when deploying online, you will not see it in the Unity editor, or in a test web build on your own computer—it loads too quickly from your hard drive to ever present you with loading information.

To avoid you having to test on a server yourself, here is an example of what the loading info will look like right now, without styles:

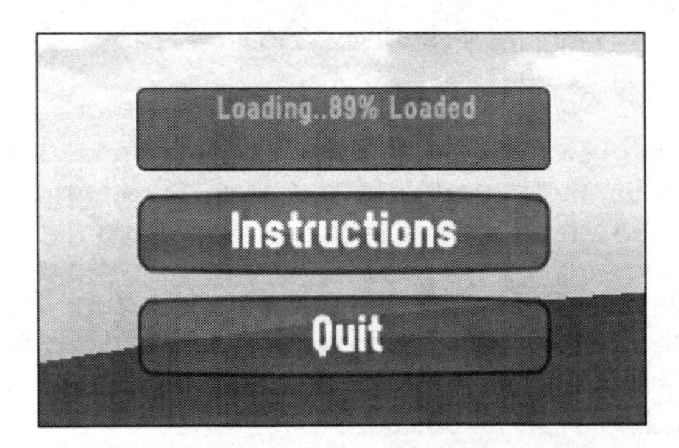

Pretty ugly right? And it doesn't fit in with the existing menu style, so let's fix it!

Save your script and return to Unity, then select the **Menu2** object in the Hierarchy. This displays the **Main Menu GUI (Script)** component, which will allow you to see the GUI Skin we are using—**Main Menu**. Select this here or in the Project panel to see the properties of the GUI Skin in the Inspector.

As we wish to style the `GUI.Box` part of our menu code, expand the properties for **Box** at the top of the list of styles by clicking the grey arrow to the left of its name.

There are three properties that we should change in order to make the info loading box match our menu's style:

- The background of the box itself
- The font size and color used
- The positioning of the text within the box

To do this, first ensure that the **Normal** property of the **Box** is expanded, so that you can see the **Background** and **Text Color** properties.

Drag the texture **guiBtnActive** from the **Book Assets | Textures** folder in the project panel to the **Background** property of **Box** in order to replace the default Unity black box background look. This texture will be appropriate for the box as it is a shade of red, suggesting to the player that something is not ready.

Next click on the **Text Color** block and choose black from the color picker window that appears, closing it when you are done. Further down the **Box** settings, assign your chosen font to the **Font** parameter and also set the **Font Size** to a value of **22**

Finally, find the property for **Alignment**—this is where Unity renders the content of the box, in this case, our loading info text. Set this to **MiddleCenter** so that we need not worry about padding our text within the box. Once complete, your GUI Skin settings for the box should look like this:

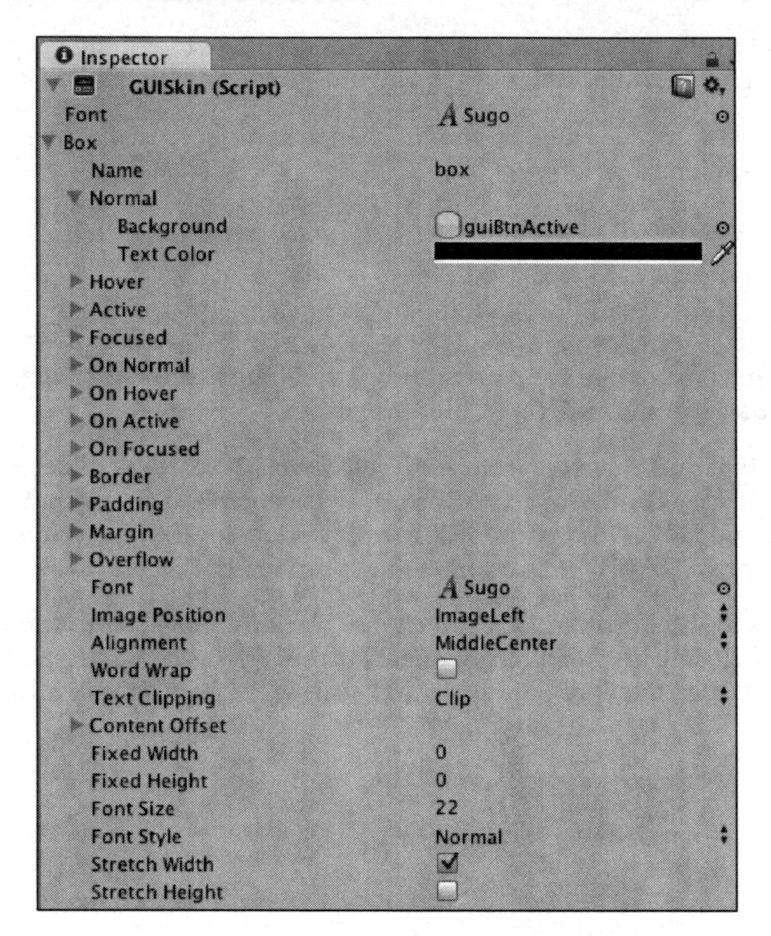

In practice, this will cause your loading bar to display like this:

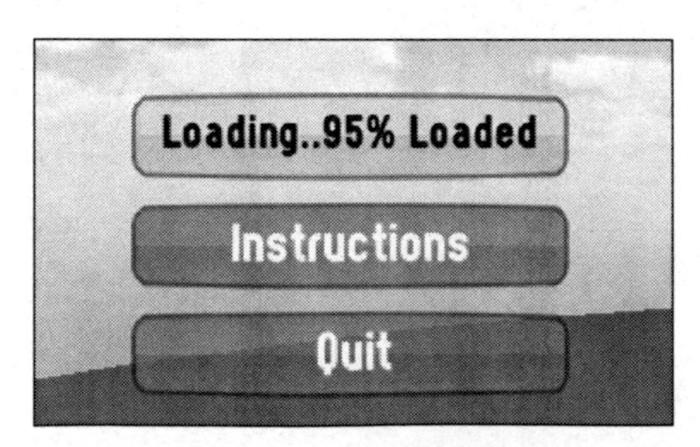

Once the bar reaches 100%, it will immediately be replaced by the Play button—allowing the user to start the game.

And that's it! You now have a piece of GUI code that will present the user with progress, but give them time to read the instructions part of the menu whilst they wait. Remember that this is only testable with a built version of the game deployed online so that streaming is in effect, and it will not be seen within the Unity editor, or as part of a Standalone build. Save your progress in Unity by choosing **File | Save Project** from the top menu.

Now let's take a look at building both the web and standalone versions of the game.

First Build

Having put our finishing touches to our code to ensure that it is ready for both of our deployment platforms, we're ready to create our first build. Exciting huh? So without further ado, let's create our Standalone version of the game, so that you can get your first look at the game in a packaged application.

Building the Standalone

Go to **File | Build Settings**, and ensure that your two scene files are listed in the **Scenes to build** area:

- **Menu.unity**
- **Island.unity**

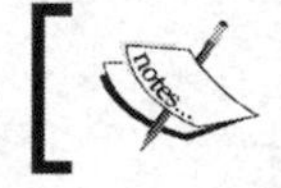

If any scenes do not appear in the list, remember that they can be dragged and dropped from the **Project** panel to the **Build Settings** list.

It is important that **Menu** is the first scene in the list as we need this to load this first, so make sure it is at index position **0**—the top of the **Scenes in Build** list. If it is not first in the list, remember that you can drag scene names to re-order them in the list.

In the **Platform** area of the **Build Settings**, the Unity logo next to a particular platform indicates that you have selected it as your intended platform to build for. If it is not currently set to PC and Mac standalone, highlight **PC and Mac Standalone** in blue and then in the bottom right-hand side of the window, click on **Switch Platform**.

> We are switching platform here for consistency, and to allow you to see the resolution in the Game View list of preview dimensions, but it is not necessary to switch platform for building, if you are working on a game and regularly switching platforms. Be aware that Unity switches for you when building depending on which platform is currently highlighted anyway.

The Unity logo should now appear to the right-hand side of **PC and Mac Standalone**.

Now simply select which **Target Platform** you'd like to build for:

- Windows
- Windows 64-bit
- Mac OS X Universal
- Mac OS X Intel Only
- Mac OS X PowerPC Only
- Mac OS X Dashboard Widget

Click on the **Build** button at the bottom of this dialog window, and you'll be prompted for a location to save your game. Navigate to your desired location and name your built game in the **Save As** field. Then press the **Save** button to confirm.

Wait while Unity constructs your game! You'll be shown progress bars showing assets being compressed, followed by a loading bar as each level is added to the build. Once building is complete, your game build will be opened in an operating system window to show you that it is ready.

On Mac, double-click the application to launch it, or on PC, open the folder containing the game and double-click the `.exe` file to launch your game. Bear in mind that if you build a PC version on a Mac or vice versa, they cannot be tested natively.

Free versus Pro

When building your game with the free version of Unity, you should be aware that a **Powered by Unity** splash screen will be shown before your game loads. This watermark is not present when building with the Pro version of Unity:

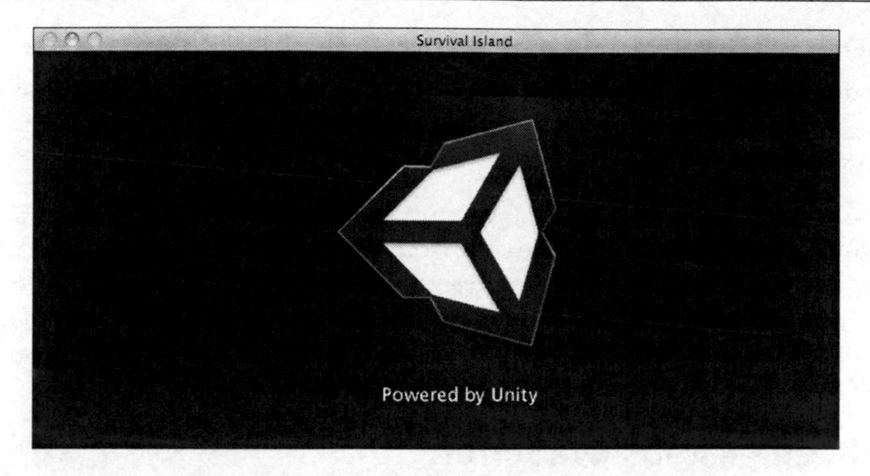

Other Free versus Pro differences, such as the lack of dynamic shadows in the free version, can be found in a full table at the following URL:

`http://unity3d.com/unity/licenses.html`

Building for the Web

In Unity, open the **Build Settings** by going to **File** | **Build Settings**, and highlight **Web Player** in blue under **Platform**. Ensure that **Streamed** is checked on the right-hand side of the settings for Web Player, as this is key to allow the Island level to stream whilst our menu is shown.

As stated in the previous information box, there is no need to hit **Switch Platform**, as Unity will switch whilst building to whatever platform is highlighted in blue. With this in mind, simply click on **Build** now. Unity will handle the relevant conversions and compressions necessary to create a build that will run well on the Web, and create this to the specifications we made earlier in the **Player Settings**.

You'll be prompted to specify a name and location to save the file. So enter this and then press the **Save** button at the bottom to confirm.

When complete, the operating system will switch to the window your build is saved in, showing you the two files that make the web build work—the game itself (a `.unity3d` extension file), and an HTML file containing the embedding code and JavaScript required to load the `.unity3d` file or if the Unity Web Player plugin is not installed, prompt download of the plugin.

To play the game, open the HTML file in a web browser of your choice, and this will launch the game. You need not install the Web Player yourself as this was installed on your computer when you installed Unity for the first time.

Embedding web player builds in your own site

This section shows you how to take a web build from Unity and include it in your own pages. Should you not wish to do this, you can simply skip ahead to the *Sharing your work* section.

Should you want to place HTML or Javascript code into your own HTML or CSS web pages, you'll simply need to take the code from the `<head>` and `<body>` areas of the page to place this build into your own design. This is because the default Unity build provides you with the necessary code to include the `.unity3d` file in a web page. If you are not interested in embedding web players into your own web page designs, then you may skip ahead to page 31, under *Sharing your work*.

The <head>—web JavaScript

The `<head>` of the document contains two pieces of Javascript. Bear in mind that this is JavaScript for the web, and not the Javascript you may have been using for Unity; it simply uses a similar syntax.

The first is a call to the web player download script on Unity's own servers. This is designed to assist the user if they do not have the player already installed:

```
<script type="text/javascript" src="http://webplayer.unity3d.com/
download_webplayer-3.x/3.0/uo/UnityObject.js"></script>
```

The next is the call that manages loading the content if the player is installed; it is written directly into the HTML page and looks like this:

```
<script type="text/javascript">
  <!--
  function GetUnity() {
    if (typeofunityObject != "undefined") {
      return unityObject.getObjectById("unityPlayer");
    }
    return null;
  }
  if (typeofunityObject != "undefined") {
    unityObject.embedUnity("unityPlayer",
      "SurvivalIsland.unity3d", 800, 600);
  }
  -->
</script>
```

In this example note that the script is loading a piece of content called `SurvivalIsland.unity3d`, though your function may differ depending upon the name you chose to save your web player files as. This function simply looks for an element on the page called `unityPlayer` using function `getObjectById()`, and if found, sends it the content of our `.unity3d` file.

Making the <head> code portable

Let's simplify this code so that we can make it more portable—at the moment we would need to copy the above function into the HTML page we wish to place our unity content within. Instead, by placing it into its own Javascript file, we can simply call that file in a single line.

Open the build's accompanying HTML page in the script editor that comes with Unity (MonoDevelop) or your favored HTML editor, for example, Dreamweaver, Coda, SciTE, TextMate, or TextWrangler.

Select all code of the `function` of the JavaScript within the `<head>` part of the HTML:

```
function GetUnity() {
  if (typeofunityObject != "undefined") {
    return unityObject.getObjectById("unityPlayer");
  }
    return null;
  }
  if (typeofunityObject != "undefined") {
    unityObject.embedUnity("unityPlayer",
      "SurvivalIsland.unity3d", 800, 600);
}
```

Now copy this to a new Javascript document, saving it as `UnityLoader.js` in the same folder as your web pages and include this JavaScript in your page by calling it in the `<head>`of your own page with the following line of code:

```
<script type="text/javascript" src="UnityLoader.js"></script>
```

Simple huh? Now whenever you need to embed your Unity content, you can simply include the above line, along with the existing call to the Unity player detection, as shown below:

```
<script type="text/javascript" src="http://webplayer.unity3d.com/
download_webplayer-3.x/3.0/uo/UnityObject.js"></script>
<script type="text/javascript" src="UnityLoader.js"></script>
```

Remember that in order for this to work, this code assumes that the `.unity3d` file is in the same directory as the HTML which calls it. If you wish to store your `.unity3d` files elsewhere, simply alter the `embedUnity` command in the code above, for example:

```
unityObject.embedUnity("unityPlayer", "http://www.yoursite.com/
afoldername/SurvivalIsland.unity3d", 800, 600);
```

Object embedding from the <BODY>

The JavaScript outlined above is looking for an element on the page named `unityPlayer`. In web development terms this is usually a `<div>` tag—a division (put simply, a space) on the web page with an ID, an identifier, simply a string as a name to identify this space. Looking further down the example page that Unity exports, you will see this division:

```
<div id="unityPlayer">
  <div class="missing">
    <a href="http://unity3d.com/webplayer/"
      title="Unity Web Player. Install now!">
    <img alt="Unity Web Player. Install now!"
      src="http://webplayer.unity3d.com/installation/getunity.png"
      width="193" height="63" />
    </a>
</div>
</div>
```

This is the piece of HTML that places the content on the page, and to place the visible player on your own page, you should copy this piece of html. You will also note that it includes a tag with a class (another form of identifier) named `missing`. This is to allow the space to display a button to prompt the user to install the unity player if their computer does not have it installed. You will not need to host the image of this button yourself, as you should note that it is hosted on Unity's server also.

Styling your Unity embed with CSS

You will note that in the example HTML export, Unity gives you some CSS to style the embed part of the page. CSS stands for Cascading Style Sheets, and is used by web designers to style their html-based information. In the example page Unity exports, there is a large amount of CSS within <style> tags.

However, there are two things to note about this - firstly, you should always place your CSS style code into its own document, known in web design terms as a style sheet. Secondly, some of the code seen here is used to design this page, and not specifically style the Unity embed discussed above. With this in mind, simply select the following part of the CSS:

```
div.missing {
  margin: auto;
  position: relative;
  top: 50%;
    width: 193px;
}
div.missing a {
  height: 63px;
  position: relative;
    top: -31px;
}
div.missingimg {
    border-width: 0px;
}
div#unityPlayer {
    cursor: default;
    height: 600px;
    width: 800px;
}
```

Now create a new file with the extension `.css`—perhaps saving it as `UnityStyle.css`, and paste the above code in.

This file can be included in your page by writing the following line of HTML into the `<head>` area of code:

```
<link href="UnityStyle.css" type="text/css" rel="stylesheet" />
```

Now that we have the necessary three calls to make your game run in an HTML web page more portably! The `<head>` of the page you embed your Unity content into should now simply look like this:

```
<head>
<title>Survival Island</title>
<script type="text/javascript" src="http://webplayer.unity3d.com/
download_webplayer-3.x/3.0/uo/UnityObject.js"></script>
<script type="text/javascript" src="UnityLoader.js"></script>
<link href="UnityStyle.css" type="text/css" rel="stylesheet" />
</head>
```

As you can see, we have the `<title>` tag, a prerequisite for any web page, followed by the call to the Unity web player Javascript file on Unity's servers, and our two local file references, one Javascript call for the `UnityLoader.js` file we created, and one for the `UnityStyle.css` stylesheet file.

By placing these three references into the `<head>` of your document and the HTML from the Object embedding from the `<body>` section above, you can easily embed your content into any web page you create.

Sharing your work

It is important that you share your work with others, not only to show off your development skills but also to get feedback on your game and allow members of the public with no prior knowledge of your project to test how it works. Also consider the value of social media in sharing your work—a strong community for Unity exists both on Facebook through various groups, and on Twitter using the hashtag `#unity3d`.

In addition to sharing your game with your audience on your own website, there are also several independent game portal sites available that act as a community for developers sharing their work.

Here are some recommended sites you should visit once you are ready to share your work with the online community:

- `www.kongregate.com`
- `www.facebook.com` (as an app)
- `www.shockwave.com`
- `www.indiegamepub.com`
- `www.tigsource.com` (The Independent Gaming source)
- `http://forum.unity3d.com` (Showcase area)
- `www.learnunity3d.com` and `www.unity3dstudent.com`
- `www.unitybook.net` (the support site for this book)

Sharing on Kongregate.com

The simplest method for beginners is to publish to portal site `Kongregate.com`, as it allows you to upload the .unity3d file that Unity exports quickly and easily, and removes the need to host your own html file embedding the content.

Simply visit the site, register for an account, and then choose **Games | Upload a Game** from their top menu. Fill in the form to upload your content to the Kongregate community, and then share the link to your game via twitter or Facebook.

Sharing your game in this way is a great way to get feedback, and you can even receive comments, ratings and upload new versions to your audience, and chat with others currently playing your game.

This kind of unbiased feedback is crucial as it allows you to weed out bugs and troubleshoot unintuitive parts of your game that may make sense to you but baffle the ordinary player.

Also, be aware that some portal sites may not be able to host your game in `.unity3d` format but maybe willing to link to your own blog with the game embedded or host a standalone version for download.

Summary

In this chapter, we've looked at how you can export your game to the Web and as a standalone project.

In the conclusion, we'll look back at what you have learned over the course of this book and suggest ways in which you can progress further with the existing skills you have developed and where to look for continued assistance with your Unity development.

13
Testing and Further Study

Over the course of this book, we have covered the essential topics to get you started in development with the Unity game engine. In working with Unity, you'll discover that with each new game element you develop, new avenues of possibility open up in your knowledge. Fresh ideas and game concepts will come more easily as you add further Unity development and scripting knowledge to your skill set. In this chapter, we'll conclude your introduction to Unity by looking at:

- Approaches to testing and finalizing your work
- Optimizing your game
- Measuring performance data from test users
- Where to go for help with Unity and what to study next

With this in mind, when looking ahead to where to continue extending your skills, you should take time to expand your knowledge of the following areas:

- Scripting
- Scripting
- Scripting

That's right, it's no joke—while Unity prides itself on providing an intuitive toolset for developing in a visual manner and using the Editor's GUI to build scenes and game objects, there is no substitute for learning the classes and commands that make up the Unity engine itself.

By reading through the Unity manual, followed by the Component Reference and Script Reference—available both online and as part of your Unity software installation—you'll begin to understand how best to create all types of game elements, which may not apply to your current project but should flesh out your understanding to help you work more efficiently in the long term:

- Component Reference (`http://www.unity3d.com/support/documentation/Components/`)
- Scripting Reference (`http://www.unity3d.com/support/documentation/ScriptReference/`)
- Unity Manual (`http://www.unity3d.com/support/documentation/Manual/`)
- MSDN C# Reference (bypass the visual C# information) (`http://msdn.microsoft.com/en-gb/vstudio/hh341490`)

Learn by doing

In addition to referring to the Unity manual, component, and scripting references, one of the most valuable approaches to improving your game development skills that you can take is that of *rapid prototyping*. Rapid prototyping is the process of creating simplified versions of game ideas quickly and with basic visuals—focusing on the gameplay of the idea itself.

Try to think of simple game mechanics, and then set yourself the task of finding out how to build them. By using idea generation to drive your learning, you will find that motivation will help you to maintain your concentration, as you will be focused on goals instead of an overall intangible leveling up of your knowledge.

Testing and finalizing

When considering game development, you should be very aware of the importance of testing your game amongst users who have no preconceptions of it whatsoever. When working on any creative project, you should be aware that in order to maintain creative objectivity, you need to be open to criticism and that testing is just as much a part of that as it is a technical necessity. It is all too easy to become used to your game's narrative or mechanics, and often unable to look at the game in a detached manner—in a similar way to how a player might respond to it. Always try and place yourself in the position of the player, instead of looking at the game you're making as a game designer—there are bound to be parts of the game that are obvious to you, but may not make sense to a player.

Public testing

When looking to test your game, try and send test builds to a range of users who can provide test feedback for you with the following variations:

- **Computer specification**: Ensure that you test on differently configured hardware, and get feedback on performance.
- **Format**: If working on a Standalone build, try sending a build for both Mac and PC where possible.
- **Language**: Do your test users all speak the same language as you? Can they tell you if your game interface makes sense?
- **Experience**: What kind of games do your testers play ordinarily—are they casual or hardcore gamers, and how do they find your game in terms of difficulty? What parts of the game are causing issues for them?

After testing your game in **alpha** form, a test version you and other developers test, you should hand your game over to a collection of public testers. You are handing them what is referred to as a **beta** test of your game. By formalizing the process, you can make the feedback you get about your game as useful as possible—draw up a questionnaire that poses the same questions to all testers while asking not only questions about their responses to the game, but also information about them as a player. In this way, you can begin to make assertions about your game, such as:

"Players aged 18 to 24 liked the mechanic and understood the game but players of 45+ did not understand it without reading the instructions."

"Casual gamers found that the game didn't have points of interest close enough together to keep them playing; consider level design changes."

In addition to technical information such as:

"Players with computers under 2.4 GHz processing speed found the game to respond sluggishly, averaging 15 to 20 frames per second; consider model detail and texture compression."

Frame rate feedback

As you test your game in the editor, you have access to the statistics of performance using the **Stats** overlay on the **Game View** (click the **Stats** button!). However as a player of your test build, a member of the public won't be able to see this, so we should consider building such tools into our game.

In order to provide testers of your game with a means of providing specific feedback on technicalities such as frame rate (speed at which game frames are drawn during play), you can provide your test build with a GUI element telling them this information.

To add this to any scene, let's take a look at a practical example. Open the scene you wish to add a frame rate screen overlay to—in our example, the **Island** scene—and create a new GUI Text object to display the information. Go to **GameObject | Create Other | GUI Text** or click the **Create** button on the Hierarchy panel and choose **GUI Text** from there. Rename the newly created GUI Text object **FPS display**, and then in the **GUI Text** component of the **Inspector,** set the **Anchor** to **upper center**, and the **Alignment** to **center**. To keep things consistent, drag and drop the font you've been using for the game so far from the Project panel onto the **Font** parameter.

In the **Transform** component, set the value for the **Y** position to **0.9**.

Now create a new script in your **Project** by selecting the **Scripts** folder, then click **Create**, and select **C# Script** or **Javascript** from the drop-down menu. Rename your script **FPSdisplay**, then double-click its icon to launch it in the script editor; as usual, C# users ensure that your class is also named **FPSdisplay**.

Since the frame rate your game runs at is variable depending upon hardware and software configuration, we need to perform a sum which takes into account how many frames were rendered within the game's time scale each second. We'll start by establishing the following variables at the top of the script—remember that for C# users, this means at the start of the class:

C#:

```
float frames = 0;
float fps = 0;
```

Javascript:

```
private var frames : float = 0;
private var fps : float = 0;
```

We establish these two variables here for the following reasons:

- `frames`: A number incremented each frame, therefore storing the amount of frames rendered.
- `fps`: A number to store the frames per second, which will be assigned the current fps value by taking the rounded value of the `frames` variable and dividing it by the time since the start of the scene.

Now, in the `Update()` function, place the following code:

C# and Javascript:

```
frames++;
fps = Mathf.Round(frames / Time.realtimeSinceStartup);
guiText.text = "Frames Per Second: " + fps;
```

Here we do the following:

- Increment the `frames` variable by 1 each time the `Update()` function occurs (after each frame).
- Set the `fps` variable to the Rounded value of frames, divided by the time since the scene began, which means that you get a realistic representation of the performance that the test player's computer is giving them.
- We address the `guiText` component's `text` property, and set it to a string saying "`Frames Per Second :`", and add the value of the `fps` variable to the end.

Now because we might wish to make this a script that we re-use for other games, we should ensure that it can be dropped onto an object in another project and work perfectly. Part of doing this is ensuring that the script contains `RequireComponent` commands to ensure a GUI Text component is present. We have used these before, so hopefully you remember how, but if not, here is what you need to do:

C#:

At the top of the script, after `using System.Collections;` add the following line:

```
[RequireComponent (typeof (GUIText))]
```

Javascript:

After the closing of the `Update` function, ensure that you include the following line:

```
@script RequireComponent(GUIText)
```

Go to **File | Save** in the script editor, and switch back to Unity. Ensure that the **FPS display** object is still selected in the **Hierarchy** and then go to **Component | Scripts | FPS display** or simply drag-and-drop the script from the Project panel onto the object in the Hierarchy. Now test your scene, and you will see the GUI Text displaying the frame rate at the top of the screen.

Your game will perform differently outside of the Unity editor. As such, readings from this FPS displayer should only be noted once the game is built and run either as a web player or standalone version; ask your test users to note the lowest and highest frame rates to give you a range of readings to consider, and if there are particularly demanding parts of your game, for example complex animation or particle effects, then it could be worth asking for readings from these times separately.

Because the game performs differently outside of the Unity editor, the values from this frame rate display will be different from those given in the in-built **Stats** tab of the **Game** view:

Optimizing performance

Improving the performance of your game as a result of testing is easily an entire field of study in itself. However, to improve your future development, you'll need to be aware of basic economizing in the following ways:

- **Spotting bottlenecks**: Your game's performance may suffer in due to a number of things, the key is spotting where this is happening—is a certain scene causing lower performance? Is the game only slower when encountering a high detail model or high output particle system? Try and be systematic when searching for what might make your game run slowly, and always ask your test users for a scenario you can reproduce in order to spot the problem.

- **Polygon counts**: When introducing 3D models, they should be designed with low polygon counts in mind. So try and simplify your models as much as possible to improve performance.
- **Draw distance**: Consider reducing the distance of your Far Clip Plane in your cameras to cut down the amount of scenery the game must render.
- **Occlusion culling**: Only available in the Pro version of Unity, occlusion culling helps avoid overdraw—rendering of unnecessary objects that are in front of one another in your camera view. There's more on this in the Unity manual (`http://unity3d.com/support/documentation/Manual/OcclusionCulling.html`).
- **Texture sizes**: Including higher resolution textures can improve the visual clarity of your game, but they also make the engine work harder. So try and reduce texture sizes as much as possible, using both your image editing software and using the Import settings of your texture assets.
- **Script efficiently**: As there are many approaches to differing solutions in scripting, try and find more efficient ways to write your scripts. Start by reading the Unity guide to efficient scripting online (`http://unity3d.com/support/documentation/ScriptReference/index.Performance_Optimization.html`).

Approaches to learning

As you progress from this book, you will need to develop an approach to further study, which keeps a balance between personal perseverance and the need to ask for help from more experienced Unity developers. Follow the advice laid out below, and you should be well on your way to helping other community members as you expand your knowledge.

Cover as many bases as possible

When learning any new software package/programming language, it is often the case that you are working to a deadline, be it as part of your job or as a freelancer. This can often lead to a "take only what you need" approach to learning. While this can often be a necessity due to working demands, it can often be detrimental to your learning, as you may develop bad habits that stay with you throughout your time working with the software—eventually leading to inefficient approaches.

Taking this on board, I recommend that you take time to read through the official documentation whenever you can—even if you're stuck on a specific development problem, it can often help to take your mind away from what you're stuck with. Go and read up on an unrelated scenario, and return with a fresh perspective.

Don't reinvent the wheel

This may seem incongruous to the previous point but as you start to tackle more complex tasks in your game development, you'll learn that there is little point reinventing the wheel—recreating something that another developer has already solved and offered to the community.

For example if you are tackling the task of enemy AI or even just pathfinding, it is worth looking at the various solutions available to you for this, rather than writing your own code from scratch.

There are many plugins and ready-made assets for Unity available to solve almost any task, available primarily from the **Asset Store** window inside the editor (**Window | Asset Store**) and from various sites across the web.

I recommend that you check out the following sites for content that has already been created, and may well help you out with your game development:

- **iTween**—This useful plugin by *Bob Berkebile* (aka pixelplacement) gives you some really simple scripting classes to make fantastic animation effects with minimal code: `http://itween.pixelplacement.com/`
- **Prime31**—This site offers many useful plugins that extend Unity, especially for mobile development; `http://www.prime31.com/unity/`

If you don't know, just ask!

Another useful approach to learning is, of course, to look at how others approach each new game element you attempt to create. In game development, what you'll discover is that often there are many approaches to the same problem—as we learned in *Chapter 5*, when making our character open the outpost door. As a result, it is often tempting to recycle skills learned solving a previous problem, but I recommend always double-checking that your approach is the most efficient way.

By asking in the Unity forum (`forum.unity3d.com`), Answers page (`answers.unity3d.com`), or on the IRC (Internet Relay Chat) channel (`irc.freenode.net`, room `#unity3d`), you'll be able to gain a consensus on the most efficient way to perform a development task—and sometimes even discover that the way you first thought of approaching your problem was more complicated than it needed to be!

When asking questions in any of the aforementioned places, always remember first of all to search—has your question been asked before? It most likely has! But if not, remember when asking to include the following points whenever possible:

- What are you trying to achieve?
- What do you think is the right approach?
- What have you tried so far?

This will give others the best shot at helping you out-by giving as much information as possible, even if you think it may not be relevant, you will give yourself the best chance of achieving your development goals. If asking for help with scripting always remember to make use of a pasting site such as `http://www.pastebin.com`, in order to show others your code without taking up pages of chat room space.

The great thing about the Unity community is that it encourages learning by example. Third party Wiki-based site (`www.unifycommunity.com/wiki`) has wide ranging examples of everything from scripts to plugins, to tutorials, and more. There you'll find useful free-to-use code snippets to supplement the examples of scripted elements within the script reference and even information on how to implement it with example downloadable projects.

Summary

In this chapter, we have discussed ways that you should move on from this book, and how you can gather information from test users to improve your game.

Remember that this isn't the end of your learning with this book; you can visit the support site `http://www.unitybook.net` and raise a question, or check on any updates to Unity that might differ from the processes in this book.

All that remains is to wish you the best of luck with your future game development in Unity. From myself and everyone involved with this book, thanks for reading, and I hope you enjoyed the ride—it's only just the beginning!

Index

Symbols

A

B

C

F

G

H

I

J

K

L

M

N

O

P

Q

R

S

T

U

V

W

Y

Z

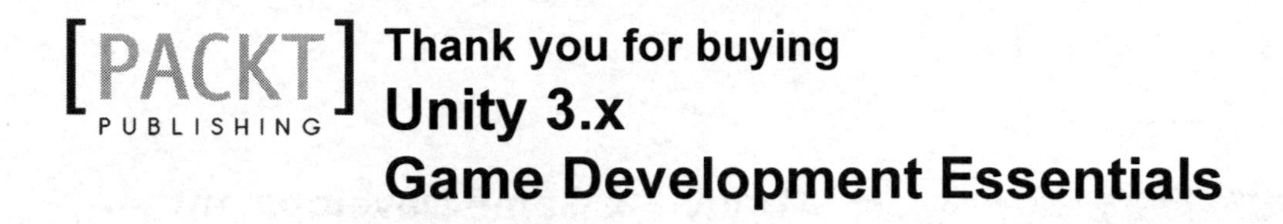

About Packt Publishing

Packt, pronounced 'packed', published its first book "*Mastering phpMyAdmin for Effective MySQL Management*" in April 2004 and subsequently continued to specialize in publishing highly focused books on specific technologies and solutions.

Our books and publications share the experiences of your fellow IT professionals in adapting and customizing today's systems, applications, and frameworks. Our solution based books give you the knowledge and power to customize the software and technologies you're using to get the job done. Packt books are more specific and less general than the IT books you have seen in the past. Our unique business model allows us to bring you more focused information, giving you more of what you need to know, and less of what you don't.

Packt is a modern, yet unique publishing company, which focuses on producing quality, cutting-edge books for communities of developers, administrators, and newbies alike. For more information, please visit our website: `www.packtpub.com`.

Writing for Packt

We welcome all inquiries from people who are interested in authoring. Book proposals should be sent to `author@packtpub.com`. If your book idea is still at an early stage and you would like to discuss it first before writing a formal book proposal, contact us; one of our commissioning editors will get in touch with you.

We're not just looking for published authors; if you have strong technical skills but no writing experience, our experienced editors can help you develop a writing career, or simply get some additional reward for your expertise.

[PACKT]
PUBLISHING

Unity iOS Game Development Beginner's Guide

ISBN: 978-1-84969-040-9 Paperback: 432 pages

Develop iOS games from concept to cash flow using Unity.

1. Dive straight into game development with no previous Unity or iOS experience
2. Work through the entire lifecycle of developing games for iOS
3. Add multiplayer, input controls, debugging, in app and micro payments to your game
4. Implement the different business models that will enable you to make money on iOS games

---

Unreal Development Kit Game Programming with UnrealScript: Beginner's Guide

ISBN: 978-1-84969-192-5 Paperback: 466 pages

Create games beyond your imagination with the Unreal Development Kit

1. Dive into game programming with UnrealScript by creating a working example game.
2. Learn how the Unreal Development Kit is organized and how to quickly set up your own projects.
3. Recognize and fix crashes and other errors that come up during a game's development.

Please check **www.PacktPub.com** for information on our titles

Lightning Source UK Ltd.
Milton Keynes UK
UKOW040319231211

184259UK00002B/55/P